Business Continuity and Risk Management:
Essentials of Organizational Resilience

By

Kurt J. Engemann, PhD, CBCP

Douglas M. Henderson, FSA, CBCP

ISBN 978-1-931332-54-5

(1-931332-54-1)

Rothstein Associates Inc., Publisher
Brookfield, Connecticut USA
www.rothstein.com

*Business Survival™ Weblog: Business Continuity for Key Decision-Makers
from Rothstein Associates at www.rothstein.com/blog*

ISBN 978-1-931332-54-5

(1-931332-54-1)

Library of Congress Control Number
(LCCN) 2011933801

PUBLISHER:
Philip Jan Rothstein, FBCI
Rothstein Associates Inc.
The Rothstein Catalog on Disaster Recovery
4 Arapaho Rd.
Brookfield, Connecticut 06804-3104 USA
203.740.7444
203.740.7401 fax
info@rothstein.com
www.rothstein.com

Keep informed of the latest business continuity news. Sign up for
Business Survival™ Weblog: Business Continuity for Key Decision-Makers
from Rothstein Associates at www.rothstein.com/blog

Foreword

As a business continuity professional serving New York's Wall Street firms, I have been an active part of how the profession has evolved. Not that long ago, business continuity was viewed as an afterthought by many organizations - a form to complete and a box to check off. The defining moment, however, for me and many senior managers now leading business resiliency and risk programs in major corporations - as well as our firms' senior leaders - was the crucible of the World Trade Center disaster – September 11th. This unimagined tragedy of unimaginable proportions taught us that no threat is impossible. Planning and preparation for both the possible and impossible, we learned, are essential for any organization.

Many of us learned business continuity and risk management by doing it, strengthened along the way by a growing international body of experience and knowledge drawn from practitioners and academicians. Kurt Engemann and Douglas Henderson have made a fundamental contribution with their focus on resiliency issues. In an "open source" format, they have assembled a core curriculum spanning a discipline that traditionally took major portions of a career to experience and understand. A blend of theory, common sense, best practice and cases, this versatile textbook provides a structured learning tool and encyclopedic reference guide for business continuity and risk management students, teachers, practitioners, and executives.

One of my favorite chapters focuses on awareness and exercises. In March 2001, at the Wall Street firm where I headed Business Continuity at the time, we completed a major disaster recovery exercise for a scenario covering the complete loss of our primary data center near the World Trade Center. This scenario and much worse was realized six months later. On that day our preparation and exercises rewarded us with the restoration of key information processing capabilities at a backup location in just over two hours. Through resilient operations and people, these efforts played a key role in helping restore basic functionality to the markets and the financial services industry affected by 9-11.

No one can foresee the future. But I believe that this can be no excuse for lack of preparation, management support or exercises that improve awareness and continuously sharpen our organizational and technical response to adversity. We repeatedly experience the unimaginable - whether Mumbai terror attacks, tornado clusters, earthquakes or tsunamis. Crises will continue to arise, as will our need to understand and practice the essentials of organizational resilience.

Roseann McSorley

Roseann McSorley
Managing Director
Global Business Resiliency Head
JPMorgan Chase & Co.
New York City

Note: The writer is not necessarily representing the views or opinions of JPMorgan Chase & Co.

Foreword

Business Continuity Management has been around for the best part of 30 years through its antecedents in Disaster Recovery and Emergency Preparedness. Arguably Risk Management has an even longer pedigree given its evolution from insurance and loss control. Together they form the backbone of how a business or public body protect themselves from threats and hazards of all types.

Given their importance in an increasingly risky world and their relative maturity as business disciplines, it is strange that little has been done to structure the subject in a way that is accessible to students and the wider academic community. Most relevant books and professional journals are targeted at either the professional practitioner or those with general interest in the topic. Most relevant books and professional journals are targeted at either the professional practitioner or those with general interest in the topic. What has been missing is a college core textbook that covers the basic body of knowledge for aspiring students wishing to gain academic qualifications en route to a professional career in Business Continuity or Risk Management.

This new book by Kurt Engemann and Douglas Henderson does much to redress this deficiency in our arsenal of published literature. Written at a level which is very comprehensive but still easily readable it provides a route-map through the terminologies, methodologies and philosophies of the subject. It is impossible to define the subject matter as precisely as many would like; there are many sources of good practice and national standards circulating globally and many competing views about what constitutes best practice. There are even many debates about the intrinsic nature of BCM and Risk. Are they really about Regulation and Compliance or are they about the improvement of Organizational Resilience? Some might argue they are about both.

Given these still unanswered questions, Engemann and Henderson has given us a fair picture of the "state of the art" and one in which most subject matter experts could feel reasonably comfortable. They have combined the formal coverage of traditional topics like Business Impact Analysis and Strategy Development with some strong content particularly suitable to those set on a career in Risk Management. Their treatment of Risk Modeling as a specialized area in the book is challenging and interesting. Although not all will want to delve too deeply into the theoretical basis for such techniques, the Chapter on Probability and Statistics makes enlightening reading for those who do.

Alternatively for those of a more practical bent, the range of case studies included are informative and provide ample evidence of the value and importance of the topics covered and their application. As Technical Director at the Business Continuity Institute, one of my specific duties is to encourage the inclusion of BCM as a serious topic in graduate and masters business programs. I believe this book will form a cornerstone of many such programs and I look forward to it facilitating the discussions I plan to have with many academic bodies in the coming months and years. The Business Continuity Institute welcomes this book and wishes the authors well in their efforts to engage with both the business and academic communities in a language that both will understand.

Lyndon Bird

Lyndon Bird, FBCI
Technical Director and Board Member
The Business Continuity Institute

Foreword

Businesses can be interrupted and destroyed by a number of threats – manmade and natural. Engemann and Henderson have done something about it with this book. For years, Business Continuity Planning Professionals have passionately attempted to address these issues, often working with knowledge gained from years of experience, trials, failures and limited resources.

Kurt Engemann and Doug Henderson decided to actively recruit talented learners into the field through their research, experience with real clients, writing and the graduate certificate program at Iona College. In this book, they provide the facts and examples on which decisions should be made, not knee-jerk reactions to crises, but researched, professional practices that produce informed decisions prior to, during and following a business interruption or crisis. The book cements the notion that BCP professionals will achieve greater success if they collaborate with external resources.

The integration of NIMS and ICS into the private sector has been the hallmark of my professional practice, and Engemann and Henderson endorse this practice.

This is a book that will inform the novice, support the expert and enhance every business continuity planner's efforts to create a resilient organization. The book is well organized as an instructional tool, a reference guide, and as a toolkit for practitioners. The outlines provided in the Appendices are worth the price of the book. Students at both the undergraduate and graduate levels will find what they need to build a strong foundation for business resiliency, regardless of the nature of the business career they seek.

Adult learners, and those already BCP practitioners, will find solid support and proven practices to enhance and improve their work. Most of all, an executive, a student, or a practitioner who absorbs the content of this book will be better prepared to function in a field where preparedness is absolutely essential. This book will serve you well in your education and practice.

Dr. Thomas D. Phelan

Dr. Thomas D. Phelan
Program Director
Emergency and Disaster Management and Fire Science
American Public University System

Brief Contents

Table of Contents

Section I: Development

Section II: Implementation

Section III: Maintenance

Section IV: Risk Modeling

Section VI: Additional Information

Preface

Objective

The viability of an organization can be seriously challenged by a disaster. Numerous recent events have focused attention on the need to be prepared for such events. The objective of this text is to provide a comprehensive study of the critical field of business continuity and risk management with particular emphasis on decision making using a holistic approach. The coverage of the book is derived from the growing body of knowledge of practical methods, experiences and research to lead an organization in the process of systematic decisions to protect people, the environment, assets and operations from disastrous events.

Because business continuity and risk management often deals with events that are improbable, analyzing these risks is challenging. Risks come in many varieties, and there is a growing concern and associated effort for organizations to respond to the challenge. Organizational resiliency can be accomplished through an effective program in business continuity and risk management based on an understanding of risk methodologies and technologies.

This book can serve as a primary text in an undergraduate or graduate level course that focuses on business continuity and risk management or as a supplemental text in a closely related field. Business students majoring in any concentration, including operations, information systems, management science, finance, accounting, marketing, human resources, management and international business will find the material both interesting and useful. In addition, emergency management students and management engineering students will also find this book very valuable.

A wide range of educational and training needs are addressed by the book. In addition to being a text for college courses, this book is also intended for use in professional training programs and as a self-study manual.

Contents

The main portion of the book is divided into the sections entitled: Development, Implementation, Maintenance, and Risk Modeling.

Section I: Development

Chapter I: Fundamentals of Business Continuity Management overviews the essential components of business continuity and risk management.

Chapter II: Business Continuity Management Organization analyzes the organizational structure that needs to be in place to effectively prepare for, respond to and recover from a crisis event.

Chapter III: Business Impact Analysis determines the importance of the organization's activities by assessing the impact over time of their interruption and establishes continuity and recovery objectives.

Chapter IV: Risk Assessment examines threats and prioritizes planning by assessing the likelihood of events and their potential impact on critical functions.

Chapter V: Strategy Development examines strategy identification, selection and implementation necessary for an organization to effectively respond to a crisis event.

Chapter VI: Disaster Recovery for Information Technology examines alternate site selection, data center controls, information management procedures and information technology principles to provide continuation and recovery of the systems and communication capabilities of an organization.

Chapter VII: Information Systems Security reviews security controls and auditing considerations and applies these concepts to various information technology applications.

Section II: Implementation

Chapter VIII: Emergency Response defines the immediate actions taken during a crisis event with the prioritized objectives of life-safety, environmental protection and asset protection.

Chapter IX: Enhancing Coordination with External Agencies examines how an organization should interface with external agencies during disaster mitigation, preparation, response and recovery phases.

Chapter X: Business Continuity Plan discusses the central plan documentation that defines continuity and recovery procedures for crisis events.

Chapter XI: Crisis Communication investigates the importance of emergency communication, media communication plus the devices and systems used to conduct crisis communication.

Chapter XII: Crisis Information Management Systems reviews the role that information systems play in the process of managing emergency information before, during and after an event.

Section III: Maintenance

Chapter XIII: Sustaining Organizational Resilience discusses the importance of awareness and training, testing and exercising, and maintaining and updating to ensure that plans remain operable and current.

Section IV: Risk Modeling

Chapter XIV: Fundamentals of Probability and Statistics develops a foundation in probability and statistics that is very useful in business continuity and risk management.

Chapter XV: Statistical Applications in Risk Management explores forecasting techniques, regression analysis and reliability modeling.

Chapter XVI: Simulation Modeling and Supply Chain Risk examines simulation modeling in business continuity and risk management with application to supply chain analysis.

Chapter XVII: Risk and Decision Modeling examines decision making techniques under risk and uncertainty.

Case Studies and Discussion Topics

Several case studies are incorporated in the book to provide a practical application of the material. The case studies are designed to enhance the connection between business continuity and risk management concepts and practical applications. Two of these case studies are examined throughout the book, providing a comprehensive view of business continuity management.

In addition to the case studies, review topics are presented at the end of each chapter. These review topics examine the primary subjects covered in the chapter. There are also discussions embedded within the text of several chapters that relate business continuity principles to practical application.

Application

This book is designed to be used in a variety of courses and its modular design allows for the inclusion of topics based upon the objective of each course.

Sections I, II and III comprise the core material for an introductory course focusing on the basics of business continuity management. The inclusion of Chapters VII and XII in a course is dependent on the extent to which the foundational material is to be enhanced with a more comprehensive coverage of information systems. Likewise, Chapter IX extends coverage of emergency management beyond the basic level.

Section IV may be included in a course if a more comprehensive approach that includes risk modeling is the intent.

Supplementary Materials

Instructor Resources are available including: PowerPoint presentations, discussion - suggested solutions, review topics - suggested solutions, case studies - suggested solutions and a test bank. Contact the Publisher at info@rothstein.com for details.

Contributing Authors

> Shoshana S. Altschuller, PhD
> Daniel P. Iradi, JD
> José M. Merigó, PhD
> Holmes E. Miller, PhD
> Donald R. Moscato, PhD, CDP
> Ore A. Soluade, PhD.

Conclusion

We hope that our text provides a solid foundation for and appreciation of the importance of business continuity and risk management.

Kurt J. Engemann, PhD, CBCP

Douglas M. Henderson, FSA, CBCP

September, 2011

About the Authors

Kurt J. Engemann is the *Director of the Center for Business Continuity and Risk Management* and *Professor of Information Systems in the Hagan School of Business at Iona College.* He has consulted professionally over the past thirty years in the area of risk management decision modeling for major organizations and has been instrumental in the development and implementation of comprehensive business continuity management programs.

Dr. Engemann is a Certified Business Continuity Professional (CBCP) with the Disaster Recovery Institute International. Professor Engemann is the editor-in-chief of the *International Journal of Business Continuity and Risk Management* and the *International Journal of Technology, Policy and Management.* He teaches courses in the areas of Business Continuity and Risk Management, Systems Analysis and Design, Operations Management, Statistics and Decision Analysis. He has a PhD in Operations Research from New York University and has published extensively in the area of risk management and decision modeling.

Douglas M. Henderson, *President of Disaster Management, Inc.*, has 20 years of experience in management with major consulting firms. In August of 1992, Doug was the key associate of the Emergency Response Team for a consulting firm located in South Miami-Dade County. Inspired by the real life business experience with Hurricane Andrew and concerned about the lack of preparation within the business community, Mr. Henderson founded Disaster Management, Inc. in 1993.

Mr. Henderson's clients include Bombardier Capital Group, CP Ships, Discovery Channel Latin America, Intek Plastics, Kemper-NATLSCO, Professional Golfers' Association (PGA), University of Miami, United Educators Insurance Company and numerous other organizations of all sizes. The activities he has undertaken on behalf of these organizations includes conducting site inspections and writing Risk Assessment reports, Business Impact Analysis reports, Business Continuity Plans, Emergency Response Plans and the facilitating of tabletop exercises.

Mr. Henderson has a Degree in Mathematics from the University of Arizona. His professional credentials include FSA – Fellow, Society of Actuaries, and CBCP – Certified Business Continuity Professional. He is the author of the book *Is Your Business Ready for the Next Disaster?* and is the author of the *Comprehensive Business Continuity Management Program*, the *Continuity of Operations Plan for Colleges and Universities*, the *Hurricane and Flood Plan,* and several other planning templates.

SECTION I: DEVELOPMENT

Development begins with senior management's commitment to a Business Continuity Management program and commitment to improve organizational resiliency. The main components of development begin with the program initiation and the allocation of resources and assignment of responsibilities. Development includes the identification and analysis of the organization's operations, the assessment of natural and man-made threats to the organization, and the selection of the strategies needed to meet the established response, continuity and recovery objectives. Development also includes an analysis of information technology and other organization controls and exposures to manage risks.

CHAPTER 1

Fundamentals of Business Continuity Management

Objectives

» Define Business Continuity Management (BCM)

» Define the relationship between BCM and risk management

» Review BCM responsibilities

» Identify BCM benefits, costs and the commitment required

» Examine the BCM development process

» Review the use of a project management approach within BCM

» Review the data collection process for BCM

» Present an overview of professional standards and terminology

» Review the relationship between information technology and business continuity

» Define Green BCM.

Business Continuity and Risk Management

Planning for disasters may take a backseat to more immediate concerns, especially for a manager who considers such events as improbable and who has not thought through the potential impact of being unprepared. However, a prudent manager will develop contingency plans to provide for the continuation of essential operations. Senior managers should review the criticality of the organization's products and services to determine priorities and when operations must resume in order to avoid significant losses.

Operations will be disrupted if one or several required resources are unavailable. The event of the loss of a resource can be due to any one of several potential disasters. Identifying these possible events requires a review of all internal and external resources required to deliver an organization's products and services.

Planning must focus on those events that can result in significant losses. Such events are identified by comparing the expected recovery time associated with the event to the length of time operations can be interrupted before incurring significant losses.

Alternative strategies can reduce the risk of an event. The selection of the set of alternatives to be used will depend on their respective costs and benefits. In certain cases the decision is obvious. When the selection is not obvious a cost-benefit analysis may be required.

Business continuity refers to the actions taken to sustain and/or resume operations impacted by crisis events. Frequently the term **business continuity** by itself also implies recovery. **Business Continuity Management (BCM)** is a holistic management program that identifies potential events that threaten an organization and provides a framework for building resilience with the capability for an effective response that safeguards the interests of its key stakeholders, the environment, reputation, brand and value creating activities. **Resilience** is the ability of an organization to withstand the impact of a crisis event.

Risk management consists of the processes of risk assessment, risk communication and risk treatment. Risk management and BCM are sometimes mistakenly seen as competing fields. However, risk management and BCM are strongly tied together and viewing the fields separately is unhelpful. Risk management tends to be preventative, whereas BCM tends to deal more with consequences. Risk management processes provide important inputs for BCM and also deals with control for risks. On the other hand, BCM goes beyond risk management to plan for the inevitable disaster. Utilizing business continuity and risk management in an integrated fashion is coherent and productive.

There are multiple purposes for BCM. BCM is used to prevent serious disruptions, if possible, and to mitigate the impact of occurring disruptions. BCM is designed to provide safety for people and the environment, minimize the interruption of operations, mitigate damages, maintain customer service standards, maintain quality controls, reduce legal exposures and comply with regulations.

Risk management is the foundation of comprehensive BCM and provides an analytic basis and an economic justification for decision making regarding the allocation of resources. Risk management is a continual process of decisions resulting in how risks are treated, whether accepted, avoided, reduced or transferred.

Conceptually, risk management decisions are extremely difficult. The difficulty arises because these decisions must come to grips with uncertainties surrounding highly unlikely events with major, potential adverse impact upon the operation of an organization. The use of risk management for contingency planning can provide an organization with considerable savings through effective use of insurance and implementation of cost-effective loss reduction strategies.

BCM Responsibility

There are many challenges facing organizations regarding BCM. Communication of the benefits of BCM and similarly communication of the risk of not having a BCM program are foremost among these challenges. BCM should be partnered strategically with the organization to be most beneficial and the effectiveness of the program should be thoroughly evaluated. There is a need for regulations to ensure compliance, and likewise, there is a need for industry standards to promote widespread implementation of BCM.

The Board of Directors is an organization's highest management authority and has ultimate responsibility for the organization's performance. The Board of Directors must establish policies and objectives to ensure the organization's survival and fulfillment of its mission. Law imposes strict duties on directors because they exercise control and management over the organization. Internal control is the direct responsibility of the directors and these duties apply to each director separately.

Senior management holds specific powers conferred by the authority of the Board of Directors and has the responsibility of managing the organization. Senior management is responsible to initiate and oversee BCM to ensure the organization's preparedness and resiliency for a broad spectrum of critical events. It is the responsibility of all employees of an organization to understand their role in BCM and to actively participate as directed.

If there is a management of money or property among two or more parties a fiduciary responsibility is created. Although fiduciary responsibilities vary somewhat between different countries, a fiduciary is required to perform duties to the highest standards and to avoid any conflicts of interest.

BCM Benefits

Communication is a critical factor in obtaining support for BCM. Senior management should be made aware of the dangers of not having BCM. Examples of disasters in relevant industries are useful in establishing the necessity of BCM and obtaining support. Highlighting actual incidents that could have been disasters is also most useful.

There are many benefits to an organization to have comprehensive BCM. Effective BCM decreases exposure, reduces downtime, secures assets and improves security. The process of developing BCM improves employee understanding and provides cross-functional training. Also, BCM protects markets, provides legal compliance and helps avoid liability.

A presentation to senior management should relate BCM to the organization's mission, explain the risks to which the organization is vulnerable, explain management's accountability and liability and provide a foundation to develop BCM policy.

BCM Costs

The cost-justification of BCM is similar to the cost-justification of a good insurance policy: there is an initial outlay of a modest amount of money that will lessen the financial impact of a possible future crisis. Similar to an insurance policy, the financial benefit of BCM must be viewed from a long-term prospective. BCM is not a vehicle that will likely produce a short term return on investment. However, as with any other venture, BCM must ultimately be cost effective to remain funded. Many of the important benefits of BCM (for example, employee goodwill and customer satisfaction) are clearly important but are difficult to measure. All of these factors contribute to the challenge of securing a financial commitment from senior management for BCM.

The cost of establishing and maintaining BCM includes both initial and ongoing expenses related to various activities and assets, including:

- Developing BCM analysis and documentation.
- Backup facilities and equipment.
- Organization assets dedicated to emergency response.
- Physical improvements designed to mitigate damages.
- Training programs for employees.
- Exercising the BCM program.
- Maintaining BCM documentation.
- Insurance.

BCM Commitment

Before any program can commence and be successful, a commitment must be secured from the highest levels of the organization. Significant senior management-level participation at the corporate level is needed to oversee the program. Sufficient authority and resources have to be allocated to the BCM program for it to be successful.

A senior executive should act as sponsor and champion of the BCM program. Management is typically aware of the need for business continuity planning but may need assistance in many aspects of project initiation and management.

Senior management should ensure that prudent precautions are in place to prevent or mitigate a crisis, with the primary emphasis being on having the organization prepared to respond to safeguard people. Fundamentally, senior management is responsible for protecting the organization.

Senior management needs to develop and implement a business continuity policy tailored to its needs. The organization should define a BCM policy so that all operational components have documented and exercised plans for the full range of resources required. A generic example of such a statement is: 'We are committed to providing continuous operations for our entire organization under normal circumstances and rapid recovery from disruptive events.'

BCM is not a short term project that comes to completion, but rather it is an ongoing, continuous program. BCM should be comprehensive across the entire organization and prioritized by operational needs. To be effective, BCM should always be current and properly tested to ensure that the proper measures are taken in the event of a situation requiring BCM activation. It is necessary to develop an approach with a budget and a timeframe. Key decisions are needed to resolve several questions as follows:

- Do we have the internal expertise to complete the program? Do we want to use the services of a consultant? The consultant may shorten the time necessary to develop the BCM program and also add much value to it.
- Which software should be utilized for the BCM program? Word processing templates come in a variety of packages from basic to rather comprehensive. More expensive menu-driven software packages may be a better value for organizations with more complex planning needs.

BCM Development Process

BCM should strive to determine and implement the most cost-effective strategies that accomplish the business continuity objectives. Identifying potential events that threaten an organization and providing a framework for building resilience with the capability for an effective response involves actions before an event, during an event and after an event.

BCM should be based on operational requirements and led by an empowered team. The deliverable is a verified plan that modifies the impact of crisis events to acceptable levels.

The first priority of BCM must always be the protection of human life. BCM must also have as a priority the protection of the environment. BCM enables effective decisions during a crisis, minimizes asset loss, facilitates timely recovery and maintains the organization's reputation.

Business Continuity Phases are the steps to be taken before, during and after a crisis and include: prevention, mitigation, response, recovery and restoration. **Prevention** steps are designed to lessen the likelihood of a crisis event. **Mitigation** steps are designed to make the impact of an event less severe. **Response** is the reaction of an organization to an event to address immediate effects. **Recovery** is the stabilization and resumption of operations. **Restoration** is the process of returning to normal operations at a permanent location.

BCM is a program consisting of three major stages: **development, implementation** and **maintenance**. As depicted in Figure 1.1, the program is continuous and cycles through these steps for the various entities of an organization.

Figure 1.1 - The Cycle of BCM Stages

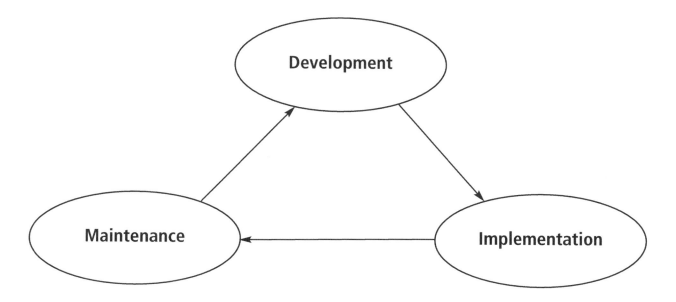

Development begins with senior management's commitment to a BCM program and involves the determination of business continuity strategies based upon an understanding of the organization. Senior management assesses organizational objectives and determines the critical products and services necessary to satisfy these objectives. The main components of development are:

▶ **Program Initiation** commences with a commitment by senior management to allocate resources and assign responsibilities for BCM.

▶ **Business Impact Analysis (BIA)** identifies the importance of the organization's activities by assessing the impact over time of their interruption and establishes continuity and recovery objectives. BIA establishes objectives before, during and after crisis events and examines the infrastructure necessary to conduct operations.

▶ **Risk Assessment (RA)** begins with a systematic process of identifying events, and determining their causes, probabilities and consequences. RA then compares risk levels with established risk criteria. RA and BIA are often conducted simultaneously.

▶ **Strategy Development** determines the strategies needed to meet the response, continuity and recovery objectives established during BIA.

Implementation involves putting the strategies in place, finalizing, documenting and, as necessary, activating the plans. The main components of implementation are:

▶ **Emergency Response Plan (ERP)** defines the action steps to be taken to respond to hazard-specific crisis events with the prioritized objectives of life-safety, environmental protection and asset protection.

▶ **The Business Continuity Plan (BCP)** is the central plan documentation that documents continuity and recovery procedures for crisis events. The ERP and the BCP are often developed simultaneously.

Maintenance involves creating an education and awareness culture of BCM and ongoing testing, auditing and change management to ensure the plans remain operable and current. The main components of maintenance are:

▶ **Awareness and Training** provides awareness to respond to crisis events and training to execute plans.

▶ **Testing and Exercising** assesses the viability of plan.

▶ **Maintaining and Updating** ensures consistency between the plan and the changes affecting the organization.

The BCM development process is implemented through a series of highly integrated projects as depicted in Figure 1.2.

Figure 1.2 - BCM Development Process

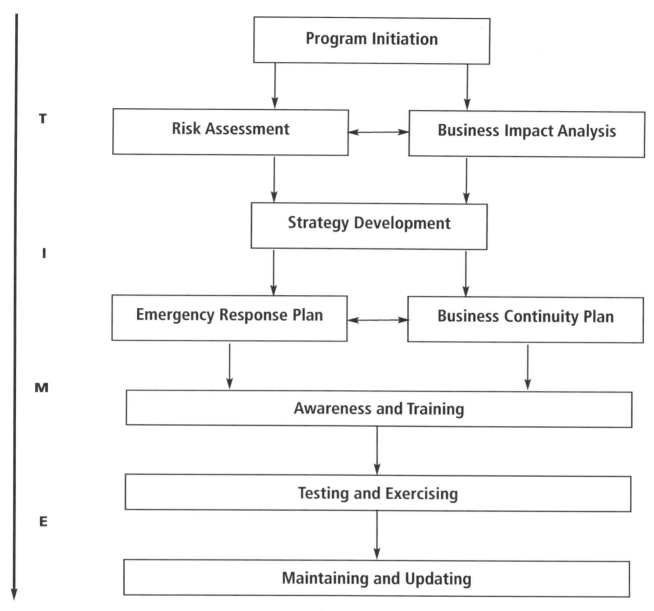

Project Management

BCM consists of numerous interrelated projects for which standard project management methodologies are most useful. Each project consists of data collection, analysis, documentation of findings and recommendations, management review and approval. Tasks that comprise a project, task duration times, precedence relationships and dependencies need to be defined in order to plan schedules. Additionally, resources need to be secured in order to undertake each project. Project management software is beneficial in tracking changes, establishing and reporting on project progress and making adjustments to meet management direction.

Every project has inherent risks of not fulfilling the intended objectives. Prior to initiating a project it is important to validate the expectations, evaluate the initial plans, assess the feasibility of schedules and resources and assess the project risk. A project manager should keep the project within scope, report variances in schedule and cost, update plans with management approval, validate the ability to meet revised goals and reschedule a revised project as necessary.

BCM should use a comprehensive approach that is formalized through a detailed methodology. The methodology should include methods of performing cost-benefit analysis and methods of handling uncertainty and determining the probability of rare events. The methodology establishes the rationale to determine the control alternatives to be implemented in a holistic fashion.

Project reviews are used to document task completions and to identify resource consumption. A well-designed methodology reduces the risk of project failure. Although some areas of an organization may have contingency plans, there is a need to have a consistent approach to business continuity planning across the entire organization using a standard methodology with articulated standards.

Data Collection

The objective of BCM is to limit the impact of major disruptions to an acceptable level. This involves determining the criticality of organization functions, operations and processes, identifying interrelationships and dependencies, identifying critical time frames and determining exposures over time. Data collection is an important activity throughout the BCM development process.

Data are obtained from various sources, including from documentation, meetings, interviews, workshops, questionnaires and site inspections. Existing documentation, such as organizational charts, flow charts, process diagrams, floor plans, engineering diagrams, financial statements and inventory records provide much useful information. Distributing questionnaires can be convenient and inexpensive. Individual interviews with key personnel can be useful but are also time-consuming. Group meetings may provide a more efficient means of collecting data. Site inspections are an integral part of the data collection process and are used to identify controls and exposures. Comprehensive checklists should be used to ensure that important points are not missed. Topics that should receive particular attention are: facilities, operations, IT, controls and procedures.

Discussion: Site Inspection – Site Unseen

An organization with multiple locations wants to utilize the services of a consultant but wants to save money by not having the consultant travel to and spend several days at each individual location. The organization believes that designated employees at each location can collect the information. Consider the following:

> ▶ Under what circumstances would this approach be most feasible?

> ▶ Under what circumstances would this approach be most difficult?

> ▶ What information and training would have to be provided to representatives from each location?

Certainly safety and security issues are of paramount importance to any organization. Business continuity professionals are typically not extensively trained to conduct detailed safety and security evaluation. For this reason, the site inspections conducted by business continuity professionals should review safety and security issues but should not be considered as a comprehensive safety and security analysis. If safety or security concerns are identified, then a trained safety and security professional should be contacted to address the situation.

Professional Standards

There are several organizations that have established professional standards and provide credentialing. At the international level, three of these organizations are the Disaster Recovery Institute International (www.drii.org), headquartered in the United States, the Business Continuity Institute (www.thebci.org) and the Institute of Risk Management (www.theirm.org), both headquartered in England. Qualified professionals are used worldwide for their expertise in business continuity and risk management to ensure that established standards are met.

There are also other organizations that have established standards. Perhaps the most widely recognized standard in the United States is the *NFPA 1600 Standard on Disaster/Emergency Management and Business Continuity Programs*. This standard has been established by the National Fire Protection Association (www.nfpa.org). The American Society for Industrial Security (www.asisonline.org) provides business and critical infrastructure with security standards, including SPC-2009 *Organizational Resilience: Security, Preparedness and Continuity Management Systems*. The *BS 25999 Standard for Business Continuity Management* was developed by the British Standards Institution (www.bsi-global.com) and is widely recognized internationally and within the United States. *HB 221-2004 Business Continuity Management and HB 292-2006 A Practitioners Guide to Business Continuity Management*, both developed by Standards Australia (www.standards.org.au), are widely recognized.

In the United States, Congress has directed the Department of Homeland Security (www.dhs.gov) to develop and implement a voluntary program of accreditation of private entities to promote preparedness in disaster management, emergency management and business continuity. The program is the Voluntary Private Sector Preparedness Accreditation and Certification Program (PS–Prep). Three standards have been adopted for assessing private sector preparedness as follows:

- *SPC-2009*
- *BS 25999*
- *NFPA 1600*

The National Accreditation Board, the accreditation body selected by the Department of Homeland Security, will oversee a certification process. The program will include a periodic review process, a public listing of accredited organizations and there will be special consideration given to small businesses.

Professional Terminology

As organizations became increasingly aware that disruptions have a severe negative impact, the business continuity profession arose to manage interruptions in IT and non-IT operations. As the business continuity profession developed, business terminology was blended with IT terminology. Over time the professional organizations have attempted to foster a more standard terminology to be used in BCM.

Federal, state and local emergency services have also developed terminology, much of which focuses on life-safety and emergency response. Government agencies use the terms 'Continuity of Operations Plan' and 'Continuity of Government Plan' rather than 'Business Continuity Plan.' Sometimes the continuity of operations planning segments for non-business entities are incorporated into an overall 'Emergency Operations Plan' or other similar term. Colleges and universities may or may not adopt business-related terms.

The Federal Emergency Management Agency (www.fema.gov) and the Emergency Management Institute (www.training.fema.gov/emi) has published an extensive collection of terms, definitions, acronyms, programs and legislative descriptions.

Information Technology and Business Continuity

The continuity and recovery of information technology (IT) services is vital to every organization. The term **disaster recovery** is generally used in the IT area to indicate business continuity activity. IT disaster recovery planning is part of overall business continuity planning and should be closely coordinated with business objectives. Information technology planning is completed by analysts with specialized training.

Executives need to know the capabilities and limitations of the IT Disaster Recovery Plan. Activation of the IT Disaster Recovery Plan as a result of a crisis event should return the organization's critical functions to stability and enable the continuity of those activities. A comprehensive IT Disaster Recovery Plan can be very expensive to maintain and execute. It is important for management to select the most cost-effective solution that accomplishes the established business continuity objectives.

Executives and IT personnel both need to keep current on IT trends that are constantly changing. IT personnel need to be thoroughly versed in technical matters. Most importantly, senior IT management needs to communicate very technical matters into understandable terms. Senior IT management needs to be able to analyze and communicate both the cost and the benefits of various IT solutions to the organization's business executives.

Green BCM

Sustainability is a central theme in decision making for organizations pursuing long term strategies. **Green BCM** is the conducting of the BCM program in a manner that is consistent with the objectives of reducing environmental impact, promoting sustainability, and conserving energy and other resources. Careful analysis is necessary to ensure that implemented strategies do not have unintended consequences which are hazardous in some unseen fashion.

Review Topics

1. What is the relationship between business continuity and risk management?
2. Identify the benefits of BCM that are easy to quantify and those that are not easy to quantify.
3. Identify the initial and ongoing expenses related to the BCM program.
4. Once completed, why would a BCP ever change?
5. Define the three stages in the BCM cycle.
6. Define the five phases of business continuity.
7. Why are comprehensive checklists and questionnaires beneficial during the site inspection and management interview process?
8. Why should senior management rather than IT managers have final approval over the IT Disaster Recovery Plan?

Case Studies

Case Study A-1: Alpha Investment Services (AIS) considers BCM

Information on Alpha Investment Services is located in Case Study A. Based on the Operations and Resource Requirements information provided in Case Study A, consider the following:

A-1.1   How would you collect information from management?

A-1.2   A key management person has a background in emergency response from prior military service and suggests using terminology used by FEMA rather than business oriented terminology. What are your thoughts on this idea?

A-1.3   The IT Department suggests that they should work on their IT Disaster Recovery Plan independently. What are your thoughts on this idea?

Case Study B-1: Beta Widget Makers (BWM) considers BCM

Information regarding Beta Widget Makers is located in Case Study B. Based on the Operations and the Resource Requirements information provided in Case Study B, consider the following:

B-1.1   How would you collect information from management?

B-1.2   A key management person has a background in emergency response from prior military service and suggests using terminology used by FEMA rather than business oriented terminology. What are your thoughts on this idea?

B-1.3   The IT Department suggests that they should work on their IT Disaster Recovery Plan independently. What are your thoughts on this idea?

Bibliography

American Society for Industrial Security, www.asisonline.org.

British Standards Institution, www.bsi-global.com.

Business Continuity Institute, www.thebci.org.

Disaster Recovery Institute International, www.drii.org.

Engemann, K. J., "Advancing Business Continuity and Risk Management," *International Journal of Business Continuity and Risk Management*, Vol. 1, No. 1, pp. 1-4, 2009.

Henderson, D. M., "Selection of Projects for Damage Mitigation using a Valuation Approach," *International Journal of Business Continuity and Risk Management*, Vol. 1, No. 2, pp. 197-210, 2010.

Institute of Risk Management, www.theirm.org.

Orlando, J., "Is Business Continuity a Moral Duty?," *Disaster Recovery Journal*, Fall 2008.

National Fire Protection Association (NFPA), www.nfpa.org.

Sarbanes Oxley, www.sarbanes-oxley.com.

Shaw, Gregory L., "Business Crisis and Continuity Management," in *Disciplines, Disaster and Emergency Management: The Convergence and Divergence of Concepts, Issues and Trends form the Research* Literature, (Ed. David A. McEntire), Federal Emergency Management Agency, Emergency Management Institute, Spring 2006.

CHAPTER II

Business Continuity
Management Organization

Objectives

» Determine the organizational requirements to plan for crisis events

» Identify individuals and teams needed to execute response and recovery plans

» Define the relationship between the various teams and individuals in the BCM program.

Overview of BCM Organization

Various individuals, teams and committees have roles in BCM before, during and after a crisis event - developing strategies, establishing the operation requirements and identifying resources needed. The BCM organizational structure selected should be functionally scalable and ready to expand or contract to meet the needs of all crises. All relevant organizational functions should be analyzed and represented (Appendix A: Organizational Functions). Some teams may be organization-wide while others are designated for particular locations. Teams may be composed of sub-teams suitable to various organizational situations.

Teams play a major role in BCM. Each business continuity team has a designated team leader and alternates. To keep the size of the teams to manageable levels, certain employees will often be assigned multiple responsibilities. It should also be kept in mind that some individuals may not be available to perform certain responsibilities during a crisis due to personal situations and alternates should be identified. Where possible, it may be beneficial to assign multiple alternate members, particularly for organizations subject to community-wide disasters.

In strategy development, teams identify the duration and scope of outage events, service priorities and key resources on which plans rely. To establish the operation requirements, it is necessary to define the type of service to be provided, the time by which service should be provided and the customers to whom service should be provided.

At the onset of a crisis, an organization must shift emphasis from normal operations to safety and security concerns. For most employees, plan execution responsibilities will likely be very different than normal responsibilities. Quick decisions need to be made and key employees need to execute response and recovery plans. It is not possible to effectively execute plans in a crisis situation if decisions are being made by committee.

Teams provide for recovery of affected parts of the organization and carry on the normal operations for unaffected parts of the organization.

Discussion: Management by Committee

Some organizations such as colleges, universities and associations prefer to conduct normal operations by committee. A 'management by committee' approach ensures that everyone knows the plan of action and all participants have the opportunity to express their ideas.

▶ What are the problems associated with management by committee during actual crisis events?

Key BCM Individuals and Groups

The BCM program is under the authority of the Chief Executive Officer (CEO). The CEO or designated alternate is responsible for declaring a disaster on behalf of the organization.

The **Business Continuity Management (BCM) Steering Committee** is the primary decision making group for the BCM program, has oversight for BCM at the corporate level and reviews and approves the BCM program. The BCM Steering Committee, which consists of senior management representing all primary functional and support areas, determines the scope, provides resources, develops timeframes and defines responsibilities for the BCM program.

Business Continuity Planning Team is responsible for providing professional guidance throughout the development, implementation and maintenance of the BCM program. The Business Continuity Planning Team develops the guidelines, methodologies, standards and best practices to be used in the BCM program. This group is responsible for adherence of all planning activity to the organizational protocols and standards. The Business Continuity Planning Team works with functional and technical individuals throughout the organization to develop plans at the business unit level.

A **Business Continuity Management (BCM) Coordinator** is an individual who has overall responsibility for BCM at each specific location. The BCM Coordinator ensures that the BCM program is properly planned. This includes assisting management in defining objectives and scope, and developing schedules and budgets. The BCM Coordinator utilizes project task forces and reports to senior management on the program's accomplishments. The BCM Coordinator performs regular updates to plan documentation and arranges for periodic plan exercises and actively participates in actual crisis events. The BCM Coordinator provides frequent feedback to management while acting on its behalf.

The BCM Coordinator should ideally be a business continuity professional who can work well within an organizational setting and has excellent communication skills to coordinate the work of teams and motivate individuals. The BCM Coordinator should possess strong analytical ability, technical competence, leadership skills and organizational knowledge. The BCM Coordinator has key responsibilities in responding to crisis events and is closely involved with the development, implementation and maintenance of the BCM program.

The **Crisis Management Team (CMT)** has overall responsibility to manage crisis events. The CMT includes senior management with the authority to manage active crisis events and is responsible to:

- Gather facts and analyze conditions regarding a crisis.
- Make decisions during a crisis.
- Allocate internal resources.
- Obtain needed external resources.

Organizations should develop a team to communicate with interested parties regarding crisis events. A **Crisis Communication Team** should be designated at the corporate level to maintain consistent communications and contact with the media. The Crisis Communication Team communicates with stakeholders and conducts all media communications.

The Crisis Communication Team is typically a group at the corporate level with liaison members designated at major organization locations. Crisis communication requires extensive planning and should always involve clear statements so that everyone involved receives consistent information. The most critical individuals are the employee in charge of overall communications and the 'spokesperson' in charge of media communications; a single individual often performs both functions.

The Crisis Communication Team should develop emergency plans and materials to prepare for crisis events. The Crisis Communication Team is responsible for the coordination of all information disseminated to employees, customers, the press, the public and other interested parties during times of crisis.

An **Emergency Response Team (ERT)** is an assembly of primary and alternate members at each major location responsible for the response to a crisis. All members are personnel who are familiar with their department's responsibilities. Alternate members execute their responsibilities in the absence or unavailability of the primary member.

All primary and alternate members need to be knowledgeable of overall BCM operations. Members must also be available during a crisis. ERT members and/or ERT alternate members are required to attend plan exercises organized by the BCM Coordinator.

These points should be considered regarding ERT membership:

- ▶ Team members should be drawn from a range of geographical locations to reduce the probability of severe impact to multiple members from a community-wide crisis.
- ▶ Team members should be capable of handling physically and emotionally stressful situations.
- ▶ Renters and single employees will likely have fewer personal responsibilities after a community-wide crisis.
- ▶ Vacations should be coordinated so that a large number of ERT members are not out of the area at any given time.

The organization's **Incident Commander** is in charge of the ERT. The Incident Commander is the individual responsible for the command and control of all aspects of a crisis. The Incident Commander must have the authority and ability to make quick decisions in critical situations. As the person who is in charge of the response efforts, the Incident Commander should be an officer of the organization. For a significant, organization-wide crisis event, it is not uncommon to find the Chief Operating Officer (COO), and not the CEO, at the top of the chain-of-command for emergency response purposes.

It is important for the organization to identify several individuals to serve as the Incident Commander and to specify a chain-of-command. The **chain-of-command** is the order of authority within the organization. During a crisis, the chain-of-command is not necessarily the same organizational command order used during times of normal operations. The actual Incident Commander will be the available individual who is highest on the chain-of-command.

The ERT is headed by the Incident Commander and consists of management personnel representing areas of the organization that have critical plan execution responsibilities. Overall incident command is relinquished to responding civil authorities at their request.

Other teams are involved in the BCM organization. The **Damage Assessment Team** assesses and documents damages caused by a crisis. The **Recovery Team** is designated to provide for stabilization and resumption of operations caused by a crisis. Other teams to perform specific functions may be designated by individual departments as necessary.

Figure 2.1 - BCM Organization

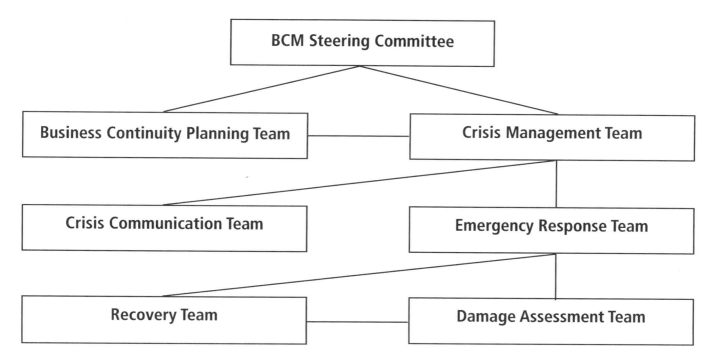

Review Topics

1. Identify reasons why quick decisions are often needed during the initial stages of a crisis event.

2. What are the significant differences between the responsibilities of the CMT and the ERT?

3. What are the characteristics of a person who would be a good leader during a disaster?

4. Does the BCM Coordinator need to be an employee at the senior management level?

Case Studies

Case Study A-2: Alpha Investment Services (AIS) considers BCM Organization

Based on the information previously provided in Case Study A, consider the following:

A-2.1   Is there a need for a CMT and an ERT at AIS?
A-2.2   Is there a need for an Incident Commander at each building?
A-2.3   Is there a need for an ERT at each building?

Case Study B-2: Beta Widget Makers (BWM) considers BCM Organization

Based on the information previously provided in Case Study B, consider the following:

B-2.1   Is there a need for a CMT and an ERT at BWM?
B-2.2   Is there a need for an Incident Commander at each Plant?
B-2.3   Is there a need for an ERT at each Plant?

Bibliography

Borodzicz, E., *Risk, Crisis and Security Management,* John Wiley and Sons, 2005.

Burtles, J., *Principles and Practices of Business Continuity: Tools and Techniques*, Rothstein Associates Inc., 2007.

Department of Homeland Security (DHS), www.dhs.gov.

Emergency Management Institute, IS-700.a National Incident Management System, 2009.

Federal Emergency Management Agency (FEMA), www.fema.gov.

Graham, J. and Kaye, D., *A Risk Management Approach to Business Continuity,* Rothstein Associates Inc., 2006.

Henderson, D. M., *The Comprehensive Business Continuity Management Program*, Rothstein Associates Inc., 2008.

Hiles, A. N., *Business Continuity: Best Practices: Aligning Business Continuity with Corporate Governance*, Rothstein Associates Inc., 2004.

National Incident Management System (NIMS), www.nimsonline.com.

Wong, W., and Shi, J., "The Role of Business Continuity Management in Organizational Long Range Planning," *International Journal of Business Continuity and Risk Management,* Vol. 1, No. 3, pp. 247-258, 2010.

CHAPTER III

Business Impact Analysis

Objectives

» Examine objectives of Business Impact Analysis (BIA)

» Define resource, outage, disruption and impact

» Define Recovery Time Objective (RTO)

» Define Recovery Point Objective (RPO)

» Review operations from the perspective of BCM

» Define supply chain and process flow

» Define single-point-of-failure

» Identify organization infrastructure and physical support operational requirements

» Review the relationship between BIA and BCM

» Determine the cost of BCM.

Organization Objectives and Business Impact Analysis

Through Business Continuity Management (BCM) an organization builds resilience to threats. To do this it is necessary to first understand the organization, the organization's deliverables which are its products, services, activities and resources that are essential to ensure continuity of critical activities at an appropriate level. Questions to be answered include:

▶ What are the objectives of the organization?

▶ What are the deliverables of the organization?

▶ What resources do these deliverables require?

Senior managers determine the criticality of the organization's deliverables and set priorities for the resumption of operations. **Business Impact Analysis (BIA)** determines the importance of the organization's activities by assessing the impact over time, if they are interrupted, and establishes continuity and recovery objectives.

BIA forms the foundation from which the BCM process is built. It quantifies the impact over time of a disruption and provides the rationale upon which appropriate continuity and recovery strategies can be formulated. The activities of BIA include: planning the project, collecting the data, analyzing the data, documenting the findings and recommendations, and obtaining senior management acceptance of the findings and recommendations.

The objectives of BIA are to:

▶ Determine the priority of the objectives of the organization.

▶ Determine the critical deliverables of the organization.

▶ Identify the critical resources required by the deliverables.

▶ Determine the impact over time of disruptions.

▶ Determine resumption timeframes for critical operations following disruptions.

▶ Provide information from which appropriate recovery strategies can be determined.

Organizations depend on resources being available in order for operations to function properly. A **resource** is an asset used to conduct operations. Resources include personnel, facilities, equipment, inventory, utilities and systems. An **outage** is the unavailability of a resource which may cause a disruption in operations. This may be due to destruction, disablement or denial of use of a resource. **Disruption** is an interruption of operations. Generic scenarios which may result in disruptions are used to assess the impact over time on the organization. BIA is conducted without reference to specific causes of disruption. **Impact** is the effect of an event. The level of impact depends on factors such as loss of life, environmental damage, asset damage and duration of disruption. Both financial and non-financial impacts may result from a disruption.

Recovery Time Objective

It is generally not practical for organizations to immediately recover all operations following a disruption. A **Recovery Time Objective (RTO)** is the prospective point in time when an operation must be resumed before a disruption compromises the ability of the organization to achieve its objectives. Establishing the RTO for each critical operation is a key activity of BIA. Various critical operations may have a different RTO and a single critical operation may have a staggered RTO allowing the operation to gradually recover over time, for example, 50% capability within two days and 100% capability within seven days. The business continuity process after a disruption should be conducted focusing on recovering operations with the shortest RTOs first.

Each RTO may be tentatively determined early in the BIA based on 'ideal' recovery objectives. After further review, short RTOs are often adjusted to reflect the financial realities of executing a fast recovery. Short RTOs will typically require more expensive strategies. As with any program, BCM must fit within the organization's budget.

In order to assess the impact of a crisis to the organization and prioritize operations, the entire supply chain, including internal process flow, must be understood. Establishing the RTO for each operation requires balancing the impact over time to the organization against the cost to recover within the RTO. Senior management makes the final RTO determinations.

BIA determines the resource requirements over time to enable each function within the organization to achieve continuity and recovery within established timeframes. It identifies requirements regarding resources including:

- air conditioning
- communications
- data
- equipment
- facilities
- gas
- information technology
- inventory
- materials
- personnel
- power supply
- sewer
- supplies
- systems
- vital records
- water

Recovery Point Objective

Unless information is secured on an ongoing basis utilizing redundant remote operations, there is a risk of information loss. For example, if information is secured in the evening of every business day, then information created during the next day and before the next evening backup will be subject to loss.

A **Recovery Point Objective (RPO)** is a retrospective point in time to which information must be recovered to ensure objectives can be met. Each RPO is determined in a cost-benefit analysis balancing the value of information at risk and the cost of controls that can be utilized to minimize information loss. The RPO establishes the pre-crisis period of acceptable information loss. Senior management makes the final RPO determinations.

Operations

For BCM purposes, there are two levels of information that need to be collected and analyzed to develop an understanding of the operations of an organization. The first level contains information common to all operations at a specific location and includes building construction and utilities such as electricity, communication, water, air conditioning and heating. The second level addresses information specific to each operation, such as daily volumes, equipment used, functions performed, relationships with other operations and external interfaces. This information helps in identifying some of the threats that must be addressed when developing alternative strategies.

All critical areas of the organization that must remain operational or rapidly recover for normal activities to continue need to be identified. **Critical operations** are activities that are necessary to safely support the primary mission of the organization. Critical operations are determined based on two variables: the importance of the operation and the time sensitivity of the operation. Generally critical operations include life-safety and environmental controls, customer service support-related operations, revenue-generating operations or operations that directly support revenue-generating operations. Within the domain of revenue-generating operations, some operations are more critical than others. The most profitable operations should receive special attention.

There are many operations that are important but not time sensitive and therefore are not identified as critical operations. For example, marketing operations are an important long-term function for nearly every organization, yet nearly all marketing operations can be suspended for a few days. On the other hand, there are many activities that are time sensitive but not critical. For example, a general staff meeting at 10am is time sensitive but typically general staff meetings are not critical.

Senior management reviews the level of importance of operations as assessed by each department. Occasionally, individual departments overestimate the importance of their activities; the management team will likely have to make a number of downward revisions.

Interdependencies

Supply chains and process flows illustrate interdependencies in operations. The emergence of a deliverable to the final customer is dependent on all operational components functioning properly.

A **supply chain** is a sequence of operations conducted by a system of organizations involved in the creation and distribution of a deliverable. Supply chain management includes the activities that procure materials and services, transforms them into intermediate goods and finished products and delivers them to customers. With an increasing reliance on supply chains comes more risk. Increasing globalization, specialization and reliance on fewer suppliers exacerbates the situation. The current approach of low-inventory supply chains operating across political boundaries adds a new dimension to risk.

A **process flow** (internal supply chain) consists of the sequence of operations by which an organization creates a deliverable. The process flow of a manufacturer converts raw materials into physical products as its deliverable. An information service organization transforms raw data into useful information as its deliverable.

Supply chain management integrates supply and demand management within and across companies. With Just-in-Time (JIT), materials arrive only when they are needed. JIT inventory is the minimum inventory necessary to keep a perfect system running. This can present challenges for the business continuity planner who must cope with the interdependency of supply chain and process flow. For example, in Figure 3.1, if the Raw Materials Supplier was unable to deliver, Manufacturing would shortly not have the raw materials to continue operations. Other interdependencies are also present. For example, if Fabrication were disabled, Assembly would be disabled within a short period of time and Test and Quality Control would be disabled somewhat later, and so forth. Practically all manufacturing operations exhibit this type of interdependency.

Manufacturing operations are also dependent on major support provided by other departments such as Human Resources, Information Technology and Facilities. Many support functions can be briefly suspended without impacting manufacturing operations. However, Information Technology is one support function that is time critical for many manufacturers where manual override is not always a feasible option.

Service industries are also a type of supply chain with many interdependencies. Data is collected, verified, analyzed with some value added and sold to a client. The entire process is sometimes completely void of paper or other physical object.

Case Study C presents an analysis of a supply chain.

Figure 3.1 - Basic Supply Chain

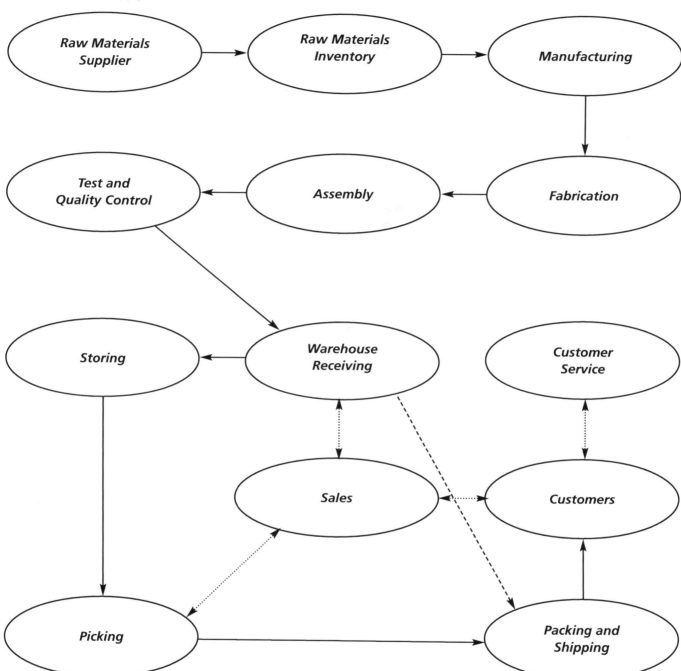

Single-Point-of-Failure

A **single-point-of-failure** is a unique resource, the failure of which will interrupt critical operations. Any operation that relies on 'one and only one' item of equipment or 'one and only one' method of processing or any 'one and only one' resource, represents a single-point-of-failure. Sometimes there are less-efficient alternate procedures or manual overrides that can be employed and sometimes there are no realistic alternatives. BIA must identify each single-point-of-failure, identify alternatives and define the potential impact to the organization associated with each single-point-of-failure.

For example, a manufacturer may have a single piece of equipment that is critical to operations and there are no manual overrides or other alternatives available if the equipment fails. If the equipment takes three months to replace, then the organization is at risk to be inoperative for three months. Management may decide to have backup equipment available, which is perhaps a very expensive alternative. If possible, management may arrange to use a competitor's equipment. Alternately, management may make a highly undesirable decision to produce a lower quality product. If none of these options are feasible, management may choose to protect the equipment to the maximum extent possible to reduce the possibility of destruction. The business continuity planner's responsibility is to develop the options and not select the option of choice – selecting the option of choice is the responsibility of senior management.

Support Infrastructure and Physical Environment Requirements

Buildings and Building Systems

Some organizations require general office space that is easily replaced. Other organizations, such as manufacturing industries, may require buildings with special features and systems that cannot be readily replaced. Building replacement time in this later case is measured in months. The destruction or denial of access to buildings, even ones that are easily replaced, could disable normal operations for a period of time.

BIA should document the important building requirements of the organization. For all important building requirements, the replacement time and any alternative options need to be identified.

Building Contents and Manufacturing Equipment

Some organizations require building contents such as furniture and office supplies that are easily replaced. Other organizations require specialized equipment that cannot be readily replaced. Certain organizations will have contents or manufacturing equipment that are of very high value. Special pre-crisis protection measures for high value or specialized equipment should be part of the planning process.

BIA should document the important building content and manufacturing equipment requirements. For all important building content and manufacturing equipment requirements, the replacement time and any alternative options need to be identified.

Community Infrastructure

Essential community infrastructure services include:

▶ **Fire** – Before any building can be utilized, basic fire and emergency services need to be available.

▶ **Police** – In order to conduct any normal operation, a general state of law and order must exist in the area.

▶ **Transportation** – For most organizations, employees live outside the immediate area and rely on public road access or public transportation.

▶ **Utilities:**

  ❖ **Communications** – Without voice and data communications, normal operations would cease for many organizations.

  ❖ **Electricity** – For most organizations without a backup electric generator, reliable electrical supply is essential to virtually all operations.

  ❖ **Natural Gas** – This is typically used to heat buildings.

❖ **Sewer** – For sanitation reasons, adequate sewer system operations are necessary for all employees.

❖ **Water** – Potable water is obviously essential to maintain human life and water is necessary for sanitary reasons.

There may be some, often low-tech, solutions that can be used to replace normal utility services on a temporary basis.

External Dependencies

External dependencies include other organizations that provide important services, supplies or raw materials. Special importance must be placed on any single or sole-source providers of critical services or raw materials. These providers represent a single-point-of-failure. BIA must identify each single-point-of-failure and identify some type of alternative or define the impact of a crisis event to the organization if this particular source fails.

BIA Provides Direction for BCM

BIA provides direction for BCM by providing an overall rationale for the program. Information assembled during BIA development identifies processes and assets that require the most protection, determines recovery timeframes, determines minimum resource requirements and provides decision support for strategies.

It is necessary to understand the impact of disruptions over time by identifying critical functions and operations, identifying potential impacts and determining when impacts begin. An event may be designated as a disaster if the disruption continues beyond the RTO, or is expected to continue beyond the RTO, and if the disruption's impact is extensive and very costly.

The cost of BCM increases as the RTO decreases. For example, a short RTO may require standby duplicate backup equipment, standby building or dedicated space and these controls can be very expensive. If a short RTO is not required, then less expensive strategies can be explored.

Financial Losses Resulting from a Crisis

The loss of the ability of the organization to provide services has a direct and indirect financial impact; in particular, indirect losses are sometimes difficult to measure exactly. Insurance can cover, at least to a large extent, financial losses associated with downtime and the destruction of organization assets. Insurance does not cover most indirect losses or the loss of revenue.

Direct financial losses can include:

▶ Destruction of organization assets.

▶ Loss of revenue.

Indirect financial losses can result from:

▶ Decrease in customer and client satisfaction.

▶ Decrease in investor confidence.

▶ Damage to reputation and brand.

▶ Adverse media coverage.

- Reduction of competitive capabilities.

- Legal exposures.

- Missed filing and reporting deadlines.

- An increase in risk rating by financial institutions.

- Loss of business opportunities.

Many of these losses become more pronounced if the crisis results in an extended period of inactivity or a decrease of normal organization service/production levels. Losses resulting from a crisis increase the longer the organization remains operating at less than normal levels.

Discussion: Let's Skip BIA

Encountering an organization that has a BCM program but has never conducted a formal BIA is not that uncommon. Management is often interested in having comprehensive BCM but believes that performing BIA may be an unnecessary expense.

- What reasons might be given for skipping BIA?

- Why is it important to conduct a thorough BIA?

BIA Results

Findings from BIA should be validated and documented. Any missing information is determined and findings are confirmed and reviewed for consistency before any recommendations to senior management are made.

A properly conducted BIA provides insight through an understanding of critical functions and operational dependencies. The time sensitivity of operations, resource requirements for recovery and resumption, resource replacement times and financial exposures are determined. Senior management is responsible to confirm recovery time objectives, the order of recovery of operations, recovery point objectives and the prioritization of critical functions. BIA provides crucial information to support decision making regarding business continuity planning.

Review Topics

1. Define and explain the differences between resource, outage, disruption and impact.

2. Why are all important operations not considered to be critical operations?

3. Define and explain the differences between supply chain and process flow.

4. Identify reasons why an operation with a short RTO will require a more expensive BCM than a similar operation but with a longer RTO.

Case Studies

Case Study A-3: Alpha Investment Services (AIS) conducts BIA

Based on the Operations and Resource Requirements information provided in Case Study A, consider the following:

A-3.1 For AIS, what are the most critical operations for each operational group and support department?

A-3.2 Identify the major interdependencies within AIS operations.

A-3.3 What are the Recovery Time Objectives for the following operations?

Department	Operation	RTO
Custom Research	Research and Analysis	
Equity Selection Services	Research for Printed Reports	
Data Operations	Data Acquisition	
	Data Verification	
Facilities	Utility Services	
	Environmental Controls	
	General Building Maintenance	
Finance and Accounting	Financial Reporting	
	Crisis Communication	
Human Resources	Payroll	
Information Technology	IT for Data Operations	
	IT for Operational Groups	
	IT for Payroll	
	Communication Technologies	
Sales and Marketing	Marketing Program	
Security	Building Protection	

A-3.4 Is it logical to set initial Recovery Time Objectives for support operations equal to something less than 100% for certain responsibilities?

A-3.5 Identify the major single-points-of-failure in the supply chain and process flow.

Case Study B-3: Beta Widget Makers (BWM) conducts BIA

Based on the Operations and Resource Requirements information provided in Case Study B, consider the following:

B-3.1 For BWM, what are the most critical operations for each operational group and support department?

B-3.2 Identify the major interdependencies within BWM operations.

B-3.3 What are the Recovery Time Objectives for the following operations?

Department	Operation	RTO
Manufacturing	Manufacturing	
R and D	New Product Design	
	Testing	
Supply Chain Mgmt.	Acquisition of Raw Materials	
	Fulfillment Mgmt.	
Warehouse	Receiving	
	Shipping	
Facilities	Utility Services	
	Environmental Controls	
	General Plant Maintenance	
	Plant Protection	
Finance and Accounting	Financial Reporting	
	Crisis Communication	
Human Resources	Payroll	
Information Technology	IT Manufacturing Support	
	IT Sales and Customer Service Support	
Sales and Customer Service	Marketing Program	
	Direct Sales	

B-3.4   Is it logical to set initial Recovery Time Objectives for support operations equal to something less than 100% for certain responsibilities?

B-3.5   Identify the major single-points-of-failure in the supply chain and process flow.

Bibliography

Aven, T., "A New Scientific Framework for Quantitative Risk Assessments," *International Journal of Business Continuity and Risk Management*, Vol. 1, No. 1, pp. 67-77, 2009.

Aven, T., *Risk Analysis-Assessing Uncertainties Beyond Expected Values and Probabilities*, John Wiley and Sons, 2008.

Bell, J. K., *Disaster Survival Planning*, Disaster Survival Planning, Inc., 1991.

Burtles, J., *Principles and Practices of Business Continuity: Tools and Techniques*, Rothstein Associates Inc., 2007.

Carreira B., *Lean Manufacturing that Works*, American Management Association, 2005.

Cullinane, T. P., *How to Plan and Manage Warehouse Operations*, American Management Association, 1994.

Dailey, K. W., *The Lean Manufacturing Pocket Handbook*, DW Publishing Co., 2003.

Engemann, K. J., Miller, H. E., and Dengler, N., "Managing Supply Chain Risk in Financial Services," *Emerging Themes in Supply Chain Risk Management: A Collection of Case Studies and Practices* (ed. O. Khan and G. Zsidisin), J. Ross Publishers, 2011.

Engemann, K. J., Miller, H. E. and Yager, R. R., "Decision Making with Attitudinal Based Expected Values," *International Journal of Technology, Policy and Management*, Vol. 4, No. 4, pp. 353-365, 2004.

Fulmer, K. L., *Business Continuity Planning: A Step-by-Step Guide With Planning Forms*, Rothstein Associates Inc., 2005.

Graham, J. and Kaye, D., *A Risk Management Approach to Business Continuity*, Rothstein Associates Inc., 2006.

Haimes, Y., *Risk Modeling, Assessment, and Management*, John Wiley and Sons, 2008.

Heizer, J. and Render, B., *Operations Management*, Prentice Hall, 2011.

Henderson, D. M., *The Comprehensive Business Continuity Management Program*, Rothstein Associates Inc., 2008.

Hiles, A. N., *Business Continuity: Best Practices: Aligning Business Continuity with Corporate Governance*, Rothstein Associates Inc., 2004.

Hiles, A. N., *Enterprise Risk Assessment and Business Impact Analysis*, Rothstein Associates Inc., 2002.

Kirschenbaum, A., "The Missing Link in Business Continuity," *Disaster Recovery Journal*, Fall 2006.

Miller, H. E. and Engemann, K. J., "A Supply Chain Simulation to Examine the Effects of Mitigation and Disaster Recovery Strategies," *Advances in Decision Technology and Intelligent Information Systems, Volume IX* (ed. K. Engemann and G. Lasker), pp. 56-60, The International Institute for Advanced Studies in Systems Research and Cybernetics, 2008.

Miller, H. E., Engemann, K. J., and Yager, R. R., "Disaster Planning and Management," *Communications of the International Information Management Association*, Vol. 6, Issue 2, pp. 25-36, 2006.

National Fire Protection Association (NFPA), www.nfpa.org.

National Safety Council, www.nsc.org.

Philpott, D., and Einstein S., *The Integrated Physical Security Handbook*, Don Dickson, 2006.

Reese, A. K., "Disaster-Proofing the Supply Chain," *Supply and Demand-Chain Executive*, April/May, 2007.

Rojas, B., "Securing Your Supply Chain," *Continuity Insights*, March/April, 2009.

Society for Human Resource Management, www.shrm.org/pages/default.aspx.

Supply and Demand-Chain Executive, www.sdcexec.com.

United States Department of Labor (DOL), Occupational Safety and Health Administration (OSHA), www.osha.gov.

Vose, D., Risk Analysis: *A Quantitative Guide*, 3rd Edition, John Wiley and Sons, 2008.

Risk Assessment

Objectives

» Define risk terminology

» Define the purpose of Risk Assessment (RA)

» Review the RA process

» Review how threats to an organization are identified

» Identify and evaluate controls

» Explore event probability estimation

» Identify methods of impact estimation

» Analyze risk measurement

» Identify the risks of greatest concern

» Examine the options to manage risks.

Risk

Risk management is the basis of BCM and provides an analytical foundation for decision making regarding the treatment of risk. A key tenet of risk management is that risk cannot be eliminated but that it can be controlled. The appropriate control to employ depends both on the likelihood of the risk occurring and the magnitude of the loss if the risk does occur. Often risk can be quantified; however, when risk cannot be quantified, either because the underlying information does not exist or because it is too expensive to collect, principles of risk management can still be applied. These principles include:

1. Identifying what can go wrong by analyzing the underlying threats and possible crisis events;

2. Identifying what controls are currently in place;

3. Evaluating the current exposure to the organization;

4. Identifying new controls that can be implemented to reduce this exposure;

5. Evaluating whether these controls should be implemented by investigating the costs and benefits.

An **event** (incident) is an occurrence that could have an impact upon the organization. Because BCM deals with events that are improbable, analyzing risks is challenging. It can be difficult to come to grips with uncertainties surrounding highly unlikely events with major potential adverse impact upon the operation of an organization.

The core of the analysis involves specifying a set of encompassing crisis events which represent 'what can go wrong.' A **threat** (hazard) is a source of potential negative impact. A **crisis** (crisis event) is a manifestation of a threat. If not handled properly, a crisis may have a severe negative impact. A **minor crisis** has limited impact and does not affect the overall functioning capacity of an organization, whereas a **major crisis** has the potential to seriously disrupt the overall operation of an organization. A **disaster** is a major crisis event which imperils an organization. An event may be deemed to be a disaster due to factors such as loss of life, environmental damage, asset damage and duration of disruption. A **catastrophe** is an extreme disaster.

Risk is the possibility of experiencing an event, measured in terms of probability and impact. **Probability** is a measure of the likelihood of an event. A **risk event chain** describes the transition from threat to crisis to disruption to impact. Figure 4.1 depicts a risk event chain. As an example, fire is a threat and a crisis would be a fire affecting a particular facility. The fire can cause a disruption of the processing facility for a length of time. The disruption can result in an impact of asset damage and revenue loss.

Figure 4.1 - Risk Event Chain

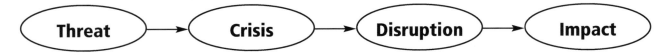

The paradigm of the risk event chain provides flexibility in the level of detail to use in analyzing risk. For example, using a broad view during an initial study, an impact can be thought of as resulting from a threat without explicitly studying the transitions through crisis and disruption.

Controls can reduce the probability of transitioning through the risk event chain and can mitigate the resultant impact. It is possible for different crisis events to result in the same disruption; for example, a data center could be destroyed by a fire, flood or explosion. Because identifying all possible crisis events is difficult and impractical, the events chosen for analysis should represent the most significant exposures faced by the organization.

Risk analysis is the process of identifying events, determining causes, and estimating probabilities and impact. **Risk evaluation** is the process of comparing risk levels with established risk criteria. **Risk Assessment (RA)** is the process of risk analysis and risk evaluation. The purpose of RA is to prioritize planning by assessing the likelihood of events and their potential impact on critical functions. RA is fundamental to identifying vulnerability and is a basis for resource allocation and exposure mitigation. **Vulnerability** is a measure of exposure to a threat that increases as the probability and impact of the event increases. **Risk tolerance** is the amount of risk that an organization is prepared to accept. Risk tolerance drives the level of action an organization will take to control identified threats. **Risk management** is comprised of the processes of risk assessment, risk communication and risk treatment. **Risk communication** is the exchange of risk information among stakeholders and **risk treatment** is the selection of procedures for managing risk.

RA is used to determine the most significant threats to an organization and to direct hazard-specific planning to address these threats by prioritization. RA activity should be focused on the most urgent business functions identified during the BIA.

The steps of RA are:

- Identify significant threats to critical operations.
- Identify and evaluate controls.
- Estimate event probabilities.
- Estimate impacts.
- Determine a risk measure combining impact and probability.
- Prioritize risks.

Senior management reviews the findings of RA and information developed during RA provides a basis for managing risk.

Threat Identification

Threats are ubiquitous and represent possible sources of negative impact to an organization. Threats can be natural, accidental or man-made and can lead to disruptions in operations which can adversely impact an organization. Significant threats that warrant further consideration are identified during RA.

Generic threats to consider include:

Acts of war	Flood	Radiation leak
Armed attack	Freeze	Riot
Blackmail	Hostage situation	Terrorism
Blizzard	Hurricane	Tornado
Chemical spill	Insurrection	Transportation disruption
Contamination	Kidnapping	Tsunami
Earthquake	Power outage	Volcano eruption
Fire	Product defect	Workplace violence

There are other categories of threats that can have a negative impact on an organization. A holistic approach towards risk management needs to include an analysis of all threats such as those of financial, economic, market, fraudulent and negligence origin. The relevance of a threat depends upon many factors including:

geographic location, infrastructure, political conditions and economic conditions. A systematic way to collect and analyze threat data is to begin with a broad view and then continue to a detailed view. For example, using a sequence such as region, community and building may be useful. Threats can be identified in the general region (e.g. hurricane), in the community (e.g. power outage) and in the building (e.g. fire).

For natural threats, the gathering of data with sufficient detail and accuracy can usually be accomplished by research on the Internet. General information for weather and seismic threats is usually easily obtained. When evaluating man-made, accidental and other non-natural threats, there are often a large number of variables involved. Information for man-made, accidental and other threats tend to be less location-specific and more judgment is often required.

The manifestation of a threat as a crisis may lead to a disruption. In identifying possible disruptions it is helpful to draw upon the information gathered in the BIA. Some outages that should be addressed include:

- Destruction of a processing area due to fire or bomb.
- Destruction of a building by fire, bomb or earthquake.
- Flooding of a processing area or adjacent areas due to hurricane, storm or ruptured water pipe.
- Inaccessibility to a building due to fire or bomb threats.
- Outages in communications, electric power, steam supply or air conditioning due to fire or flood.
- Lack of processing personnel due to a strike, transportation problems or snowstorm.

Those specific events which impact operations and cause disruptions beyond the RTO are then identified.

Part of the difficulty in assessing certain threats is a result of the type of organization under analysis. The two business case studies included in this book illustrate these differences. Another part of the difficulty in assessing certain threats is a result of a large number of controls, exposures and variables.

Consider the following examples:

- **Example 1** – An organization with a technology department that has an IT alternate site plan and backup data center that can be activated rapidly will be able to recover quickly from a major crisis. An organization without these planning and resources available will most likely not be able to recover quickly. Also, a technology department with good physical controls (e.g. raised floors, fire suppression system, dedicated HVAC, and backup electric generator) at the data center is less likely to experience a major crisis than an organization that does not have good physical data center controls in place.

- **Example 2** – An organization with good security controls (e.g. proper procedures, monitored security system, dedicated security personnel) can avoid many security breaches. Security will also be impacted by the general crime rate in the area and the exact nature of the organization.

- **Example 3** – A manufacturing organization that requires the use of hazmat materials can reduce the likelihood of a hazardous release and can contain a release better if a good hazard response plan is in place. Many other factors are important. Has the hazmat team been properly trained and properly equipped? What types of chemicals are used? How are the chemicals stored?

- **Example 4** – The RA of a terrorist attack is most difficult to make. The type, level and location of the event will all be factors that are often hard to pinpoint. RA must consider the likelihood of a terrorist attack on the organization and in the immediate area. Plus RA must consider the impact, if any, of a major terrorist attack at a distant location. Certain organizations may be impacted by overseas terrorist attacks.

Controls Identification and Evaluation

Controls are devices and procedures that prevent the occurrence of a crisis event or mitigate the impact of a threat. Controls include physical security, preventive maintenance, information security and personal procedures. The effectiveness of existing controls should be evaluated. The evaluation of controls includes determining the benefits of the controls, identifying costs, developing options and improving the controls. After determining any outstanding risks to the organization, potential cost-effective controls are identified and recommended for management approval.

Some controls reduce the probability that an event will occur; other alternatives reduce losses by providing some business continuity during a disaster or improving workplace safety. Generic control checklists are useful in exploring alternatives. For each function, the generic alternatives are further developed with appropriate details for the specific location. The annualized cost of each alternative is calculated and compared to the reduction in the expected annualized risk exposure. Some decisions are obvious; others require more detailed quantifications and sensitivity analysis. Recommendations regarding additional planning, improvements to existing procedures and physical controls to mitigate damages, injuries and loss of life should be identified.

Building Evacuation and Safety Procedures

The two most common safety procedures are building evacuation and shelter-in-place. Most individuals understand how to conduct a building evacuation as these procedures have been regularly practiced in the school system. Shelter-in-place procedures have historically not been practiced as frequently as building evacuation procedures.

It is important that formal plans be developed to address both building evacuation and shelter-in-place procedures. Plans should include the identification of safe gathering areas, routes to gathering areas and procedures to make a headcount at the gathering areas.

The need to communicate emergency instructions during a crisis event is central to the effectiveness of executing the procedure. Communicating accurate and sufficiently detailed information presents an important challenge. Typically alarms alert everyone to conduct a building evacuation.

At a minimum, some type of siren is needed to alert everyone that a dangerous condition exists and a shelter-in-place needs to be performed. In addition to a siren, it is very important to utilize an intercom or other communication system. Emergency information regarding a hostile intruder, hazardous release or tornado cannot be effectively communicated by a siren alone.

Depending on the specific threat there are important differences in the exact shelter-in-place procedures. For a hostile intruder threat, doors need to be locked, windows and window treatments should be closed, and everyone should get out of sight. For a tornado threat, with time permitting, employees in outside rooms should relocate to interior corridors – this procedure is not recommended in a hostile intruder situation.

Hazardous Materials

Organizations may have some level of hazardous materials (hazmat) and should review the following:

▶ Have all hazardous materials been identified?
▶ Is there an MSDS (Material Safety Data Sheet) for every hazardous material maintained by the organization? **Material Safety Data Sheet (MSDS)** is a summary of information regarding hazardous materials.

▶ Are all employees trained in utilizing emergency action plans, evacuation routes and alarm activation?

Organizations with large amounts of hazmat present in the workplace require special planning to avoid environmental contamination and health hazards. Planning should contemplate the following:

▶ Has the organization identified and trained Hazardous Response Teams in compliance with federal and state Hazardous Materials First Responder regulations with:

   ❖ Plant shutdown?

   ❖ Use of fire extinguishers?

   ❖ Chemical spill control?

   ❖ Search and rescue procedures?

   ❖ First aid?

▶ Does training occur initially upon hire, at least annually thereafter, and whenever new equipment or materials are introduced?

▶ Have personal protection equipment (PPE) such as respirators, boots and whole body coverings for adverse environmental conditions been considered?

▶ Unless the facility is near a hospital or other medical treatment facility, are there on-site personnel properly equipped and trained in first aid?

▶ Are hazardous materials stored in approved containers, in properly ventilated areas where volatile chemicals cannot interact and away from heat sources?

▶ Are non-smoking policies established and enforced?

▶ Are all hazardous wastes disposed of properly?

▶ Is every incident investigated?

Personnel Concerns

As employees are one of the critical keys to the success of any organization, employee safety and security issues are important components of BCM. Particularly after a community-wide crisis event, the recovery of the workforce is a high priority and a challenge.

After a community-wide crisis event, employees may not be able to work for a wide range of reasons. Employees and their families may be injured or be living in a 'survival mode.' Transportation to and from work may be very difficult or impossible. Back to work policies and payroll policies will need to be developed to address all these contingencies. Providing employees with some level of crisis assistance will help with workforce recovery. Management needs to address the following:

▶ Can the organization function with a skeleton staff?

▶ How highly trained and educated is the workforce?

▶ Can temporary replacement workers be found and quickly trained?

▶ Are certain critical responsibilities being performed by only one employee – essentially representing a 'single-point-of-failure?'

▶ Is cross-training being performed?

▶ Is there a good 'Disaster Assistance Plan' (Appendix B) in place to define crisis payroll and time-off policies plus help employees affected by the crisis?

For organizations with unionized labor employees, the possibility of a strike, work slowdown or other labor action needs to be considered. Management needs to address the following:

▶ Is there a plan in place to deal with a strike?

▶ Can non-union employees or management employees maintain critical operations without union employees?

▶ Does the organization have a good relationship with the labor union?

▶ Does the organization have a plan to either maintain or improve labor union relations?

▶ What has been the history of work stoppages and strikes?

▶ What are the key labor issues that are currently in dispute and when does the current labor contract expire?

Discussion: Conducting Operations with a Skeleton Staff

What if a crisis event occurred that did not significantly damage assets but prevented a large segment of the workforce from working? This scenario actually happened to many organizations in Miami, Florida in August 1992 after Hurricane Andrew.

On August 24, 1992 a very strong Category 5 and compact by hurricane standards, Hurricane Andrew struck south Miami-Dade County. Most major organizations in Miami are not located in the southern part of the county and were only partially impacted with minor building damage and a few days of power outages. However, many employees lived in residential south Miami-Dade County and experienced incredible damage. Damage included massive residential home damage or destruction, a complete breakdown of community infrastructure such as communications, electricity and potable water, and no gasoline for vehicles that survived the storm. In summary, a large segment of the workforce was in a survival mode, isolated and unable to commute to work.

▶ How did organizations cope with this situation?

▶ What actions can an organization take to recover the workforce?

Property and Technology Protection

Protection of property and technology is an important element of BCM. An organization should: utilize systems to detect abnormal situations, control all hazardous materials, establish procedures for securing buildings, establish procedures for securing equipment, identify and stock backup equipment and materials. Technology protection includes: establishing preventive maintenance schedules, establishing orderly shutdown procedures and determining the need for backup systems. Plans to protect equipment from contaminants, smoke, water, humidity, mold and corrosion should be in place.

Security

For protection of both employees and organization assets, all organizations need some level of physical security protection. The level of protection largely depends on the environment surrounding the location of the organizations and the value of physical assets. The nature of the organizations as well as the nature of other nearby organizations will also be factors as certain organizations may be targets of attack. All organizations need to address the following and select appropriate security controls:

- Does the security system have:
  - ❖ Door sensors?
  - ❖ Window sensors?
  - ❖ Motion detectors?
  - ❖ A panic alarm at the switchboard, reception desk and other critical locations?
  - ❖ Surveillance cameras in buildings?
  - ❖ Surveillance cameras on grounds?
  - ❖ Emergency alert stations with alarms and intercom systems on grounds and in parking lots?
- Is there a designated security officer?
- Are security guards present during normal operating hours?
- Are security guards present during non-operating hours?
- Are security guards armed?
- How easy is access to the building during operational hours? During non-operational hours?
- How many entrances are there to the building?
- Is there a special entrance for deliveries where packages are checked?
- Are packages brought in by employees checked?
- Are all occupants required to wear badges? With pictures for employees? Numbered for visitors?
- Are all occupants required to execute sign-in sheets? Electronic for employees? Manual for visitors?
- Are escorts required to accompany visitors – to all areas, to restricted areas, other?
- Are employees sufficiently security conscious to question strangers whether or not they have badges?
- Are all windows and doors locked during non-operating hours?
- Are roof openings always secured?
- Are parking lots and building grounds sufficiently illuminated at night?
- Do security threat monitoring responsibilities include:
  - ❖ Weather threats?
  - ❖ Physical security threats in the general area?
- What equipment is available for threat monitoring?
- Have there been any serious crisis events in the past?

Most of the previously listed security questions fall within the responsibility of or are supervised by either the Security Department or the Security Subcontractor. There are several other important security responsibilities that typically fall at least partly with other departments. The responsible departments must coordinate the following security issues:

- For all valuable equipment:
    - Is the model number recorded?
    - Is the serial identification number recorded?
    - Is the purchase date recorded?
    - Is the price recorded?
- Are there secure areas for important documents and personal valuables?
- For small, valuable equipment such as computers, is the equipment secured with bolts, lockdown plates, cables or alarms to prevent theft or damage during and after an earthquake?
- When discarded, are all reports, worksheets, confidential documents either shredded or incinerated? Note that shredding is environmentally preferred.
- When hiring employees, does the organization perform:
    - Background checks?
    - Drug Checks?
    - Credit Checks?
- When terminating an employee does the organization:
    - Conduct exit interviews?
    - Collect keys, badges and all borrowed company materials?
    - Review any projects in progress?
    - Escort the former employee out of the building and off-site?
    - Notify IT to remove the former employee's access to computer systems?

Event Probability Estimation

Risk analysis can be qualitative or quantitative in terms of determining the probability of events. For example, a qualitative valuation of probability may use designations such as high, medium or low, while a quantitative approach would develop numerical probabilities.

Estimating the probability of events involves reviewing historical data and discussing the events with relevant groups such as the fire department, weather bureau, utility companies, computer virus incident monitoring agencies, police departments, building engineers, reliability engineers and government agencies. In determining what data are necessary to collect, it is important to consider the risk factors including: weather, topography, population, transportation, infrastructure, facilities and supply chain. Data can be obtained from a variety of sources, including: interviews, questionnaires, workshops, documents, observation, data repositories and internal audit.

Once threats have been identified, the next step is to assign a probability of occurrence. Threats that have a significant probability of occurrence and/or have a significant impact are selected for further analysis. Because probabilities of threat occurrence may be quite difficult to determine exactly, estimating the probability of threat occurrence within a range is a reasonable approach. A threat probability classification system is useful to aid in prioritizing threats for further analysis. This is illustrated in Case Study D.

Probabilities can be obtained from historical data and by system modeling. Probabilities also can be estimated by using computer simulation, which allow for the blending of historical data and subjective opinion to arrive at intuitively acceptable estimates for the occurrence rates for events.

Judgment is often used when data are unavailable and also to incorporate risk attitudes of decision makers. Probability estimates for some events are difficult to obtain because their occurrence is rare.

Impact Estimation

The impact of a disruption on an organization may be measured quantitatively or qualitatively and may be expressed in various units such as downtime or dollars. The level of impact may be based upon various criteria such as loss of life, environmental damage, asset damage and duration of disruption.

The impact of an event may be measured in terms of downtime of a critical resource. For example, a severe winter storm might cause little damage but completely shutdown all organizations in a given area for one day. For organizations with time-sensitive operations (e.g. medical facilities, customer service centers, or delivery services) the loss of a day is important. For some other organizations (e.g. a private school or a civic association), a one-day loss of operations will have little impact. Although the impact of any given crisis will be a function of the organization itself, using downtime as a measure of impact is valid prior to performing a more thorough analysis of the impact in financial terms.

Disruptions in operations can result in losses, both direct and indirect. Although direct losses may be significant, they may not have a lasting impact on earnings. Direct losses include losses due to physical damage, expenses related to incremental personnel and losses resulting from failure to process deliverables in time.

Indirect losses include the loss of future business due to the disruptions, for example, customers who switch their business to competitors. These may be the biggest potential losses and may be the most difficult to estimate.

Estimates of direct and indirect losses may be obtained from extensive interviews with operations and business managers. The expected annualized losses for an event are the sum of annualized losses for all areas affected by the event. For example, if four processing divisions are affected by a fire, the expected losses would be the sum of their individual expected losses. Naturally appropriate steps must be taken to insure common losses are not double counted.

Consider the following illustration of impact categories utilizing life-safety threat, environmental damage, asset damage, and disruption time as criteria:

Impact	Life-Safety	Environmental Damage	Asset Damage	Disruption Days
1 - Low	low	low	low	1
2 - Moderate	some	some	some	2 to 4
3 - Serious	medium	medium	medium	5 to 10
4 - Extreme	significant	significant	significant	> 10

For impact classification, 'expected' and not 'worst case' scenarios are used, otherwise virtually every risk would be assigned an 'extreme' impact, making it difficult to determine which risk actually is the most important.

Note that the definition of the impact level will need to be adjusted from organization to organization. For organizations that have time-critical services, such as an organization that relies heavily on customer service or call center operations, a 'serious' impact might be a downtime of only one day or less. For college or university academic operations, a 'serious' impact might be a week.

Organizations with multiple significant operations may find it necessary to analyze each significant operation separately. For example, a manufacturing industry may have a certain RTO for manufacturing operations and a shorter RTO for sales and customer service operations.

Worst Case Scenario

Planning for scenarios representing typical crisis events may not prepare an organization for more devastating events. Some organizations consider worst case scenarios to be more fully prepared. However, worst case scenarios are difficult to envision and it may not be possible to cost-justify preparations for such situations. Nevertheless, consideration should be given to worst case scenarios.

Discussion: The 'Smoking Hole' Scenario

A worst case scenario commonly considered is the 'smoking hole' scenario. The 'smoking hole' scenario assumes that without warning on Monday morning the entire workplace is a smoking hole – complete destruction of the physical structure and all building contents. What actions should the organization take? Clearly this is a useful exercise to consider but also consider the following:

▶ Is this really the worst case?

▶ Will BCM that responds well to the 'smoking hole' scenario also respond well to all types of crisis events?

Discussion: Hurricane Pam

In the summer of 2004, FEMA conducted a week-long simulation exercise of a fictional category 3 Hurricane Pam striking the New Orleans area. After the exercise, FEMA felt reasonably well prepared for an actual event. A year later a very similar Hurricane Katrina actually struck the New Orleans area with devastating consequences.

A key missing assumption in the crisis scenario failed to capture the worst case scenario. The Hurricane Pam scenario assumed that the levees would be topped and excessive rain would cause major flooding problems. FEMA had developed plans to drain the city. Unfortunately, the actual Hurricane Katrina breached the levees and draining the city could not commence until the levees were repaired. FEMA was not prepared to repair the levees quickly and New Orleans was flooded for an extended period.

With all the problems of poor communication and plan execution at the federal, state and local level, it is unclear if an effective levee repair plan would have entirely corrected the situation. Nevertheless, the inability to rapidly repair the levees was a devastating factor.

▶ Is it realistic to envision in advance all the possible consequences of a major crisis event?

Multiple Crisis Events

The previous discussion also illustrates the compounding problems associated when one specific crisis event triggers another, perhaps more serious, crisis event. Hurricane Katrina did impact the City of New Orleans with hurricane force winds and heavy rainfall. However, the real disaster occurred when the levees were subsequently breached causing massive flooding.

Another example is the 2011 earthquake in Japan. The earthquake itself did cause significant damage from ground movement. However, the subsequent tsunami and subsequent nuclear power plant disaster probably caused more damage than the earthquake.

Risk Measure Evaluation and Risk Prioritization

There are several methods of classifying risks, but most approaches use some measure of risk involving event probabilities and the resultant impacts. Risk estimation can be quantitative or qualitative in terms of probability and impact. Different organizations will find that different measures of probability and impact will suit their needs best. For example, a very basic method would score both impact and probability as low or high. This can be presented as a 2 x 2 matrix.

Risk can be prioritized as:

1. High impact and high probability.
2. High impact and low probability.
3. Low impact and high probability.
4. Low impact and low probability.

Risk Estimation Matrix

	Low Impact	High Impact
Low Probability	Low Risk	Moderate Risk
High Probability	Moderate Risk	High Risk

Most organizations require a more detailed method of assessing impact and probability, perhaps requiring a 5 x 5 matrix, or by actually calculating impact in dollars and determining true probabilities. **Risk Measure** is a quantitative summary value of risk based on probability and impact. A common method is to score both probability and impact on numerical scales and use the following formula:

Risk Measure = Probability x Impact

RM = P x I

This score can then be used to prioritize risks. With a dollar impact and a true probability the risk measure would be an expected value, which could be used in cost-benefit analysis.

The RM = P x I effectively evaluates a crisis of high probability and low impact (such as a thunderstorm) equivalent to a crisis of low probability and high impact (such as an earthquake or a hurricane). This result may not be satisfactory for some organizations. When risks are evaluated, if it is appropriate, consider the impact to be more important than the probability (P), the following formula may be used:

$RM = P \times I^2$

In actual practice, this method is easily understood and reasonably accurate. Other formulas can be used to evaluate risks and there is no single standard recommended by all the professional bodies.

Discussion: Risk Assessment Illustration

Case Study D presents an illustration of RA for an organization.

What are the merits of the approach used in the risk assessment? Would an alternate approach add any value? Suggest a modification to the formula used for risk measure and provide a rationale.

▶ Apply your revised risk measure to Case Study D.

Discussion: Evaluating Multiple Severe Disasters

For the purpose of this discussion let's define 'major natural threat' as a large, community-wide natural threat that can cause catastrophic damage. In the continental United States very few regions of the country are subject to more than one major natural threat. In the South Pacific, including Hawaii, several regions are at risk for multiple natural disasters such as hurricanes, earthquakes, tsunamis and volcano eruptions.

Referring to Case Study D, both a major hurricane and severe seismic event would justify a 'level 4 extreme impact' for most organizations. Largely due to the lack of a lengthy warning period, a severe seismic event would likely present a much greater threat than a major hurricane. However, the risk evaluation process as described herein would not recognize any difference in the final evaluation.

> ▶ How would you adjust the risk measure formula or data to correct this problem?

Risk Treatment

Risk treatment includes:

▶ **Avoidance** – activities causing the risk are eliminated.

▶ **Transfer** – the risk in part or in totality is assigned to another.

▶ **Reduction** – the likelihood and/or impact of the risk is reduced.

▶ **Acceptance** – the risk is retained.

Risk Avoidance

Given the four approaches available for risk treatment, being able to completely avoid the risk appears to be the ideal solution. Unfortunately completely avoiding a risk might not be possible or may be possible only if extreme measures are taken. For example, if the organization is located along the coast of the Gulf of Mexico, the organization is going to have some level of hurricane risk. Storm shutters can be installed, roofs can be reinforced, extensive planning can be completed and many other steps can be taken to reduce the risk. Unfortunately, unless the organization is willing to move, the hurricane risk cannot be completely eliminated.

Risk Transfer

The most common type of risk transfer is to pay a premium to an insurance company to cover the financial exposure. 'Business Interruption Insurance' can compensate for the direct cost of damage, business continuity/recovery expenses and downtime. Although lost revenue can be covered, insurance will not be able to cover the indirect 'cost' of lost customers or customer dissatisfaction. Basic questions to be addressed with an insurance professional include the following:

▶ Are coverage limits and deductibles appropriate?

▶ What types of threats (perils) are covered and what threats are specifically excluded?

‣ Does the insurance provide adequate protection for senior management against litigation resulting from insufficient business continuity planning?

‣ Does coverage contemplate inflation, improvements and building code changes?

‣ Is coverage for 'replacement cost' or 'actual value' (cost less depreciation)?

‣ Does business interruption insurance cover loss of income and payroll expenses?

‣ Is documentation (serial number, date of purchase, cost, receipts, photographs, etc.) current and sufficiently detailed for the insurance company?

‣ Are copies of all insurance policies secured in a safe location?

‣ Does coverage include loss from an interruption of power or other critical services?

‣ Does coverage include loss from a denial of access order issued by civil authorities?

‣ Does the insurance cover losses incurred as a result of a disruption of transportation services?

‣ If a 'disaster declaration' is made to activate the alternate site:

   ❖ Does insurance cover the costs charged by the alternate site vendor?

   ❖ Does insurance cover all the extra personnel and other costs associated with activating and operating the alternate site?

‣ Is there sufficient life insurance coverage for key executives?

‣ Has coverage been reviewed with a professional insurance advisor during the past year?

‣ If an effective BCM is implemented, will the insurance premiums go down?

Risk transfer is not limited to insurance. Many organizations located in office buildings transfer security and facility risks to building management. Payroll processing is commonly outsourced to other organizations. For business continuity planning purposes, it is unimportant whether the organization is directly responsible or the responsibility has been assigned to another party. It is important that all organization processes and infrastructural requirements are protected and alternate procedures and infrastructural resources are identified.

Risk Reduction

Risk reduction can include either the introduction or enhancement of physical controls. An example of a physical control would be the installation of a sprinkler system to suppress fires. The introduction of surveillance cameras and a full perimeter alarm system is another example of a physical control that reduces risk. The introduction of physical controls will involve an initial expense and possibly an ongoing expense as well.

Risk reduction can also include either the introduction or enhancement of existing procedures. Developing and practicing formal fire evacuation plans will reduce the life-safety risk associated with fires. Training employees to report obvious security exposures is another example of a procedural control that reduces risk. Unlike most physical controls, most procedural controls have a minimal cost impact; however, procedural controls will typically require some level of time investment.

Risk Acceptance

To the extent that a risk cannot be avoided, transferred or reduced, the risk is accepted. As a practical matter, it is almost impossible to completely eliminate certain risks. As discussed earlier, if the organization is located along the coast of the Gulf of Mexico, the organization is going to have some level of hurricane risk and unless the organization is willing to move, the hurricane risk cannot be completely eliminated. Moreover, wherever the organization relocates there will likely be some new type of risk encountered.

Common reasons for accepting some level of risk are as follows:

- There is a low frequency of crisis occurrence.
- The value of the asset being protected is not that high.
- The cost of reducing the risk is high.
- The impact to operations and life-safety is minimal.

Review Topics

1. Define and explain the difference between threat and crisis.

2. Define and explain the difference between risk analysis, risk evaluation and risk assessment.

3. What are some approaches to assess event probabilities?

4. Describe some of the difficulties associated with determining the probability and impact of a terrorist attack.

5. When considering disruptions, how important are building structure and building contents for a typical service-related organization?

6. When considering disruptions, how important are building structure and building contents for a typical manufacturing-related organization?

7. What are the four options for risk treatment?

Case Studies

Case Study A-4: Alpha Investment Services (AIS) conducts Risk Assessment

Based on the Operations and the Resource Requirements information provided in Case Study A, along with your knowledge of the general area and based on the RA procedures illustrated in Case Study D, consider the following:

A-4.1   Natural Threats at Grand Office Park.
   A. Possible Natural Threats: Flood, Severe Winter Storm, Thunderstorm, Tornado, Wildfire.
   B. Identify the four most important Natural Threats to be analyzed.

A-4.2   External Threats at Grand Office Park.
   A. Possible External Threats: Fire, Hazmat Release, Pandemic Outbreak, Security Breach, Terrorist Attack, Transportation Accident, Utility Failure.
   B. Identify the four or five most important External Threats to be analyzed.

A-4.3   Internal Threats at Grand Office Park.
   A. Possible Internal Threats: Fire, Hazmat Release, Security Breach, Utility Failure.
   B. Identify the three or four most important Internal Threats to be analyzed.

The AIS management team has defined numerical categories to be used for probability classification and impact classification.

The probability classification assigned to each crisis event is as follows:

- ▶ 5 = at least a 10% chance of annual occurrence
- ▶ 4 = at least a 5% but less than a 10% chance of annual occurrence
- ▶ 3 = at least a 2% but less than a 5% chance of annual occurrence
- ▶ 2 = at least a 1/2% but less than a 2% chance of annual occurrence
- ▶ 1 = less than a 1/2% chance of annual occurrence.

The impact classification for a given disruption is as follows:

- ▶ 4 = Extreme (expected downtime over two days)
- ▶ 3 = Serious (expected downtime one hour to two days)
- ▶ 2 = Moderate (expected downtime five minutes to one hour)
- ▶ 1 = Low (expected downtime under five minutes).

Based on these Probability and Impact classifications and the threats selected in A-4.1, A-4.2 and A-4.3, complete questions A-4.4 through A-4.10.

A-4.4   Determine the crisis event that best represents the manifestation of each threat. Then assign a probability classification to each crisis event and summarize the results in the table below.

The Probability Classification (P) assigned to each Crisis Event

Probability Classification (5)
Probability Classification (4)
Probability Classification (3)
Probability Classification (2)
Probability Classification (1)

A-4.5   Determine the level of resource unavailability due to each of the crisis events. Resources include the following: personnel, building structure, building access, building contents, IT services, utility services and community resources. For each crisis event, determine numerical values (5 = Very High, 4 = High, 3 = Medium, 2 = Low, 1 = Very Low) for the resource unavailability and summarize in the following table. This information is useful in establishing disruption levels for impact classification.

Levels of Resource Unavailability

Crisis Event	Resources						
	Personnel	Building Structure	Building Access	Building Contents	IT Services	Utility Services	Community Resources

A-4.6   Based on the life-safety, environmental, disruptions and other factors, determine the impact classification for each crisis event. Then summarize the results in the table below.

Impact (I)

Extreme (4)

Serious (3)

Moderate (2)

Low (1)

A-4.7   Use the formulas $P \times I^2$ and $P \times I$ to measure risks.

Risk Measure

Crisis Event	Probability (P)	Impact (I)	$P \times I^2$	$P \times I$

A-4.8   Using the P x I^2 formula, what are the significant conclusions?

A-4.9   Using the P x I formula, what are the significant conclusions?

A-4.10   If we change the Impact numerical classification as follows:

- 8 = Extreme (expected downtime over two days)
- 4 = Serious (expected downtime one hour to two days)
- 2 = Moderate (expected downtime five minutes to one hour)
- 1 = Low (expected downtime under five minutes).

Using the P x I formula, what are the significant conclusions?

Risk Measure

Crisis Event	Probability (P)	Impact (I)	P x I

A-4.11   Identify significant physical or procedural weaknesses/exposures at AIS.

A-4.12   Determine the actions (if any) AIS can take to reduce the probability of occurrence and/or impact of these risks.

A-4.13   Are we finished with RA or are there any important components that we still need to analyze?

Case Study B-4: Beta Widget Makers (BWM) conducts Risk Assessment

Based on the Operations and the Resource Requirements information provided in Case Study B along with your knowledge of the general area and based on the RA procedures illustrated in Case Study D, considering the following:

B-4.1   Natural Threats facing at Grand Office Park.
        A. Possible Natural Threats: Flood, Severe Winter Storm, Thunderstorm, Tornado, Wildfire.
        B. Based on your knowledge of the general area, identify the four most important Natural Threats to be analyzed.

B-4.2   External Threats at Grand Office Park.
        A. Possible External Threats: Fire, Hazmat Release, Pandemic Outbreak, Security Breach, Terrorist Attack, Transportation Accident, Utility Failure.
        B. Based on the information provided, identify the four or five most important External Threats to be analyzed.

B-4.3   Internal Threats at the Grand Office Park Central Plant.
        A. Possible Internal Threats: Fire, Hazmat Release, Security Breach, Utility Failure.

B. Based on the information provided, identify the three or four most important Internal Threats to be analyzed.

The BWM management team has defined numerical categories to be used for probability classification and impact classification.

The probability classification assigned to each crisis event is as follows:

- 5 = at least a 10% chance of annual occurrence
- 4 = at least a 5% but less than a 10% chance of annual occurrence
- 3 = at least a 2% but less than a 5% chance of annual occurrence
- 2 = at least a 1/2% but less than a 2% chance of annual occurrence
- 1 = less than a 1/2% chance of annual occurrence.

The impact classification for a given disruption is as follows:

Manufacturing-Related Operations

- 4 = Extreme (expected downtime over ten days)
- 3 = Serious (expected downtime over three days and up to ten days)
- 2 = Moderate (expected downtime over one day and up to three days)
- 1 = Low (expected downtime one day or less).

Sales and Customer Service-Related Operations

- 4 = Extreme (expected downtime over two days)
- 3 = Serious (expected downtime one hour to two days)
- 2 = Moderate (expected downtime five minutes to one hour)
- 1 = Low (expected downtime under five minutes).

Based on these Probability and Impact classifications and the threats selected in B-4.1, B-4.2 and B-4.3, complete questions B-4.4 through B-4.10

B-4.4   Determine the crisis event that best represents the manifestation of each threat. Then assign a probability classification to each crisis event and summarize the results in the following table.

The Probability Classification (P) assigned to each Crisis Event

Probability Classification (5)

Probability Classification (4)

Probability Classification (3)

Probability Classification (2)

Probability Classification (1)

B-4.5   Determine the level of resource unavailability due to each of the crisis events. Resources include the following: personnel, building structure, building access, building contents, IT services, utility services and community resources. For each crisis event, determine numerical values (5 = Very High, 4 = High, 3 = Medium, 2 = Low, 1 = Very Low) for the resource unavailability and summarize in the following table. This information is useful in establishing disruption levels for impact classification.

Levels of Resource Unavailability

Crisis Event	Resources						
	Personnel	Building Structure	Building Access	Building Contents	IT Services	Utility Services	Community Resources

B-4.6   Based on the life-safety, environmental, disruptions and other factors, determine the impact classification for each crisis event. Then it summarize the results in the table below.

Impact (I) – Manufacturing—Related Operations

Extreme (4)

Serious (3)

Moderate (2)

Low (1)

Impact (I) – Sales and Customer Service-Related Operations

Extreme (4)
Serious (3)
Moderate (2)
Low (1)

B-4.7   Use the formulas $P \times I^2$ and $P \times I$ to measure risks.

Risk Measure
For Manufacturing-Related Operations

Crisis Event	Probability (P)	Impact (I)	P x I²	P x I

For Sales and Customer Service-Related Operations

Crisis Event	Probability (P)	Impact (I)	P x I²	P x I

B-4.8   Using the P x I² formula, what are the significant conclusions?

B-4.9   Using the P x I formula, what are the significant conclusions?

B-4.10   If we change the Impact numerical classification as follows:

Manufacturing-Related Operations

▶ 8 = Extreme (expected downtime over ten days)

▶ 4 = Serious (expected downtime three to ten days)

▶ 2 = Moderate (expected downtime one day to three days)

▶ 1 = Low (expected downtime under one day).

Sales and Customer Service-Related Operations

▶ 8 = Extreme (expected downtime over two days)

▶ 4 = Serious (expected downtime one hour to two days)

▶ 2 = Moderate (expected downtime five minutes to one hour)

▶ 1 = Low (expected downtime under five minutes).

Using the P x I formula, what are the significant conclusions?

Risk Measure for Manufacturing-Related Operations

Crisis Event	Probability (P)	Impact (I)	P x I

Risk Measure for Sales and Customer Service-Related Operations

Crisis Event	Probability (P)	Impact (I)	P x I

B-4.11   Identify significant physical or procedural weaknesses/exposures at BWM.

B-4.12   Determine the actions (if any) BWM can take to reduce the probability of occurrence and/or impact of these risks.

B-4.13   Are we finished with RA or are there any important components that we still need to analyze?

Bibliography

Aven, T., "A New Scientific Framework for Quantitative Risk Assessments," *International Journal of Business Continuity and Risk Management*, Vol. 1, No. 1, pp. 67-77, 2009.

Aven, T., *Risk Analysis-Assessing Uncertainties Beyond Expected Values and Probabilities*, John Wiley and Sons, New York, NY, 2008.

Burtles, J., *Principles and Practices of Business Continuity: Tools and Techniques*, Rothstein Associates Inc., 2007.

Engemann, K. J. and Miller, H., "Operations Risk Management at a Major Bank," *Interfaces* Vol. 22: No. 6 pp. 140-149, November-December 1992.

Engemann, K. J., Miller, H. E. and Yager, R. R., "Computational Intelligence for Risk and Disaster Management," *Proceedings of the IEEE International Conference on Fuzzy Systems at the World Congress on Computational Intelligence*, Vancouver, pp. 6900-6906, July 2006.

Engemann, K., Miller, H. and Yager, R., "Sequential Decision Making Using Interval Probabilities: An Operations Risk Example," *Proceedings of the Northeast Decision Sciences Institute 2000 Annual Meeting*, pp 114-116, March 2000.

Federal Emergency Management Agency, Natural Hazards, www.fema.gov/areyouready/natural_hazards.shtm.

Graham, J. and Kaye D., *A Risk Management Approach to Business Continuity*, Rothstein Associates Inc., 2006.

Haimes, Y., *Risk Modeling, Assessment, and Management*, John Wiley and Sons, 2008.

Henderson, D. M., *The Comprehensive Business Continuity Management Program*, Rothstein Associates Inc., 2008.

Henderson, D. M., *The Comprehensive Continuity of Operations Management Program for Colleges and Universities*, Rothstein Associates Inc., 2007.

Henderson, D. M., Is *Your Business Ready for the Next Disaster?*, Dorrance Publishing Co., Inc., 1996.

Hiles, A. N., *Business Continuity: Best Practices: Aligning Business Continuity with Corporate Governance*, Rothstein Associates Inc., 2004.

Hiles, A. N., *Enterprise Risk Assessment and Business Impact Analysis*, Rothstein Associates Inc., 2002.

Monahan, G., *Enterprise Risk Management*, John Wiley and Sons, 2008.

Mooney, S., *Insuring Your Business*, Insurance Information Institute Press, 1992.

National Flood Insurance Program, www.FloodSmart.Gov.

Puri, S., Khurana, A. and Seth, N., "TDCP: A Scale to Measure Technological Dimensions of Crisis Preparedness," *International Journal of Business Continuity and Risk Management*, Vol. 1, No. 3, pp. 283-300, 2010.

Risk and Insurance Management Society, www.rims.org.

Risk Management Association, www.rmahq.org.

United States Geological Survey, www.usgs.gov/hazards.

Vose, D., Risk Analysis: A Quantitative Guide, 3rd Edition, John Wiley and Sons, 2008.

Yager, R., Engemann, K. J. and Filev. D., "On Immediate Probabilities," *Proceedings of the Fifth International Conference on Information Processing and Management of Uncertainty in Knowledge Based Systems*, pp. 423-428, July 1994.

CHAPTER V

Strategy Development

Objectives

» Examine strategy development

» Examine factors used to select strategies

» Identify specific strategies

» Review strategy implementation.

Developing Strategies

A consistent methodology should be used across an organization to study how disruptions may cause losses, and also to identify and select cost-justified BCM strategies. A **strategy** is an approach used by an organization to treat risk in order to accomplish resiliency objectives.

Strategies may prevent disasters, provide backup for lost resources or specify alternative resources to deliver products and services. A strategy may provide protection against only one event or against several. Continuity strategies enhance the organization's capability to respond to events in order to continue operations. Recovery strategies enhance the organization's capability to return to stable operations following an event. During the analysis process, crisis scenarios are useful. While developing strategies, focus is placed on what needs to be accomplished. Organization activities are divided into business as usual for unaffected areas and recovery activities for affected areas.

The set of preferred strategies to meet BCM objectives is selected in developing the overall strategy. For each critical function, the available recovery strategies need to be evaluated. The selection of a set of strategies depends on costs and benefits. In certain cases, the decision is obvious. This is in situations where the strategies provide protection for most events and are relatively inexpensive. Occasionally, a strategy may be the only one that could provide for the continuation of a service in case of all major events and the service is so vital that its disruption is not acceptable as a risk. Sometimes, the additional expenditure required for contingency planning is small because it can be combined with other plans, for example, the decision to place operations at two or more locations is made at the same time as additional space is being acquired for expansion.

The BCM program must provide backup against all major events unless senior management makes an explicit business decision to exclude certain events. Some strategies cover multiple events and cover several operations. Offsite strategies provide coverage for the broadest range of events. Additional backup sometimes still proves worthwhile even if the offsite alternative selected covers all the functions. For example, onsite backup could be a cost effective and convenient solution for localized events. The evaluation is performed across services when appropriate to determine the usefulness in other operations. Some events may result in consequences which are unacceptable to management, such as the loss of key markets, restrictions from regulatory agencies or very high losses. Obtaining commitments and advising on contractual agreements is a key part of strategy development.

Management selects strategies by reviewing and rating various combinations of strategies. Some of the evaluation criteria include: cost, service level provided, time to switch over, reliability and manageability. Each combination of strategies may be evaluated by assigning relative ratings with respect to each criterion. The ratings of excellent, good, fair and poor respectively, provide a qualitative evaluation useful in comparing strategies. Management judgement is used in both assigning the ratings and selecting the strategies.

The advantages and disadvantages of the strategies should be determined and the suitability of the strategies should be assessed against the BIA. Senior management commitment should always be obtained on the proposed strategy before proceeding.

When the selection of a set of strategies is not obvious, a more detailed cost-benefit analysis is useful. A structured format to perform cost-benefit analysis is most beneficial. In performing this analysis, the criteria used to rate strategies are taken into account.

A strategy usually entails both one-time costs and recurring costs. As one time costs are determined for each component of a strategy, these costs are annualized to allow for comparison of strategies. This is done by dividing the one time cost by the useful life of the component. Depreciation guidelines are helpful in determining the useful life of each component. One time costs include: the cost of facilities, site construction, equipment, computer hardware, furniture, air conditioners plus the staff and consultants required in order to implement the strategy. Recurring costs include the costs of: renting/leasing, maintenance, contracted services, personnel, supplies and utilities. The total annualized cost is the sum of the annualized one-time costs and the annualized recurring costs.

Quantifying the benefits of a strategy requires reviewing all the events for which the alternative provides some protection and estimating how it reduces the expected loss of each of these events. For each alternative strategy, the losses resulting from the various events are estimated. The service level provided under each strategy may impact these losses. Direct losses include asset losses such as computers, furniture and buildings along with financial losses such as fees, interest and compensation. Indirect losses include the loss of future revenue and consequential damages. Estimation of these losses should be performed in the context of the country risk, the expected response of competitors, the strength of customer relationships and the impact on image. All losses should be considered in conjunction with insurance coverage. This entails incorporating deductibles, maximum limits and future premium increases as a result of a disaster in the estimates.

The benefit of a strategy is the reduction of potential losses compared to the base case. The impact of an event depends upon its extent and duration. The expected loss from an event is the product of the losses from that event and its probability. The net benefit of an alternative is obtained by subtracting the total annualized cost of the alternative from its benefit.

Alternatives with positive net benefit are considered for selection as part of the overall strategy. While a structured and quantitative approach to selecting strategies is beneficial there are difficulties in estimating probabilities and in determining costs and losses. Sensitivity analysis should be used to determine how changes in the estimates of costs, losses and probabilities would affect the selection of a strategy.

While developing strategies, related factors such as future business volume, planned facility relocation and planned expansion of processing capacity should be considered. Such factors may have a significant impact on the available strategies. For example, if the data center plans to install an additional computer, a strategy alternative resulting from this plan could be to establish a second data center housing the new acquisition. This provides the planned increase in computer capacity while also providing a backup for each of the two data centers.

Selecting strategies involves: reviewing business continuity objectives, identifying potential strategies, assessing strategies against the BIA, consolidating strategies across the organization, determining advantages and disadvantages, conducting cost-benefit analysis and presenting findings for senior management approval.

Selecting Strategies

Before selecting strategies, it is necessary to establish parameters under which the BCM program must operate. It is important to review the resources required to conduct operations. In addition to the requirements necessary to conduct operations, it is also important to assess the level of organization resources that are available. Strategies focus on the maintenance and recovery of critical operations and do not necessarily attempt to replicate existing procedures.

Planning Parameters

The type of organization plus the human resource, physical and technical environment necessary to conduct operations must be defined. If the organization requires the use of valuable, specialized equipment or if there are special requirements/building systems of the physical environment, a crisis that damages assets could result in an extended period of downtime. When determining the appropriate planning assumptions, consider the following:

▶ What are the facility requirements of the organization? Some service industry businesses require only general office space but other manufacturing businesses require specialized facilities.

▶ What are the facility content requirements of the organization? Note that insurance can cover the cost of replacing expensive equipment but will not be able to guarantee quick replacement of specialized manufacturing equipment.

▶ What are the community infrastructure support services that are necessary to support the organization? Nearly every organization will require police, fire, water and other essential services to be available. Organizations without backup generators will likely be reliant on public electrical services. Some organizations can operate in the short term without normal communication services while others cannot.

▶ What is the reliance on IT? Is IT crucial for the operational groups or just certain support departments with non-critical operations? In today's environment, IT support services are likely needed to support many, if not all, critical operations.

Crisis Impact

When considering the appropriate strategies it is important to review the RA and the BIA. Based on the crisis events that are the most important, consider the following:

▶ Does the crisis provide a warning period? It may be possible to protect organization assets by, for example, pre-positioning equipment to a safer location. Employees can also be pre-positioned to remote locations and perhaps work from these locations.

▶ Can the crisis affect a large area, essentially a community-wide crisis? In addition to direct organization damages, the normal community infrastructure support system may be degraded. Employees may not be able to return to work. Relocation of the organization within the community may be difficult or impossible in the short term.

▶ Does the crisis damage organization assets or does it just deny access to the workplace?

▶ Does the crisis pose a life or health hazard? Special measures should be given to safety and security concerns.

Resources Available

Finally, consider the resources available for BCM. Many, if not most, strategies require some amount of time and level of financial commitment. No properly run organization works with an unlimited budget. It is necessary for management to determine strategies based on the cost as well as the effectiveness of each individual strategy. Based on the resources available, consider the following:

▶ What types of alternate sites are available? Have vendor sponsored alternate sites been secured? Does the organization have other alternate locations that can be used in a crisis? Consider IT and non-IT aspects separately.

▶ What is the budget available to spend on strategies? Again, consider IT and non-IT aspects separately.

▶ How are resources allocated between strategies designed to prevent or mitigate a crisis and strategies designed to respond to a crisis? Effective strategies designed to prevent or mitigate a crisis could reduce the cost of responding to a crisis or, better yet, eliminate the need to respond to a crisis.

Specific Strategies

Specific strategies include the following:

▶ **Alternate Sites** – These are remote locations where work can be conducted. Alternate sites are an important component of any good strategy. An IT alternate site represents a location where IT functions can be performed and an office alternate site represents a location where non-IT personnel can work. For a specific organization, the IT alternate site and the office alternate site are sometimes the same physical location. Office alternate sites are often multiple sites for larger organizations.

▶ **Backup Equipment** – Additional equipment is often secured if the equipment is critical, not overly expensive or represents a single-point-of-failure. This practice is often used for specialized manufacturing equipment, electrical power generation and IT hardware.

▶ **Buffer Stock** – Securing additional inventories, often at off-site locations, will provide a cushion if supplies of raw materials are interrupted. This strategy is for manufacturing industries but unfortunately introduces idle asset inefficiencies in times of normal operations.

▶ **Building Fortification (Bunker Approach)** – The fortification of the facility or critical areas of the facility is a pre-crisis event strategy. This is an important planning component especially for organizations that require specialized facilities or have expensive critical equipment to protect.

Fortification can be broken into two distinct categories: permanent fortifications that are constantly in place and temporary fortifications that are deployed when necessary. Examples of permanent fortifications are levees and check valves for flood control or the installation of wind resistant glass for hurricane protection. Temporary fortifications include the deployment of sandbags for flood control or the deployment of storm shutters for hurricane protection.

Appendix C identifies several types of structural and non-structural building fortification planning initiatives.

Discussion: Fully Fortified Building

Consider a fully fortified building capable of withstanding the maximum possible natural crisis that can reasonably be expected, such as a building that can withstand a category 5 hurricane, an EF 5 tornado or a great earthquake. The building also has self-contained and redundant utility systems. A building that will always be available for operations; therefore, no IT alternate site or office alternate site is needed.

- The building is clearly a great asset but is it foolproof?

- Can you think of any situations where such a facility could be disabled or even rendered useless?

- **Distributive Manufacturing/Processing** – Organizations with multiple locations can provide some internal redundancy by performing identical tasks at multiple locations. Distributing critical operations to multiple locations will ensure critical operations at some minimum level in the event of the destruction or disablement of one location. This is a powerful strategy for organizations with multiple locations but unfortunately often introduces inefficiencies by making it difficult to minimize inventories in times of normal operations.

- **Distributive Warehousing** – This is most closely associated with the warehousing of finished products at some location other than where it was manufactured. This procedure will help ensure that some finished products will be available if manufacturing operations are disrupted. Distributive warehousing can also be utilized for raw materials. This strategy is most appropriate for manufacturing industries but unfortunately introduces idle asset inefficiencies in times of normal operations.

- **Insurance** – Insurance will typically play an important role in the BCM strategy and should be assessed. Although insurance may pay a portion of the loss, it should be considered as part of a comprehensive approach. Self-insurance is not a complete solution. Insurance payments providing for a loss of profits is usually assessed on profits immediately before a disaster. Insurance companies are getting more selective about accepting claims as valid.

- **Manual Overrides** – There are often less-efficient manual procedures that can be utilized if equipment is damaged or destroyed or if IT services are disrupted.

- **Maximize Work Hours** – Expanding work hours or hours of operations can be an important strategy that has multiple applications.

  - ❖ For an organization with multiple operations, after a crisis at one location, it might be possible to add an additional shift to another undamaged location.

  - ❖ It may be practical to expand the work hours to include overtime for unaffected employees. This strategy is most effective for organizations with multiple operations, but is equally effective for single site employers that have an operational alternate site.

- **Multiple/Alternate Suppliers** – As an ongoing practice, utilizing multiple suppliers will help to insure a continuous supply of raw materials. All manufacturing industries should have alternate suppliers available in the event of a disruption of raw materials from the primary supplier. Many manufacturers are reluctant to use this strategy and prefer to use single source suppliers for volume discounts and quality control reasons.

- **Mutual Aid Agreements** – An agreement between two or more organizations to provide a resource when one of the organizations experiences an outage.

Business Alliances are similar except the agreement is between organizations that have a mutual business interest. For example, a business alliance is an agreement between a manufacturing business that supplies critical components to another manufacturing business. Business alliances are more likely to be effective after an actual crisis than the typical mutual aid agreements.

▶ **Outsourcing** – Having other organizations perform certain work functions is referred to as outsourcing. This strategy is usually an additional or supplemental rather than a primary strategy. Many organizations have certain ancillary operations such as internal print shops, mail distribution and employee cafeterias which could be outsourced.

The effectiveness and efficiency of outsourcing should be explored. Factors to consider regarding outsourcing parts of business continuity analysis and planning include organizational knowledge, expertise and experience. Factors to consider regarding outsourcing include cost, commitment, availability, response and risk.

▶ **Personal Protection Equipment (PPE)** – These are personal devices designed to reduce or eliminate the contact of hazardous materials to an individual. The most likely use of PPE is for employees who handle hazardous materials in manufacturing industries and for any employee during a pandemic outbreak.

▶ **Portable Equipment** – Portable equipment can sometimes be used to supply critical services such as compressed air and chilled water normally supplied by permanent building systems. Portable generators can have important application for most any organization. Portable equipment can generally be secured quickly – often much faster than severely damaged building systems can be repaired or replaced.

▶ **Pre-Positioning** – Pre-positioning involves the relocation of physical assets or employees to a safe location prior to a crisis event. This is a powerful strategy for organizations facing a serious risk that provides an extended warning period such as a hurricane or a flood. When relocating employees out of the area, it will be necessary to consider transportation, lodging, employee families, overtime and other logistical factors in advance.

Pre-positioning also includes the relocation of physical assets to a higher floor or to a distant higher elevation location if a flood threatens.

Discussion: Pre-Positioning

In the Case Study Section, Case Study E presents a plan designed to pre-position employees in a phased manner and allow for uninterrupted operations.

▶ What are your thoughts about this plan?

▶ What are the assumptions that are necessary for this plan to work?

▶ What problems might occur in the actual execution of this plan?

▶ **Quick Re-Supply (Just-In-Time (JIT))** – This is the rapid replenishment of inventory, supplies or equipment. This is a cost-effective strategy for manufacturing industries. However, this approach will probably not be effective for replacing highly specialized and expensive manufacturing equipment. There is also a reliance on the transportation infrastructure which may be disabled by a community-wide crisis.

▶ **Redundant Operations (Continuous Processing)** – This is a mirror-image operation being performed at another location. This strategy is often extremely expensive as it requires redundancy of personnel, equipment and infrastructure.

▶ **Remote-Site Storage** – This is most closely associated with the securing of information records both in electronic and in hardcopy format at another location. This is a critical ongoing crisis avoidance strategy.

Materials vital to operations should be backed up and retrievable. Vital materials include: Business Continuity Plans, software and data, procedures, agreements, contracts, leases, insurance policies, supplies, forms, plans, drawings, blueprints, keys, passwords, check books, credit cards and cash.

▶ **Social Distancing Policies (SDP)** – These are personal procedure policies designed to reduce or eliminate the exchange of hazardous infections between individuals. The most likely use of SDP is during a pandemic outbreak. Basic SDPs are identified in Appendix D.

▶ **Subcontractors** – The availability of subcontractors is a critical component of a good strategy. Subcontractors should be readily available for facility clean-up and repair work such as equipment replacement or repair, building content replacement and communication infrastructure repair. An organization should not place undue emphasis on small, local subcontractors that are subject to the same community-wide crisis events. Consider backup subcontractors, out-of-the-area subcontractors and large subcontractors with multiple locations.

▶ **Temporary Structures (Modules)** – Arguably this is a special type of alternate site that is rapidly deployed to replace damaged or destroyed facilities. Mobile Sites would also fall into this category.

▶ **Work from Customer or Client Location** – This strategy is usually an additional or supplemental rather than a primary strategy. Although it is probably not possible to relocate the entire organization to a customer or client location, it is often possible to send customer service representatives to key customer/client operations. Arguably this is a subset of the Business Alliance strategy described earlier.

▶ **Work from Homes and Hotels** – With the Internet, cloud computing and other technological advancements, this strategy is becoming increasingly important. This strategy has more application within service industries where substantial operations can be provided by individuals with laptop computers, power supply and communication access. To rely on this strategy, it is advisable to have an IT alternate site that will remain operational or can be activated quickly. The ability to access data and applications over the Internet will be critical. Sufficient laptop computers, air-cards, cellular phones, a few satellite phones, PDAs and other resources need to be planned for and secured in advance. Note that there is application within manufacturing industries for sales, customer service and certain other support departments.

Working from home is less effective or completely ineffective for a community-wide crisis. Communication and electrical power services may be degraded or disabled. It may be possible to transition working from home into working from other distant locations as a result of a community-wide crisis. Hotels can usually function as temporary homes in these circumstances. If relocating employees out of the area is contemplated, it will be necessary to consider additional logistical factors in advance, such as: transportation, lodging, employee families and overtime, as well as employee willingness to relocate.

Working from Homes and/or Hotels is often less expensive than internally or externally provided alternate sites.

Implementing Strategies

Some strategies include obtaining business continuity services from external vendors. In such cases, a Request for Proposal (RFP) needs to be developed. The steps involved with a RFP include: clarify assumptions, specify requirements, issue RFP, review submitted proposals, interview vendors, check references, tour sites and negotiate and award contracts. Contract negotiation includes factors such as services and fees, IT, testing, exclusivity, declaration determination, liabilities and early termination. These service level agreements are written documents between organizations that specify services and/or performance levels to be provided. After senior management has selected the strategies, actions must be taken to implement the strategies. Implementing the strategies will take time, effort and likely involve a financial commitment; in certain instances, the financial commitment can be significant.

Implementing the strategies usually involves activities such as: acquiring additional equipment, arranging for contractual agreements, physical changes to the workplace environment, preparing backup and off-site facilities to ensure that appropriate documentation is in place. Since the strategies define business continuity procedures of an organization, these strategies need to be implemented either prior to or simultaneously with the drafting of the plan documents.

Forward-looking organizations are creating infrastructures resilient enough to eliminate or reduce the impact of disasters. BCM needs to be involved in long-term planning to foster this approach.

Review Topics

1. Identify the one time and recurring costs that should be examined to determine the total cost of a strategy.

2. Consider facility, personnel and IT resources. In general, all the resource components identified above are necessary for most organizations. Can you think of organizations that can operate without any one of the identified resource components at least temporarily?

3. Identify the business continuity problems associated with the following types of crisis events:

    a. Community-wide crisis events.

    b. Crisis events that provide no warning.

    c. Crisis events that destroy manufacturing equipment.

4. Identify and discuss strategies that are effective for hurricanes but ineffective for earthquakes.

5. Identify strategies that can introduce inefficiencies to a manufacturer in times of normal operations.

Case Studies

Case Study A-5: Alpha Investment Services (AIS) develops Strategies

Based on the Information Technology and Revised Recovery Time Objectives and other Case information previously provided in Case Study A, consider the following:

A-5.1   For AIS business operations, how important are building systems, building contents, IT services, utility services and access to Grand Office Park?

A-5.2   Which strategies are likely to be most effective for AIS?

A-5.3   Identify the additional resources and procedures that are needed for AIS to achieve the Revised Recovery Time Objectives.

A-5.4   AIS management is considering moving the business to Southern California. There would be only one office building for all operations. The building is to be of modern design and construction. Although not located directly above a fault line, earthquakes are a very serious concern. Essentially the flood, tornado and severe winter storm risks have been replaced with the earthquake risk; all other significant risks are essentially the same. How would this change the strategies?

Case Study B-5: Beta Widget Makers (BWM) develops Strategies

Based on the Information Technology and Revised Recovery Time Objectives and other Case information previously provided in Case Study B, consider the following:

B-5.1   For BWM business operations at the Central Plant, how important are building systems, building contents, IT services, utility services and access to Grand Office Park?

B-5.2   Which strategies are likely to be most effective for BWM?

B-5.3   Identify the additional resources and procedures that are needed for BWM to achieve the Revised Recovery Time Objectives.

B-5.4   BWM management is considering moving the business to Southern California. There would be only one Plant for all operations. The Plant is to be of modern design and construction. Although not located directly above a fault line, earthquakes are a very serious concern. Essentially the flood, tornado and severe winter storm risks have been replaced with the earthquake risk; all other significant risks are essentially the same. How would this change the strategies?

Bibliography

Borodzicz, E., *Risk, Crisis and Security Management*, John Wiley and Sons, 2005.

Burtles, J., *Principles and Practices of Business Continuity: Tools and Techniques*, Rothstein Associates Inc., 2007.

Engemann, K. and Miller, H., "A Taxonomy for Managing Global Operations Risk," *Proceedings of the Twenty-sixth Annual Meeting of the Northeast Decision Sciences Institute*, pp.117-119, April 1997.

Engemann, K. J., and Miller, H. E., "Critical Infrastructure and Smart Technology Risk Modeling using Computational Intelligence," *International Journal of Business Continuity and Risk Management*, Vol. 1, No. 1, pp. 91-111, 2009.

Graham, J. and Kaye, D., *A Risk Management Approach to Business Continuity: Aligning Business Continuity With Corporate Governance*, Rothstein Associates Inc., 2006.

Henderson, D. M., *The Complete Hurricane and Flood Plan for Business*, Rothstein Associates Inc., 2006.

Henderson, D. M., *The Comprehensive Business Continuity Management Program*, Rothstein Associates Inc., 2008.

Hiles, A. N., *Business Continuity: Best Practices: Aligning Business Continuity with Corporate Governance*, Rothstein Associates Inc., 2004.

Ishikawa, A., and Tsujimoto, A., *Risk and Crisis Management – 101 Cases*, World Scientific Publishing Co., 2009.

Kelly, P., "Conceptualizing Business Risk Culture: A Study of Risk Thinking and Practice in Contemporary Dynamic Organizations," *International Journal of Business Continuity and Risk Management*, Vol. 1, No. 1, pp. 19-37, 2009.

Miller, H. E., Engemann, K. J., and Yager, R. R., "Mitigating Natural Disasters," *Advances in Decision Technology and Intelligent Information Systems, Volume VII* (ed. K. Engemann and G. Lasker), pp. 18-22, The International Institute for Advanced Studies in Systems Research and Cybernetics, 2006.

Monahan, G., *Enterprise Risk Management*, John Wiley and Sons, 2008.

Philpott, D. and Einstein, S., *The Integrated Physical Security Handbook*, Don Dickson, 2006.

CHAPTER VI

Disaster Recovery for Information Technology

Objectives

» Define the scope of Disaster Recovery Planning

» Identify alternate site type

» Provide a method of selecting alternate site providers

» Determine the alternate site location

» Identify controls at the data center

» Identify the steps needed to recover the data center

» Review information management procedures

» Review information security measures.

Overview of Disaster Recovery Planning

Information Technology (IT) – IT consists of the hardware, software, telecommunications and other technologies used in computer based information systems. The IT department of an organization is responsible for storing, protecting, processing and retrieving information. IT is a critical resource for most organizations.

Disaster Recovery Plan (DRP) – A DRP is a plan for the IT department to provide continuation and recovery of the systems and communication capabilities of an organization. A DRP includes planning in the following areas:

- **IT Alternate Site** – An IT alternate site is the backup data center where IT services can be performed in the event of the destruction or disablement of the primary data center.

- **Data Center Controls** – These are the controls in the data center designed to prevent or mitigate the impact of a data center crisis event.

- **Data Center Recovery Plan** – This is a plan to resume data center operations.

- **Information Management Plan** – This is a plan to classify and retrieve electronic information and critical applications.

- **Information Security Plan** – This is a plan to secure data and other critical information from internal and external threats.

Senior management determines the level of planning and resources that will be devoted to the DRP. This decision is based on the established Recovery Time Objectives, acceptable levels of service degradation and the cost of the planning.

IT Alternate Site

If a crisis event occurs at the main data center, is there an available alternate location where IT services can be performed? Such a location is generally referred to as an 'IT alternate site' or an 'IT recovery site' and there are several categories of sites that need to be identified as follows:

- **Redundant Site** – This is a completely functional separate operation that continually duplicates every activity of the primary data center. Under this environment, the primary data center can be completely shut down without any interruption of service as the redundant site is fully staffed, equipped and continually operational. This is often a very expensive alternative that is beyond the budget and requirements of many organizations. Note that it may be possible to operate the redundant site remotely without onsite staff at least temporarily. It is also possible to conduct redundant operations on a selective basis. For example, some organizations will perform real-time data backups at remote locations or ensure the availability of e-mail communications by having redundant servers operating at remote locations.

- **Hot Site** – This is a separate operation that is ready on a standby status. Compatible hardware, power, communications and other necessary assets are all available and ready to be activated. The site must be regularly tested to assure readiness. Hot sites can generally be made fully operational within a day or two.

- **Cold Site** – This is a separate facility that is not operational but can be made operational within a reasonable period of time. Electric power and communication access is available, although computer hardware is not in place. Other basic requirements such as raised floors and security may be available. As additional features and hardware are added, the cold site becomes a **Warm Site**.

IT Alternate Site Support Requirements

Type of Site	Duplicate Staff	Duplicate Hardware	Duplicate Space
Redundant	Yes	Yes	Yes
Hot	No	Yes	Yes
Warm	No	Partial	Yes
Cold	No	No	Yes
None	No	No	No

The important question for senior management is how long the organization can reasonably afford to be without IT services. Once this Recovery Time Objective is established, the type of site desired can be determined by the site recovery time associated with each type of site.

After an organization identifies the type of site that is desired, the organization needs to identify the cost of the site and the cost associated with other acceptable solutions. Maintaining the IT alternate site plan can require a substantial financial commitment and the cost of the various solutions needs to be carefully examined and a cost-benefit analysis is often performed.

As the cost of the IT alternate site increases, the recovery time decreases as illustrated below:

Recovery Time: Redundant (shortest) < Hot < Warm < Cold < No Site (longest)

Cost of Site: Redundant (most expensive) > Hot > Warm > Cold > No Site (least expensive)

There are many variables that determine IT alternate site recovery times and it is generally difficult to specify recovery times exactly. However, a rough guideline of recovery times is as follows:

IT Alternate Site vs. Recovery Time Illustration

Type of Site	Recovery Time
Redundant	Instantaneous
Hot	24 – 36 Hours, Certain Critical Applications Perhaps Faster
Warm	Certain Critical Applications 24 – 36 hours, Full Recovery 5+ Days
Cold	Partial Recovery 5+ Days, Full Recovery Longer
None	10 – 20 Days or Longer

IT Alternate Site Provider

Once the type of IT alternate site needed is identified, it will be necessary to select a provider. Providers basically fall into one of three categories; vendor provider, internally provided or mutual aid agreement.

Vendor Provided

Many organizations engage vendors to provide IT alternate sites. Vendors can be engaged to support hardware, space and, at least to some extent, personnel services. A typical hot-site vendor will provide the space and supporting infrastructure with appropriate controls and redundancies. Hardware requirements for each client are stipulated by contract with the vendor and the necessary hardware will be made available as needed.

Once a major crisis event occurs or threatens, the organization will alert the vendor that the IT alternate site needs to be activated and the IT team will be dispatched. This action is referred to as a disaster declaration. **Disaster Declaration** (Invocation, Activation) is the statement used to announce the activation of BCM. Upon receiving a disaster declaration, the vendor's employees configure the hardware with the goal of having the hardware setup completed by the time the IT team arrives. Certain other actions, such as acquiring data, will also simultaneously commence. The organization's IT team will have to load data, test data and software upon arriving at the vendor provided site.

Note that vendors will charge a declaration fee for site activation services. If for some reason a disaster declaration is made and subsequently determined that it was unnecessary, the declaration fees will still be payable. To avoid a frivolous declaration, it is important that only a few key executive managers have the authority to make a disaster declaration.

A **co-location site** is an alternate site where the vendor provides the facility and infrastructure support and the organization provides the hardware. The hardware is secured inside compartments at the vendor's location. Since the cost of a co-location site is based on the volume of space leased, in addition to hardware costs, hardware size is also a cost factor. Over the last several years, hardware costs and the physical size of most hardware has decreased. As such, co-location sites have become increasingly popular.

Aside from the costs and technical requirements of the IT alternate site, the following should be considered before a vendor is selected:

- The number and locations of sites potentially available.
- The primary assigned site.
- Other vendor clients in the immediate area.
- Other vendor clients with any priority commitments.
- Back-up power supply and alternate communication capability.
- Annual testing hours.
- Additional services and support.

Internally Provided

For many large organizations with multiple locations, an internally provided IT alternate site is the option of choice. When comparing the cost of an internally provided IT alternate site against the cost of utilizing a vendor, a primary determining factor will be the cost of hardware. A vendor will basically share computer hardware with multiple companies. If hardware buying or leasing costs are low, the cost of using a vendor will typically save little money and may even be more expensive when vendor profits and overhead are considered. Contrarily, if hardware costs are high, then the cost of using a vendor should be less expensive.

With the cost of hardware decreasing over the last several years, internally provided IT alternate sites have become increasingly popular. Many smaller and medium sized organizations with multiple locations are now finding this approach to be cost-effective.

Mutual Aid Agreement

A **mutual aid agreement** is a service level agreement between two or more organizations to provide a resource when one of the organizations experiences an outage. In an actual crisis these arrangements frequently fail for information technology services for one or more of the following reasons:

▶ **Hardware is Incompatible** – Even if the hardware is identical at the initial point of agreement, equipment changes by either organization will ruin compatibility.

▶ **Insufficient Capacity** – Most data centers have resources to meet the needs of their normal operations and will not have sufficient excess capacity for another organization of similar size.

▶ **Lack of Availability** – Most data centers are in operation for extended hours and there simply isn't time available for another organization that also needs usage for extended hours.

▶ **Both Data Centers Disabled** – Mutual aid agreements are often arranged between organizations in the same local area and these organizations are all subject to the same community-wide crisis events.

IT Alternate Site Location

Classic thinking is that the IT alternate site should be located a sufficient distance away from the primary data center to avoid multiple destruction or denial of access to both locations. This classic thinking is still widely accepted. However, it does require relocating personnel to test, activate and maintain the IT alternate site. Relocating staff will result in travel expenses, travel time and inconvenience to IT personnel. The approach also assumes that travel to the distant location is possible and for most crisis events this is a valid assumption. Possible exceptions include severe community-wide crisis events such as earthquakes, terrorist attacks or other sudden crisis events. Note that hurricanes and most other severe weather crisis events provide sufficient warning time to safely pre-position personnel at distant locations before the weather event strikes.

Some organizations have opted for local IT alternate site locations in heavily fortified buildings. In addition to having self sustaining and redundant utility systems, these buildings are hardened to withstand the maximum community-wide crisis event that can reasonably be expected in the region. Theoretically, this approach removes all the travel problems associated with IT alternate sites located at distant locations. In reality, this approach removes most of the travel problems associated with IT alternate sites located in distant locations. During certain major community-wide crisis events, local travel may be impossible and unsafe due to crisis event damage, curfews and/or a possible breakdown of law and order. IT mobile sites with self sustaining and redundant utility systems are also vulnerable to these problems.

If the organization is located in an area where community-wide crisis events are unlikely, then a local IT alternate site is an option that should be seriously considered. On the other hand, if the organization is located in an area where major community-wide crisis events are possible, then a distant IT alternate site is the option often selected.

Discussion: Logistical Problems with Distant IT Alternate Sites

Alarge organization headquartered along the coast of the Gulf of Mexico is threatened by a major hurricane. Operations around the country are dependent on IT services located at the company headquarters. The organization has an IT alternate hot site located in Pennsylvania and makes a disaster declaration 48 hours in advance of the hurricane strike.

> ▶ What are the logistical problems in making the IT alternate site operational that are facing this organization before the hurricane strike?
>
> ▶ Should a disaster declaration have been made 72 hours in advance of the hurricane strike?
>
> ▶ What are the logistical problems in maintaining the IT alternate site operational that are facing this organization during and after the hurricane strike?

There are several other subjects that senior management should discuss with the organization's IT professionals. These questions include the following:

▶ How often is the IT alternate site tested?

▶ What types of tests are being performed?

▶ Can the IT alternate site be activated remotely?

▶ For recovering applications, has a recovery sequence been developed and is it compatible with the overall RTO for the organization?

▶ How well documented is the IT alternate site plan?

Cloud Computing is anything that entails the delivery of hosted services over the Internet and a '**Private Cloud**' is a proprietary network that delivers hosted services to designated users. Cloud computing has important application for communications between the data center and the organization users – also between the IT alternate site and the organization users.

A successful operational IT alternate site must be able to communicate with the organization users and a private cloud is a most useful communication approach. The Internet has many infrastructural redundancies and is considered to be highly reliable and location independent. These are important factors in an environment where the community-wide communications infrastructure is damaged. Communication between the distant IT alternate site and the organization users can likely be continued by relocating employees to any location where the communication infrastructure is not damaged.

Data Center Controls

Regardless of the IT alternate site planning in place, it is important to incorporate as many data center controls as financially feasible to avoid an IT crisis event in the first place. Some of the key physical controls commonly found in modern data centers are discussed below.

Electrical Equipment Protection and Power Backup

Data center hardware and ongoing operations are dependent upon reliable electrical power. Long-term power requirements are handled by backup diesel powered electrical generators. Generators should be designed to automatically kick-in when a power disruption is initially detected. There needs to be fuel adequate for several days of operation and generators need to be regularly tested under load and serviced according to manufacturer's recommendations.

Short term power disruptions and power fluctuations are covered by surge protectors and uninterruptible power supply (UPS) systems. UPS systems should be designed to maintain electrical power long enough for a controlled shutdown of data center operations. This is obviously important for data centers without a backup generator. This is also a good 'rule of thumb' for data centers with backup generators as backup generators are not 100% reliable. In addition, UPS systems can bridge the gap while a backup generator is cycling up.

Fire Suppressant Systems

Handheld, gas-based fire extinguishers are only marginally effective in suppressing a fire. Nonetheless, handheld gas-based fire extinguishers are typically found in data centers for use on small fires. Regular 'ABC' fire extinguishers are effective in fire suppression but may damage electrical components. Regular fire extinguishers should never be located in the data center – they can do more damage than a fire.

Probably the most common data center fire suppressant system is the same water-based system that is typically used for the rest of the building. The major concern here is an accidental breakage or malfunction of a sprinkler head resulting in the discharge of water in the data center. Probably the best fire suppressant system is a dry-pipe water system in the data center that virtually eliminates the possibility of an accidental release. The dry-pipe system will not discharge water unless a sprinkler head is open and another 'trigger' activates the system. Other triggers might include the activation of a smoke or heat sensor. Installation of a dry-pipe system will involve additional expense.

Older data centers are often equipped with a gas-based fire suppressant system. These systems are generally effective but could present an unwanted chemical exposure to the data center personnel and create environmental concerns. These concerns are somewhat dependent upon the exact chemical being used but, for our purposes it is safe to say, there are no perfect chemicals. These systems are also expensive to install.

Gauges and Alarms

Temperature and humidity gauges monitor atmospheric conditions to ensure that the environment remains within the operational range of data center hardware. Smoke and heat sensors detect any fire danger. It is important that all alarms and gauges be monitored continuously. If a problem occurs when the data center is not in operation, a designated off-site data center team member needs to be alerted.

Physical Security

The importance of data center physical security is a topic that really needs no discussion and should go well beyond door key locking mechanisms. A keypad entry system provides an increased level of security but is not 100% foolproof and typically does not record the user. Ideally there should be a swipe-card access system that records all data center access activity. Surveillance cameras in the data center are also a powerful security tool. Swipe-card systems coupled with surveillance cameras can be of great security forensic value should a problem occur.

Raised Floors, Wiring and Cabling

Historically, data centers were designed with a raised floor to protect data center hardware from flooding. Wires and cables were also located under the floor and this offered protection from accidental physical damage.

While this classic design is still viable, the preferred choice for most modern data centers is to run the wires and cables in the ceiling. Overhead wiring and cabling is easier to access, not subject to being submerged after a water pipe-burst and is less vulnerable to accidental physical damage. Data center hardware is generally supported on racks and raised floors may also be used.

Miscellaneous Controls

Dedicated climate control systems are preferred for data centers to prevent data center climate needs being compromised with general building needs. Fortified walls protect the data center from crisis events that occur in the building outside of the data center. Emergency lighting should be available in case normal and backup electrical controls both fail. An emergency shutoff switch or button should be placed near the data center exit door and a plastic cover should shield the switch to avoid accidental activation.

Data Center Recovery

Regardless of the IT alternate site plan in place, an organization will likely want to have a plan to recover the main data center. This is especially true if the organization is using an outside vendor, as maintaining operations at an outside vendor's location is likely to be expensive. If no IT alternate site is available, then rapidly recovering the data center will be even more imperative.

Data center recovery plans should address:

- Data center hardware and hardware configuration needs to be well documented.
- Contracts need to be in place with outside service providers to rapidly replace damaged or destroyed equipment. These contracts are relatively inexpensive to secure.
- Contracts need to be in place with outside service providers to rapidly assist with data center recovery. These contracts can usually be secured at little or no cost.
- Documentation needs to be developed to define the timeline, major steps and assign personnel to perform the following:

  1. Damage assessment to data center infrastructure and hardware.
  2. Engage subcontractors.
  3. Recover the data center infrastructure.
  4. Order replacement hardware.
  5. Data center infrastructure recovery.
  6. Hardware replacement.
  7. Data and software loaded and tested.
  8. Applications recovered.

Information Management

For most organizations data can be divided into two categories – hardcopy and electronic. Because of the physical nature of hardcopy data, hardcopy data is more cumbersome to store.

Hardcopy Data

Certain industries such as law firms, lenders and others do need to maintain large volumes of hardcopy data. If there is a high volume of hardcopy data, original copies of hardcopy data are often digitized. In many organizations, once hardcopy data is digitized the original hardcopy document is discarded. Many organizations are moving towards paperless environments where all data is created or scanned and captured in an electronic format.

Hardcopy-only data is information that has not been electrically secured. Assuming that the data is important, one of the following precautions should be taken for hardcopy-only data:

1. The data should be duplicated and disbursed.

2. The data should be scanned or converted into an electronic format.

3. The data should be secured in a fire-resistant safe.

The most fail-safe approach to secure hardcopy-only data is to duplicate and disburse. The two physical locations of duplicated hardcopy-only data should be sufficiently distant to avoid multiple destruction. The least failsafe approach to secure hardcopy-only data is typically a fire-resistant safe. Note that fire-resistant safes are not fireproof safes as there is no such thing as a fireproof safe. Fire-resistant safes may also be subject to damage from certain non-fire crisis events such as explosion, flood and theft or fail because someone forgot to close the door. Denial of access can also be an issue for any data secured at only one physical location.

Discussion: Disbursing Hardcopy Records

How far apart should an original and backup hardcopy record be separated? Clearly the backup records should be located far enough away to avoid the destruction of both records. However, the farther apart the records are located the more difficult and expensive it is to manage.

▶ What is your opinion on the correct distance between original and backup hardcopy records?

▶ In addition to distance between the two records, what other factors should be considered when separating the records?

Electronic Data

Unless there is an unusual feature of the data, such as an original signature or hand written amendments, a document can usually be easily captured, stored, classified and retrieved by IT. Backup electronic data can be duplicated and disbursed without requiring more than minimal physical space and energy consumption. For these reasons, electronic data is generally considered to be more environmentally friendly than hardcopy data.

A most important point centers around how often data is captured. Practices vary largely depending on how important the data is to the organization. Sometimes the shear volume of data places practical limits on how frequently data backups are performed. Probably the most common frequency of performing data backups is once daily; usually being performed overnight after normal working hours.

An important point that is sometimes overlooked for data is how often the backup information is taken off-site. Senior management generally knows the frequency of data backups but often does not know the frequency of storing backups off-site. Clearly data not stored off-site is subject to many of the same exposures that could damage or deny access to the original data. Accomplishing the established Recovery Point Objective (RPO) requires both data backups and off-site storing of the backups. Storing data off-site involves an additional step and expense but it is an important control.

The location of where backup information is secured also needs to be assessed. Data is occasionally secured at the home of a trusted employee. This is inexpensive but it lacks sufficient security and other controls. Electronic data does not require extensive space for storage and this allows for data storage at hardened, climate-controlled secured locations at moderate cost. Another important question is data access. Bank vaults are secure but not always available; therefore, they should not be used to store data that requires immediate accessibility. Professional records management companies have all the controls and access issues covered. For many organizations, the use of a professional records management company is a cost-justified expense.

Today's technologies also allow for ongoing or real-time data backups. This procedure is becoming increasingly popular and can backup data at an off-site location as it is being captured.

Information Security

The information security plan is based upon management's objectives, the value of the information being protected, the perceived threat levels, audit requirements and costs. A security breach could lead to legal actions, lost business or, in an extreme case, bankruptcy. Basic questions that management should address with the individual in charge of information security are:

- Has anyone been assigned the position of Information Security Officer?
- In smaller data centers without a full time Information Security Officer, is the employee assigned to this position able to allocate sufficient time to perform the job correctly?
- Has senior management approved the information security plan?
- Has an adequate information threat assessment been performed?
- Are administrative controls such as written policies, standards and procedures in place?
- Have information security classifications such as public, sensitive, private and confidential been established for all information?
- Are access controls in place for non-public information?
- How complex are the usernames and passwords?
- How often are passwords changed?
- Is data encryption used when information is transferred or stored?
- Are there firewalls in place?

Review Topics

1. Discuss the reasons why the use of a vendor provided hot site is better than the use of an internally provided hot site.

2. Discuss the reasons why the use of an internally provided hot site is better than the use of a vendor provided hot site.

3. Identify the logistical problems associated with using a local IT alternate site location in heavily fortified buildings during a major community-wide crisis event.

4. Identify the logistical problems associated with using a distant IT alternate site location during a major community-wide crisis event.

5. If a good IT alternate site plan is in place, why is it important to have a data center recovery plan for the main data center?

6. Identify the environmental benefits of electronic data over hardcopy data.

Case Studies

Case Study A-6: Alpha Investment Services (AIS) IT Disaster Recovery Planning

Assume that you are an executive officer of AIS and not an IT professional making a review of overall IT department procedures and controls. Be sure to provide a brief explanation for your answers. Based on the information previously provided in Case Study A, consider the following:

A-6.1   Identify the major controls in place and rate as Excellent, Good, Fair or Poor in each of the following areas:

    A. IT Alternate Site

    B. Data Center Controls

    C. Data Center Recovery

    D. Information Management

    E. Information Security.

A-6.2   List the improvements (if any) that you would suggest at AIS in each of the following areas:

    A. IT Alternate Site

    B. Data Center Controls

    C. Data Center Recovery

    D. Information Management

    E. Information Security.

Case Study B-6: Beta Widget Makers (BWM) IT Disaster Recovery Planning

Assume that you are an executive officer of BWM and not an IT professional making a review of overall IT department procedures and controls. Be sure to provide a brief explanation for your answers. Based on the information previously provided in Case Study B, consider the following:

B-6.1   Identify the major controls in place and rate as Excellent, Good, Fair or Poor in each of the following areas:
A. IT Alternate Site
B. Data Center Controls
C. Data Center Recovery
D. Information Management
E. Information Security.

B-6.2   List the improvements (if any) that you would suggest at BWM in each of the following areas:
A. IT Alternate Site
B. Data Center Controls
C. Data Center Recovery
D. Information Management
E. Information Security.

Bibliography

Burtles, J., *Principles and Practices of Business Continuity: Tools and Techniques*, Rothstein Associates Inc., 2007.

Engemann, K. and Miller, H., "A Simulation Approach to Managing Risk for Money Transfer Telecommunications Lines," *Proceedings of the Twentysecond Annual Meeting of the Northeast Decision Sciences Institute*, pp.81-83, April 1993.

Engemann, K. and Miller, H., "Measuring Information Technology Investment Payoff for Electronic Commerce," *10th International Information Management Conference*, October 2009.

Fulmer, K. L., *Business Continuity Planning: A Step-by-Step Guide With Planning Forms*, Rothstein Associates Inc., 2005.

Henderson, D. M., *The Comprehensive Business Continuity Management Program*, Rothstein Associates Inc., 2008.

Hiles, A. N., *Business Continuity: Best Practices: Aligning Business Continuity with Corporate Governance*, Rothstein Associates Inc., 2004.

Miller, H. E. and Engemann, K. J., "Information Security Management Planning," *Proceedings of the Twentyfourth Annual Meeting of the Northeast Decision Sciences Institute*, pp. 435-437, March 1995.

Sun Microsystems, "Linking Disaster Recovery Time Objectives to Business Requirements," 2006.

CHAPTER VII

Information Systems Security[*]

Objectives

» Examine the security of IT assets of an organization

» Characterize threats to IT assets

» Review the control of IT assets in a systematic way

» Examine audit objectives and control objectives

» Describe substantive tests and compliance tests

» Describe presenting material findings to executive management

» Review operating systems and systems software security

» Define applications security, database security and network security

» Review mobile devices and security

» Examine the growth of social networking.

*Chapter prepared by Donald R. Moscato PhD, CDP.

The Control Environment

What is a control?

In this section, we discuss several concepts that form the basis of understanding some of the primary ways for an organization to think about control. It is convenient and effective to view controls from a very simple perspective. There is a fundamental statement of the control which is followed by a discipline over that control. An example would be the control to keep all doors locked. That would be the basic control statement discipline. However, unless an auditor verifies that the doors are indeed locked, then there is no compliance with that basic control statement. It is the surrounding control that makes it effective. Merely stating the control is never enough.

Controls as a Layering Process

A useful way of implementing controls in any situation is to view them as a multilayered process of controls. In the first instance we try to *prevent* an incident from happening that would breach a system. Often, most controls are set at this layer. Unfortunately, an adversary is able to penetrate a system and, if successful, has free reign over the target areas. To counter this possibility, controls are placed to *detect* a breach to the system. In this manner, if a perpetrator gains access we are at least able to know that something improper has occurred. Finally, provision must be made to *correct* the problem resulting from the breach to that part of the system. These three layers: preventive, detective and corrective, form the basis of layering controls on a particular information technology asset to be protected.

The following is an example of layering the controls on a system. Take the example of a "man trap" entry system to a building. The double door system tries to prevent improper entry by unauthorized personnel. If the person is able to enter the first door and announces them self to the intercom and that person should not be given entry, then the second door prevents further access and locks the first door behind the individual. The system prevented the person from entering the building. It detected an unauthorized person trying to enter. Finally, a security guard can proceed to the entry way and take corrective action.

It is good practice to recognize that these layers of control support the recognition that threats to a system asset can occur from several different intentions. A threat could be active on the part of the perpetrator (Newman, 2010); (Solomon and Chapple, 2005). An example would be the deliberate destruction of a server farm in a datacenter. The threat can be passive. An example would be the benign neglect of backing up an important database asset at regular intervals. The absence of properly timed backups could compromise the system in the event of system failure. Finally, a threat can be accidental (Easttom, 2006). This category includes acts of nature such as floods, tsunamis and earthquakes as well as acts of people including electrical fires and liquids spilling on electronic devices.

Characterizing Threats to IT Assets

In implementing any control system for a targeted asset it is imperative to understand the nature of any exposure. On some occasions your concern could be *disclosure* of the state of a particular asset. An example would be the balance in a bank account or the fact that a person knows that an alarm to an area is in an inactive mode at a point in time. Other times, the exposure is an asset that could be *modified*. Examples would be when a perpetrator could change the direction of an inquiry to a dangerous web site or when a firewall is set to an 'off' mode unbeknownst to an organization. A third type of exposure would be when the intent is to *destroy* an asset (Pipkin, 2000). The goal is destruction and it could be as large as an entire intranet of a corporation to something as minor as the contents of a person's hard drive on their computer.

In order to facilitate the creation of a control system and its efficacy, we can follow a straightforward process. There are many names given to this exercise, and many variations of it, but we present the following as one of many options to inform our actions. It makes little sense to insert controls at random in a system. This action can result in inefficiencies, poor control and wasted expense and frustration on the part of system's users. The first step is to systematically attempt to identify the types of breaches to the system that might occur. Examples could be a fire, robbery, etc. The next step is to ascertain at what point in the system (a control point) there should be a control inserted. Again, this control could be any one of the three types discussed previously -- preventive, detective or corrective. The auditor must be assured that these controls are in fact in place as part of a formal audit. Finally, depending upon the importance of the audit target, a step-by-step approach must be designed to perform the audit in an expeditious manner.

There are many design principles that must be considered in designing an effective control system. These include: requisite variety, redundancy, granularity, protocols and standards, encryption and trust (Raval and Fichadia, 2007).

Information Systems Auditing Considerations

Audit Objectives and Control Objectives

There is a very simple process that an auditor follows when on a site visit. It involves asking a series of questions and reflecting on the answers to them. The questions are as follows: who, what, when, where, why, how and which (Moscato, 1995). However, an audit is far more complex than simply asking a few basic questions and reporting the results. The auditor must be guided by a clear control objective and audit objective or countless resources will be wasted.

Each audit has a control objective. Its purpose is to ensure that an asset is properly protected at the desired level. In order to ascertain this state, the auditor establishes a specific audit objective. The ultimate purpose of the audit objective is to be able to determine whether or not the control objective has been met. It should be noted that a control objective might be financial in nature (are assets properly valued?), non-financial in nature (is data archived?) or operational (is a facility properly secured?). The audit objective eventually is translated into an audit program that is drilled down to the audit steps necessary to carry out the actual site audit.

Substantive Tests and Compliance Tests

Typically, the auditor performs tests on the targeted system. These tests are either substantive or compliance in nature. A substantive test is a test of data values and usually involves accessing a company's data base and verifying balances contained therein. Emphasis is placed on material values and not always a direct enumeration of all the data. A compliance test is one that is concerned with a review of operations with the purpose of rendering an opinion on whether or not a proper policy or procedure is being followed at a data center. In this chapter, we are concerned only with compliance testing of the controls in place at the physical site and not with any data contained within databases.

Statement of Audit Findings

The Institute of Internal Auditors (IIA) has developed a series of guidelines that are to be followed in presenting the audit results to corporate management in a concise and standardized manner. As part of an audit review, the auditors are expected to follow these guidelines in presenting their audit findings as a result of their site visits to the data center. Each audit finding is documented and then prioritized in terms of risk exposure to the organization. The following five points constitute the architecture of the audit findings framework.

1. The Statement of Condition

This contains the factual (observed) evidence of the current state. It can be thought of as the "what was" part of the report.

2. The Criteria

This is our reference point or standard/protocol that is used to measure against the current condition observed by the auditor.

3. The Effect

Preferably stated with a monetary value, it represents the degree of risk or exposure incurred as a result of the deviation from the standard.

4. The Cause

This is the auditor's opportunity to explain why there is a deviation from the stated standard. Often, this is the result of someone not performing their assigned duties but can also be the result of no one person being held responsible for an entity.

5. The Recommendation

This is the opportunity for the auditor to state to management what actions could be taken to rectify the identified exposure. In other words, what to do now! (IIA, 2010).

By following this audit findings template all identified risk exposures are presented in a uniform format to executive management. Each audit finding could be ranked in terms of corporate impact. Its design facilitates communication and keeping the focus on the facts of the audit and the generally accepted standards of the profession. It is important to note that it is not the responsibility of the auditor to set standards but, rather, to identify any deviations from those standards identified in the audit of the data center.

In order to assist the information systems auditor in carrying out their responsibilities it is incumbent upon each professional to have a competency level on a basic skill set. We can identify several of these skills and requirements. There are guidelines and standards provided in COBIT, ISO and from the IIA (Whitman and Mattord, 2008); (Dhillon, 2007). Audits of data centers are carried out by having formal site visits. The time of these visits is a judgmental call -- during work hours or when the site is closed. Conducting a physical site visit can be expensive in both time and money. Often, there is a need to have interaction with key people and the actual site itself. Care should be taken to make sure the site is available at the time the auditor is going to visit. In this case study, the visit is carried out after hours when only a security person is staffing the front desk of the building. The auditor is to observe the site looking for both exposures resulting from errors of commission as well as errors of omission.

Information Technology and Security Considerations

In this section, we discuss various information technology applications using concepts discussed earlier in this chapter.

Operating Systems and Systems Software Security

Every computer system has an operating system that serves to handle major tasks that enable applications to be processed. The degree of security of any operating system is something that can be engineered by an organization to ensure that the appropriate level of trust is achieved. Applications involving national security require what is referred to as "trusted" systems. Most businesses implement general purpose operating systems that, although having some degree of security, are not intended to possess an inordinate level of security. Operating systems such as Windows, Linux, OS/390 and Unix are examples of these.

Since the major purpose of any operating system is to control the processing of tasks it is important to understand that most of the work carried out by the operating system is out of sight of most computer users. Often the end user interfaces with the operating system when they sign on to the computer. The operating system manages the functions of identification, authentication and authorization of all end users. For most applications this involves the use of a login name and password. The operating system contains tables created by the data manager to verify that the person trying to access the computer is indeed a valid user. A serious security threat to any operating system occurs when unauthorized users gain access to the computer. Once inside the computer aberrant activities such as malware (viruses, worms, spyware, trojan horses and adware) could wreak havoc with valid organizational activities.

With the growth of the Internet, attacks on operating systems have proliferated. The information on vulnerabilities of certain operating systems is widely available and shared across national boundaries. Certain people have as their objectives financial gain whereas others are simply out to disrupt the operations of businesses.

Most operating systems have embedded security modules, whereas older systems had to rely on external modules that were purchased separately. In most organizations there is a specialist whose responsibilities are to manage all aspects of the operating system. They set security parameters commensurate with the specific objectives of the organization. One of their most important tasks is to ensure that all current upgrades are installed in a timely manner. The number of patches required varies with the discovery of serious security or operating flaws detected by users in the field. Another task is to backup all files on the servers in a timely manner and to test the recovery policies that have been established by management.

Some organizations function in a 24/7 environment and cannot afford to have any universal system downtime. The ultimate goal of the systems manager is to "harden" the system so that it is resilient to attacks and can keep the organization functioning in an effective and efficient manner. The principal means to secure operating systems is through real-time monitoring and the use of event logs. The latter is an after-the-fact control that allows systems managers to look for breaches in the system and to track any patterns that might be an indication of abuse. (Marko, 2010)

Applications Security

The major purpose of using computers is to perform useful work. This work is done by applications software (often referred to as apps). In large organizations applications are designed by systems analysts and designers. Typically, some form of project management techniques are employed to manage costs and time as well as the quality of the finished product. With the advent of microcomputers more development work was delegated to end users whose task it was to build spreadsheets, document generation, databases and presentations. These applications are executable programs that perform many tasks required by the organization. If care is not taken to make certain that the programs are secure then serious breaches can occur in the security of the organization.

These application programs provide windows into the company's nerve center. They often use existing files (open, read and modify data) and provide reports and analyses to management at all levels of an organization that is used daily for decision-making. If proper security procedures in developing these applications are not taken, then the quality of decision-making could be seriously compromised. For example, a spreadsheet program has embedded within itself to perform calculations accurately, present attractive graphics and to prepare attractive looking reports. However, there is no guarantee that the developer is using the data properly. Bad data and bad analysis are major security risks for any organization that uses computers to support decision-making. Therefore, it is incumbent upon any organization to properly train application developers in the rudimentary principles of control and security if they are charged with supporting the organization decision processes. A "runaway" application could alter other system resources and have a far greater impact than to its own local application.

A final concern with applications is the management of changes to any system. Only authorized users should be allowed access to an application and be given the ability to make any changes to it. Once the need is established for a change to an application, someone must authorize the change. The change to the application must be thoroughly tested and, if acceptable, it should be properly documented and then implemented. In large organizations there is a formal change configuration process in place. However, in smaller organizations changes to applications are often done in a very informal manner thus increasing the security risk from any changes made by end users.

A recent study identified these five threats as the most dangerous programming errors:

1. Cross-site scripting

2. SQL Injection

3. Classic buffer overflow

4. Cross-site request forgery

5. Improper access control (authorization) (Higgins, 2010).

Database Security

Databases have evolved over time from traditional file management approaches. In the latter, a file was assigned to its own computer program where there was a one-to-one mapping. Whenever the data changed there was a commensurate change in the file specifications of the program to match the change. This approach resulted in several security issues. Data was disaggregated and often out of sync with the business needs since there was a lag between real-time status and the update of the data. End users were never aware of the current business situation often resulting in ineffective decision-making. Since all data was tied to the application program there was often redundant data within the organization causing unnecessary expense for storage and updates occurring at different intervals.

During the 1970's and continuing to the present, databases have emerged to rectify some of these concerns. Over time several different database architectures have been in favor in the field of information technology. The goal of a database management system is to organize the data so that data redundancy is optimized. Since management relies on timely, accessible data for decision-making, databases must be reliable, available, secure and efficient.

In discussing database security we must take two different perspectives. The first perspective is that of the database creator or designer. In setting up the database, one must determine who has access and how people will have access to the data, who will update the data and which constituent owns the data. Since the database administrator is responsible for securing the data, many organizational questions must be addressed. Some of these are technical and some are political. The primary concern of the administrator is efficiency in design that translates into rapid access retrieval speeds and low overhead on the system.

It is helpful to think of databases as an important link in processing transactions. These transactions are created by applications (birth) and during their existence often become a component of a database. While resident in the database they can be modified (updated) and undergo various transformations. At some point they are archived (death). This birth/death metaphor emphasizes the importance of maintaining audit trails of all activities affecting a database. The database administrator is the custodian of the data as it moves through each stage of materialization in the life of a transaction. Federal laws dictate how long certain business data must be maintained; however, some companies may choose to archive their data for longer periods of time.

The second perspective belongs to the end user. Typically, they are not aware of the behind-the-scenes technical issues. They are concerned with the efficacy of the user interface. The end user accesses the database in a natural language interface by a series of queries. The power of the particular database system determines the extent of the functionality that is available to users. Access for each person is pre-determined and entered into the system by the database administrator. Security is enforced via a user sign on procedure. The complexity of the password rubric employed (number of characters, special symbols, case sensitivity, frequency of change) all contribute to the quality of security. Passwords are ranked on a scale from weak to strong.

Other controls could include a timeout feature enforced when there is a lack of keyboard activity, encryption of all data in transmission to and from the database server and encryption of all data in storage. Depending upon the perceived risk inherent in each system application, one or more of these security features can be implemented. The inherent tradeoff that exists is between user friendliness of the interface versus the robustness of the security employed

Network Security

A convenient way to understand the direction in network technology is to focus on the delivery of services to the end user. Microsoft uses the idea of three screens and the cloud to emphasize its strategic direction. Users rely on the television screen, the computer screen and the handheld device screen to interact with the universe. All of these devices are linked through cloud computing. (Mackinnon, 2010) The plethora of network devices and their projected improvements create a significant security risk for all organizations. These risks run the gamut from loss or theft of the smaller devices to hacking and cracking of corporate or government networks.

To understand network security one must be aware of the various exposures and where they occur. Network standardization is facilitated via the OSI (open systems interconnect) seven-layer network model: application layer, presentation layer, session layer, transport layer, network layer, data link layer and physical layer. This model allows various forms of security to be implemented at each level of the conceptual model. Security controls can be placed on the physical layer all the way to the application layer discussed earlier in this chapter. In practice, the more familiar TCP/IP model is the basis for Internet activity and one term that many end users are somewhat familiar with as they interact with wider networks in practice. The TCP/IP model is composed of four layers (application layer, transport layer, Internet layer and network access layer). You can think of it as a mapping to the conceptual design of the OSI model.

Behind the scenes of network activity lies a host of technical decisions not the least of which are security concerns. These networks can be LANs (local area networks), WANs (wide area networks) and can be called intranets (within organizations) or the Internet (public network). The networks can be wired or wireless. Each choice involves complex security tradeoffs for the network designers.

Every network must have a designed level of reliability so that organizations can function in a global environment with an expected level of service to its customers. Therefore, choices in technology must be made regarding "pathways" the data will traverse. Will the data channels be public or private? Will they be secured (encrypted) or unsecured? Will there be a single control center or will the control be distributed across several computers? The network designers must determine a network that contains redundancies in the event one channel is out of service or compromised.

In certain cases an organization might want to utilize a public network but want a higher level of built-in security. In order to satisfy this requirement virtual private networks (VPNs) were created. The process is effective in that the end user initiates contact with the Internet as a first step. Then via a client software program the user's data is encrypted at the sending location. This encrypted data is then transmitted over the public Internet until it arrives at its target destination. At that location a VPN switch is utilized to decrypt the transmission and forward it to another user in the corporate network. A good way to understand this process is by means of a metaphor. The message is loaded into an armored car (a process referred to as encapsulation) and that car passes through a private, secured (encrypted) data tunnel that has been carved out virtually through the superhighway (Internet). Each designer must select the appropriate level of security to achieve the organization's security goals. These policies range from the use of static passwords all the way up to dynamic passwords and digital certificates or signatures.

The increased use of wireless and Bluetooth technology raises additional security concerns for an organization. Their primary advantage is that they do not require a network of wires or cables to implement. Rather they use airwaves or radio frequency technology. This becomes a two-edged sword, in that specific security technologies, namely encryption, become a virtual requirement in a business context. Instead of wiring, a series of access points are strategically located at various locations in a building. These access points gather a signal which is used by each computer connected to the network. Network routers are also employed to pass the data on down the network paths. From a security standpoint, wireless transmission enables a non-authorized user to recognize transmissions so that they can intercept them often from outside the premises. This process is referred to as "sniffing" and unless the data is encrypted can result in a compromise to the corporate system.

Mobile Devices and Security

The easiest security approach to take for an organization is to prohibit all mobile devices that could be connected to the corporate network. These smart devices are carried by "road warriors" as part of their desire to be in continuous communication with their customers as well as their colleagues. It is inevitable that the functionality that is present on desktop computers would be demanded and eventually ported to mobile devices (Dolezalek, 2010). Since they are usually small, compact devices that can fit in a pocket or purse, they can easily be lost or even stolen.

Once taken from legitimate owners they can be used to target an organization's information assets. Unless proper protection is taken like encryption of device contents and robust sign-on procedures, the holder of these devices could have a straight shot into the company's assets (Gain, 2010). One way to think about security for mobile devices is to appreciate the fact that these devices are actually computers and, as such, should be taken as seriously as any other corporate computer whether it is a desktop or laptop.

It is good security practice to educate all users of wireless mobile devices about the specific security risks inherent with these devices. In addition to end user education, IT can also implement practices such as password management, auto-disable and remote wipe as well as centralized encryption (Brandel, 2010).

There is another possible security threat that utilizes the GPS and advanced mapping features present in many smartphones. A perpetrator could use these features to locate an individual and know where that person is going. The implication is ominous in that this information can be used in tandem with plots to either rob or physically harm someone (Brenner, 2010).

Growth of Social Networking

There has been an unprecedented growth in the number of social networking sites and users of those services around the world. Members of these services provide personal data to the systems in exchange for the ability to communicate with a larger community. There are numerous security issues inherent in the use of these systems for personal use but the risks increase dramatically when they become part of a corporate enterprise.

In an attempt to reach out to customers, many organizations have incorporated these social networking sites into their marketing and human resources initiatives. They are used to receive feedback from their customers regarding products and services offered in the marketplace. Each of these social networking sites provides for a designated level of security regarding the storage of the member's personal data and the use of that same data. Within the application, each user is able to set their own parameters with respect to their personal data that is made available to other subscribers.

There are several new features that are being added to these sites on a continuous basis. In addition to traditional texting and photo sharing is the ability to combine GPS technology to the social networking site. This process is called "check-ins." By combining the two capabilities, a person is able to discern the location of the person they are communicating with. Businesses are recognizing the revenue generating potential by tying in advertisements and other promotional opportunities. From a security perspective, organizations are finding it increasingly problematical to keep their employees off these sites during working hours resulting in a demonstrable loss of productivity. There is also the concern that corrupted data can enter a system via interactions with outsiders who wish to do harm. The obvious security policy is to issue a corporate ban on using these sites during work hours. But herein lies the conflict when the organization itself is a corporate user of that social networking site. Its employees must monitor the site on a continuous basis.

Networking sites like Facebook, Twitter, MySpace and Flickr provide both a security challenge and organizational challenge to corporations trying to understand and harness the new social networking options available to both customers and employees. Corporate executives often take the position that social networking sites are just another opportunity for employees to waste time while at work. To this end, corporations have instituted policies to block these sites. "An April, 2009 study by Deloitte LLP found that 22% of employees use social networking sites at work five times a week, and 53% feel these activities are none of the company's business." (Marko, 2010b)

Conclusion

In this chapter, the concept of controls and auditing IT assets was discussed. These topics provided a framework that can be implemented by any organization that has an interest in determining a unique approach to securing its information assets. After discussing these important considerations, various components of security and controls were presented.

The challenge for any organization that wants to protect its information technology assets is to inculcate within its employees a fundamental awareness and vigilance toward security. This process starts with new hires and is reinforced on a daily basis. As end users clamor for ease of use it is critical that a company balance its security concerns with enhanced productivity tools that do not compromise the economic viability of the enterprise.

Review Topics

1. What are the benefits of thinking of controls in terms of a layering approach?

2. Identify three examples of IT threats for each of the following exposures: disclosure, modification and destruction.

3. Choose an auditing instance concerning the physical security of an IT center and develop a brief control objective and an auditing objective for it.

4. You have just conducted a site visit to a data center and discovered that the main entrance had a card key entry system installed as a security feature. Unfortunately, the system was inoperable so the door was propped open with a piece of wood. Using the IIA audit findings template prepare an audit finding for your observed event.

5. Discuss why it might be impractical to have all operating systems in business rated for the equivalent of military trusted systems.

6. Discuss why the role of a database administrator in any large organization has both political and technical dimensions

7. Discuss the salient issues in permitting employees in business organizations access to social networking sites.

Bibliography

Brandel, M., "Smartphones Need Smart Security," *Computerworld*, pp.20-23, January 18, 2010.

Brenner, B., "Why Your Smartphone Is Stupid Easy to Hack," *CSO*, pp. 14, March 2010.

Dhillon, G., *Principles of Information Systems Security*, John Wiley, 2007.

Dolezalek, H., "Security on the Go," Processor.com, pp. 26, September 11, 2009.

Easttom, C., *Computer Security Fundamentals*, Pearson Prentice-Hall, 2006.

Gain, B., "Tightening Mobile Security," *Processor.com*, October 23, 2009.

Higgins, K. J., "Should Vendors Be Liable for Bugs," *Information Week*, February 22, 2010.

Institute for Internal Auditors, www.iia.org.

Mackinnon, C. A., "Security in the Cloud," *Processor.com*, pp. 12, February 26, 2010.

Marko, K., "Best Practices for Windows Log Monitoring," *Processor.com*, pp. 1, 8, February 12, 2010.

Marko, K. (b), "Threat Protection in the Age of Social Networking," *Processor.com*, pp. 1, 8, February 26, 2010.

Moscato, D. R., *Computer Assisted Auditing Techniques*, Metamation Systems, 1995.

Newman, R. C., *Computer Security: Protecting Data Resources*, Jones and Bartlett, 2010.

Pipkin, D., *Information Security*, Prentice-Hall, 2000.

Raval, V. and Fichadia, A., *Risks, Controls, and Security: Concepts and Applications*, John Wiley, 2007.

Michael G. Solomon and Mike Chapple, *Information Security Illuminated*, Jones and Bartlett, 2005.

Whitman, M. E., and Mattord, H. J., *Management of Information Security* 2nd. Ed., Thomson Course Technology, 2008.

Implementation

Implementation involves putting the strategies in place, finalizing, documenting and activating the plans. Implementation includes planning to respond to hazard-specific crisis events with the prioritized objectives of life-safety, environmental protection and asset protection. Planning includes the central plan documentation for continuity and recovery procedures for the organization that are needed to return to normal operations following a crisis event. Implementation also includes a review of the internal and external communication systems and procedures necessary to effectively respond to a crisis event.

CHAPTER VIII

Emergency Response

Objectives

» Overview emergency response

» Identify crisis phases

» Define emergency response objectives

» Define emergency operations center

» Review threat monitoring

» Review notification and activation procedures

» Identify emergency actions

» Examine the role of civil authorities.

Emergency Response Overview

An **emergency** is a crisis that requires immediate action. **Emergency response** is the set of immediate actions taken during a crisis event with the prioritized objectives of life-safety, environmental protection and asset protection. An **Emergency Response Plan (ERP)** documents the actions to be taken to respond to hazard-specific crisis events with prioritized objectives. The ERP is designed for use by individuals and teams involved with emergency response including initial responders, the ERT and the Incident Commander. An **initial responder** to a crisis is an individual who encounters the crisis and is the first to take action. The ERP should detail the response to hazard-specific crisis events as identified in RA and BIA. Each important preparation and response step should be stated in chronological order and assigned to the appropriate individual team or department.

Successful emergency response requires proper planning and preparation for each crisis phase. **Crisis phases** include the following three phases:

▶ **Pre-Strike phase** – The period of time when there are indications that the manifestation of a threat is credible. Crisis events may have an extended, brief or nonexistent pre-strike phase.

▶ **Strike phase** – The period of time when the crisis has the most direct impact to the organization.

▶ **Post-Strike phase** – The period of time after the crisis has been contained and controlled, and before all operations are fully recovered.

Emergency Response Objectives

At the onset of a crisis, the Incident Commander takes charge and normal operations may cease. The emergency response objectives to the crisis are to:

1. Protect life and prevent injuries.

2. Protect the environment.

3. Mitigate damages.

4. Contain and control the crisis.

Level of the Crisis

In responding to any crisis, it is important for the Incident Commander to classify the level of the crisis. Crisis levels are broadly classified as follows:

▶ **Minor crisis** has limited impact and does not affect the overall functioning capacity of an organization.

▶ **Major crisis** has the potential to seriously disrupt the overall operation of an organization.

Major crisis events may be further classified as follows:

▶ **Disaster** is a major crisis event which imperils an organization. An event may be deemed a disaster due to factors such as loss of life, environmental damage, asset destruction and duration of disruption.

▶ **Catastrophe** is an extreme disaster.

Emergency Operations Center (EOC)

The **Emergency Operations Center** (EOC) is the location where the teams gather and execute the ERP and BCP. The primary EOC should contain emergency supplies, emergency equipment (Appendix E) and should ideally be fortified with reinforced walls, electric generator back-up and other controls.

The primary EOC should be located on the property. The first backup EOC is generally located outside of the primary facility but in the immediate area. It is used when the primary EOC is inaccessible or destroyed but the crisis was not community-wide. The second backup EOC should be located some distance away so that it is unlikely to have been affected by the same community-wide crisis that rendered the other locations inoperative.

Having a virtual EOC where members are connected by communication devices as a designated backup EOC has become popular. There are limitations inherent with not having a fixed location where everyone can be present. There is also a reliance on communication infrastructure, even when redundant communication systems are in place.

Emergency Command Post (ECP)

The **Emergency Command Post** (ECP) is a designated area near the site of the crisis but located a safe distance from and generally upwind of the crisis site. In an isolated crisis the Incident Commander may instruct ERT members to report directly to the ECP. The Incident Commander will direct response activities and work assignments from the ECP.

Pre-Crisis Activities

Pre-crisis activities include: identifying potential emergencies, determining emergency procedures, planning the EOC, coordinating with civil authorities, documenting the ERP and integrating emergency response with the BCP.

Threat Monitoring

Organizations should continuously monitor threats as a prelude to plan activation. If the organization maintains a security force, the security force will likely monitor man-made threats. Sometimes security forces may not be particularly well trained to monitor weather related threats and the monitoring of weather threats is assigned to another department. Certain specific situations may also be handled by other departments. For example, the Facilities Department will likely monitor utility systems and the IT Department will likely monitor the data center. Additionally, all employees should be encouraged to monitor and report any events that pose a threat to themselves, other employees or the organization.

Many organizations subcontract security and facility services. Organizations should confirm that all parties, including subcontractors, are handling their threat monitoring responsibility.

Notification Procedures

Once a crisis event is detected, the situation needs to be reported. It is recommended that a central point of contact be responsible for receiving initial crisis information, investigating the crisis and communicating the information as necessary. Generally the Security Department handles this responsibility for a larger organization. For some organizations, Human Resources, the receptionist or someone else will receive crisis information. Regardless of who functions as this central point, the following must be in place:

> The central point must be continuously accessible.

> The central point must be able to quickly evaluate or investigate the threat.

> The central point must have the authority to either directly respond or assign someone to respond to the threat and take whatever action is necessary.

> The central point must have access to the Incident Commander.

Any employee can act as an initial responder and may also contact other appropriate entities such as the Police Department and take immediate actions such as activating the fire alarm.

Plan Activation

Plan activation begins at the discretion of the Incident Commander upon the receipt of information regarding a current or pending crisis. Based on information received by the Incident Commander from appropriate entities, plan activation occurs to the extent necessary.

The Incident Commander reviews the circumstances of a crisis and determines the appropriate response. Upon activation, the Emergency Response Team members will be notified typically by Security and should report to the designated Emergency Operations Center or Emergency Command Post as directed.

Some crisis events provide a pre-strike phase. Plan activation may occur during this pre-strike phase. A most important situation occurs if there is an immediate danger from a sudden crisis. In this case, certain emergency response actions such as building evacuation and shelter-in-place procedures must occur automatically.

Evacuation and Shelter Procedures

All employees need to know what actions are to be taken in the event of a crisis. At a minimum, all employees should be able to conduct building evacuation and shelter-in-place procedures. For these procedures to be executed correctly, organizations need to develop, distribute and review crisis guidelines and to conduct periodic exercises.

Employee guidelines should be distributed which present building evacuation and shelter-in-place procedures. Employee guidelines often define employee responsibilities after a crisis, provide contact information and provide important information regarding workplace events such as medical emergencies and workplace violence. Employee guidelines may communicate special payroll and time-off policies that are in effect during and after a crisis. Appendix B presents a sample 'Disaster Assistance Plan.'

Guidelines for evacuation of a typical building are provided in Appendix F. Certain types of buildings and special circumstances require special evacuation procedures as follows:

> In high-rise buildings, individuals located above the floor of a fire or hazmat release should not automatically evacuate – the evacuation route may be dangerous. Properly conducting an evacuation in a high-rise building requires a special alarm system that activates on selected floors and an intercom system that can relay specific information to selected floors.

> 'Vertical Evacuation' is a procedure in which individuals on lower floors relocate themselves to higher floors. This type of evacuation is conducted when there is a danger on the lower floors and there is either a danger in passing through the lower floors or the outside environment is dangerous. The most likely use of a vertical evacuation is when a chemical spill occurs either outdoors or within the building on a lower floor. Vertical evacuations are also used as an evacu-

ation of last resort in a flooding or hurricane event.

▶ 'Silent Evacuation' is a procedure conducted when it is advisable to evacuate without causing alarm. This procedure is most likely used during some type of crime or crime-threatening emergency. Conducting a silent evacuation properly takes a great deal of practice and very few organizations have a silent evacuation plan in place.

▶ A complete evacuation of a hospital is very difficult to safely execute. Hospitals depend, at least to some extent, on relocating individuals vertically and horizontally to safe zones.

A detailed discussion of the special procedures is beyond the scope and purpose of this book. However, everyone should be aware that special procedures exist. All building evacuation plans and procedures should be reviewed with Fire Department officials.

There are a number of emergency situations where an evacuation of a building or area is not advisable such as hostile intruder, hazardous release, terrorist attack, tornado or earthquake events. Certain crisis events may require shelter-in-place procedures to be executed. Shelter-in-place situations often constitute life-threatening events and conducting a building evacuation or failing to respond properly could be a fatal mistake.

Appendix G provides shelter-in-place guidelines. Note that, depending upon the type of threat, there are subtle but important differences in procedures.

Figure 8.1 illustrates these emergency actions

Discussion: Conflicting Emergency Response Recommendations

Standard emergency response steps for an earthquake are outlined in Appendix G. Alternative emergency response procedures for an earthquake were recently advanced by the American Rescue Team International, including:

▶ Lie down next to large objects rather than under large objects to avoid being crushed.

▶ In order to have a shorter escape route, seek safety near outer walls of a building rather than interior areas.

▶ What are your thoughts on these recommendations?

▶ Are any recommendations clearly 100% correct?

Figure 8.1 - Emergency Actions

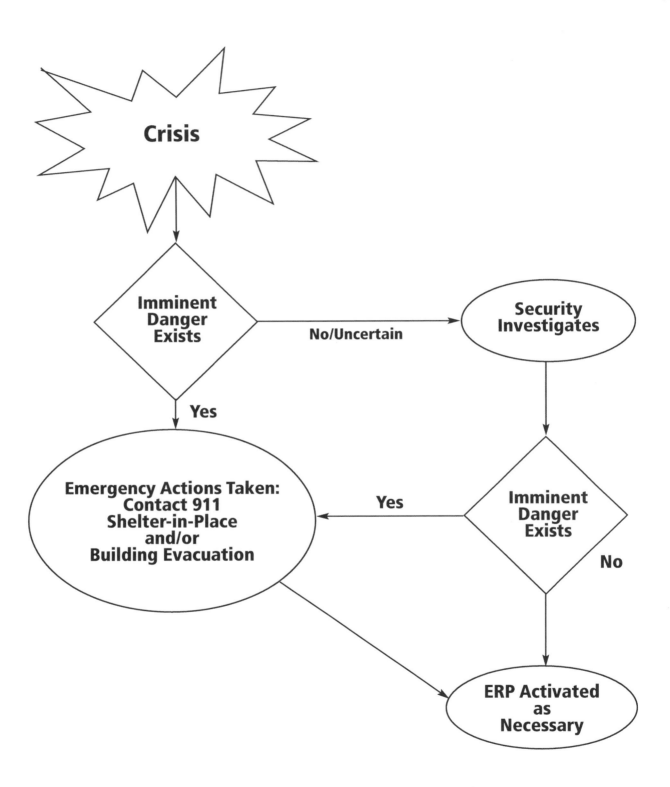

Actions during the Pre-Strike Phase

For a crisis that has a pre-strike phase, emergency actions may be taken before the crisis strike to prevent loss of life, prevent injuries, environment damage and asset damage. The Incident Commander is notified of a crisis and the situation is monitored closely.

Exact pre-strike actions will be different for various crisis events. Weather crisis events are often preceded by a warning period allowing an organization to implement actions to save lives. If there is sufficient warning, actions can be taken to mitigate damages. Appendix H identifies recommended pre-strike actions to be taken for a hurricane, Appendix I identifies recommended pre-strike actions to be taken for a tornado and Appendix J identifies recommended pre-strike actions to be taken for a severe winter storm. The possibility of a pandemic outbreak is a serious concern and special planning is needed. Appendix D identifies recommended pre-strike actions as well as actions to be taken during a pandemic outbreak.

Actions during the Strike Phase

To the extent that some emergency actions are not taken during the pre-strike phase, the Incident Commander has the responsibility to take emergency actions during the strike phase as necessary.

Escalation actions include:

- Activate the EOC.
- Declare a disaster.
- Assemble the Emergency Response Team.
- Alert the Crisis Management Team.
- Alert the Crisis Communication Team.

Life-safety actions include:

- Disseminate emergency messages.
- Address life-safety issues.
- Evacuation and shelter-in-place.
- Release employees.
- Determine building safety.
- Cordon off any dangerous areas.
- Assist with search and rescue.

Environmental protection actions include:

- Address environmental issues.
- Secure hazardous materials.
- Shut down dangerous utilities.

Asset protection actions include:

- Deploy emergency equipment and supplies.
- Enhance facility protection.
- Enhance security.
- Contain and control the incident.

Communication and notification actions include:

- Contact civil authorities.
- Contact relatives of affected employees.
- Contact utility companies.
- Contact legal counsel.
- Contact insurance companies.
- Maintain communications with employees.
- Maintain communications with media.
- Maintain communications with clients, suppliers and other stakeholders.

Emergency Response and Business Continuity

As the crisis becomes contained and controlled, emphasis shifts from emergency response to business continuity. During the post-strike phase, activities focus on stabilizing and resuming operations. Some organizations with good planning in place can direct attention to maintaining or rapidly recovering critical operations during certain crisis events.

Interfacing with Civil Authorities

In order to effectively respond to a major crisis, there may be a need to summon outside civil authorities and it will thus be necessary for an organization to interface with the responding authorities. In addition to coordinating emergency response efforts, an organization needs to be aware of the laws and scope of power of civil responders. Organizations must recognize that the organization's BCM is subordinate to the plans of the civil responders.

Organizations are encouraged to develop positive relationships with civil authorities. This will require an investment primarily of time by the organization. The local Offices of Emergency Management are good places to meet civil responders and to observe as well as participate in emergency response exercises.

Coordinating with external agencies requires developing public-private partnerships to help the organization prepare for a disaster. This includes establishing procedures and policies for coordinating continuity and recovery activities with external agencies, ensuring compliance with applicable laws and regulations, and developing and facilitating exercises with external agencies. Public-private partnerships involve the development of processes to identify critical dependencies, determine information to be shared and collaborate on training and exercise. The benefits include access to response resources, recovery resources and vital information.

In emergency response planning organizations identify potential emergencies and appropriate responses, determine emergency command and control procedures, plan the command center during emergency, coordinate with public authorities and integrate emergency response with BCM.

External agencies include: local, state and federal agencies; health and safety agencies; environmental authorities; police and fire departments; hospitals and ambulance services; compliance authorities and regulators; voluntary organizations and the military.

Department of Homeland Security (DHS)

DHS was established by the U.S. Homeland Security Act of 2002. The DHS was established to consolidate into one single department the various security responsibilities of more than 100 different government bodies. The DHS is a cabinet department of the federal government with the primary responsibilities of protecting the U.S. from terrorist attacks and responding to natural disasters. The DHS is the primary contact for state and local officials on matters related to homeland security planning, equipment, training and exercises. One of the agencies brought into the DHS was the U.S. Federal Emergency Management Agency.

On April 20, 2011 the DHS introduced the National Terrorism Advisory System together with a sample alert that is presented in Appendix K. This system replaces the DHS Advisory Code System that was established on March 11, 2002 in response to the September 11, 2001 terrorist attacks. The original system was often criticized for being too general, poorly understood by the public, subject to political manipulation and not having specific guidelines for changing the threat level. The DHS National Terrorism Advisory System focuses on specific threats in geographical areas, provides more detail and should be more easily understood than the old system.

Federal Emergency Management Agency (FEMA)

FEMA is the federal agency responsible for domestic disaster mitigation and disaster response. During a major crisis, FEMA coordinates both national level and field level response. In catastrophic situations, FEMA has extremely broad powers designed to allow the agency to effectively control or commandeer any resource that it needs.

Local Authorities

Major crisis events at the workplace such as fires, accidents and shootings will involve the assistance of police, fire, emergency medical services and perhaps other local public resources. These entities practice responding to crisis events and are well trained to respond to emergencies in a coordinated and orderly manner. The designation of the Incident Commander is dependent on the type of crisis and is established by preset protocols between these entities. When civil responders are present at the workplace, the Incident Commander is determined by the civil responders and not by the organization.

National Incident Management System (NIMS)

NIMS establishes a nationwide framework designed to coordinate the efforts of federal, state, local and non-government entities during domestic crisis events. NIMS is a structured framework used nationwide for both governmental and nongovernmental agencies to respond to natural disasters and terrorist attacks. NIMS is based on an appropriate balance of flexibility and standardization. NIMS standard incident command structures are based on the Incident Command System.

Incident Command System (ICS)

The ICS is an organizational structure using a set of policies and procedures to improve emergency response operations. It is a flexible and scalable response organization providing a common framework within which people can work together effectively. The ICS includes terminology, hierarchy and methodology, and provides the structure to coordinate public and private sector efforts.

Phases of Emergency Management

As defined by the Post-Katrina Emergency Management Reform Act of 2006, Title VI National Emergency Management, FEMA utilizes Phases of Emergency Management defined as follows:

Phase 1 - Mitigation

Mitigation actions include taking sustained actions to reduce or eliminate long-term risks to people and property from hazards and their effects.

Phase 2 - Preparedness

Preparedness actions include planning, training and building the emergency management profession to prepare effectively for, mitigate against, respond to and recover from any hazard.

Phase 3 - Response

Response actions include conducting emergency operations to save lives and property through positioning emergency equipment, personnel and supplies; through evacuating potential victims, through providing food, water, shelter and medical care to those in need and through restoring critical public services.

Phase 4 - Recovery

Recovery actions include rebuilding communities so individuals, businesses and governments can function on their own, return to normal life and protect against future hazards.

The Phases of Emergency Management is a term used by FEMA; Business Continuity Phases is the corresponding term typically used by business entities.

Review Topics

1. If an organization has subcontracted threat monitoring services, does the organization need to review the actual actions being taken by the subcontractor?

2. Identify key earthquake mitigation steps.

3. Identify key hurricane mitigation steps.

4. List the most common 'social distancing policies' that can be used in the workplace if a pandemic outbreak occurs.

5. List the most common 'personal protection equipment' that can be used in the workplace if a pandemic outbreak occurs.

6. An intercom message is received stating that a hostile intruder situation exists in the building and that a shelter-in-place should be performed. Subsequently a fire alarm is heard indicating the need to perform a building evacuation. Faced with this conflicting information, what would you do and why?

7. What types of crisis events provide a warning period?

8. Discuss ways an organization can interface with civil responders without making a substantial financial commitment.

Case Studies

Case Study A-8: Alpha Investment Services (AIS) Emergency Response

Based on the information previously provided in Case Study A, consider the following:

A-8.1   If a fire breaks out at the Main Building, what are the immediate actions that should be taken by the typical employee at the Main Building?

A-8.2   If a fire breaks out at the Main Building, what are the immediate actions that should be taken by employees at the Auxiliary Building?

A-8.3   What are logical locations of the primary EOC, the second EOC and the third EOC?

Case Study B-8: Beta Widget Makers (BWM) Emergency Response

Based on the information previously provided in Case Study B, consider the following:

B-8.1   If a fire breaks out at the Central Plant, what are the immediate actions that should be taken by the typical employee at the Central Plant?

B-8.2   If a fire breaks out at the Central Plant, what are the immediate actions that should be taken by employees at the West Plant?

B-8.3   For teams located at the Central Plant, what are logical locations of the primary EOC, the second EOC and the third EOC?

Bibliography

American Red Cross, www.redcross.org.

Department of Homeland Security (DHS), www.dhs.gov.

Earthquake Emergency Response Procedures:
- ▶ American Red Cross, www.redcross.org.
- ▶ American Rescue Team, www.amerrescue.org.

Federal Emergency Management Agency (FEMA), www.fema.gov.

Graham, J. and Kaye, D., *A Risk Management Approach to Business Continuity*, Rothstein Associates Inc., 2006.

Fulmer, K. L., Business Continuity Planning: *A Step-by-Step Guide*, Rothstein Associates Inc., 2005.

Henderson, D. M., *Is Your Business Ready for the Next Disaster?*, Dorrance Publishing Co., Inc., 1996.

Henderson, D. M., *The Complete Hurricane and Flood Plan for Business*, Rothstein Associates Inc., 2006.

Henderson, D. M., *The Comprehensive Business Continuity Management Program*, Rothstein Associates Inc., 2008.

Henderson, D. M., *The Pandemic Planning and Response Plan,* Rothstein Associates Inc., 2007.

Hiles, A. N., Business Continuity: Best Practices: *Aligning Business Continuity with Corporate Governance*, Rothstein Associates Inc., 2004.

National Fire Protection Association (NFPA), www.nfpa.org.

National Incident Management System (NIMS), www.nimsonline.com.

National Ocean and Atmospheric Administration (NOAA), National Weather Service, www.nws.noaa.gov.

National Safety Council, www.nsc.org.

United States Department of Labor (DOL), Occupational Safety and Health Administration (OSHA), www.osha.gov.

CHAPTER IX

Enhancing Coordination with External Agencies*

Objectives

» Identify external resources available throughout the phases of emergency management

» Review the importance of having relationships with outside agencies and partners

» Identify opportunities to develop relationships during mitigation and preparedness phases.

Chapter prepared by Daniel P. Iradi, JD.

External Relations Overview

Business Continuity Management (BCM) cannot stand alone if it is to be successful. Coordination with external agencies that can bring additional resources helps ensure that BCM is best situated to respond and recover from an emergency that impacts business operations and the community.

The key to coordination between BCM and the resources of government agencies, non-government organizations (NGOs), and businesses that are critical to the implementation of a Business Continuity Plan is relationships. "External relations" is the management of relationships with external agencies for the incorporation of their resources into BCM.

External resources may be people or materials (such as equipment and supplies), or they may be plans, policies, guidelines, best practices or other tools developed by others in BCM and related fields.

Resources are available to augment BCM from all levels of government – from the agencies active in your state under the National Response Framework (NRF) to the local building code enforcement agency; from non-profit agencies such as the American Red Cross; and from businesses that corporations rely on every day, such as utility companies and insurance companies.

This chapter will focus on the relationships every business continuity planner should have with state and local government agencies and non-government organizations (NGOs) and how to build them throughout the four phases of emergency management – mitigation, preparedness, response and recovery. By knowing what these partners bring to the table, you will understand which agencies in a community can provide the resources necessary to successfully augment BCM.

Knowing what resources are available to your business and how to access them during times of emergency is a key to continuity of operations and business recovery plans, as is the recovery assistance available to the community, employees' families and their property. An important factor for the recovery of normal business operations is the ability of employees to access recovery assistance for their families and homes.

External Relations throughout the Four Phases: Overview

The four phases of emergency management are viewed in a circle; however the phases are overlapping, not separate and distinct – as are relationships developed to enhance BCM. The intervening moment to this idea of a cyclical flow occurs when a disaster happens and focus must shift to response and recovery operations. For this reason, mitigation and preparedness are sometimes idiomatically referred to as the "peace time" phases, distinctive from the more chaotic atmosphere during the "disaster phases" of response and recovery. Remember that for a large organization, activities at some locations could be focused on response or recovery while at other sites the focus is on mitigation and preparedness activities – either because the disaster has not had an impact, has not yet had an impact or the impact has already been remediated. At these times, BCM is engaged in all four phases simultaneously and activities at a single location could have a dramatic impact on other locations' activities.

Because the phases overlap and because activities in one phase have an impact on phases that follow, it is important to focus on relationship development during all four phases. However, due to the dichotomy in atmosphere between the peace time phases and the disaster phases, it is recognized that relationships are best developed during mitigation and preparedness phases. Although it is possible to build relationships during the "organized chaos" of response or during recovery, it is not ideal.

In addition, BCM is responsible for moving operations not only from "peace time" activities to response and recovery when a disaster happens, but also for transitioning back to mitigation and preparedness activities focused on the next possible or even impending event.

Opportunities to Develop Relationships in the Mitigation and Preparedness Phases

The primary activities of BCM during the preparedness phase are planning, training and exercising the program. Identifying available resources and establishing communications for the mobilization of these resources is also part of preparedness.

Resources that are capable of meeting an emergency need and able to be deployed are said to be "ready." Readiness is a measurable factor for both human and material resources and should be tested during drills, functional and full-scale exercises.

Once available resources are identified and ready, part of BCM is to identify assets likely to be needed from external resources during the response and recovery phases. Identifying these resources and forming relationships for their mobilization is necessary if BCM expects to rely upon them as part of response and recovery operations.

Opportunities to find the right resources can be found through local emergency management, regulatory agencies, and not-for-profits involved in disaster response, as well as through networking groups for business continuity, disaster recovery and emergency management practitioners. Other relationships are already part of the company's day-to-day business and need only to be accessed as part of BCM.

External Relations throughout the Four Phases

Building relationships during Mitigation and Preparedness Phases facilitates success during Response and Recovery Phases

Forming relationships during the mitigation and preparedness phases is critical to response and recovery success. What has become an emergency management adage rings true for business continuity professionals: during the disaster is not the time to be exchanging business cards. The resources you identify and work with during mitigation and planning activities are the people and organizations that will be active during response and recovery operations.

Mitigation and Preparedness are tied together in that these are the "peace time" phases: before or after an incident impacts a community. Also many of the objectives of mitigation planning can be accomplished by preparedness planning. For example, both phases begin with an identification of the hazards facing the community and the likely impact from these hazards. Emergency management agencies and other external agencies developing continuity of operations and emergency response plans may have valuable information collected that could augment Risk Analysis and Business Impact Assessment. Also, proper training during the preparedness phase, for example in evacuation and safety protocols, will lessen the impact of a disaster and make recovery easier and less expensive -- which are goals of mitigation!

Identifying available resources to implement both mitigation and preparedness activities will often identify many of the same organizations and people. In turn, these will be the same people and organizations active during the response and recovery phases. Working with these agencies to achieve mitigation and preparedness successes for BCM will create relationships that will make response and recovery protocols easier to implement under the National Incident Management System (NIMS) and Incident Command System (ICS).

The preparedness phase, like the mitigation phase, is based on the expectation that response and recovery operations will take place at some point. Training exercises, plans and protocols and the readiness of material and human resources are all based on response scenarios. Relationship building and defining and understanding the expectations and abilities of all organizations active during response and recovery before it happens are key to success during those phases for BCM.

Understanding not only how external resources will directly impact business continuity, but how external agencies will support employees and the community during response and recovery of a community-wide crisis will also impact business resumption.

Closing the Loop

Following a crisis response and recovery operation (or an exercise simulating these actions) is the best time to initiate or re-ignite the achievement of important mitigation and preparedness goals. The interest in initiating change most readily occurs in the immediate post-disaster time period. People are more interested in taking actions to be better prepared for the next time and decision-makers are more likely to commit funding after experiencing an impact from a disaster.

BCM can initiate the move from response and recovery to mitigation and preparedness by reviewing the recent occurrences of those phases. It is important to discuss actions taken, and anticipated and actual results of the response and recovery phases in an After Action Review. Documentation of these considerations, along with action items for improvement, should be published in an After Action Report (AAR) and Improvement Plan (IP).

By including an Improvement Plan along with the After Action Report, BCM can identify actions to take, plans to develop and relationships to build throughout the four phases of emergency management as the cycle begins again. By looking forward, a company will move from being primarily in the recovery phase to being back into the mitigation and preparedness phases. Of course, ongoing recovery of normal business practices, employee well-being and community recovery may continue for longer periods of time even while the focus of BCM is on the next time.

Capitalize on Existing Relationships

In some circumstances, BCM will be interfacing with government, non-government and business organizations with whom there is already some level of relationship within the company due to regulatory, financial or community obligations. These include:

- Fire, Police, EMS and local authorities that inspect and respond to alarms.
- Fire, Police and EMS volunteer units with which company employees are affiliated.
- Security companies that provide alarm system monitoring or personnel.
- Safety companies that provide alarm and fire suppression systems.
- Regulatory agencies for hazardous material and employee safety compliance.
- Insurance companies which protect the business and provide risk management resources.
- Health insurance providers with an Employee Assistance Program (EAP) and other benefits.
- American Red Cross which provides Health and Safety training to employees such as First Aid, cardiopulmonary resuscitation (CPR) and workplace safety courses.
- Utility companies and contractors that are responsible for recovery activities.
- Community-based organizations and faith-based organizations which the company supports as a donor or for which employees volunteer either on their own or through corporate activities.

Knowing what interactions already exist and who in the company holds these relationships will have a positive impact when approaching these organizations as part of BCM. A survey of employees and on-site personnel to identify who has training such as first aid, CPR and who may be trained as a firefighter, emergency medical technician, Red Cross volunteer or other emergency personnel in the community is one way to gain this information, if it is not already documented in other places within the company.

State and Local Government Agencies

Many states and local jurisdictions are actively entering into public-private partnerships to improve their capabilities in emergency management. Some states have an Emergency Support Function (ESF) for business and industry, some include the private sector in exercises and participate in private sector exercises, and some communities have created online registries of business resources that are available to public sector responders.

According to FEMA, the operational concept for incident management involving the private sector is the concept specified in the National Response Framework (NRF) and the National Incident Management System (NIMS).

Response organizations at all levels should facilitate coordination with the private sector when:

- Determining the impact of an incident.
- Maintaining situational awareness across sectors.
- Setting priorities for incident management support and response.
- Determining appropriate recovery and reconstitution measures, particularly in cases where they may result in indemnity, liability, or business losses for the private sector.
- Obtaining goods and services necessary for the recovery and restoration of Critical Infrastructure and Key Resources (CIKR) and other elements of the economy on a priority basis.

Emergency Management Agencies (EMAs)

Coordination with Comprehensive Emergency Management Plans

One goal of NIMS is to ensure integration of emergency response plans from the local level up through the states and including Federal support as outlined in the NRF. Local planning at the county and municipal level should include private sector coordination in their comprehensive emergency management plans (CEMPs). During the response phase, emergency management Emergency Operations Centers (EOCs) should include representatives from the private sector, including industry. Therefore it is critical that BCM include coordination with local emergency management agencies and ensure that emergency plans are coordinated. Being part of exercises that test the CEMP and including emergency management in exercises that test BCM are two ways to accomplish this objective. Exercises test and identify gaps in emergency plans before an emergency occurs. By working with emergency management personnel before an emergency occurs, businesses and emergency management can ascertain what assistance may be necessary and how they can help each other. Providing assistance, particularly with non-essential employees and volunteers, to support emergency management during an emergency and throughout the recovery process can provide many benefits to the business and BCM.

Coordination between a jurisdiction's comprehensive emergency management plan (CEMP) and BCM can begin with RA and BIA. EMAs gather information and conduct hazard analysis much the same way as is necessary to complete these management reports for BCM. In a CEMP, the segment may be called a Hazard Vulnerability Analysis or have a similar designation. A jurisdiction's mitigation plan, required to receive certain funding, will also have this information and analysis. A jurisdiction's CEMP and mitigation plans can provide information to BCM such as designations of critical infrastructure and key resources (CIKR), changes to the community that may be forthcoming and other agencies, NGOs and businesses active in emergency management planning within the community.

NIMS, ICS and National Response Framework Training

Partnering with local emergency management during the preparedness phase includes ensuring that a company's ERT can effectively communicate with emergency management and first responders when an incident response includes their activation. One way to ensure this happens is to take advantage of training offered through local first responders and emergency management. BCM, although not required to be "NIMS Compliant," can nevertheless follow available guidelines, particularly when it comes to getting key personnel trained in National Incident Management System (NIMS), the National Response Framework (NRF) and the Incident Command System (ICS). These courses are typically offered frequently by first responders and EMA. Knowing when these courses are offered and/or arranging with certified trainers to bring the training to one's facility will allow ERT members to become more comfortable working with first responders and communicating with them during an actual response.

Community Emergency Response Team (CERT) and Medical Reserve Corps (MRC)

The CERT program, developed in California and expanded nationally through FEMA and federal funding is a volunteer management program to assist emergency management personnel. This program has been adapted in some circles specifically for business to create and train their own CERT teams. Other CERT teams become an arm of the EMA.

CERT members receive 18 hours of training initially in areas such as incident management, first aid and triage, disaster mental health, family preparedness, basic fire suppression and light search and rescue.

Medical Reserve Corps (MRC) is a similar program designed for responders to meet medical needs of the community after an incident. Not all MRC volunteers need to be licensed, trained medical workers or professionals, however they have to be comfortable around medical operations as that is the team's focus. MRC will either be part of the OEM, Department of Health or other entity as designated in a locality's Comprehensive Emergency Management Plan.

While BCM may not directly make use of all the skills learned through CERT and MRC, providing this training to a company's Emergency Response Team, initial responders, and emergency management committee members has great value.

Volunteer management programs such as CERT and MRC facilitate team building, provide a tangible platform for exercising emergency management principles such as ICS and allow a company's ERT and other employees to feel empowered to act – quickly and decisively and according to the BCP when an incident occurs.

In addition, having CERT or MRC training will allow employees to participate in a community response even if the business is not impacted, as well as better integrate with first responders if the company has an incident requiring outside assistance.

Local Emergency Planning Committees (LEPCs)

LEPCs have arisen in local jurisdictions from hazardous materials and hazardous waste handling regulations. These entities may sit at the municipal, county or regional level and are focused on response procedures for all entities that could be activated during an emergency in the community. LEPCs are composed of emergency management, first responders including police, fire and emergency medical services, public works, environmental protection, public health, hazmat and others that would respond to a hazardous materials release. Representatives from businesses in the community that may manufacture, store or transport hazardous materials or waste may also be part of the LEPC. Many LEPCs today focus beyond simple hazardous materials responses and address issues such as natural and manmade disasters, including terrorist events, which could have an impact on critical infrastructure and key resources – and may only relate to hazardous material releases indirectly.

LEPCs are a great way to build relationships with local regulators and responders, to learn about laws impacting businesses in the community, to understand hazards and risk in the community and to have a voice in mitigation, preparedness, response and recovery plans and projects by the government and other businesses that could impact BCM.

Police, Fire and Emergency Medical Services

It is likely that a business already has interaction, if not active relationships, with first responder agencies. This could be through safety and security inspections, routine activity such as alarms or individual emergencies, or participation in community activities such as government meetings or local emergency preparedness committees. Employees may also participate as volunteers with police, fire and emergency medical services departments. First responders will also be involved in NIMS/ICS training and on exercise planning teams.

When an incident occurs requiring outside assistance, it is likely that a first responder will take over as Incident Commander from the person designated in the BCP. During the transition briefing, it will be necessary for the BCP Incident Commander to provide to the first responder Incident Commander the information they will need to continue incident management and expand operations, if necessary. As such, the ERT and CMT must have relationships with first responder agency leadership. Understanding transition protocols and information needs and practicing these during "peace time" will make actual transitions go that much smoother during an incident response. Training and exercises that include resources from the BCP as well as from first responders is a necessary part of complete BCM.

Local Regulatory Agencies

Safety inspections are a necessary part of most companies' calendars. Essentially they are mitigation by regulation. Knowing what an inspector is looking for and keeping facilities clear of them at all times will ensure that hazardous risks are minimized all year long and not just around inspection time. While safety hazards in most industries and facilities are not the same as the hazards associated with natural and manmade disasters, having a good worker safety program in place can benefit BCM. First, risks associated with safety hazards can be exacerbated when combined with facing a disaster response. Second, tools and resources put in place to minimize the impact of safety hazards such as alarms, response teams, first aid kits, fire suppression apparatus and personal protective equipment (PPE) will often be utilized during the initial response to a disaster other than a technological disaster.

While businesses are sometimes reluctant to invite in representatives from regulatory agencies due to their ability to levy fines for compliance purposes, having a relationship with these agencies can benefit BCM in the mitigation and preparedness phases. Many regulatory agencies provide benefits for proactive safety programs which ensure companies won't get fined if violations are found while engaged in these safety activities.

These prevention programs help companies reduce risk and lessen the impact of hazards. To begin, agencies may provide inspectors or self assessment tools for a company to conduct an internal audit of safety procedures, protocols, training and equipment.

Non-Government Organizations (NGOs)

When disasters strike a community, a large portion of the relief provided is through the work of volunteers and through donations of money, goods, and services. Charitable organizations that utilize these resources are often referred to as voluntary agencies (VOLAGs) or NGOs meaning non-government organizations.

Because the recovery of a company's employees and their families is crucial to returning business operations to normal, knowing which agencies are providing disaster relief services in an impacted community is necessary to BCM.

National Voluntary Organizations Active in Disaster (VOAD), Points of Light and Hands-On Network are NGOs that coordinate relief efforts and capabilities of other voluntary agencies.

These groups include within their systems agencies that have a disaster mission throughout the four phases of emergency management – such as the American Red Cross – as well as those agencies whose focus may shift to response and recovery operations when resources are needed.

Becoming familiar with which agencies are members of coordinating organizations, providing opportunities for employees to learn how they can get involved with voluntary agencies before a disaster strikes and what services are available through charitable organizations when disasters do impact a community are all ways to augment BCM, as is partnering with organizations such as the American Red Cross and VOAD.

American Red Cross

The American Red Cross is a non-government organization (NGO) that is part of the International Red Cross Movement and has a congressional charter to operate within the United States of America as an independent, not-for-profit agency. The American Red Cross mission extends throughout the four phases of emergency management helping people prevent, prepare for and respond to emergencies. ARC has a large disaster relief program active in chapters throughout the United States. It also has a preparedness program for individuals, families and businesses.

Health and Safety Training

The American Red Cross and other organizations offer training in first aid, cardiopulmonary resuscitation (CPR) and the use of automated external defibrillators (AEDs). Having sufficient staff trained in these skills, identifying who they are, and making the necessary tools available to provide these services can achieve important mitigation goals through preparedness training, planning and implementation in partnership with the American Red Cross.

Corporate Preparedness Program Suite

The American Red Cross has a progressive program available for companies to purchase called the Ready Rating Program Guide for Business and Organizations. The program uses five steps in order to strengthen a company's Continuity of Operations Plan and engage executive decision makers in understanding the need to be prepared. While larger companies may have the personnel and resources to thoroughly manage BCM for those that cannot, partnering with the Red Cross is one way to engage in table top exercises, develop a preparedness planning program and improve upon existing procedures. www.readyrating.org

Disaster Services / Ready When the Time Comes (RWTC) Program

 The American Red Cross Ready When the Time Comes program is designed to partner with businesses by creating teams of volunteers trained in Disaster Services. Like CERT, having employees trained as Red Cross volunteers has as many direct advantages to BCM as it does indirect advantages.

Ready When the Time Comes volunteers typically get trained to provide Mass Care services such as sheltering, bulk distribution of disaster relief supplies and fixed or mobile feeding during a community disaster response. Companies with specialized employees could receive training in disaster assessment or logistics; licensed professionals could be trained as Disaster Health Services or Disaster Mental Health.

Volunteers trained to help their community are typically more prepared for themselves and their families to have disaster supply kits, a family evacuation and communication plan and to be aware of hazards potentially impacting the community. If a Red Cross volunteer is essential to company response and recovery procedures, they are more likely to be successful facing a crisis because of their training and their preparedness efforts. If they are not part of response and recovery, employees can participate in community recovery efforts after taking care of themselves and their neighbors. This ability to help gives a person focus and an outlet for their energy while the company is working to resume operations.

If a company's Disaster Assistance Plan includes continuing to pay employees, even while their function is not online, partnering with the Red Cross could have a financial advantage. If non-working employees are volunteering for the Red Cross and still getting paid, the company could consider their time as an in-kind donation to the American Red Cross and receive tax benefits for donating their employees' time. Having a written Memorandum of Understanding with the local chapter and reviewing procedures with counsel and tax advisors would be necessary steps to ensure this benefit is achievable.

Voluntary Organizations Active in Disaster (VOAD)

A group dedicated to organizing charitable organizations who respond to disasters is called the National Voluntary Organizations Active in Disaster (NVOAD or VOAD). VOAD coordination also occurs at the state and local level. By being a participant in VOAD, charitable organizations can ensure their resources are put to the best use during a response and spontaneous volunteers and donors that best fit their mission can contribute to their activities.

VOAD includes non-government organizations that provide disaster relief on a regular basis such as the American Red Cross, the Salvation Army and Catholic Charities, as well as other charitable organizations that provide social services assistance on a regular basis and make their services available to those impacted by a disaster during response and recovery operations in the community.

Among NGOs are two segments which participate in VOAD that may or may not typically provide social services on a normal basis that can have a positive impact during a disaster: Faith Based Organizations (FBOs) and Community Based Organizations (CBOs). Faith-Based Organizations are churches, mosques, synagogues and other religious institutions which are central to a community's identity and seek to participate in disaster response and recovery activities. FBOs have access to large numbers of volunteers through their memberships. CBOs are advocacy groups that provide representation and sometimes services to particular segments of the community. CBOs may or may not be voluntary agencies, usually with small staffs, that understand the demographics and dynamics of the area and the people in it. CBOs often expand their services to people impacted by a disaster that might not otherwise get help by their agency.

Supporting VOAD, their member agencies, and other Non-Government Organizations that provide disaster assistance can augment BCM due to their breadth of resources. Steering company philanthropy to these organizations, as well as volunteers, helps assure that a community will recover after a disaster impacts it.

Networking Opportunities

Just as its important to form relationships with emergency managers and first responders, it's important to form relationships with other business continuity practitioners. Networking opportunities can take many forms, but each has similar advantages:

- keep up to date with current trends and regulations in the field,
- share best practices and lessons learned,
- meet vendors of business continuity and disaster recovery tools and resources, and perhaps most importantly -
- form relationships with emergency management, business continuity, disaster recovery, disaster preparedness and relief agency professionals.

Networking opportunities can include trade associations and educational groups, conferences and online forums.

Trade Associations

Trade associations have different missions, membership and organizational structures. They may define themselves as networking groups, educational groups or lobbying groups. Ultimately, business continuity or disaster recovery trade associations have as their goal the promotion of the field and the opportunity to network and learn from fellow practitioners and those that have an impact on its work such as emergency management, vendors, partners and clients.

Two of the most well-known and respected such groups in the United States are ACP and CPE.

Association of Contingency Planners - ACP has 44 chapters in the United States. Each chapter has their own membership rate structure, schedule of presentations and networking opportunities. ACP's stated mission is to provide a powerful network for the advancement of the industry and the development of business continuity professionals. According to their website, the benefits of joining ACP include opportunities to:

- Share knowledge with and gain insight from a network of industry practitioners.
- Expand your skills through an extensive knowledge base of resources.
- Earn professional education credits for membership and meeting attendance.
- Advance your career through increased visibility and leadership opportunities.
- Receive discounts on conferences, products, services, and training.

www.acp-international.com

Contingency Planning Exchange – *CPE* has chapters in and around New York City and in Washington, DC. With the breadth of businesses and business continuity practitioners in those areas that bring their experience to CPE meetings and roundtables, CPE attracts members from up and down the East Coast. CPE's website also includes a members-only area which allows new members to catch up on past meeting topics and for all members to share their best practices, lessons learned and presentation topics; giving CPE all the advantages of educational and networking groups and online forums.

According to its website, Contingency Planning Exchange (CPE) strives to provide its members with ideas and resources to continually enhance business continuity, disaster recovery and crisis/emergency management strategies and tools through high profile educational programs, and by encouraging relationships with peers and working with government to promote public/private sector interaction. www.cpeworld.org

To find a local trade association or chapter, a targeted online search may be the best route or, alternatively:

www.edwardsinformation.com/listing/guide/trade_associations/disaster_recovery_business_continuity_associations

Conferences

There are many conferences available for business continuity, disaster recovery, and emergency management practitioners. Conferences can last from one day to a full week and often include additional pre- or post-conference training sessions available to registrants. Conferences typically invite top experts from various fields to discuss important updates and features of BCM. Breakout sessions often focus on more specific areas of practice and allow a more intimate setting for learning about new techniques, models, practices and equipment.

The Disaster Resource GUIDE (www.disaster-resource.com) maintains an annually updated list of worldwide conferences that includes contact links.

Online Forums

There are a number of online forums and list-servers available to business continuity, disaster recovery, and emergency management personnel. Forums and list-servers allow members via e-mail and websites to post questions, comments, articles and items for discussion and to get feedback. These virtual conversations are often driven by leaders in the field. They can provide good information for brand new, as well as experienced, practitioners. Best practices, new ideas and debate can all be found on online forums and list-servers.

Yahoo groups and the International Association of Emergency Managers are two of the most well known sources for these networking opportunities. Typically membership is free, however sometimes a screening process is employed by the network controllers.

The All Hands Dot Net Network (www.all-hands.net/network) and Emergency Management Discussion List (http://health.groups.yahoo.com/group/Emergency-Management) together form a growing online community for business continuity, disaster recovery and emergency management professionals. Utilizing these resources provides practitioners with easy access to relevant news, important updates for the field and a growing network of subject matter experts, products, service providers and practitioners to augment BCM."

Other Businesses with resources for BCM

Businesses that corporations rely on every day, such as utility companies and insurance companies, can provide valuable external resources to BCM.

Alarm, security and safety supply companies all likely have programs or ideas to strengthen mitigation, preparedness, response and recovery plans and resources.

Insurance companies often have risk management programs available to their customers to identify and mitigate risk and negative consequences to business operations, facilities and employees. Like the resources available from regulatory agencies, insurance programs may take the form of audits conducted by experts hired by the insurance company or self assessment tools that a company can utilize independently to assess strengths and shortfalls.

It's not just the insurance companies providing risk management coverage but also health insurance providers that can be incorporated into BCM. Health insurance coverage often includes Employee Assistance Programs

(EAP) and Wellness Programs. An EAP provider typically has resources for mental health, legal and other advisors available to members who, after a disaster impacts a community, could play a vital part in the recovery process for employees and their families. These resources should be included as part of a company's Disaster Assistance Program. Wellness programs, designed to get employees healthier and safer, may provide for training such as first aid, CPR and AED, but may also include recovery programs for employees after a disaster. Remember that the sooner employees and their families return to normal lives, the sooner business operations can return to normal, too.

Utility companies are another type of business where it is beneficial to have relationships with their representatives during response and recovery operations. Utility companies will typically have their own external affairs, government affairs and emergency management personnel – all of whom are good people to know as part of BCM. Utility companies will often have liaisons in municipal or county EOCs. These representatives will be accessing and providing damage assessment and recovery information. Priorities for the recovery of utility services will depend on the number of customers affected and proximity to critical infrastructure and key resources in the impacted area. Having a relationship with utility company representatives can help ensure a quicker return to service than those who do not. At a minimum, know how local providers tally outage areas and the way they rely on customers to report occurrences. Ensure that reporting an outage is a priority of response and recovery operations and how to do so is addressed in your BCP.

Review Topics

1. What other advantages can BCM gain from partnering with EMAs, NGOs and other business continuity professionals?

2. What BCM activities crossover among two or more phases or emergency management?

3. What other activities in one phase affect activities in another?

4. What other emergency preparedness skills might the company already have on hand either through existing relationships, employee involvement or through corporate involvement in the community?

5. In addition to RA and BIA, what other information is found both in BCPs and CEMPs?

6. Besides the American Red Cross what other charitable organizations have a mission that spans across all four phases of emergency management?

7. Is there a VOAD in your community? How is it organized? What agencies are members? What agencies in the community are not members?

8. What trade associations, educational groups or networking groups for business continuity professionals exist in the area? Do they have student membership or allow new members to attend a free session?

9. What conferences are coming up that could provide value to BCM?

10. What other online forums have you found to be valuable?

11. What other educational resources exist for business continuity practitioners?

12. In addition to utility and insurance companies, what other businesses that already support companies – outside the supply chain – need to be included in BCM coordination with external agencies? What resources do they bring to a BCM? How can relationships with these entities and BCM be initiated?

13. What are examples in the news of coordination between emergency management, NGOs and the private sector? What is the nature of these relationships and their involvement through the four phases of emergency management?

Bibliography

Burtles, J., *Principles and Practices of Business Continuity: Tools and Techniques*, Rothstein Associates Inc., 2007.

Department of Homeland Security (DHS), www.dhs.gov.

Disaster Resource GUIDE, www.disaster-resource.com.

Emergency Management Institute (EMI), www.training.fema.gov/emi.

Federal Emergency Management Agency (FEMA), www.fema.gov.

Graham, J. and Kaye, D., *A Risk Management Approach to Business Continuity: Aligning Business Continuity with Corporate Governance*, Rothstein Associates Inc., 2006.

Henderson, D, M., *The Comprehensive Business Continuity Management Program*, Rothstein Associates Inc., 2008.

Hiles, A. N., *Business Continuity: Best Practices: World-Class Business Continuity Management*, Rothstein Associates Inc., 2004.

National Incident Management System (NIMS), www.fema.gov/emergency/nims.

CHAPTER X

Business Continuity Plan

Objectives

» Examine the objectives of the BCP

» Summarize operational requirements

» Document strategies

» Review activation procedures

» Identify business continuity actions

» Identify crisis communication procedures.

Business Continuity Plan Overview

The **Business Continuity Plan (BCP)** is the central plan that documents continuity and recovery procedures during and after a crisis. The BCP provides sufficient detail regarding the deployment of appropriate strategies for the resumption of operations according to predetermined priorities. Pre-crisis activities include: implementing strategies, documenting the BCP and integrating business continuity with the ERP.

The BCP must be supported by senior management and have organizational commitment. Successful plans are comprehensive, coordinated, and adaptable and part of a strategic effort. BCP mistakes to avoid include: obsolete strategies, complicated procedures, out-of-date information, unidentified alternatives, incorrect recovery times, flawed communications, inaccessible facilities, unsynchronized data and incorrect insurance.

To be effective, the BCP must be clearly defined and thoroughly documented. An organization should develop guidelines and standards for the proper documentation of the BCP. To provide a consistent approach to business continuity planning, an outline for documentation for the BCP should be used. The information required for the BCP can be provided in formats such as written descriptions, flowcharts, graphs, computer reports or tables.

The purpose of the BCP is to provide a vehicle for disseminating information, ensuring that all parties are aware of their responsibilities. The documents summarize the plan and its objective, provide an outline of the actions required in the response, alternate processing and full recovery phases, and identify responsible individuals. The level of detail provided in the BCP should be consistent with the complexity and time frame of the operations. The BCP appendices contain team details, contact information, recovery site details, vendor contracts, vital records list, supply sources, support agreements, notification lists, building plans, resource lists and a glossary. The BCP documentation should be structured so that it is easy to use. It must include all vital information and should integrate interrelated plans.

The BCP should contain audit procedures to use following a disaster. After a disaster there will be claims, counter-claims and regulatory implications. An audit trail must document actions undertaken in recovery to respond to inquiries.

Document control is very important to ensure that all parties are working with the most current plan. Document control establishes appropriate distribution procedures, controls confidentiality of the documentation and ensures version control. To control distribution, each copy should be uniquely numbered and copies of the old version should be destroyed upon distribution of new version.

Before final approval, the BCP needs to be verified that it is consistent with the BIA report. Responsibilities should be clearly defined, needed resources should be available and the plan should be implementable. Final plans are reviewed and approved by senior management. The following major sections are typically included in the BCP:

- Objectives
- Organization
- Requirements
- Strategies
- Activation
- Actions
- Communication
- Maintenance.

There should be one master BCP for the organization which acts as the overall documentation repository. Any changes should take place only in this master BCP to avoid inconsistencies. Organizations with multiple locations typically document each location's plan in a separate section of the master BCP.

Business continuity planning development software can help structure planning and documentation. Planning software is based on the experience of business continuity experts. Planning software contains checklists to aid completeness, utilizes templates to support analyses and may be industry specific. Software supports, but does not replace, management decisions.

BCP Objectives

The BCP is intended to document an organization's approach to manage recovery from crisis events that are of sufficient magnitude to cause significant disruption. Certain organizations with BCM programs in place may be able to continue critical operations despite an ongoing crisis. The BCP actions should be consistent with emergency response and follows through to the recovery of operations.

The ERP, containing emergency actions for hazard-specific events, may be considered a subset of the BCP. Emergency actions to be taken during a crisis event are documented in the BCP. Emergency response is reviewed in a separate chapter in this book.

The BCP objectives are as follows:

1. Protect life and prevent injuries.
2. Protect the environment.
3. Mitigate damages.
4. Contain and control the crisis.
5. Continue and recover operations.

The BCP should explicitly state its assumptions and limitations. For example, assumptions and limitations include statements regarding:

▶ The possibility of loss of life.

▶ The possibility of a complete community-wide breakdown of law and order.

▶ Recovery times required at alternate sites.

Organization

The BCP documents the organizational structure including committees, teams and individual assignments that comprise the BCM program. The BCM organization is reviewed in a separate chapter in this book.

Requirements

The BCP should include a summary of operations, supply chains and process flows. The personnel, physical and IT requirements of the organization need to be defined. This information should be recorded in sufficient detail to enable the organization to recover from a disaster that could destroy, disable or substantially degrade the workforce, workplace buildings, building content, IT systems and communication services. Much of this material is contained in the BIA and is reviewed in a separate chapter in this book.

Strategies

An organization makes use of strategies to treat risk and meet established objectives. These strategies are documented in the BCP. Business continuity strategy development is reviewed in a separate chapter in this book.

Activation

The BCP is activated either simultaneously with or subsequently to the activation of the ERP. For a minor crisis, the event may be completely handled by the ERP making the activation of the BCP unnecessary. Figure 10.1 illustrates the ERP and BCP activation process.

Strategy Activation

Once the BCP is activated, it is necessary for an organization to initiate specific strategies to recover normal operations. Examples of strategy activation are as follows:

Example 1 – Strategy Activation by Scope of Crisis

This first example illustrates a method to activate strategies that are effective for an organization with critical IT support requirements that also faces, in addition to a localized crisis, the possibility of a community-wide crisis. This organization has a very short RTO for critical operations. Note that IT has an alternate data center that can be activated remotely; critical IT support services can be recovered almost immediately and the alternate data center can be fully operational within 6 to 8 hours. This organization is a service industry and does not require physical needs beyond general office space and equipment.

Crisis events in this example fall into one of three categories as follows:

1. IT Failure – The data center is disabled.

2. Building Failure – The building and the main data center are disabled or access is denied.

3. Community-Wide Crisis – The building and the main data center are disabled and employees cannot work from home or from anywhere in the general area.

Figure 10.2 illustrates the actions by scope of crisis approach for an organization that can rapidly work with laptops from remote locations with electrical power, cloud computing and Internet access.

Example 2 – Strategy Activation by Duration of Disruption

Figure 10.3 illustrates a method to activate strategies that are effective for a manufacturing facility with two Manufacturing Plants: a North Plant and a South Plant. This business has a two-day RTO for critical operations. Community-wide crisis events are unlikely and it is assumed that both plants would not be simultaneously disabled for a significant period of time. Also note that IT has the main data center in the North Plant with a backup data center located in the South Plant.

All crisis events basically fall into one of three categories as follows:

1. Operations are suspended for a period of time not to exceed 48 hours. Limited business continuity aspects of the plan need to be executed in this short period of time.

2. Operations are suspended for a 2 to 60 day period of time. A substantial level of business continuity efforts need to be executed.

3. Operations are suspended for a period of time in excess of 60 days. Full business continuity efforts need to be executed.

Figure 10.1 - ERP and BCP Activation

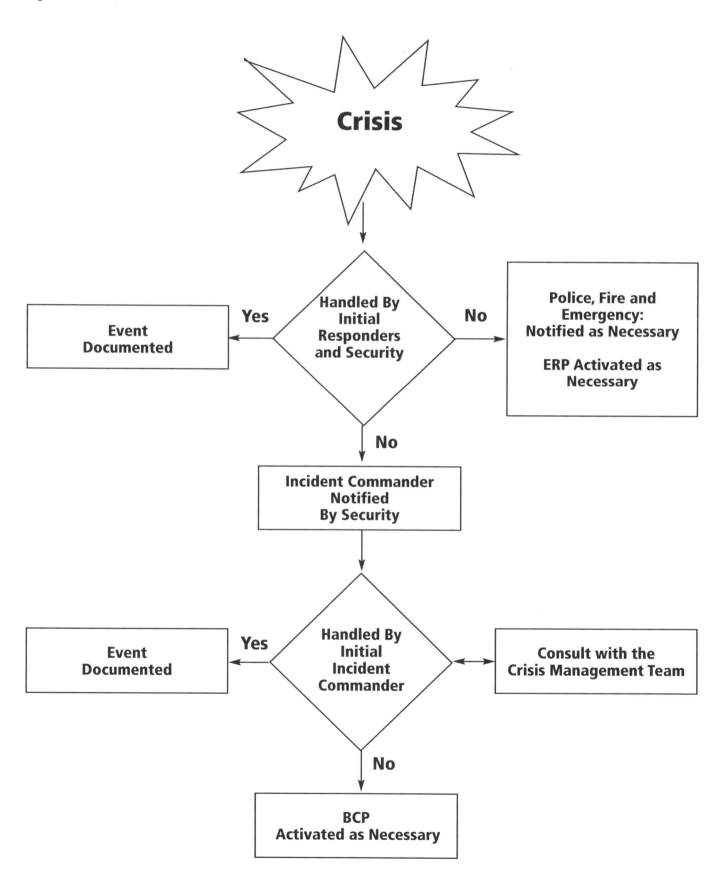

Figure 10.2 - Strategy Activation by Scope of Crisis

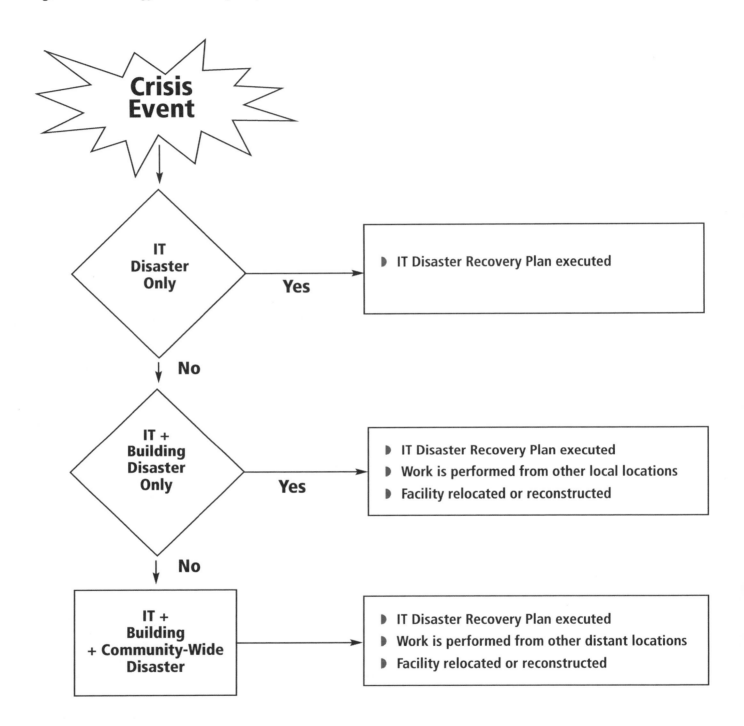

Figure 10.3 - Strategy Activation by Duration of Disruption

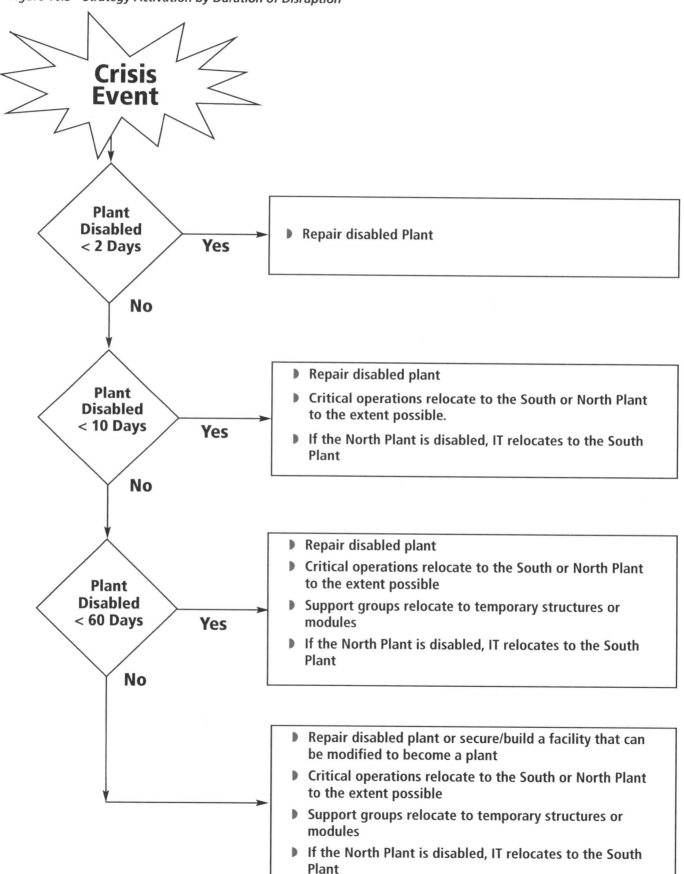

Actions

Actions during the Pre-Strike Phase

Crisis events are sometimes preceded with some warning period. The Incident Commander is notified of the crisis and the situation is monitored closely. If there is sufficient warning, actions may be taken to minimize the interruption of operations. Exact business continuity pre-strike actions will be different for various crisis events. These actions include deploying equipment and materials, activating alternate sites and pre-positioning employees. In some cases, general operations may be discontinued and actions to provide for continuity of critical operations may be taken. Appendix H identifies recommended pre-strike actions to be taken for a hurricane, Appendix J identifies recommended pre-strike actions to be taken for a severe winter storm. Appendix D identifies recommended pre-strike actions as well as actions to be taken for a pandemic.

Discussion: Prepare for a Hurricane Strike

Appendix H provides general information for preparing an organization for a hurricane strike. Combine the pre-positioning information provided in Case Study E with the general information given in Appendix H and develop a pre-hurricane strike plan of action. Identify steps to be taken at the following pre-hurricane strike periods: 72 – 64 hours, 64 – 56 hours, 56 – 48 hours, 48 – 40 hours, 40 – 32 hours, 32 – 24 hours, 24 – 16 hours, 16 – 8 hours and 8 – 0 hours. Be sure to include the significant actions and location of each of the four employee groups listed below:

> ▶ Group A: This group consists of employees who are assigned to travel to the alternate site. Employees who are designated to travel to alternate sites are obviously identified well in advance of the crisis. However, employee assignment adjustments may be necessary as some employees may have sustained injuries and will not be able to travel. During a community-wide crisis, employee families may be placed in a dangerous situation and employees may be unwilling to travel.

> ▶ Group B: This group consists of employees who intend to travel to locations at least 100 miles away. Group B employees should pre-position themselves at multiple different and distant locations. Nevertheless, it is acknowledged that some Group B employees may not be able to work during or immediately after the storm.

> ▶ Group C: This group consists of employees who intend to remain in the general area – either at home, in shelters or other nearby safe locations.

> ▶ Group D: This 'storm personnel' or 'essential personnel' group is assigned to stay at the facility during the storm.

You can assume that the 72 hour point is 8:00am Monday morning and that a major hurricane will strike at 8:00am on Thursday morning. Weather conditions for highway travel will remain good until the eight hour pre-hurricane strike point. Airline travel will be possible up to the 24 hour pre-hurricane strike point.

You can also assume that employees will be given eight hours of personal time per day from midnight until 8:00am, eight hours for personal hurricane preparation time and eight hours to travel to the alternate site or to travel to hotels and other locations at least 100 miles away. Normal hours are from 8:00am to 4:00pm, Monday through Friday.

This case study starts with Group A employees being called at home and instructed not to report to work on Monday Morning.

Complete the following Table. Hint: The significant actions and the locations of the Groups have been partly completed.

Time Period	Group A	Group B	Group C	Group D
72 – 64 Hours, Monday: 8:00 am – 4:00 pm	Personal Preparations and Travel Plans			
64 – 56 Hours Monday: 4:00 pm – Midnight	Traveling to the Alternate Site			
56 – 48 Hours Tuesday: Midnight – 8:00 am	Personal Time	Personal Time	Personal Time	Personal Time
48 – 40 Hours Tuesday: 8:00 am – 4:00 pm	Working from the Alternate Site			
40 – 32 Hours Tuesday: 4:00 pm – Midnight	Overtime Work and Personal Time			
32 – 24 Hours Wednesday: Midnight – 8:00 am	Personal Time	Personal Time	Personal Time	Personal Time
24 – 16 Hours Wednesday: 8:00 am – 4:00 pm				
16 – 8 Hours Wednesday: 4:00 pm – Midnight				
8 – 0 Hours Thursday: Midnight – 8:00 am	Personal Time	Personal Time	Personal Time	Stationed at the Main Location

Actions during the Strike and Post-Strike Phases

To the extent that not all business continuity actions are taken during the pre-strike phase, the Incident Commander has the responsibility to take actions during the strike and post-strike phases as necessary. Actions follow the priorities developed during the BIA and include:

- Preliminary damage assessment.
- Recovery of critical operations.
- Comprehensive damage assessment.
- Recovery of general operations.

Escalation actions include:

- Activate the EOC.
- Declare a disaster.
- Assemble the Emergency Response Team.
- Alert the Crisis Management Team.
- Alert the Crisis Communication Team.
- Alert the Damage Assessment Team.
- Alert the Recovery Team.

A recovery plan and timeframe, based on damage assessment, is selected and executed. This may involve decisions regarding making repairs, utilizing alternate facilities and relocating employees. Contact with headquarters and the Board of Directors is essential.

Business continuity actions within each function for a typical organization (Appendix A) include:

- Operations
- Maintain workplace safety and security.
    - Maintain environmental controls.
    - Perform damage assessments.
    - Assess utility services.
    - Facilitate cleanup.
    - Perform and supervise repairs.
    - Direct and redirect shipments in transit.
    - Maintain inventory control.
    - Maintain quality controls.
    - Facilitate alternate sites.
- Finance
    - Activate payroll procedures.
    - Activate purchasing procedures.
    - Contact legal counsel.
    - Coordinate insurance.
    - Contact parties with financial interest.
- Marketing
    - Maintain contact with clients and prospects.
    - Maintain contact with suppliers and distributors.
    - Maintain contact with advertisers and other interested parties.

- ❖ Utilize alternate sites.
- ◗ Information Technology
    - ❖ Maintain IT security controls.
    - ❖ Assess IT damage.
    - ❖ Utilize alternate sites.
    - ❖ Commence repairs.
- ◗ Communications
    - ❖ Maintain communications with employees.
    - ❖ Maintain communications with media.
    - ❖ Maintain communications with clients, suppliers and other stakeholders.
- ◗ Human Resources
    - ❖ Contact all employees.
    - ❖ Assess workforce capabilities.
    - ❖ Execute the Disaster Assistance Plan.
    - ❖ Maintain payroll processing.
    - ❖ Maintain critical employee benefit services.

All the above actions may be taken by BCM teams supported by departments and individuals (Appendix L: Assigning Actions by Department).

All employees should maintain contact with their supervisors. Some employees may be assigned to assist with damage assessment and cleanup. Relocated employees work from alternate sites.

Communication

The BCP needs to document crisis communication teams and team member responsibilities, as well as crisis communication equipment, systems and procedures. Crisis communication topics are reviewed in a separate chapter in this book.

Maintenance

The maintenance program is to be documented in the BCP. Ongoing maintenance requirements of awareness and training, testing and exercising, and maintaining and updating are reviewed in a separate chapter in this book. In addition to these ongoing maintenance requirements, the following debriefing actions should occur after every major crisis event:

- ◗ Review the actions taken by the teams.
- ◗ Review the actions taken by the various departments.
- ◗ Review the actions taken by individual employees.
- ◗ The BCM Coordinator drafts changes to the documentation and procedures for review by the ERT and approval by the CMT and, if applicable, the BCM Steering Committee.

Review Topics

1. What is the difference between emergency response and business continuity?

2. Is there a clear point in time when emergency response ends and business continuity begins?

3. What is the difference between business continuity and business recovery?

4. What additional information could a comprehensive damage assessment provide that was not available in the preliminary damage assessment?

5. Why should department responsibilities be assigned on an enterprise-wide basis?

Case Studies

Case Study A-10: Alpha Investment Services (AIS) Business Continuity Plan

Based on the information previously provided in Case Study A, consider the following:

A-10.1 What are the Revised Recovery Time Objectives for the following operations?

Department	Operation	RTO
Custom Research	Research and Analysis	
Equity Selection Services	Research for Printed Reports	
Data Operations	Data Acquisition	
	Data Verification	
Facilities	Utility Services	
	Environmental Controls	
	General Building Maintenance	
Finance and Accounting	Financial Reporting	
	Crisis Communication	
Human Resources	Payroll	
Information Technology	IT for Data Operations	
	IT for Operational Groups	
	IT for Payroll	
	Communication Technologies	
Sales and Marketing	Marketing Program	
Security	Building Protection	

A-10.2 If a Disaster occurs, how important is the fact that there are two building locations?

A-10.3 If the Main Building is destroyed; highlight the initial major business continuity steps to be taken.

A-10.4 If the Auxiliary Building is destroyed; highlight the initial major business continuity steps to be taken.

A-10.5 If both the Main Building and the Auxiliary Building are destroyed; highlight the initial major business continuity steps to be taken.

A-10.6 Under the crisis event described in A-10.5, can the Recovery Time Objectives be met?

A-10.7 AIS management is considering moving the organization to Southern California. There would be only one office building for all operations. The building is to be of modern design and construction. Essentially the flood, tornado and severe winter storm risks have been replaced with the earthquake risk; all other significant risks are essentially the same. Although not located directly on a fault line, earthquakes are a very serious concern. If a Disaster occurs from an earthquake: describe the major business continuity response steps to be taken and determine if the Recovery Time Objectives can be met.

Case Study B-10: Beta Widget Makers (BWM) Business Continuity Plan

Based on the information previously provided in Case Study B, consider the following:

B-10.1   What are the Revised Recovery Time Objectives for the following operations?

Department	Operation	RTO
Manufacturing	Manufacturing	
R and D	New Product Design	
	Testing	
Supply Chain Mgmt.	Acquisition of Raw Materials	
	Fulfillment Mgmt.	
Warehouse	Receiving	
	Shipping	
Facilities	Utility Services	
	Environmental Controls	
	General Plant Maintenance	
	Plant Protection	
Finance and Accounting	Financial Reporting	
	Crisis Communication	
Human Resources	Payroll	
Information Technology	IT Manufacturing Support	
	IT Sales and Customer Service Support	
	IT for Payroll	
	Communication Technologies	
Sales and Customer Service	Marketing Program	

B-10.2   If a Disaster occurs, how important is the fact that there are two Plant locations?

B-10.3   If the Central Plant is destroyed; highlight the initial major business continuity steps to be taken.

B-10.4   If the West Plant is destroyed; highlight the initial major business continuity steps to be taken.

B-10.5   If both the Central Plant and the West Plant are destroyed; highlight the initial major business continuity steps to be taken.

B-10.6   Under the crisis event described in B-10.5, can the Recovery Time Objectives be met?

B-10.7   BWM management is considering moving the business to Southern California. There would be only one Plant for all operations. The Plant is to be of modern design and construction. Although not located directly on a fault line, earthquakes are a very serious concern. Essentially the flood, tornado and severe winter storm risks have been replaced with the earthquake risk; all other significant risks are essentially the same. If a Disaster occurs from an earthquake: describe the major business continuity response steps to be taken and determine if the Recovery Time Objectives can be met.

Bibliography

Burtles, J., *Principles and Practices of Business Continuity: Tools and Techniques*, Rothstein Associates Inc., 2007.

Carreira, B., *Lean Manufacturing that Works*, American Management Association, 2005.

Cullinane, T. P, *How to Plan and Manage Warehouse Operations, American Management Association*, 1994.

Dailey, K. W., *The Lean Manufacturing Pocket Handbook*, DW Publishing Co., 2003.

Engemann, K. and Miller, H., "Business Continuity Planning Software," *Advances in Decision Technology and Intelligent Information Systems*, Volume VIII (ed. K. Engemann and G. Lasker), pp. 38-42, The International Institute for Advanced Studies in Systems Research and Cybernetics, Windsor, Canada, 2007.

Engemann, K., Miller, H. and Yager, R., "The Role of Decision Attitude in the Selection of Alternatives", *Advances in Decision Technology and Intelligent Information Systems*, Volume 1V (ed. K. Engemann and G. Lasker), pp.36-40, The International Institute for Advanced Studies in Systems Research and Cybernetics, Windsor, Canada, 2003.

Graham, J. and Kaye, D., *A Risk Management Approach to Business Continuity: Aligning Business Continuity With Corporate Governance*, Rothstein Associates Inc., 2006.

Henderson, D. M., *The Comprehensive Business Continuity Management Program*, Rothstein Associates Inc., 2008.

Hiles, A. N., *Business Continuity: Best Practices: World-Class Business Continuity Management*, Rothstein Associates Inc., 2004.

Miller, H. E., and Engemann, K. J., "Cyberterrorism in Perspective," *Advances in Decision Technology and Intelligent Information System*s, Volume IV (ed. K. Engemann and G. Lasker), pp. 65-69, The International Institute for Advanced Studies in Systems Research and Cybernetics, Windsor, Canada, 2003.

Miller, H. E., Engemann, K. J., and Yager, R. R., "Disaster Planning and Management," *Communications of the International Information Management Association*, Vol. 6, Issue 2, pp. 25-36, 2006.

CHAPTER XI

Crisis Communication

Objectives

» Overview crisis communication

» Examine the importance of effective crisis communication

» Identify Crisis Communication Team responsibilities

» Review the importance of media communications

» Identify communication equipment and systems

» Identify and evaluate the important features of communication equipment and systems

» Examine the need for effective communication procedures and protocols.

Crisis Communication Overview

Crisis communication includes disseminating and receiving crisis information within the organization and with outside parties. Internal communications include safety information and emergency instructions for employees in the workplace and with management at other locations. External communications include information provided to stakeholders, media, government agencies, suppliers, vendors and other interested parties.

During times of crisis, a failure in crisis communication can manifest into a problem that can cause a breakdown of the entire emergency response efforts – even for organizations that otherwise have good planning in place. It is absolutely essential that crisis messages be disseminated promptly and with sufficient detail to initiate the correct response. Sufficient planning, decision-making protocols, systems and equipment must all be in place for communications to properly occur over a wide range of environments.

Crisis Communication Team

As a key component of the entire plan, the communication effort needs extensive planning. Organizations should designate a Crisis Communication Team to communicate with interested parties. The most critical team members are the spokesperson and the employee in-charge of overall communications – a single individual may perform both functions. The employee(s) with these responsibilities must have direct contact with the CEO, Incident Commander and other key executives.

The team members and backup team members need to be selected for the following contact responsibilities:

- Media Communications
- Employees
- Employee Relatives
- Website Update
- Voicemail Update
- Clients and Customers
- Prospects
- Shareholders
- Financial Relationships
- Government Contacts
- Utility Companies
- Corporate Headquarters
- Corporate Insurance
- Insurance Companies
- IT Alternate Site Providers
- Office Alternate Site Providers
- Suppliers
- Subcontractors
- Vendors

◗ Regulators

◗ Emergency organizations

◗ Unions

◗ Neighbors.

Various methods of communication that may be used regarding crisis information include: press briefings and press releases, public and employee meetings, conference calls, websites, mailings, newsletters and advertisements.

Media Communication

Most executives are untrained to discuss a crisis with the media. Large organizations have senior executives who are professionally trained to deal with the media. Such training is also useful in a non-crisis, but otherwise newsworthy event, where there is interaction with the media.

There should be a single source for information to the media. This will help prevent conflicting reports that may occur after a crisis strike. Individuals who answer telephones need to know where to direct incoming calls from the media. All unauthorized employees need to be instructed not to speak with the media.

Media communication steps are: alert the spokesperson, gather and confirm the facts, prepare a statement, notify the stakeholders and respond to the media. Key questions that will arise include:

◗ What happened?

◗ Were there injuries or deaths?

◗ How did it happen?

◗ What is the extent of the damage?

◗ What is being done now?

◗ When will it be remedied?

In conducting press briefings and providing press releases, observe media deadlines and give media equal access. Effective crisis communication considers the target audiences, determines the key message and communicates in an appropriate way. When being interviewed, a few basic concepts to keep in mind are as follows:

◗ Be prepared for tough questions.

◗ Keep responses simple.

◗ Avoid technical terms.

◗ Be honest.

◗ Do not place blame.

◗ Respond to every question.

◗ Never speculate.

◗ Avoid 'no comment.'

◗ Never discuss matters 'off the record.'

The organization should identify a media room that can be used to communicate information to the various media sources. It is a good idea to keep reporters away from crisis scenes and away from employees who are not authorized to speak with the media. Interview guidelines include:

- Confirm that human life and safety is the top priority.
- Do not discuss injuries until family has been informed.
- Confirm that the environment is a top priority.
- Present information in an accurate, timely, and clear manner.
- State what is known and unknown, and what you intend to find out.
- Preserve security and confidentiality.
- Confirm that the organization has prepared plans to address crisis situations.
- Confirm that the organization is committed to do everything possible to remedy the situation.

Discussion: Effective and Ineffective Crisis Communication

Effective Crisis Management: 1982 Tylenol Crisis

Johnson and Johnson's handling of the 1982 Tylenol Crisis is considered to be one of the best examples of good crisis management. The 1982 Tylenol Crisis is a product tampering event that resulted in seven deaths and seriously threatened the organization's name and product line. The following two articles provide an excellent capsule summary of the crisis:

Effective Crisis Communication: www. iml.jou.ufl.edu/projects/Fall02/Susi/tylenol.htm
The Tylenol Crisis: How Effective Public Relations saved Johnson and Johnson, Tamara Kaplan, The Pennsylvania State University, 1998:
www.aerobiologicalengineering.com/wxk116/TylenolMurders/crisis.html

Based on your reading of these articles, consider the following:

- What significant steps were well handled?
- What significant steps (if any) could have been handled better?
- What was the short and long term impact of this crisis?

Ineffective Crisis Management: 1989 Exxon Valdez Crisis

Exxon's handling of the 1989 Exxon Valdez Crisis is considered to be one of the best examples of poor crisis management. The 1989 Exxon Valdez Crisis was an environmental crisis where eleven million gallons of oil were spilt into Alaska's Prince William Sound. The following two articles provide an excellent capsule summary of the crisis:

Effective Crisis Communication: www.iml.jou.ufl.edu/projects/Fall02/Susi/exxon.htm
Case Studies in Crisis Management, Mallen Baker, mallenbaker.net:
www.mallenbaker.net/csr/crisis03.html

Based on your reading of these articles, consider the following:

- What significant steps (if any) were well handled?
- What significant steps could have been handled better?
- What was the short and long term impact of this crisis?

Systems and Equipment - Key Features

Communication systems serve a wide variety of purposes as follows:

▶ Emergency warnings.

▶ Ongoing information during a crisis.

▶ Internal department communications.

Communication systems must be able to contact employees in several environments including:

▶ At the workplace.

▶ On workplace grounds.

▶ At employee homes.

▶ In transit.

▶ At alternate locations.

Key features regarding communication equipment and systems include the following:

▶ Reliability.

▶ Communication speed.

▶ Range.

▶ Two-way communication capability.

▶ Special group contact.

▶ Security.

▶ Message detail availability.

Communication systems may fail as a result of power outages or damage to telephone lines or cell towers. Communication reliability may be improved by the use of redundancy.

Systems and Equipment - Evaluation

Every organization needs to examine the communication systems and equipment currently in use. Communication systems encompass a very wide range of technologies and equipment. It is necessary to have multiple specific-purpose systems to properly communicate with users located in various environments. Each system will have at least some area of weakness, so it is important to examine each system carefully. Observations regarding some of the more common communication systems and equipment in use are as follows:

▶ **Landline and Cellular Phones** – These devices are nearly universally in use within the business community and in very wide use among employees. Both systems are fast, have excellent range and permit detailed two-way communication. Cellular phones allow for contact in nearly all physical environments. Reliability is good but landline phones are dependent on wires and cell phones are dependent on towers. Both systems have power requirements and cell phone systems can become overloaded and shutdown.

▶ **Voicemail** – Voicemail systems are in wide use for disseminating information to employees and to other interested parties. Voicemail systems should be able to handle a large number of incoming calls and have remote updating ability. Ideally the voicemail system should be located off-site to avoid disablement from a crisis that directly impacts the organization location.

▶ **Satellite Phones** – Devices that communicate directly with satellites in space are not commonly in use within the business community. Although satellite communications are too expensive for normal usage, satellite phones are extremely reliable after a community-wide crisis strike. With proper power backup, satellite phones will function when other long distance communications fail. Organizations located in regions subject to community-wide crisis events should seriously consider having a minimum number of satellite phones available for critical communications.

▶ **Email and Internet** – Email and Internet communications are nearly universally in use within the business community and in wide use among employees. These systems are fast, have excellent range and can accommodate two-way communication. Additionally, Internet access has the potential of employee access to the computer system or 'cloud computing;' this allows many employees to perform normal services in distant, undamaged locations. Although the communication infrastructures have many redundancies, the communication infrastructures and normal power supply infrastructures could be physically damaged by a community-wide crisis.

▶ **PDAs/Blackberries** – These devices combine the features of voice and data communication systems; basically combining all the advantages identified under cell phones, email and Internet communications

▶ **Two-Way Radios and Walkie-Talkies** – These devices are not in very wide use among employees but many larger organizations have these communication devices for facility and security services. Communication range is limited but with proper power backup, these systems are highly reliable. These systems are valuable for internal communications within the workplace in a crisis post-strike environment.

▶ **Social Networks** – In recent years, social networks such as Facebook, MySpace and, in particular, Twitter provide messaging services that can be used primarily for disseminating information. There is excellent capacity, possible two-way communication and, except for possible phone charges, free service. There are limitations: security is lacking and users must actively participate and have either computers or mobile phones. Considering the constraints, social networks can provide a good backup, but not primary, communication service.

▶ **Intercom, Fire Alarm and Siren** – These systems are all low-tech systems that have good reliability and are primarily used to communicate crisis information during working hours at organization locations. The systems can communicate information fast such as a fire alarm to evacuate and a siren to shelter-in-place but do not permit two-way communications or special group contact. Fire alarm and siren systems generally do not provide detailed information. Virtually all modern buildings have fire alarm systems, many buildings have intercom systems and, although sirens are not commonplace in buildings, many communities have siren systems.

High-Tech

High-Tech Emergency Notification Systems have emerged over the last few years. These systems have first been applied in the government and higher education areas.

High-Tech Emergency Notification Systems are automated mass notification systems that can deliver detailed messages fast and accurately. Communication can be made to a wide range of devices including landline, cell and satellite phones, computers, email, PDA, Blackberry and other.

During a crisis, individual communication infrastructures often fail. The ability of High-Tech Emergency Notification Systems to utilize multiple communication infrastructures is an important feature.

Crisis Communication Procedures and Protocols

When a crisis emerges, there is frequently a need to disseminate information immediately. The best planning and equipment will be ineffective at the onset of the crisis if the authority to communicate the information cannot be made rapidly.

Emergency information regarding most sudden emergencies such as a fire, shooting or severe accident is disseminated immediately by the initial responders or by the Security Department. It is important for initial responders and the Security Department to have the authority to act on any and all life threatening and/or environmental emergencies.

In larger organizations with a sophisticated BCM program that is expensive to activate, full program activation must be authorized by the Incident Commander. As stated earlier, the Security Department and the initial responders, who often act through the Security Department, must have direct access to all Incident Commanders listed on the chain-of-command.

Review Topics

1. Are there any advantages of holding a conference with the media immediately after a crisis strike before all the facts are known?

2. Satellite phones, intercom systems and two-way radios are three communication systems used for crisis event warnings or crisis event communication. Is it possible to determine which system is best?

3. Alerting employees commuting to work about a crisis event at the organization often presents a problem. Identify systems and procedures that can be used to communicate with employees commuting to work.

Case Studies

Case Study A-11: Alpha Investment Services (AIS) Crisis Communication

Based on the Crisis Communication and other information previously provided in Case Study A, consider the following:

A-11.1 Identify the major controls in place and rate as Excellent, Good, Fair or Poor the ability of AIS to conduct crisis communication to employees in following environments:

　　A. At work.

　　B. At employee homes.

　　C. In transit or working at another location.

　　D. Customers, clients, subcontractors and outside interests.

A-11.2 Identify the major controls in place and rate as Excellent, Good, Fair or Poor the ability of AIS to conduct crisis communication to employees in following situations:

　　A. Emergency warnings.

　　B. During and after a crisis.

A-11.3 In order to improve communications, what changes to existing systems or new systems would you recommend?

Case Study B-11: Beta Widget Makers (BWM) Crisis Communication

Based on the Crisis Communication and other information previously provided in Case Study B, consider the following:

B-11.1   Identify the major controls in place and rate as Excellent, Good, Fair or Poor the ability of BWM to conduct crisis communication to employees in following environments:

   A. At work.

   B. At employee homes.

   C. In transit or working at another location.

   D. Customers, clients, subcontractors and outside interests.

B-11.2   Identify the major controls in place and rate as Excellent, Good, Fair or Poor the ability of BWM to conduct crisis communication to employees in following situations:

   A. Emergency warnings.

   B. During and after a crisis.

B-11.3   In order to improve communications, what changes to existing systems or new systems would you recommend?

Bibliography

Baldwin, J., "Staying Connected," *Disaster Recovery Journal*, Winter 2007.

Burtles, J., *Principles and Practices of Business Continuity: Tools and Techniques*, Rothstein Associates Inc., 2007.

Continuity Insights Staff, "Special Report: Emergency Notification and Communication," *Continuity Insights*, July/August 2008.

Engemann, K. J. and Miller, H. E., "Smart Technologies in Critical Infrastructure," *Advances in Decision Technology and Intelligent Information System*s, Volume X (ed. K. Engemann and G. Lasker), pp. 79-83, The International Institute for Advanced Studies in Systems Research and Cybernetics, Windsor, Canada, 2009.

Graham, J. and Kaye, D., *A Risk Management Approach to Business Continuity: Aligning Business Continuity With Corporate Governance*, Rothstein Associates Inc., 2006.

Henderson, D. M., *The Comprehensive Business Continuity Management Program*, Rothstein Associates Inc., 2008.

Hiles, A. N., *Business Continuity: Best Practices: World-Class Business Continuity Management*, Rothstein Associates Inc., 2004.

Hodges, E., "Crisis Communications and the CEO's Role," *Disaster Recovery Journal*, Summer 2008.

Miller, H. E. and Engemann, K. J., "Managing Operations Risks in E-Commerce," *Proceedings of the Annual Conference of the Decision Science Institute*, Vol. 2, pp.719-721, November 1999.

Philpott, D. and Einstein, S., *The Integrated Physical Security Handbook*, Don Dickson, 2006.

The Tylenol and Exxon Valdez case study articles:

- Case Studies in Crisis Management, Mallen Baker, mallenbaker.net: www.mallenbaker.net/csr/crisis03.html.
- Effective Crisis Communication: www.iml.jou.ufl.edu/projects/Fall02/Susi/tylenol.htm.
- Effective Crisis Communication: www./iml.jou.ufl.edu/projects/Fall02/Susi/exxon.htm.
- The Tylenol Crisis: How Effective Public Relations saved Johnson and Johnson, Tamara Kaplan, The Pennsylvania State University, 1998: www.aerobiologicalengineering.com/wxk116/TylenolMurders/crisis.html.

CHAPTER XII

Crisis Information Management Systems*

Objectives

» Identify the importance of effective information management during crisis

» Identify the roles that information systems play in managing crises

» Review how information systems are used before, during and after an emergency

» Review various technologies that underlie crisis information management systems

» Examine the contributions and challenges of social media in the realm of information management during crisis

» Review some institutional initiatives that contribute to crisis response and management.

* Chapter prepared by Shoshana S. Altschuller, PhD.

Systems for Crisis Information Management

While no two emergency situations are alike, when disaster strikes, the ability to share and communicate accurate and timely information is most often a key goal in response and recovery efforts. This chapter will highlight why a typical emergency scenario creates such a dire need for the ability to effectively manage information. It will review various types of information systems and overview what role they often play in the process of managing emergency information before, during and after an event. We focus in particular on the contributions and challenges of social media in the realm of information management during crisis due to their increasing use and viability as a means of quickly and efficiently sharing information among many parties. Finally, we discuss some initiatives that have taken place on the institutional level in order to enhance the aptitude with which crisis scenarios can be addressed.

Information Management during Crisis

The Crisis Scenario

The atmosphere that ensues during a crisis situation is typically very complex and uncertain. Although we can never predict exactly how events will unfold, there are a number of elements that are common among crisis scenarios. These characteristics impact the way that information systems should be designed to help manage information during crisis.

▶ **Multiple agents with no single authority**: In many crisis scenarios, the impact of an event is multi-faceted. Especially when the effects are widespread, there will be a number of agents who assume some level of responsibility for addressing the event and its ramifications. Depending on the nature of the event, these agents might include:

  ❖ local police

  ❖ volunteer groups

  ❖ private businesses

  ❖ civilian organizations

  ❖ Federal authorities.

For any or all of these agents to collaborate effectively toward recovery, information must be shared among them. Therefore crisis information must be collected and transmitted in a format that is accessible to all potential agents. Proprietary data formats would not be conducive to this type of information sharing.

▶ **Multiple sources of data**: Data that is used by agents during a crisis comes from many different sources, oftentimes numerous sources at once. Again depending on the nature of the crisis, sources of data could include:

  ❖ civilian reports

  ❖ national weather agency

  ❖ emergency response organizations

  ❖ local governments.

When data is obtained from many different sources, it must be managed in a unified manner so that it can all be considered together. Therefore, crisis information systems must have a means to consolidate disparate information coherently.

▶ **Rapid staff turnover:** Responders to a crisis are most often operating under high levels of stress and under extreme time pressure. They will likely put in 14 to 18 hours of work at a time. Under these circumstances, it is expected that responders will take shifts so they can take breaks. In longer-term recovery efforts contract workers are stationed for a few months at a time and replaced with little or no transition. Since the group of responders continually changes, an ideal crisis information system keeps a history of the activities and communications of the responders so that newcomers can be fully informed.

▶ **Rapidly changing environment:** As crises unfold, unexpected developments are bound to occur. It is not always possible to plan for the roles that people will take during a crisis especially as the situation continues to evolve. The information management system used must be adaptive and flexible to accommodate unforeseen circumstances.

All of these aspects of the crisis scenario help define the requirements for the systems that are used to collect, disseminate, and share information among crisis responders.

Information Systems Functions During Crisis

To counteract the atmosphere that exists during crisis, as described above, information systems that are used during these times fill a number of different functions. These functions include:

Decision Making

In an uncertain environment, decisions must be made quickly. Decision support systems can be applied in numerous ways to help decision makers make either tactical or strategic decisions. For tactical decisions, for example, simulations or forecasting applications are useful in deciding how to proceed logistically in the event of a crisis. However, strategic decisions tend to be based on unique circumstances and tacit knowledge that could not have been codified into any algorithm. Decision tools to support these types of decisions might instead focus on identifying and balancing objectives.

In crisis situations decision support systems should compensate for the fact that data comes from many different sources and is highly susceptible to error. A decision support system that can identify conflicting data and report it to the decision makers will result in decisions that most accurately reflect the uncertainty involved in the situation. Further, decision support systems that monitor and record the decision-making processes and are collaborative in nature will ensure that there is a shared perspective among all the various agencies that are involved with decision making during emergency response.

Institutional Memory

In crisis environments, in order for the recovery operation to be successful, work processes need to progress in a way that is independent of the people who are carrying out the tasks. Since it is impossible to know with certainty who will be filling which roles at what times, work processes must flow from one worker to the next seamlessly. The capacity for an information system to capture and store knowledge that has already been discovered and tasks that have already been accomplished is what we refer to as *institutional memory* and is crucial to this process. Information systems that provide institutional memory help staff who is arriving on the scene to be fully informed without taking too much precious time.

In addition, although each crisis presents a unique combination of challenges, commonalities provide lessons to be learned particularly at the global level. An information system's capacity to store past decisions and the factors that contributed to them affords the global community the opportunity to not repeat mistakes that have been made in the past. This type of decision audit also can be useful in helping to understand what occurred in the aftermath of a disaster.

Coordination

The ability to share information and knowledge is extremely important to facilitate the coordination among the many agencies that are potentially all facing the same challenges. Without an organized way to coordinate their activities, resources and time can be wasted on redundant efforts while others go unaddressed. Proper communication between these agencies allows them to make plans and decisions with up-to-date information and adequate knowledge from the other parties involved.

Situational Awareness

Especially where the impact of a crisis is widespread, information systems provide the ability to gather information about the totality of the event. Keeping everybody up to date, even at distributed sites, is key to being well prepared and responding swiftly and appropriately to developments. This is also especially important in keeping independent actors aware of each other's activities.

In summary, the need for information technology during a crisis is created by the emergent and uncertain nature of a scenario where many players are involved and things are continually changing. Essentially, the ability to communicate, store, process and share information to support these circumstances is the value that information technology adds to a crisis scenario.

How Information Technology is Used

Types of Systems

In addition to having application to an organization's operations, information technology has application to community emergency response efforts. Information technology has been used in a myriad of different ways to address crises at all stages of their development. These systems are tools to assist in preparing for a crisis before it occurs, responding to it during the event and recovering after the crisis has struck. These stages of crisis management are also known as *preparedness, response* and *recovery*. (The stages of emergency management were further discussed earlier.)

Preparedness – Early Warning and Communication Systems

Part of dealing with a crisis is being prepared for it before it occurs. Information systems have been useful in this effort to increase response effectiveness in advance of an emergency situation. There are three stages of preparedness at which these *early warning systems* play a critical role. These stages are monitoring, forecasting and alerting potential victims of an impending disaster.

▶ Monitoring -- Early warning systems are designed to continuously measure and monitor the precursors of a catastrophic event. Monitoring might utilize technologies such as satellite imaging and land and sea-based sensors. Such systems have been put into place by the World Meteorological Organization, for example, to stay abreast of the precursors of weather-related events. The Indian Ocean tsunami in 2004, where hundreds of thousands of lives were lost, indicated a weakness in the early warning capabilities for other natural disasters and triggered recent progress in this area. One monitoring system (OPTIMA, created by the European Commission's Joint Research Center) uses text mining to analyze news across the Web to extract information about current events and issue warnings about them.

▶ Forecasting – Early warning systems also include the capability to conduct scientific analyses to forecast a catastrophic event based on the patterns and trends in the detected risk factors. These analyses might utilize techniques such as statistical analysis, computer modeling and simulation, machine learning, etc.

▶ Alerts – Once an early warning system has detected a potential catastrophic event, it sends out an alert to potentially affected parties. With current innovations in technology, the focus in this area has been to close the gap in the "last mile" and get the message across to the people who need it the most. This involves the utilization of existing telecommunications systems or the dedication of new ones. For example, a cell broadcasting system would send a text message to all cell phones in an affected region.

Still, getting the message out is not nearly enough. The "people-centered" approach to disaster preparedness uses information and communication technologies to ensure that early warnings get to all the people who are at risk in a way that they can be understood and trusted, and that appropriate actions are taken in response to the information. Information and education centers (actual or virtual) where people can learn about the risks they face and how to proceed in the event that an early warning is issued are one way to keep people informed. All types of broadcasting media (radio, mobile technologies, Web-based media, etc.) are also potential technologies for the dissemination of information that at-risk communities need to be prepared for an emergency.

Response – Emergency Notification and Dispatch Systems

As soon as an emergency situation arises, responders must take swift action to alleviate the impact as quickly as possible. Information systems can be used in the moments immediately following an emergency event by coordinating the response to that event. The coordination effort, which is often centralized at a command center such as an EOC or ECP, necessitates the flow of information in two directions:

▶ *Information flowing out* of the centralized location includes:

   ❖ notifying people in the affected region who might be at risk, and

   ❖ notifying the responders who should be dispatched to help them.

▶ *Information flowing into* the command center consists of receiving communications from throughout the affected area.

In both of these cases, systems must be in place to facilitate the communication and be equipped to administer instructions to those in danger.

*Emergency Notification System*s that are used by many organizations store the information needed to contact all of their members through numerous media and with various communication devices (SMS, e-mail, cell phone, etc.). Based on the circumstances of the event and its impacts, managers can use the system to blast notifications to selected people through preferred means. Advanced systems will include rules for routing, prioritizing and escalating notifications automatically.

The typical *Emergency Dispatch System* is designed to route first responders to where they are needed to provide assistance and supplies. The system typically receives communications from people in the field so that resources can be deployed most efficiently to where they are needed most. Enhanced emergency dispatch systems will also automate the ability to give callers instructions on how to proceed based on the unfolding events that they report.

The information received from people in the affected area should ideally be recorded to determine the impact of the emergency event, perhaps mapping and/or prioritizing reports of impact throughout the area. Collecting this information through a centralized system is a crucial step for the further analysis of the incident and coordination of response actions. A *Crisis Information Management System (CIMS)* is a computer application that is used for the aggregation and analysis of facts about a crisis as it develops. In fact, often these systems are robust enough that they can be used to support many of the functions of a command center responding to an incident. While each actual implementation includes different features, some common CIMS features include: an event log, reporting capabilities, response planning, resource management, notifications, situational awareness management and organizational communications.

An important criterion for a CIMS is to be flexible so it can meet the needs of emergencies of various types, sizes and scopes. It should also be based on open standards so that it can work together with the systems of other agencies and allow for the possibility that all users can't necessarily gain access to the same system during an emergency event. In many cases the CIMS is Web-based and perhaps even compatible with handheld devices. An added benefit of this is that it can serve as a virtual command center where people can update, retrieve and communicate crisis-related information from distributed locations.

Since emergency response depends on two-way communications over telecommunication systems that are not always available or intact after an emergency, much technology research in emergency management has focused on how to transport and set up telecommunication centers as quickly as possible.

Recovery

Once a crisis is under control, focus turns from mitigating immediate danger to recovering normal life and rebuilding affected areas. Information systems are playing an important role in this stage as well. Many of the systems that are used for early warning also have uses at this stage. Systems that monitor and collect information about the risk factors in an area continue to identify risks and monitor the safety of the area. Mapping, imaging, and geographic systems are used to report the current status of infrastructure so that damage can be assessed and recovery activities allocated appropriately. They can also be used to monitor displaced persons and coordinate continued aid.

Many of the systems that are being put in place to help devastated communities rely on SMS message technology and cellular phones. These are two technologies that can be implemented to provide communication capabilities despite massive infrastructure damage. They are also being used in other innovative ways. In combination with Internet-based services they can match humanitarian aid with the people who need them and work with the people in search of jobs after a crisis strike. Another innovation uses mobile phones for fund raising and other financial transactions in disaster areas.

Technologies

These are some of the technologies that underlie the systems described above, allowing them to meet the information needs of emergency management.

Geospatial Systems

A majority of the information that is managed before, during and after an emergency is geographic in nature. Sources of danger move rapidly, effect large areas and require intricate knowledge of the effected and surrounding areas in order to be addressed. Therefore, the ability to create an association between data and geography is crucial in emergency management and response. *Geographical Information System (GIS)* technology facilitates this association, creating an interface to visualize, analyze and model combinations of spatially referenced data.

Many areas of emergency management depend on geospatial systems – those that use GIS technology to capitalize on the location elements of data. For example:

  ▶ **Hazard Analysis** – Computer-generated maps help emergency managers better understand the
     geographic area under their jurisdiction. In the planning stages, emergency management can use
     the maps to locate hazards (such as earthquake faults and flood zones) and identify potential
     emergencies. A *map overlay* feature will allow analysts to simultaneously map more than one

geographic dataset. By analyzing combinations of spatial data, emergency management personnel can identify areas of high risk where mitigation efforts and response plans might be focused. For example, a map that combines information about earthquake faults with information about pipelines and power lines can determine opportunities for utility companies to invest in mitigation to secure or bypass potentially affected areas. On the Web, *mashups* are applications that reuse and combine information from disparate sources and use it in different ways. *Location mashups* are those that visually combine data with geographic information and similarly prove beneficial in the context of hazard analysis.

▶ **Risk Assessment** – *Data modeling and geostatistics* are capabilities of geospatial systems that allow them to determine the probabilities and potential damage of certain events. By mapping multidimensional information (such as topology) and combining it with other temporal data (such as rainfall levels over time), a geospatial system could model what the results of various conditions would look like (such as areas of flooding). Geospatial systems that also incorporate geostatistical analysis tools will further allow observed patterns to be interpolated, measuring the probability of events to help predict events and assess risk. During an actual emergency, modeling the speed and direction of environmental movement (such as wind) can determine the next locations that will be in danger and require assistance (such as from a spreading fire).

▶ **Operational Decisions** – Rapid access to visually displayed geospatial information can also be instrumental in logistical operations during an emergency. They can help quickly plan response procedures so that geographical factors (such as fire hydrant locations or floor plans) can be easily considered in creating evacuation routes and rescue strategies. *Geocoding*, a technique that allows geospatial systems to associate geographic locations with addresses, is also useful in managing emergency operations in residential areas.

▶ **Real-time Monitoring** – Situational awareness is enhanced when a geospatial system can be updated in real-time giving a visual representation of the situation as it changes. Management can then use this information to coordinate and make decisions about the next steps for response. *Advanced Vehicle Locating (AVL)* can track deployed responders' locations, responsibilities and find the nearest mobile units to be dispatched. Mobile, GPS and wireless technologies are all instrumental in creating dynamic geospatial information gathering, analysis and distribution.

Geospatial information is not constrained by political boundaries. On a global level, geospatial systems are used:

▶ by the Center for Disease Control (CDC) to track and control the spread of diseases,

▶ by the UN to analyze satellite images of remote disaster sites,

▶ to assess the need for humanitarian aid after crises via high resolution Unmanned Aerial Vehicle (UAV) images, and

▶ to monitor major natural hazards and consolidate their information into global early warning systems.

Knowledge Management Systems

We have seen that collecting, storing, analyzing and disseminating information in an accurate and timely manner is the main goal of crisis information management. However, the combination of that information with experience and intuition is what we call knowledge. Encapsulating that knowledge in a systematic way so that it can be transferred from one person to another, reused and applied to new situations is one of the challenges in a disaster management scenario.

Knowledge management systems are systems that help decision-makers apply information to situations in meaningful ways. *Case-based reasoning* is one technique that has been recommended to be applied in disaster management cases. This is a computer-based technique that applies knowledge management by systematically taking into account the circumstances of past cases to help apply solutions in current cases.

Other emergency management systems implement knowledge management by enhancing communication between experts and responders so knowledge from past experience can be shared. In addition, systems that are dynamic, allowing for the editing of rules, policies and procedures based on experiences and lessons learned, also help responders share and obtain knowledge.

Artificial Intelligence Systems

As discussed in the previous section, decision support systems, especially those that apply knowledge management techniques, can capture and process some knowledge based on previous experiences. Disaster scenarios, however, are at times so uncertain and non-routine that there is no previous experience to call upon. High risks, time pressure and limited resources create a scenario where decision makers must act quickly based upon their intuition and implicit knowledge, which is much more difficult to automate.

Artificial intelligence (AI) systems are systems that can be programmed to behave as a human being would. An *expert system*, for example, is designed to emulate the thought processes of a human expert. Expert systems have been implemented for disaster management using subject matter experts and building systems to model their decision-making processes for all stages of disaster management. PortBlue is an example of a company that does this for incident management at hospitals.

Artificial intelligence has also been applied to disaster management by applying AI planning technology to crisis management tasks. *AI planning* systems are designed to make choices to achieve a goal. They need to make predictions and assumptions to reach the goal. In uncertainty, as in disaster management, they must continually change their plans as circumstances change, mimicking reasoning under uncertainty. For example, since in real emergencies decision makers are continually improvising their plans in this way, the cognitive process of improvisation has been studied, modeled and implemented into a computer program.

Challenge — Interoperability

One of the major challenges faced in the crisis management community is *interoperability* among the systems used by the various agencies that are on the scene. Crises are complex and require the involvement of an unpredictable set of distributed teams from many different organizations and emergency managers from different jurisdictions. Therefore, it is not feasible to expect that everybody who needs to partake in a crisis management effort will be able to access the same system. Differing technology platforms and organizational procedures among the various organizations make this very unlikely. To meet this challenge, efforts have begun to create a standard protocol to facilitate communication between different CIMS and between CIMS and other systems used by crisis management organizations.

The Organization for the Advancement of Structured Information Standards (OASIS), in 2005, developed an XML-based standard called *Common Alerting Protocol (CAP)* to standardize alerts and warnings. The goal is to eventually be able to distribute warnings consistently over all available channels and to be able to monitor the whole picture of local, state and national warnings at any one time. In addition, OASIS is producing a group of XML standards, called *Emergency Data Exchange Language* (EDXL) to standardize the transmission of various types of emergency information.

Social Media in Crisis Management

The systems discussed above are predominantly run and used by those who are providing emergency response and humanitarian aid and relief. They focus on a "top-down" flow of information. In "bottom-up" systems, however, information flows from within the community affected by the disaster. The combination of increased availability of communications devices (especially mobile devices), and the Web 2.0 trends of sharing user-generated content has allowed social media to become a viable tool in information management during crisis.

Social Media Concepts

The goal in crisis information management is to aggregate, analyze and share information easily, efficiently, and quickly. Yet traditional crisis information systems are closed, proprietary and centralized, relying on members of the crisis management organizations to contribute information. The Internet, however, in recent years has proven to be a tool that can gather all forms of information from anybody who has access to it very quickly. The current and potential implications for crisis information management abound.

Citizen Journalism and Crowdsourcing

Recall that situational awareness is one of the goals of crisis information management systems. Response efforts are best directed by real-time information about the current situation. What better way to get real-time status than from the people who are witnessing it first hand? The current Web trend of sharing user generated content creates a medium where people can let other people know what is going on through many different media. Using these tools, individuals engage in *citizen journalism* as they share:

- Experiences (blogs),
- Short text updates (SMS) (e.g., Twitter),
- Photos (e.g.. Flickr),
- Video (e.g. YouTube), and
- Video streams (e.g. Bambuser, uStream.tv).

The Internet has afforded us the opportunity to *crowdsource* situational awareness information. This means that its creation is outsourced to the general public. The benefit of gathering information this way is that information collection is not restricted to designated officials. Information is gathered and shared by anyone and with everyone without interoperability issues, speeding up the process manifold. For example, citizen journalism was seen on Flickr following hurricane Katrina in the US Gulf Coast in 2005 and using Twitter during the terrorist attacks on Mumbai, India in 2008 and during the Middle East unrest in 2011.

Collective Intelligence and Wikis

It has been said that a whole is greater than the sum of its parts when it comes to knowledge creation. This implies that when an information-based effort is crowdsourced the result reflects a more robust product and efficient process than if an individual had been assigned to obtain the information alone. The power of *collective intelligence* for the creation of situational awareness was evident in 2007 when a Facebook group successfully compiled an accurate list of the casualties in the shooting at Virginia Tech hours before this information was available from local Blacksburg authorities.

This is the concept behind any *wiki* where many people contribute to the creation and perfection of a knowledge base or problem-solving task. Crowdsourcing tools have been applied to the creation of knowledge for crisis information management. For example, OpenStreetMap.org is a Web-based application through which the "crowd" can update a map of the world. This can be used as a crisis unfolds to maintain a real-time awareness of the geographic impacts of the crisis. This tool was used after the 7.0 magnitude earthquake that devastated Haiti in January of 2010. A call to the OpenStreetMap community spurred them to go to work updating the map of Haiti based on any information that they had access to. The up-to-date map could then be used in response and relief efforts.

Socially-produced situational awareness was taken one step further with the Ushahidi application. This open source, Web-based service allows maps to be updated with SMS messages and photos to depict a picture of a crisis scene. This is also useful in that it can feed this information back to the people who need it most via e-mail or SMS alerts.

Social Networks

The prevalence of online social networks also proves to be useful for crisis management. An online social network is characterized by shared connections between people who are organized into groups and share information objects such as messages, photos, videos, notifications, current activities, etc. Capitalizing on these links between people, social networking sites have already been used as notification systems to get urgent messages out to groups of people through "status updates," "wall postings," group discussion and photo threads. The sheer numbers of users of social networking sites and the volume of information they share, make social networking a premium opportunity for information gathering and as a repository of relevant information during a crisis. The ability to "tag" information objects further provides a user-generated cataloging system that helps organize and filter the volumes of aggregated information.

Challenges – Accuracy and Verifiability

The use of social media for crisis information management is in its infancy and continues to evolve. The opportunities are many but challenges do exist. The main challenge that we face in adapting social media to the crisis information context is the accuracy and verifiability of information. To rely on information for crisis response, it must be trustworthy and authoritative. While user-generated crisis information is much more quickly obtained, there is an inherent trade-off between speed and verifiability. Opening the information gathering process to the general public opens opportunities for fraud and sabotage that can even exacerbate the crisis. Furthermore, the power of social media to spread information quickly among social networks intensifies the impact of "bad" information.

Some potential solutions to this challenge are to continue use of the technology but restrict its use to a bounded group of trusted individuals or to devise a technique for real-time validation. Cross references to the same information on multiple platforms are some form of validation. Since pictures are harder to fabricate than text, they too can validate reports on some level. Swift River developed by Ushahidi (www.swift.ushahidi.com) verifies information by virtue of the fact that it is collected across multiple types of media. As social media continues to be applied to crisis management, further developments in verification remain to be seen.

Institutional Initiatives

Progress in the area of systems for the management of crisis information is continually underway. As globalization progresses, technologies advance and crises occur, global crisis management initiatives will be an arena that is worthwhile to watch. Many large technology organizations are investing in development in crisis management technology. Some of these initiatives follow.

▶ **Microsoft** – In 2006 Microsoft Corporation established a group that is dedicated to serving humanitarian causes, bringing expertise and assistance in the form of collaboration software to areas throughout the world that are affected by disaster. What is unique about this group, *Microsoft Humanitarian Systems (MHS)*, is that they develop their humanitarian software – in situ – at the actual site of the disaster. Software developers actually live among the rescue workers. Knowing what the disaster response community is going through helps Microsoft's developers understand the real needs of the crisis situation and the users of the systems they develop. The belief is that the stressful development environment helps spur innovative solutions to support the collaboration and coordination of disaster relief groups.

▶ **IBM** – IBM's *Crisis Response Team* has been on the disaster response scene since 1993, responding to disasters worldwide with technology resources, solutions and volunteers. One of their notable contributions has been an open source, Web-based disaster management system that tracks information such as victim identification and donations of relief goods. IBM's team has also devised systems to help in other ways such as finding missing persons and helping victims find jobs.

▶ **CISCO** – CISCO Systems, Inc. has been active worldwide in supplying post-disaster communities with relief. For example, their *Community Voice Mail (CVM)* program is a simple idea with a big impact. CVM gives a phone number and voice mailbox to people who have lost everything in a disaster to help them as they try to rebuild. In addition, CISCO's worldwide *Networking Academy* makes networking and communications education available to communities around the world so that struggling communities can obtain the tools to help themselves.

▶ **Strong Angel III** – *Strong Angel III* was the most recent in a series of training efforts in which a diverse group of first responders, military officials, and software and wireless network experts got together to simulate a disaster experience. The drill, which lasted several days was designed to practice collaboration among the different types of disaster response organizations, showcase and try new disaster response technologies and teach the disaster response communities some lessons that could be applied for real disaster response. The event was unstructured to closely simulate an actual disaster environment where groups must self-organize in the absence of one leader.

Review Topics

1. Information systems are crucial management tools during crisis, but for small or medium-size organizations they can be costly. What factors should an organization consider in justifying the cost of a system that will be used only during crisis?

2. Decisions made during a crisis often have significant consequences. In what ways do information systems help or hinder the reliability of these decisions? What attitude must decision makers take when relying on information systems to help them make life altering decisions?

3. White et al. (2009) propose a social network as a "one stop shop" solution for global information dissemination and communication during all stages of an emergency. How feasible is this? What challenges are involved?

Bibliography

CISCO Systems, Inc., "CISCO Corporate Citizenship Report," 2005.

Coyle, D. and Meier, P., "New Technologies in Emergencies and Conflicts: The Role of Information and Social Networks," Washington, D.C. and London, UK: UN Foundation-Vodafone Foundation Partnership, 2009.

de Leon, JVC., Bogardi, J., Dannenmann, S., and Basher, R., "Early Warning Systems in the Context of Disaster Risk Management," www.unisdr.org, 2006.

Desimone, R., "The Application of AI Planning Technology to Crisis Management Tasks," *IEE Colloquium on Intelligent Planning and Scheduling Solutions* (Digest No. 1996/197), 2002.

Environmental Systems Research Institute, Inc., "GIS for Emergency Management." U, www.esri.com/library/whitepapers/pdfs/emermgmt.pdf, 2002.

French, S. and Turoff, M., "Decision Support Systems," Communications of the ACM, Vol. 50, No. 3, 2007.

Iannella, R., Robinson, K., Rinta-Koski, O., "Towards a Framework for Crisis Information Management Systems (CIMS)," 14th Annual Conference of the International Emergency Management Society (TIEMS), Trogir, Croatia, 2007.

IBM Corporation., "IBM's Global Disaster Response: Helping People, Leveraging Technology, Skills," 2007.

Karpovich, G., "Crisis Information Management Software: Information Sharing During a Disaster," www.officer.com, 2007.

Lang, G. and Benbunan-Fich R., "The Use of Social Media in Disaster Situations: Framework and Cases," International Journal of Information Systems for Crisis Response Management, Vol. 2, No. 1, pp. 11-23, 2010. Vol. 2, No. 1, pp. 11-23, 2010.

Liu, S. B., Palen, L., Sutton, J., Hughes, A. L., and Vieweg, S., "In Search of the Bigger Picture: The Emergent Role of On-Line Photo Sharing in Times of Disaster," *Proceedings of the 5th International ISCRAM Conference*, (F. Fiedrich and B. Van De Walle, eds.), pp. 140-149, Washington, DC, 2008.

Malykhina, E., "Maps Meet Mashups," *Information Week*, March 19, 2007.

Markoff, J., "Technology; This Is Only a Drill: In California, Testing Technology in a Disaster Response," *The New York Times*, August 28, 2006.

Mendonça, D. and Wallace W.A., "A Cognitive Model of Improvisation in Emergency Management," *IEEE Systems, Man and Cybernetics*, Part A, Vol. 37, No. 4, pp. 547 – 561, 2007.

Microsoft Corporation, "MHS Charter: 'Do good, learn, build solutions'," 2006.

Mount Carmel Foundation, "New Emergency Medical Dispatching System," www.mountcarmelfoundation.org.

Murphy, T. and Jennex, M. E., "Knowledge Management, Emergency Response, and Hurricane Katrina," *International Journal of Intelligent Control and Systems*, Vol. 11, No. 4, pp. 199-208, 2006.

OASIS Emergency Interoperability, www.oasis-emergency.org/cap.

Otim, S., "A Case-Based Knowledge Management System for Disaster Management: Fundamental Concepts," *Proceedings of the 3rd International ISCRAM Conference* (B. Van de Walle and M. Turoff, eds.), Newark, NJ, 2006.

Public Technology Institute (PTI) and Geospatial Information and Technology Association (GITA), "Geospatial Systems That Support Emergency and Disaster Operations: A Case Study Guide for Local Government and Utility First Responders," 2009.

Rinkineva, K., "The Role of Information Technology in Crisis Management," The 14th EINIRAS Conference, www.einiras.org, 2004.

Turoff, M., "Past and Future Emergency Response Information Systems," *Communications of the ACM*, Vol. 45, No. 4, 2002.

U.S. Department of Justice, "Crisis Information Management Software: Feature Comparison Report," www.ncjrs.gov/pdffiles1/nij/197065.pdf, 2002.

White, C., Plotnick, L., Kushma, J., Hiltz, S.R., and Turoff, M., "An Online Social Network for Emergency Management," *International Journal of Emergency Management*, Vol. 6, No. 304, pp. 369-382, 2009.

Maintenance

Maintenance involves creating an education and awareness culture of BCM with the goal of improving organizational resiliency by ensuring the program will be effective in an actual emergency situation. The main components of maintenance include awareness to respond to crisis events and training to execute plans, testing and exercising to assess the viability of the plan, and maintaining and updating to ensure consistency between the plan and the changes affecting the organization.

CHAPTER XIII

Sustaining Organizational Resilience

Objectives

» Review the role of awareness and training in BCM

» Define the types of tests and exercises

» Review BCP maintaining and updating.

Making BCM Effective

To develop comprehensive BCM, an organization has likely spent a significant amount of time and money on performing analysis and creating documentation. Unfortunately, all this effort alone will not guarantee that the BCM program will be effective during an actual emergency situation. Additional actions are required to prepare the BCM program ready to effectively respond to an emergency.

Maintenance involves creating an education and awareness culture of BCM and ongoing testing, auditing and change management to ensure the plans remain operable and current. BCM readiness is sustained through the maintenance components.

▶ **Awareness and Training** provides awareness to respond to crisis events and training to execute plans. Awareness ensures that everyone is knowledgeable of BCM and the importance senior management has placed on this program. Training ensures that everyone has the skill, knowledge and experience to execute their responsibilities.

▶ **Testing and Exercising** assesses the viability of the plan. Testing checks the operability of equipment, while exercising is practicing individual and team roles in order to improve skills to execute plans effectively.

▶ **Maintaining and Updating** ensures consistency between the plan and the changes affecting the organization. Maintaining the BCP involves reviewing and auditing to determine if all the elements of the plan are in place and accurate. Updating improves the BCP and keeps it current.

Awareness and Training

For BCM to be effective all employees should be aware of the program and all participants in the organization should be thoroughly trained. All personnel are to know the necessary emergency response actions and new employees are to be informed of relevant procedures. In addition, a process should be in place to ensure that supervisors and managers responsible for tasks understand the overall BCM and their particular responsibilities within it.

As a first step, the objectives of the BCM awareness and training program should be specified. Senior management needs to be in full support of the awareness and training program. Functional awareness and training requirements should be identified. The awareness and training program helps provide employees with a thorough understanding of their role in BCM.

Awareness requires knowledge and alertness, while training requires instruction in order to be proficient. Awareness and training should be designed to meet the needs of the organization. The objectives are to provide awareness to respond to crisis events and to provide training to execute BCM. The process of an awareness and training program includes raising awareness, determining training requirements, developing the training methodology, training the team leaders, members and alternates, and evaluating the results.

The questions that should be addressed in an awareness program include:

▶ What is BCM?

▶ Why is BCM important?

▶ Who participates in BCM?

▶ How is BCM activated?

The awareness and training program may include posters, pamphlets, a web site and wallet cards detailing emergency procedures. Emergency procedure booklets inform personnel of the actions to take during an emergency. The emergency procedures booklets contain information of evacuation, emergency assembling areas, emergency organization, safety and security procedures and the emergency call list. More information can be provided in a detailed emergency preparedness manual. Seminars are useful to promote BCM awareness. Questionnaires and checklists can be used to assess vulnerabilities, the current state of recovery preparedness and knowledge of associated risks. The goal is to ensure employees are familiar with their roles and responsibilities.

Once recovery teams are determined, they are provided training related to their specific functions. This is accomplished through meetings of individuals responsible for tasks outlined by the program. The meetings explore the participants' knowledge of BCM, ability to respond in an emergency situation and ability to perform duties involved with alternate processing and full recovery.

The training methodology should focus on individuals' skills initially and then build up to team training with team leaders being trained first. Training topics include:

▶ Notification procedures.

▶ Escalation procedures.

▶ Emergency response procedures.

▶ Evacuation and shelter procedures.

▶ Safety and security measures.

▶ Emergency equipment.

▶ Hazardous materials.

Various training methods and approaches can be employed including computer-based, workshops, courses and conferences. A consultant can be a valuable resource in this process.

Training should be documented and evaluated. To thoroughly evaluate the program, it is necessary to review objectives, evaluate the approach, define gaps, assess employees and review the budget.

Testing and Exercising

Crisis events present challenges that are different from the challenges employees face during normal times of operations. Moreover, a crisis will frequently involve dangerous situations. Without practicing plans and procedures there is a real risk that the business continuity efforts will fail and, most importantly, that injuries or loss of life may result.

The goal of testing and exercising is to determine how the BCP can fail and then take action to solve the problem to ensure success in an actual event. Other reasons for conducting tests and exercises include:

▶ Prevent loss of life and injuries.

▶ Prevent environmental damage.

▶ Promote increased BCM awareness.

▶ Identify any gaps in planning.

▶ Identify any gaps in the skills necessary to execute BCM.

▶ Practice working together under unusual circumstances.

▶ Identify any mistakes in program execution.

▶ Test equipment.

What is the difference between 'testing' and 'exercising?' The term 'testing' is used when equipment, such as a computer, is involved. The term 'test' may have a negative tone to some, so the term 'exercise' is used when people are involved, for example in an evacuation. During certain exercises equipment will be *tested* simultaneously with individuals *exercising* their responsibilities.

Types of Exercises

All exercises will require some outlay of money and time. The organization must strike a balance between exercise needs and organization budgets. The following types of exercises are commonly conducted:

▶ **Talk Through Exercise** – This exercise is a presentation and discussion of a particular topic. Talk Through exercises are typically used when new planning or procedures are introduced. Talk Through exercises are often followed by a Tabletop exercise at a later date. Talk Through exercises require a minimum financial commitment, a minimum amount of time and do not interfere with most normal operations.

▶ **Walk Through Exercise** – This exercise is a Talk Through exercise but is more physical. For example, the presenter may be describing a new fire evacuation route while actually walking through the evacuation route with the participants. Walk Through exercises are often followed by an Exercise Drill at a later date. Walk Through exercises require a minimum financial commitment, a minimum amount of time and do not interfere with most normal operations.

▶ **Tabletop Exercises** – In a Tabletop exercise a crisis is described followed by questions regarding the proper actions that should be taken. In the first phase of the Tabletop exercise the initial crisis is described. Specific questions regarding the initial response are then asked. After the questions are analyzed and then discussed, the crisis situation is updated and the process is repeated.

Typically the participants are broken into small groups and each group will work on the questions as a team. The Tabletop exercise will require generally about two- to four-hours of time by each member of the ERT and as many members of the EMC who can attend. The exercise will also require the use of a facilitator and the development of an exercise workbook. Facilitating a Tabletop exercise may be complicated and, if no one at the organization has experience being a facilitator, the use of an outside consultant should be considered. Tabletop exercises require a time commitment, a possible moderate financial commitment but do not interfere with most normal operations.

▶ **Drills and Full Scale Exercises** – These exercises actually require the organization or a segment of the organization to cease normal operations and practice a response to an announced crisis. Some exercises, such as fire evacuation drills or shelter-in-place drills, may shut down normal operations for a short period of time.

Other Full Scale exercises, such as activating the IT Hot Site, may require teams traveling and recovering operations at a distant location. For this type of IT Hot Site exercise, exercises are conducted during non-working hours or other teams remain at the main data center during the exercise to maintain normal technology support to the organization.

Full scale exercises involve role play scenarios and use great detail. Participant scripts, the timing of incidents and reports on damage assessment are meant to provide a realistic situation that will promote the participants believing in the exercise. A full scale exercise is high-profile and challenges BCM. Full Scale exercises require a time commitment, a possible significant financial commitment and may briefly suspend normal operations.

Exercise Frequency

For ERT members, exercises should be conducted at the BCP inception and at least annually thereafter. Annual exercises for ERT members often alternate between Tabletop exercises and Full Scale exercises. More frequent exercises should be held whenever new procedures or new team members are introduced. These interim exercises are often a Walk Through or Talk Through.

Full Scale Exercises for the IT Department should be conducted at least once a year. Drills that involve all employees are typically conducted once or twice a year. Exercise frequency is also a function of criticality and exposure to loss.

Approach to Exercising

An organization should not be placed at risk from a test or exercise. Exercises should start simply and build up in complexity. Eventually, all aspects of the BCP should be included in the testing and exercising program. The scope and objective should be realistic, and the assumptions and limits should be clear. Testing and exercising should be practical and cost-effective. An external facilitator can add much value to an exercise. The purpose of testing and exercising is to increase the effectiveness of BCM and to build confidence.

Decisions need to be made regarding the involvement of emergency services in exercises. An exercise should not be mistaken for a real disaster, resulting in invoking emergency services accidentally. On the other hand, emergency services should be able to respond if a real disaster actually would occur during the exercise.

Typically, all parties will be informed of the day and the approximate or exact time of an exercise. Frequently, parties will know the type of crisis event that will be exercised. For example, many organizations in hurricane-prone areas will conduct a hurricane exercise at the beginning of or slightly before the start of the hurricane season. However, details of the exercise scenario are generally kept confidential.

A more challenging exercise can be constructed if the type of crisis event being examined is unknown to the participants. Arguably, this is a more realistic scenario as many crisis events are not preceded by a warning period. An unannounced or 'surprise exercise' will add another layer of realism and difficulty. A surprise exercise should not be considered until BCM is very mature.

Exercise Evaluation

The idea behind conducting an exercise is not to check a box on the 'things to do' list, rather to ensure that procedures, awareness levels, skill levels, training, equipment and planning are adequate. Each exercise should conclude with a debriefing to document any problems and, if necessary, explore solutions. If the problems require additional exercise or training the BCM Coordinator should make appropriate recommendations for formal approval by senior management.

Testing and exercising is important to assess the viability of the BCP, identify areas that need improvement, satisfy audit and legal requirements and keep the BCP up-to-date.

Maintaining and Updating

Changes to operations can result from acquisitions and the introduction of new technologies, processes, products and services. Changes to organization priorities, the competitive environment, the supply chain and other outside influences need to be examined. The BCP needs to be maintained and updated accordingly. The objective of the maintenance program is to ensure that the BCP remains accurate, relevant and operable under current conditions. There should be consistency within the documentation and between the documentation and the organization.

For the BCP to be used effectively in an emergency, it must be timely and complete. It is imperative therefore that the program be reviewed and exercised regularly and modified as necessary. An organization should develop guidelines for BCP maintenance and apply these guidelines to verify that plans are valid.

Reviewing the BCP determines if all the elements of the plan are in place and accurate. Reviewing precedes exercising since it identifies weaknesses which would lead to unsatisfactory exercises. Exercising determines how well a program works when executed. The review program begins by validating assumptions. Assumptions underlying the criticality of operations are reviewed by management. Assumptions made in selecting planning strategies are reviewed and involve the potential disasters and associated operational impact. Assumptions should be validated regarding the availability and adequacy of resources required to provide the planned service levels through discussions with operations managers, supervisors, vendors and other parties with whom agreements have been made. Reviews also include visits to backup sites, requests for specific sample documents and examination of these documents. Checking the accuracy of information involves checking the correctness of all documented data and lists.

Establishing the maintenance program requires defining every review and exercise with respect to its objective and scope, scheduling, procedures and participants. Maintenance plans specify the reviews and exercises to be performed, responsibility for completion and target dates by which the tasks are to be completed. The results of each review or exercise are then documented.

The results are also evaluated by management to ensure the adequacy of the exercise or review performed and to develop an action plan to complete necessary modifications. A process should be established to review and exercise the BCP after software, hardware or communication changes to ensure that the change is accurately reflected at both primary and alternate sites. This process should be an integral part of the change control process.

BCP Review and Audit

Complete review of the BCP should be made at least once a year and following any major change in operations. In addition, information which may change more frequently, such as telephone numbers and the names of individuals responsible for specific tasks are to be kept current.

BCP review and audit is an essential component of program maintenance. Consistency of the documentation is critical and assessment of the program should answer questions such as:

▶ Is the plan valid?

▶ Is the scope of the plan correct?

▶ Are the plan's assumptions reasonable?

▶ Is the plan structure appropriate?

▶ Are the teams up to date?

▶ Are the components of the plan integrated?

▶ Are the procedures executable?

▶ Does the plan support the organizational objectives?

Review and audit areas include: recovery time objectives, notification, invocation, teams, contact numbers, assigned recovery tasks, recovery procedures, contingency strategies and resources, service agreements and off-site procedures.

BCP review and audit approach includes: determining consistency, reviewing administrative aspects, reviewing documentation control and developing conclusions regarding the program meeting its objective. The review process and any issues that are encountered are documented.

Maintenance responsibilities include the involvement of many individuals. Auditors determine if programs meet objectives; the BCM Coordinator is responsible for program maintenance; team leaders are responsible for team sections; department managers are responsible for their departments; and senior management reviews and approves the program.

During the updating process, each plan needs to remain coordinated with all associated plans. Utilizing an established process, the updated BCP should be validated as complete. Established procedures for document control and security are vital.

In order to meet the objectives, an accurate, current and executable BCP is critical for an organization to recover from a disaster. The maintenance plans contain a summary of all the tasks that must be performed to ensure the BCP remains accurate, relevant and operable. Included in the maintenance plan are the names of the individuals responsible for completing tasks and documenting results, the target dates for completing the tasks and a brief description of the objectives of the tasks. Documenting the results of a task includes evaluating the results of the task against the objectives of the task, reporting on issues and future actions required. For the BCP to be used effectively in an emergency it is imperative that the program be reviewed and exercised regularly and modified as necessary.

Review Topics

1. All of the exercise types can be used to test emergency procedures. Which types of exercises are most effective in testing business continuity procedures?

2. When conducting a Tabletop exercise where civil responders would likely be involved, is it a good idea to invite civil responders to the exercise? What might be the downside of having civil responders attend the exercise?

3. Identify the events that determine when BCP maintenance and update should be performed.

Case Studies

Case Study A-13: Alpha Investment Services (AIS) Tabletop Exercise

In the Case Study Section, Case Study F presents a sample Tabletop exercise. The material includes additional information regarding the conducting of a Tabletop exercise. Questions should be answered for AIS.

Case Study B-13: Beta Widget Makers (BWM) Tabletop Exercise

In the Case Study Section, Case Study F presents a sample Tabletop exercise. The material includes additional information regarding the conducting of a Tabletop exercise. Questions should be answered for BWM.

Bibliography

Bell, J. K., *Disaster Survival Planning*, Disaster Survival Planning, Inc., 1991.

Burtles, J., *Principles and Practices of Business Continuity: Tools and Techniques*, Rothstein Associates Inc., 2007.

Fulmer, K. L., *Business Continuity Planning: A Step-by-Step Guide with Planning Forms*, Rothstein Associates Inc., 2005.

Gillis, T. K., *Emergency Exercise Handbook*, PennWell Books, 1996.

Graham, J. and Kaye, D., *A Risk Management Approach to Business Continuity: Aligning Business Continuity With Corporate Governance*, Rothstein Associates Inc., 2006.

Henderson, D. M., *The Comprehensive Business Continuity Management Program*, Rothstein Associates Inc., 2008.

Henderson, D. M., *Today's Exercise: Terrorist Attack, Disaster Management, Inc.*, 2006.

Herath, H., and Wijayanayake, W., "Modelling Business Readiness Frameworks," *International Journal of Business Continuity and Risk Management*, Vol. 1 No. 3, pp. 211-221, 2010.

Hiles, A. N., *Business Continuity: Best Practices: Aligning Business Continuity with Corporate Governance*, Rothstein Associates Inc., 2004.

Philip Jan Rothstein, et. al., *Disaster Recovery Testing: Exercising Your Contingency Plan*, Rothstein Associates Inc., 2007.

Risk Modeling

Risk modeling includes the development of a foundation in probability and statistics, and explores forecasting techniques, regression analysis and reliability modeling. This section then applies simulation modeling to supply chain analysis and examines decision making techniques. Risk models enhance the assessment of risk and the development of strategies through the decision support obtained from comprehensive data analysis and system modeling.

CHAPTER XIV

Fundamentals of Probability and Statistics[*]

Objectives

 » Present fundamental concepts of probability and statistics

 » Review measures of central tendency and dispersion

 » Analyze methods and applications of descriptive statistics

 » Review basic probability distributions.

* Chapter prepared by Ore A. Soluade, PhD

Fundamentals of Probability and Statistics

An understanding of the fundamentals of probability and statistics is basic to describing and interpreting data. This knowledge is also most valuable in dealing with random events and risk which is inherent in business continuity planning.

Probability is a measure of the likelihood of occurrence of an event. It could refer to the chance that a new machine will work or not; or the chance that a hurricane will occur; or the chance that a neighborhood will be hit by a heavy snow-storm. There are several ways of calculating probability, and we will explore them later in this chapter.

Statistics is the technique used to collect, describe and analyze data. For example, in order to estimate the life expectancy of a machine, one can collect the time-to-failure of a number of similar machines and compute the average time-to failure. This measure, *average*, becomes a statistic. It gives one an idea of how long a machine will last. It is also possible to obtain the *range* of values for the life expectancy of a machine. The range will give us an idea of the minimum and maximum values. Such measures as *average*, *range* and many other measures are known as *statistics*. We will develop several other statistics in this chapter.

In the study of statistics, there are two basic concepts that are crucial – the concept of *population* and the concept of *sample*. A *population* is the entity that we are interested in studying. However, it is usually not advisable to collect data on whole populations due to cost and time considerations. Normal practice is to take a *sample* from the *population*. The data collected from the sample is used to develop sample characteristics known as *statistics*. This will then be used to make inferences about the population characteristics known as *parameters*.

Data Classification

*Discrete variable*s are variables whose outcomes are counted, for example, the number of requests for emergency response per day.

*Continuous variable*s are variables whose outcomes are measured, for example, the time it takes to respond to an emergency call.

Nominal measurements have no meaningful rank order among values, for example, the classification of a weather event as a tornado, hurricane, or winter storm.

Ordinal measurements have imprecise differences between consecutive values, but have a meaningful order to those values, for example, the classification of a tornado as EF1, EF2, EF3, EF4, or EF5.

Interval measurements have meaningful distances between measurements defined, but have no meaningful zero value defined, for example, degrees Fahrenheit.

*Ratio measurement*s have both a zero value defined and the distances between different measurements defined, for example, loss measured in dollars.

Graphical Presentation of Data

One powerful way of describing data is by displaying it on a chart. With the aid of Microsoft Excel, there are several options for displaying data graphically, depending on what information one is interested in highlighting.

For a set of discrete data, one type of graphical representation is a *bar chart*. An example of a bar chart is shown in the figure below:

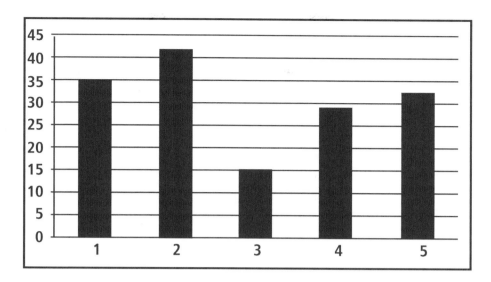

A *line graph* displays information as a series of data points connected by straight line segments. Line graphs are particularly revealing if there is trend in the data, as illustrated in the figure below:

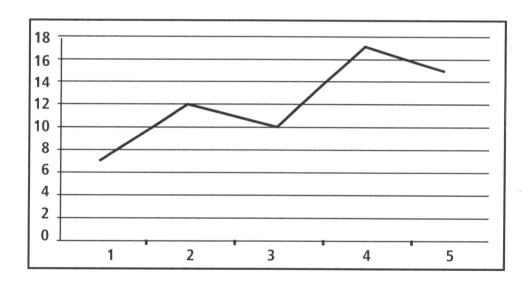

Stem and Leaf Plot

A stem and leaf plot is a graphical display of the data that lists them in ascending order and then displays the distribution within a given category. This is used as a preliminary description of the data before more detailed analysis is done. Assume we have the following set of data of the length of time (in minutes) of power outages in a city in the last year, already sorted as follows:

| 12 | 14 | 17 | 21 | 26 | 29 | 34 | 45 | 47 | 48 | 50 | 55 | 61 |

A stem-and-leaf plot of this set of data is as shown below:

1	2	4	7
2	1	6	9
3	4		
4	5	7	8
5	0	5	
6	1		

As can be seen, there are 3 data values in the teens, 3 data values in the twenties, 1 in the thirties, 3 in the forties, 2 in the fifties, and 1 in the sixties.

Frequency Distributions

Frequency distribution is a tabular summary of a data set showing the number of occurrences of each value or each class. This is true for both qualitative as well as quantitative data.

Given the following data:

12	14	17	12	26	29	34	45	17	17	50	55	50

The corresponding frequency distribution is as shown below:

X	Frequency
12	2
14	1
17	3
26	1
29	1
34	1
45	1
45	1
50	2
55	1

Measures of Central Tendency

Measures of central tendency of a set of data include the mean, the median, and the mode. The *mean* is the average value, the *median* is the middle value, and the *mode* is the value that occurs most frequently. There are two types of means – population mean, and sample mean.

Population Mean, μ, is given by:

$$\mu = \frac{x_1 + x_2 + x_3 + \ldots + x_N}{N} = \frac{1}{N}\sum_{i=1}^{N} x_i$$

where x_i = the value of the ith item and N = population size.

Sample Mean, $\bar{x}$, is given by:

$$\bar{x} = \frac{x_1 + x_2 + x_3 + ... + x_n}{n} = \frac{1}{n}\sum_{i=1}^{n} x_i$$

where n = sample size.

When working with data that is summarized in a frequency distribution comprising classes of data, the computation of the mean of the distribution is calculated using the formula:

$$\bar{x} = \frac{f_1 x_1 + f_2 x_2 + f_3 x_3 + ... + f_n x_n}{f_1 + f_2 + f_3 + ... + f_n} = \frac{\sum_{i=1}^{n} f_i x_i}{\sum_{i=1}^{n} f_i}$$

where f_i = frequency count for x_i.

Quartiles and Percentiles

Quartiles are used to split a dataset into four equal parts. One can determine the lowest 25% of the data as values below the first quartile, the lowest 50% of the data as values below the second quartile (also known as the *median*), and the lowest 75% of the data as values below the third quartile.

The pth percentile is a value such that p percent of the data are below this value.

Steps for calculating p^{th} percentile:

Step 1. Arrange the data in ascending order (rank order from smallest value to the largest value).

Step 2. Compute an index i as follows:

$$i = \frac{p}{100} \, n; \text{ where } p \text{ is the percentile of interest, and } n \text{ is the number of items.}$$

Step 3.

(a) If i *is not an integer, round up.* The next integer value greater than i indicates the position of the pth percentile.

(b) If i *is an integer*, the pth percentile is the average of the data values in positions i and $i+1$.

Boxplots are useful for revealing the center of a data set, the spread of the data, the distribution of the data, and the presence of outliers. To construct the boxplot, we require the following:

▶ The minimum value.

▶ The first quartile, Q_1.

▶ The second quartile (or median), Q_2.

▶ The third quartile, Q_3.

▶ The maximum value.

Example:

Consider a data set with the following values:

- Minimum value: 11.
- First quartile, Q_1: 33.
- Second quartile, Q_2: 60.
- Third quartile, Q_3: 75.
- Maximum value: 90.

The Boxplot is shown below:

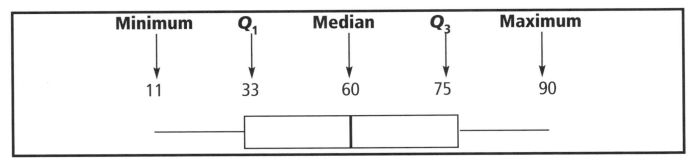

Measures of Dispersion

It is generally not sufficient to describe only the central tendency of a dataset. This does not provide any indication of the nature of the variability of the data. In order to provide this additional information, we can use measures of dispersion such as: *range*, *variance*, and *standard deviation*.

Range = Maximum value – minimum value.

Population Variance, σ², (sigma squared) is given by:

$$\sigma^2 = \frac{(x_1 - \mu)^2 + (x_2 - \mu)^2 + \ldots + (x_N - \mu)^2}{N} = \frac{1}{N}\sum_{i=1}^{N}(x_i - \mu)^2$$

Population Standard Deviation, $\sigma = \sqrt{\sigma^2}$

Sample Variance, s^2 is given by:

$$s^2 = \frac{(x_1 - \overline{x})^2 + (x_2 - \overline{x})^2 + \ldots + (x_n - \overline{x})^2}{n-1} = \frac{1}{n-1}\sum_{i=1}^{n}(x_i - \overline{x})^2$$

where (*n*-1) is called *degrees of freedom*.

Sample standard deviation, $s = \sqrt{s^2}$

We may be interested in finding out the percentage of data that falls within 1, 2, or 3 standard deviations from the mean of a set of data. The table below shows the meaning of these phrases.

Interpretation of statistical phrases:

Phrase	Meaning
Within 1 standard deviation of the mean	Between $(\bar{x} - s)$ and $(\bar{x} + s)$
Within 2 standard deviations of the mean	Between and $(\bar{x} - 2s)$ and $(\bar{x} + 2s)$
Within 3 standard deviations of the mean	Between and $(\bar{x} - 3s)$ and $(\bar{x} + 3s)$

The Empirical Rule

When it is believed that the data approximates a bell-shaped distribution, the empirical rule applies. For data having a bell-shaped distribution:

▶ Approximately 68% of the items will be within one standard deviation of the mean.

▶ Approximately 95% of the items will be within two standard deviations of the mean.

▶ Approximately 99.7% of the items will be within three standard deviations of the mean.

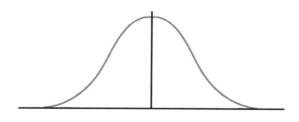

A Bell-Shaped distribution

Measures of Relative Standing: (z scores)

A *z score* is a measure of position relative to the mean. A *z* score of 2 indicates that a value is two standard deviations *above* the mean. A *z* score of -3 indicates that a value is three standard deviations *below* the mean. A *z* score is often called the *standardized value* for the item. It can be interpreted as the number of standard deviations a data point is from the mean. For example, a value *x* that corresponds to a *z* score of 1.2 is 1.2 standard deviations above the mean of *x*.

For a population, the *z* score of the ith item is given by: $z_i = \dfrac{x_i - \mu}{\sigma}$

For a sample, the *z* score of the ith item is given by: $z_i = \dfrac{x_i - \bar{x}}{s}$

Example:

The following data shows the number of calls into an emergency center every 15 minutes for 5 hours on a given day.

24	26	58	24	22	20	15	33	19	27
21	18	16	22	34	26	26	30	31	33

Compute the mean, median, mode, Q_1, Q_2, Q_3, range, inter-quartile range, variance, and standard deviation of this population.

Solution:

a. The mean is given by:

$$\bar{x} = \frac{1}{n}\sum_{i=1}^{n} x_i = \frac{525}{20} = 26.25$$

15	16	18	19	20	21	22	22	24	24
26	26	26	27	30	31	33	33	34	58

b. The median is obtained by arranging the data in ascending order.

Since the number of items is even, the median is obtained by taking the average of the 10th and 11th data points.

So the median is (24 + 26)/2 = 25

c. The mode is the most frequently occurring data value. The mode is 26.

d. Q_1 = 25th percentile. The index i = (25/100)*20 = 5. Since 5 is an integer, the 25th percentile (Q_1) is the average of the 5th and 6th data values. So Q_1 = (20 + 21)/2 = 20.5

e. Q_2 = 50th percentile. The index i = (50/100)*20 = 10. Since 10 is an integer, the 50th percentile (Q_2) is the average of the 10th and 11th data values. So Q_2 = (24 + 26)/2 = 25

f. Q_3 = 75th percentile. The index i = (75/100)*20 = 15. Since 15 is an integer, the 75th percentile (Q_3) is the average of the 15th and 16th data values. So Q_3 = (30 + 31)/2 = 30.5

g. Range = maximum – minimum = 58 – 15 = 43

h. Inter Quartile Range (IQR) = Q_3 – Q_1 = 30.5 – 20.5 = 10

i. Variance is given by

$$s^2 = \frac{1}{n-1}\sum_{i=1}^{n}(x_i - \bar{x})^2 = \frac{(x_1 - \bar{x})^2 + (x_2 - \bar{x})^2 + \dots + (x_n - \bar{x})^2}{n-1}$$

Variance = 1661.75/(20-1) = 87.46

j. Standard Deviation, $s = \sqrt{s^2} = \sqrt{87.46} = 9.35$

x_i	$(x_i - \bar{x})^2$	$(x_i - \bar{x})^2$
15	-11.25	126.5625
16	-10.25	105.0625
18	-8.25	68.0625
19	-7.25	52.5625
20	-6.25	39.0625
21	-5.25	27.5625
22	-4.25	18.0625
22	-4.25	18.0625
24	-2.25	5.0625
24	-2.25	5.0625
26	-0.25	0.0625
26	-0.25	0.0625
26	-0.25	0.0625
27	0.75	0.5625
30	3.75	14.0625
31	4.75	22.5625
33	6.75	45.5625
33	6.75	45.5625
34	7.75	60.0625
58	31.75	1008.063

$$\sum_{i=1}^{n}(x_i - \bar{x})^2 = 1661.75$$

Basic Probability Concepts

Experiment

An *experiment* is a process that yields a result or an observation. An example of an experiment is testing the functionality of a machine to determine its state.

Outcome

An *outcome* is any particular result of an experiment. An example of an outcome of an experiment is testing a machine and finding that it is in working order.

Event

An *event* is a collection of outcomes. An example is testing two machines and finding that both are in working order.

Sample Space

A *sample space* is a collection of all possible outcomes of an experiment.

Examples include:

▶ The sample space when one machine is tested: {working, not working}.

▶ The sample space when two machines are {(working, working), (working, not working), (not working, working), (not working, not working)} or if we call the working state, state 1, and the not working state, state 2, then we have {(1,1), (1,2), (2,1), (2,2)}.

▶ The sample space when the possible states of two machines are given as:

 ❖ *State 1: Working*

 ❖ *State 2 : Idle*

 ❖ *State 3: Minor repair*

 ❖ *State 4 : Major breakdown*

2nd Machine

	1	2	3	4
1	1,1	1,2	1,3	1,4
2	2,1	2,2	2,3	2,4
3	3,1	3,2	3,3	3,4
4	4,1	4,2	4,3	4,4

1st Machine

Probability

Probability is a measure of likelihood that an outcome will occur. *Relative frequency* is often used in determining probability. The probability of event A is given by the formula:

$$P(A) = \frac{\text{Number of elements in the event}}{\text{Number of elements in the sample space}} = \frac{n(A)}{n(S)}$$

Law of Large Numbers

The *Law of Large Numbers* states that as a procedure is repeated over and over again, the observed relative frequency of an event tends to approach the actual probability. For instance, if you toss a fair coin, the percentage of heads observed will tend to be approximately 50% as the number of tosses becomes larger.

Mutually Exclusive Events

Two events are *mutually exclusive* if the occurrence of one precludes the occurrence of the other. For example, it is not possible for a machine to be working and not working at the same time; therefore, they are mutually-exclusive events. If you flip a switch to turn on the light, it is not possible for the light to be on and off at the same time, so they are mutually-exclusive events.

Complementary Events

The complement of an event A is the event 'not A' denoted by $\bar{A}$. A and $\bar{A}$ are mutually exclusive and collectively exhaustive.

Probability Rules

Probability of an event cannot be negative. In other words, $P(A) \geq 0$.

The sum of the probabilities of all the events in a sample space = 1. In other words, if we have events $A_1, A_2,..., A_n$

$$P(A_1) + P(A_2) + P(A_3) +.....+ P(A_n) = 1$$

The sum of the probabilities for complementary events A and $\bar{A}$ is one.

$$P(A) + P(\bar{A}) = 1$$

Example:

Consider 3 machines, each of which can be in one of two equally likely conditions – (working, not working). Find the probability that, at least 1 of them is working.

Solution: We can develop the sample space using the schematic below:

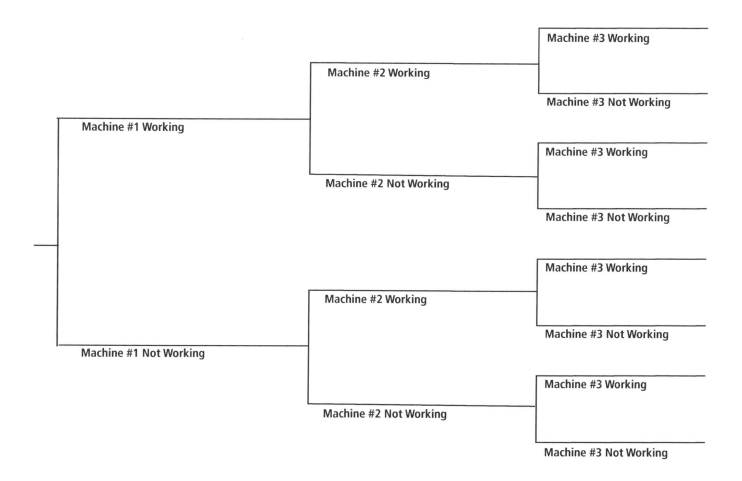

The Sample Space is shown below:

	Machine 1	Machine 2	Machine 3
1.	Working	Working	Working
2.	Working	Working	Not Working
3.	Working	Not Working	Working
4.	Working	Not Working	Not Working
5.	Not Working	Working	Working
6.	Not Working	Working	Not Working
7.	Not Working	Not Working	Working
8.	Not Working	Not Working	Not Working

The number of equally likely elements in the sample space is 8. The number of elements with at least 1 machine is working is 7.

Let *A* represent the event that no machine is working.

Then $\bar{A}$ represents the event that at least one machine is working.

Then we have:

[Probability of no machine working] + [Probability of at least one machine working] =1

$$P(A) + P(\bar{A}) = 1$$

$$P(A) = 1/8, \text{ therefore, } P(\bar{A}) = 1 - 1/8 = 7/8.$$

The Addition Rule

Consider two events *A* and *B* as shown in the Venn diagram below:

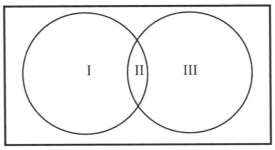

Event *A* occupies regions I and II.
Event *B* occupies regions II and III.

The *addition rule* states,

$$P(A \ or \ B) = P(A) + P(B) - P(A \ and \ B).$$

The last term ensures that region II is not counted twice.

If A and B are mutually exclusive, then

$$P(A \text{ or } B) = P(A) + P(B)$$

In general, if there are n mutually exclusive events, then

$$P(A_1 \text{ or } A_2 \text{ or } A_3 \ldots \text{ or } A_n) = P(A_1) + P(A_2) + P(A_3) + \ldots + P(A_n).$$

Example:

20 candidates apply for a business continuity position.

Let: C = event that a candidate selected at random is certified.

        N = event that a candidate selected at random is not certified.

        M = event that a candidate selected at random has a masters degree.

        B = event that a candidate selected at random has a bachelors degree.

Given the data:

	M	**B**	**Total**
C	4	7	**11**
N	5	4	**9**
Total	**9**	**11**	**20**

The corresponding Probability table is shown below:

	M	**B**	**Total**
C	.20	.35	**.55**
N	.25	.20	**.45**
Total	**.45**	**.55**	**1.00**

Find the probability that a randomly selected candidate:

    a) is certified: $P(C)$.

    b) has a masters degree: $P(M)$.

    c) has a masters degree $P(M)$ *and* is certified: $P(M \text{ and } C)$.

    d) has a masters degree *or* is certified: $P(M \text{ or } C)$.

Solution:

a) $P(C) = 11/20 = 0.55$

b) $P(M) = 9/20 = 0.45$

c) $P(M \text{ and } C) = 4/20 = 0.20$

d) $P(M \text{ or } C) = P(M) + P(C) - P(M \text{ and } C) = 0.45 + 0.55 - 0.20 = 0.80$

Marginal, Joint and Conditional Probabilities

Let:

$P(A)$ = probability of event A (*marginal probability*).

$P(B)$ = probability of event B (*marginal probability*).

$P(A \text{ and } B)$ = probability of event A and event B (*joint probability*).

$P(A|B)$ = probability of event A given event B (*conditional probability*).

$P(B|A)$ = probability of event B given event A (*conditional probability*).

Independent Events

Two events A and B are independent if the occurrence of one does not affect the probability of the occurrence of the other. For any two events A and B,

$$P(A \text{ and } B) = P(A) \bullet P(B/A) \qquad\qquad \text{Thus } P(B/A) = \frac{P(A \text{ and } B)}{P(A)}$$

$$P(A \text{ and } B) = P(B) \bullet P(A/B) \qquad\qquad \text{Thus } P(A/B) = \frac{P(A \text{ and } B)}{P(B)}$$

If A and B are independent, then

$$P(A \text{ and } B) = P(A) \bullet P(B)$$

In general, if A, B, C,..., Z are independent, then

$$P(A \text{ and } B \text{ and } C \text{ and } ... \text{ and } Z) = P(A)P(B)P(C) ... P(Z)$$

Note: Always distinguish between mutually exclusive events and independent events. Two events with non-zero probabilities cannot be both mutually exclusive and independent. If one mutually-exclusive event occurs, the probability of occurrence of the other is reduced to zero. This implies that the events are dependent.

Note: It is often convenient in computing the probability of "at least one" to use its complementary event. The probability of "at least one" is equivalent to (1 − probability of none).

Multiplication Rule

The *multiplication rule* states that the probability of events A and B occurring, $P(A$ and $B)$, is given by the equation:

$$P(A \text{ and } B) = P(A) \cdot P(B|A)$$

That is, the joint probability of A *and* B is the marginal probability of A multiplied by the conditional probability of B given A.

Basic Counting Principles: If an experiment is composed of 2 trials, where one trial has m possible outcomes and the other trial has n possible outcomes, then there are $m \times n$ possible outcomes of the experiment.

General Counting Rule: If an experiment comprises k trials where:

1st trial has n_1 possible outcomes;

2nd trial has n_2 possible outcomes;
.
.
k^{th} trial has n_k possible outcomes;

Then there are $n_1 \cdot n_2 \cdot n_3 \cdot ... \cdot n_k$ possible outcomes of the experiment.

Permutation

A *permutation* is number of ways an ordered arrangement of r objects can be selected from n distinct objects and is given by $_nP_r$.

Example:

A team leader and an alternate are to be selected from a group of 6 individuals. How many ways can this be done.

Solution:

This is a permutation since the order does matter, so we have: $_6P_2 = 30$
The Excel function PERMUT() can be used in calculating permutations.

Combination

A *combination* is the number of ways that r objects can be selected from n distinct objects, without regard to order, and is given by $_nC_r$.

Example:

In how many ways can a 5-person team be selected from a department of 30 such that there are 2 team leaders and 3 members?

Solution:

The number of ways is given by $_{30}C_2 *_{28}C_3 = 1,425,060$
The Excel function COMBIN() can be used in calculating combinations.

Bayes' Theorem

Often we perform analysis based on *prior probability* estimates. Then from sources such as a sample, a special report, or product test, we obtain additional information about the events. Given this information, we update the prior probability values by calculating revised probabilities known as *posterior probabilities*. *Bayes' Theorem* is used to make these probability calculations.

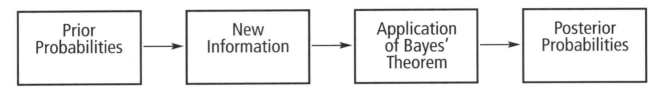

Example:
Consider that 2 different plants produce identical components.

Let D denote the event that the component is manufactured in Detroit.

Let R denote the event that the component is manufactured in Raleigh.

Assume that currently 55% of the components are manufactured in Detroit; thus $P(D)$ = .55

Assume that currently 45% of the components are manufactured in Raleigh; thus $P(R)$ = .45

Based on historical data, we have the following conditional probabilities, given the place of manufacture:

	Component State	
	Operational	**Malfunction**
Manufactured in Detroit	.98	.02
Manufactured in Raleigh	.05	.95

a. What is the probability that a randomly selected component, in an operational state, was manufactured in Detroit? What is the probability that a randomly selected component, in an operational state, was manufactured in Raleigh?

b. What is the probability that a randomly selected component, in a state of malfunction, was manufactured in Detroit? What is the probability that a randomly selected component, in a state of malfunction, was manufactured in Raleigh?

Solution:

Let:

D = Detroit

R = Raleigh

O = operational

M = malfunction.

We know

$$P(D \, / \, O) = \frac{P(D \text{ and } O)}{P(O)}$$

and

$$P(D \text{ and } O) = P(D) * P(O \, / \, D)$$

Likewise

$$P(R \, / \, O) = \frac{P(R \text{ and } O)}{P(O)}$$

and

$$P(R \text{ and } O) = P(R) * P(O \, / \, R)$$

Also,

$$P(O) = P(D \text{ and } O) + P(R \text{ and } O)$$
$$= P(D) * (O \, / \, D) + P(R) * P(O \, / \, R)$$

Combining terms, we have

$$P(D \, / \, O) = \frac{P(D) * P(O \, / \, D)}{P(D) * P(O \, / \, D) + P(R) * P(O \, / \, R)}$$

Similarly,

$$P(R \, / \, O) = \frac{P(R) * P(O \, / \, R)}{P(D) * P(O \, / \, D) + P(R) * P(O \, / \, R)}$$

In summary, we have:

Operational

Plant	Prior Probability	Conditional Probability	Joint Probability	Posterior Probability
D	$P(D) = .55$	$P(O/D)=.98$	$P(D \text{ and } O) = P(D) * P(O / D)$ $= (.55) * (.98) = .5390$	$P(D / O) = \dfrac{P(D \text{ and } O)}{P(O)}$ $= \dfrac{.5390}{.5615} = .9599$
R	$P(R) = .45$	$P(O/R)=.05$	$P(R \text{ and } O) = P(R) * P(O / R)$ $= (.45) * (.05) = .0225$	$P(R / O) = \dfrac{P(R \text{ and } O)}{P(O)}$ $= \dfrac{.0225}{.5615} = .0401$
			$P(O) = P(D \text{ and } O) + P(R \text{ and } O)$ $= .5390 + .0225 = .5615$	

Malfunction

Plant	Prior Probability	Conditional Probability	Joint Probability	Posterior Probability
D	$P(D) = .55$	$P(M/D)=.02$	$P(D \text{ and } M) = P(D) * P(M / D)$ $= (.55) * (.02) = .011$	$P(D / M) = \dfrac{P(D \text{ and } M)}{P(M)}$ $= \dfrac{.011}{.4385} = .0251$
R	$P(R) = .45$	$P(M/R)=.95$	$P(R \text{ and } M) = P(R) * P(M / R)$ $= (.45) * (.95) = .4275$	$P(R / M) = \dfrac{P(R \text{ and } M)}{P(M)}$ $= \dfrac{.4275}{.4385} = .9749$
			$P(M) = P(D \text{ and } M) + P(R \text{ and } M)$ $= .011 + .4275 = .4385$	

The probability tree below provides a graphic illustration of marginal, conditional and joint probabilities.

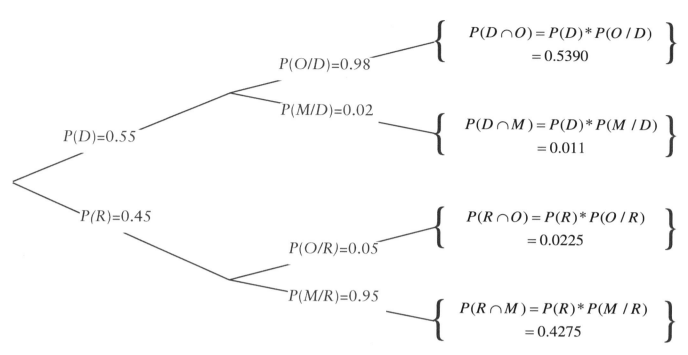

$$\left\{ \begin{array}{c} P(D \cap O) = P(D) * P(O \,/\, D) \\ = 0.5390 \end{array} \right\}$$

$P(O/D)=0.98$

$P(M/D)=0.02$

$$\left\{ \begin{array}{c} P(D \cap M) = P(D) * P(M \,/\, D) \\ = 0.011 \end{array} \right\}$$

$P(D)=0.55$

$P(R)=0.45$

$$\left\{ \begin{array}{c} P(R \cap O) = P(R) * P(O \,/\, R) \\ = 0.0225 \end{array} \right\}$$

$P(O/R)=0.05$

$P(M/R)=0.95$

$$\left\{ \begin{array}{c} P(R \cap M) = P(R) * P(M \,/\, R) \\ = 0.4275 \end{array} \right\}$$

Discrete Probability Distributions

Definition of a Random Variable:

A *random variable* is a variable that assumes a unique numerical value for each of the outcomes in the sample space of an experiment.

Examples:

a) We attempt to start a machine 5 times and observe the number of failures (failure means "does not start").

Let the random variable x represent the number of failures.

Then x: {0, 1, 2, 3, 4, 5}

Note that the possible values of x form a *finite* set.

b) Consider the number of customers that arrive at a bank in a given time period.

Let the random variable x represent the number of customers that arrive.

Then x: {0, 1, 2, 3, ...}

In this case, the possible values of x form an *infinite* set.

Discrete Random Variable

A *discrete random variable* is a random variable that has a countable number of values. It therefore has a one-to-one correspondence with the set of integers.

For example, the number of defective components in a set of components can be described as a discrete random variable. The number of students that pass a statistics examination is another example of a discrete random variable.

Continuous Random Variable

A *continuous random variable* is a random variable that can assume values corresponding to any of the points contained in one or more intervals.

Example: The time between arrivals of successive customers at a bank is a continuous random variable.

Probability Distribution

A probability distribution is a description that assigns probability values to each value of a random variable.

Probability Distribution of a Discrete Random Variable

Consider that you toss a fair coin 2 times. Define the random variable x to be the number of heads observed.

The sample space of two trials is {*TT, TH, HT, HH*}, with each outcome having a probability of $0.5 \bullet 0.5 = 0.25$.

The possible values of x are {0, 1, 2}.

Therefore:

$$P(x= 0) = P(TT) = 0.25$$

$$P(x= 1) = P(TH) + P(HT) = 0.25 + 0.25 = 0.50$$

$$P(x= 2) = P(HH) = 0.25.$$

The probability distribution is:

x	P(x)
0	0.25
1	0.50
2	0.25
Sum	1.00

Examples of discrete probability distributions are:

1. Bernoulli trial.

2. Binomial Probability Distribution.

3. Poisson Probability Distribution.

Bernoulli Distribution

A *Bernoulli distribution* has 2 possible outcomes. For example, a machine may either start ("success") or not start ("failure") in one attempt.

Binomial Distribution

The number of "successes" in *n* independent and identical Bernoulli trials follows a *binomial* distribution.

Let:

n = the number of independent trials (*n* is fixed).

p = the probability of "success" at each trial.

q = the probability of "failure" at each trial (Note $p + q = 1$, so $q = 1 - p$).

x = number of "successes" in *n* trials (*x* is a random variable).

$P(x)$ = the probability of getting exactly *x* "successes" in *n* trials ($x \leq n$).

Then $P(x)$ follows a binomial distribution with probability function given by:

$$P(x) = \binom{n}{x} p^x (1-p)^{n-x}$$

Example:

Historically, 95% of the computers in a computer laboratory are up and running. Find the probability that in a computer laboratory with 100 computers, 8 are defective.

Solution:

This is a binomial experiment so we will solve it using the binomial formula.

We have: $n = 100$, $x = 8$, $p = 5\%$ or 0.05. The probability of 8 defective computers out of 100 is:

$$P(8) = \binom{100}{8}(0.05)^8 \ (1-0.05)^{100-8} = 0.0649$$

Example:

The probability that a machine is defective is 0.1. If 10 machines are tested for their working condition, what is the probability that exactly 7 are defect-free?

Solution:

This is a binomial experiment so we will solve it using the binomial formula.

We have:

$n = 10$

$p = 0.1$

$q = (1-p) = (1-0.1) = 0.9$

$x = 3$ (If 7 are defect-free, then 3 are defective; so $x = 3$)

So we have:

$$P(3) = \binom{10}{3}(0.1)^3(1-0.1)^{10-3} = 0.05739$$

The Excel function BINOMDIST() can be used in calculating binomial probabilities.

Poisson Distribution

Often we are interested in the number occurrences of independent events in a given "space" ("space" can be time, volume, length, area, or any continuous environment). The *Poisson distribution* is useful is this case. The random variable that corresponds to these occurrences is called a Poisson random variable with parameter λ (lambda) that represents the average rate at which the event occurs.

The formula to calculate probabilities associated with a Poisson distribution is given by:

$$P(x,\lambda) = \frac{\lambda^x e^{-\lambda}}{x!}$$

where e is a constant equal to approximately 2.71828.

Example:

The average number of times a machine fails during operation in any given 6 month period is 2. What is the probability that the machine does not fail during operation in the next 6 months?

Solution:

This is a Poisson distribution in which we have: $\lambda = 2$, $x = 0$.

So we have:

$$P(0,2) = \frac{2^0 e^{-2}}{0!} = 0.1353$$

Thus, the probability that the machine does not fail during operation in the next 6 months is 0.1353 or 13.5%. Note that: $2^0 = 1$ and $0! = 1$. The Excel function POISSON() can be used in calculating Poisson probabilities.

A *cumulative Poisson probability* refers to the probability that the Poisson random variable is less than some specified upper limit.

Example:

The average number of times a machine fails during operation in any given 6 month period is 2. What is the probability that there are less than 2 machine failures in the next 6 months?

Solution:

This is a Poisson experiment in which $\lambda = 2$. Let x = number of machine failures in the next 6 months.

$$P(x < 2) = P(x \leq 1) = P(x = 0) + P(x = 1)$$
$$= \frac{2^0 e^{-2}}{0!} + \frac{2^1 e^{-2}}{1!}$$
$$= 0.1353 + 0.2707 = 0.4060$$

Thus, the probability that less than 2 machines fail in the next 6 months is 0.4060.

Continuous Probability Distributions

Continuous probability distribution models have applications in business and the social sciences. Examples of continuous probability distributions include: the time it takes to clean up a disaster; and, the loss (in dollars) incurred because of a disaster.

Normal Distribution

The *Normal Probability Distribution* is commonly used to describe continuous random variables. The normal probability distribution has the following properties:

1. It is "bell-shaped" and symmetrical in appearance.

2. Its measures of central tendency (mean, median, mode, midrange) are identical.

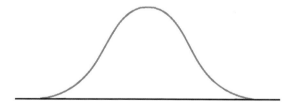

In order to be able to calculate probabilities associated with a Normal random variable, it is necessary to first obtain the corresponding *Standard Normal variable*.

Standard Normal Probability Distribution

If x is distributed normally with a mean μ, and variance σ^2, then z is a standard normal random variable with mean 0, and variance 1 and is given by

$$z = \frac{x - \mu}{\sigma}$$

Conversely, if z is a standard normal distribution, then the corresponding normal variable is given by

$$x = \sigma z + \mu$$

is a normal random variable with mean μ and variance σ².

Example:

Historically, the average duration of a power outage in a particular location is 25 minutes, with a standard deviation of 8 minutes. If the distribution of power outage durations is normally-distributed, find the probability that next year, this location will have:

    a. A power outage of at least 28 minutes duration.

    b. A power outage of between 15 and 30 minutes duration.

Solution:

    a. Let x be the duration of the power outage.

      We are required to determine the probability that x is greater than 20.

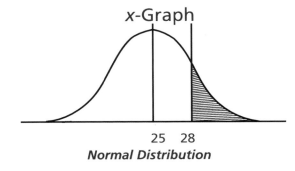

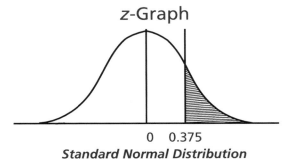

$$P(x > 28) = P\left(\frac{x - \mu}{\sigma} > \frac{28 - 25}{8}\right)$$
$$= P(z \geq 0.375) = 0.3520$$

b) The probability that x takes on the values between 15 and 30 can be written as:

$$P(15 \leq x \leq 30) = P\left(\frac{15 - 25}{8} \leq \frac{x - \mu}{\sigma} \leq \frac{30 - 25}{8}\right)$$
$$= P(-1.25 \leq z \leq 0.625) = 0.6301$$

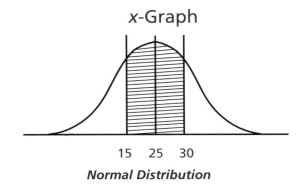

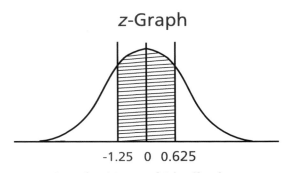

The Excel functions NORMDIST(), NORMINV(), NORMSDIST() and NORMSINV can be used in calculating Normal probabilities.

Exponential Distribution

Another continuous distribution that is useful in the analysis of risk is the *exponential distribution*. An example of an exponentially distributed random variable is the *inter-arrival time*, that is, the time between arrivals of successive events. The probability density function of the exponential distribution is given by:

$$f_T(t) = \begin{cases} \mu e^{-\mu t}, & for\ t \geq 0 \\ 0, & for\ t < 0. \end{cases}$$

where: μ = rate parameter.
$\quad\quad$ T = exponentially distributed random variable.
$\quad\quad$ t = specific value of T.

Graphically we have:

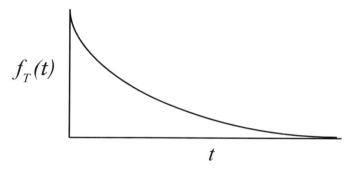

As with the normal distribution, the probability that an exponentially-distributed random variable takes on a value in any interval is given by the area under the curve of the distribution. The corresponding expression for the cumulative distribution function is given by:

$$P(T \leq t) = 1 - e^{-\mu t}$$
$$and$$
$$P(T > t) = e^{-\mu t}, for\ t \geq 0.$$

The mean or expected value of an exponentially distributed random variable T with rate parameter μ is given by:

$$E(T) = \frac{1}{\mu}$$

This makes sense; if a machine breaks down at an average rate of twice per year, for example, then we would expect it to function properly for 6 months on the average.

The variance of T is given by:

$$Var(T) = \frac{1}{\mu^2}$$

Example:

Assume that a machine breaks down at an average rate of twice per year ($\mu = 2$) and that the exponential distribution is a valid model for the situation. Find the probability that the next failure occurs:

    a. within the next year.

    b. after 4 years from now.

    c. between 3 and 5 years from now.

Solution:

    a. $P(T \leq t) = 1 - e^{-\mu t} = 1 - e^{-(2)(1)} = 1 - 0.135 = 0.865$

    b. $P(T > 4) = e^{-\mu t} = e^{-(2)(4)} = 0.000335$

    c. $P(3 \leq t \leq 5) = P(T > 3) - P(T > 5) = e^{-(2)(3)} - e^{-(2)(5)} = 0.002479 - 0.000045 = 0.00243$

The Excel function EXPONDIST( ) can be used in calculating exponential probabilities.

Review Topics

1. Describe how to calculate the mean, median and mode.

2. Define the range, variance and standard deviation.

3. What is the purpose of taking a random sample?

4. Discuss some uses of Bayes' theorem.

5. Give some applications of the binomial distribution.

6. What are the characteristics of a Poisson distribution?

7. Give some examples of the normal distribution.

8. Discuss how the exponential distribution can be applied.

Bibliography

Albright, S., Winston, W. and Zappe, C., *Data Analysis and Decision Making with Microsoft Excel*, South Western Cengage Learning, Mason, Ohio, 2009.

Anderson, D., Sweeney, D., and Williams, T., *Statistics for Business and Economics*, South-Western Cengage Learning, Mason, Ohio, 2011.

Soluade, O. A., *Computer Models in Production and Operations Management*, 3rd Edition, McGraw-Hill Publishing Company, 1996.

CHAPTER XV

Statistical Applications in Risk Management*

Objectives

» Define the fundamentals of statistical forecasting

» Explore the use of regression analysis

» Review probability applications in operations maintenance

» Examine the development and use of reliability models.

Chapter prepared by Ore A. Soluade, PhD.

Forecasting Techniques

Statistical forecasting provides useful techniques that may be used when empirical data is available. The time horizon for a forecast can be *short-range, medium-range* or *long-range*.

A *time series* is a sequence of data points evenly spaced over time. The spacing of the data points can be any consistent length of time that is suitable for the problem and the available data. Two basic time series forecasting techniques are:

▶ Moving Average.

▶ Exponential Smoothing.

Given a time series of actual values, the objective is to develop a forecast. The notation we will use is as follows:

A_t = actual value for period t.
F_t = forecast for period t.
n = number of actual values.

Forecast error measurements are used in determining the accuracy of a forecasting technique. The basic formulations of error measurements are given below:

Forecast error for period t:

$$e_t = A_t - F_t$$

Average error:

$$AE = \frac{\Sigma(A_t - F_t)}{n}$$

Mean squared error:

$$MSE = \frac{\Sigma(A_t - F_t)^2}{n}$$

Mean absolute deviation:

$$MAD = \frac{\Sigma|A_t - F_t|}{n}$$

Mean absolute percentage error:

$$MAPE = \frac{\Sigma 100|A_t - F_t|/A_t}{n}$$

Moving Average

The forecasted value using the *simple moving average* is the average of the most recent values in the time series. The *weighted moving average* is a generalization of the simple moving average where the weights applied to prior actual values may be different. Typically, newer data receives a higher weight. Each weight must be positive and the sum of the weights must sum to 1.

To illustrate, consider a 3-period weighted moving average:

$$F_t = w_1 A_{t-1} + w_2 A_{t-2} + w_3 A_{t-3}$$

where w_i is the weight used for the actual value i periods prior to forecasted period. The sum of the w_i must be one and each w_i must be between 0 and 1.

Example:

The table below shows the number of events (e.g. component failures) in the last ten periods. We will forecast the number of events for period 11 using a weighted moving average.

Period	1	2	3	4	5	6	7	8	9	10
Number of events	30	27	29	33	26	27	28	30	31	29

The results are displayed in the table below using $w_1 = 0.5$, $w_2 = 0.3$, $w_3 = 0.2$ and the model:

$$F_t = 0.5 A_{t-1} + 0.3 A_{t-2} + 0.2 A_{t-3}$$

3-period Weighted Moving Average

t	A_t	F_t	$A_t - F_t$	$(A_t - F_t)^2$	$|A_t - F_t|$	$100|A_t - F_t|/A_t$
1	30					
2	27					
3	29					
4	33	28.60	4.40	19.36	4.40	13.33
5	26	30.60	-4.60	21.16	4.60	17.69
6	27	28.70	-1.70	2.89	1.70	6.30
7	28	27.90	0.10	0.01	0.10	0.36
8	30	27.30	2.70	7.29	2.70	9.00
9	31	28.80	2.20	4.84	2.20	7.10
10	29	30.10	-1.10	1.21	1.10	3.79
11		29.80				
		Total	2.00	56.76	16.80	57.57
		Average	0.29	8.11	2.40	8.22

The forecast for period 11 using the weighted moving average is 29.80 = 30, with error measurement: *AE* = 0.29, *MSE* = 8.11, *MAD* = 2.40 and *MAPE* = 8.22%.

Exponential Smoothing

Exponential smoothing is a weighted moving average forecasting method in which the weights are determined by an exponential decay function. In this case, the forecasting formula is given by:

$$F_t = \alpha A_{t-1} + (1 - \alpha)F_{t-1}$$

where α = smoothing constant between 0 and 1.

Example:

The table below shows the number of events (e.g. component failures) in the last ten periods. We will forecast the number of events for period 11 using exponential smoothing.

Period	1	2	3	4	5	6	7	8	9	10
Number of events	30	27	29	33	26	27	28	30	31	29

The results are displayed in the table below using an exponential smoothing constant, α = 0.3, and assuming an initial F_1 = 30.00.

Exponential Smoothing

t	A_t	F_t	$A_t - F_t$	$(A_t - F_t)^2$	$\|A_t - F_t\|$	$100\|A_t - F_t\|/A_t$
1	30	30.00	0.00			
2	27	30.00	-3.00	9.00	3.00	11.11
3	29	29.70	-0.70	0.49	0.70	2.41
4	33	29.63	3.37	11.36	3.37	10.21
5	26	29.97	-3.97	15.74	3.97	15.26
6	27	29.57	-2.57	6.61	2.57	9.52
7	28	29.31	-1.31	1.72	1.31	4.69
8	30	29.18	0.82	0.67	0.82	2.73
9	31	29.26	-7.36	45.58	15.74	50.77
10	29	28.53	-0.92	5.70	1.97	6.78
11		28.44				
		Total	**-11.95**	**87.38**	**29.74**	**99.96**
		Average	**-1.33**	**9.71**	**3.30**	**11.11**

The forecast for period 11 using the exponential smoothing is 28.44 = 28, and error measurements: *AE* = -1.33, *MSE* = 9.71, *MAD* = 3.30 and *MAPE* = 11.11%.

Regression Analysis

Regression analysis is a statistical procedure for developing a mathematical equation showing the relationship between two or more variables. *Simple regression* is a statistical technique that determines the relationship between one *independent variable*, *x*, and one *dependent variable*, *y*. A *simple linear regression* is of the form:

$$\hat{y} = b_0 + b_1 x$$

where:

x = independent variable.

y = dependent variable.

$\hat{y}$ = estimated value of y.

b_0 = y intercept of the estimated regression line.

b_1 = slope of the estimated regression line.

To estimate a regression line, a sample of n values (x_i, y_i) is taken. The *sample means* of the *n* values of the variables *x* and *y* calculated from the data are:

$$\bar{x} = \frac{\sum x_i}{N}, \text{ and } \bar{y} = \frac{\sum y_i}{N}$$

The criterion used to determine the values for the b_0 and b_1 that make the regression line fit best with the data (x_i, y_i) is to minimize the *sum of the squares* of the deviations ('*least squares*') between the actual values of the dependent variable, y_i, and the estimated values of the dependent variable, $\hat{y}$, as determined by the regression. The criterion for the least squares method is:

$$min \sum (y_i - \hat{y}_i)^2.$$

Statistics useful in estimating the regression line and determining its significance are:

Slope of the regression line:

$$b_1 = \frac{\sum (x_i - \bar{x})(y_i - \bar{y})}{\sum (x_i - \bar{x})^2}$$

y-intercept of the regression line:

$$b_o = \bar{y} - b_1\bar{x}$$

Sum of squares due to error:

$$SSE = \sum (y_i - \hat{y}_i)^2$$

Sum of squares due to regression:

$$SSR = \sum (\hat{y}_i - \bar{y})^2$$

Total sum of squares:

$$SST = \sum (y_i - \bar{y})^2$$
$$SST = SSR + SSE$$

Coefficient of determination:

$$r^2 = \frac{SSR}{SST}$$

Sample correlation coefficient:

$$r = (\text{sign of } b_1)\sqrt{r^2}$$

Mean square error:

$$s^2 = MSE = \frac{SSE}{n-2}$$

Standard error of the estimate:

$$s = \sqrt{MSE}$$

Estimated standard deviation of b_1:

$$s_{b_1} = \frac{s}{\sqrt{\sum(x_i - \bar{x})^2}}$$

t test statistic:

$$t = \frac{b_1}{s_{b_1}}$$

Mean square regression:

$$MSR = \frac{SSR}{number\ of\ independent\ variables}$$

F test statistic:

$$F = \frac{MSR}{MSE}$$

Multiple regression is a statistical technique that shows the relationship between one dependent variable and several independent variables. The standard form of the *multiple linear regression* equation is:

$$\hat{y} = b_0 + b_1 x_1 + b_2 x_2 + ... + b_n x_n$$

where b_0, b_1, ..., b_n are the regression coefficients, x_1, x_2,..., x_n are the independent variables, and $\hat{y}$ is the estimated value of y.

Example:

We will estimate a regression line for the variables in the table below:

Temperature (0F)	68	75	63	80	74	60	87	90	86	73
Number of Failures	2	7	4	8	6	3	9	9	7	6

Using a simple linear regression:

$$\hat{y} = b_0 + b_1 x$$

where: x = temperature, and y = number of failures.

Excel's Data Analysis-Regression results are presented on the next page.

Regression

Regression Statistics					
Multiple *R*	0.892				
R Square	0.796				
Adjusted *R* Square	0.771				
Standard Error	1.160				
Observations	10				
ANOVA					
	df	*SS*	*MS*	*F*	*Significance F*
Regression	1	42.126	42.126	31.280	0.001
Residual	8	10.774	1.347		
Total	9	52.900			
	Coefficients	*Standard Error*	*t Stat*	*P-value*	
Intercept	-9.952	2.893	-3.439	0.009	
X Variable 1	0.212	0.038	5.593	0.001	

From the above table we observe the statistics:

$b_1 = 0.212$	$b_0 = -9.952$	$SSE = 10.774$
$SSR = 42.126$	$SST = 52.900$	$r^2 = 0.796$
$r = 0.892$	$MSE = 1.347$	$s = 1.160$
$s_{b_1} = 0.038$	$t = 5.593$	$MSR = 42.126$
$F = 31.280$	Significance of $F = 0.001$	

The estimated regression line is:

$$\hat{y} = -9.952 + 0.212x.$$

The regression is significant since the significance of $F = 0.001$ (values less than 0.05 are typically considered significant).

Maintenance Modeling

It is important to continuously monitor the activities of an organization to minimize cost as well as risk. Failure to do so can result in higher cost, greater risk, and damaged reputation. In order to improve the reliability of a system, all the components have to be working in harmony.

Maintenance is the activity involved in ensuring that all the components of a system are in proper working condition.

Typically the greater the commitment to *preventive maintenance*, the greater the maintenance cost, however the resulting system failure cost will decrease due to fewer and less costly failures. This is illustrated in the graph below. The idea behind maintenance is to ensure the continued proper functioning of a system. With preventive maintenance, activities are carried out prior to breakdown. Cost is an important factor in the decision regarding the commitment to preventive maintenance. Preventive maintenance requires proper monitoring and detailed attention to the performance of each component in a system.

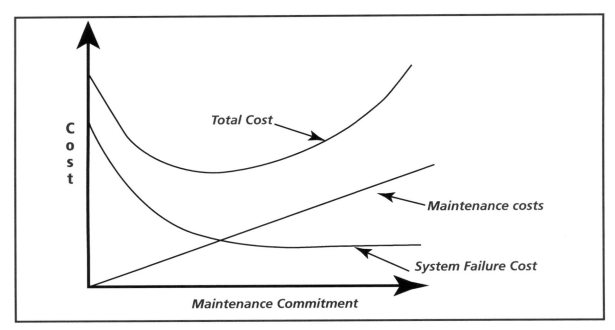

Example:

The current maintenance plan costs $100 per month and over the past 24 months the system has failed at the rate indicated in the following table:

Number of System Failures	Number of Months that Failures Occurred
0	6
1	6
2	8
3	4
	Total = 24

Each failure results in a failure cost of $400. A new proposed maintenance plan cost $200 per month and is expected to result in an average system failure rate of once every two months. Should the new maintenance plan be implemented?

Solution:

Using the current maintenance plan, the expected number of system failures per month is:

$$\begin{bmatrix} Expected\ number \\ of\ failures \end{bmatrix} = \Sigma \left[\begin{pmatrix} Number \\ of\ failures \end{pmatrix} x \begin{pmatrix} Relative \\ frequency \end{pmatrix} \right]$$

= (0) (6/24) + (1) (6/24) + (2) (8/24) + (3) (4/24) = 1.42 system failures per month

Using the current maintenance plan:

Expected cost per month = System failure cost + Maintenance cost = (400) (1.42) + 100 = $667.

Under the proposed maintenance plan, the expected number of system failures per month would be 0.5.

Using the proposed maintenance plan:

Expected cost per month = System failure cost + Maintenance cost = (400) (0.5) + 200 = $400.

The proposed maintenance plan should be implemented.

Reliability Modeling

A system is an interconnection of components, arranged to a specific design in order to perform certain functions with acceptable performance. *Component reliability* is the percentage of time that the component performs as intended. *System reliability* is the percentage of time that the system performs as intended.

Failure rate (FR) is a basic measure of reliability and may be represented as:

Failure rate percentage:

$$FR(\%) = \frac{Number\ of\ failures}{Number\ of\ units\ tested} \times 100\%$$

Number of failures per unit time:

$$FR(N) = \frac{Number\ of\ failures}{Number\ of\ units\text{-}hours}$$

The *mean time between failures (MTBF)* is given by:

$$MTBF = \frac{1}{FR(N)}$$

Example:

40 machines are tested for 1000 hours for their reliability. One failed after 300 hours, another failed after 400 hours. Find the failure rate.

Solution:

$$FR(\%) = \frac{2}{40}(100\%) = 5\%$$

To calculate *FR(N)*, we first need to obtain the number of unit-hours of operating time, which is (40) (1000) - 700 - 600 = 38,700 unit-hours.

$$FR(N) = \frac{2}{38,700} = 0.000052\ failures/unit\text{-}hour$$

$$MTBF = \frac{1}{0.000052} = 19,350\ hours$$

System Reliability

Components of a system may be arranged in series and parallel in order to achieve functionality and redundancy.

Example: Series System

Consider a system with 3 components in series as shown in the figure below:

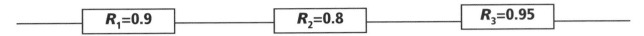

A series system fails if any of the components fails. Likewise, all components of the system must function as intended in order for the system to be successful.

Let R_i be the reliability for component i. Assuming that all the components' reliabilities are independent of each other, then:

$$\text{System Reliability} = R_1 \cdot R_2 \cdot R_3 = (0.9)\,(0.8)\,(0.95) = 0.684 \text{ or } 68.4\%.$$

It is observed that the system reliability is less than the reliability of any of its components.

Example: Parallel System

Consider a system with 3 components connected in parallel as shown in the figure below:

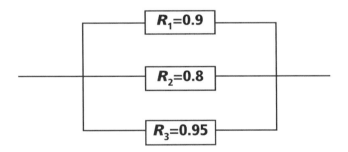

$$\begin{aligned}
\text{System Reliability} &= 1 - [(1 - R_1)\,(1 - R_2)\,(1 - R_3)] \\
&= 1 - [(0.1)\,(0.2)\,(0.05)] \\
&= 1 - 0.001 = 0.999 \text{ or } 99.9\%.
\end{aligned}$$

In general, parallel systems are used to provide redundancy in the event of component failure.

Example: Hybrid System

Assume that the series system introduced earlier now has redundant components added. We have three components whose reliabilities are R_1, R_2, and R_3 respectively, connected in series; with component R_1 having a backup component with reliability R_4, and component R_2 having a backup component with reliability R_5, as shown in the figure below:

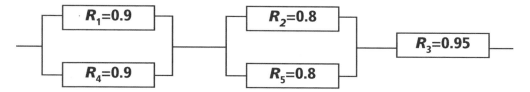

The subsystem with R_1 and R_4, has a subsystem reliability of:

$$R_{1-4} = 1 - P(both\ 1\ and\ 4\ fail) = 1 - (1 - 0.9)(1 - 0.9) = 1 - (0.1)(0.1) = 1 - 0.01 = 0.99$$

The subsystem with R_2 and R_5, has a subsystem reliability of:

$$R_{2-5} = 1 - P(both\ 2\ and\ 5\ fail) = 1 - (1 - 0.8)(1 - 0.8) = 1 - (0.2)(0.2) = 1 - 0.04 = 0.96.$$

The system reliability then is equivalently represented in the figure below:

| $R_{1-4}=0.99$ | $R_{2-5}=0.96$ | $R_3=0.95$ |

System Reliability = (0.99) (0.96) (0.95) = 0.90288 or 90.3%.

As a result of redundancy, the system reliability improves from 68.4% to 90.3%.

Review Topics

1. What is the relationship between planning and forecasting? How can statistical forecasting provide support in risk management?

2. Explore the uses of regression analysis as a tool for risk and business continuity management.

3. Discuss how improper maintenance policies lead to business continuity problems.

4. Discuss how reliability models are used to provide information to support decisions regarding systems availability.

Bibliography

Albright, Winston and Zappe, *Data Analysis and Decision Making with Microsoft Excel*, South Western Cengage Learning, 2009.

Anderson, D., Sweeney, D., and Williams, T., *Statistics for Business and Economics*, South-Western Cengage Learning, 2011.

Heizer, J. and Render, B., *Operations Management*, Prentice Hall, Upper Saddle River, New Jersey, 2011.

Soluade, O. A., *Computer Models in Production and Operations Management*, 3rd Edition, McGraw-Hill Publishing Company, 1996.

CHAPTER XVI

Simulation Modeling and Supply Chain Risk*

Objectives

- » Examine the purpose of using simulation modeling in business continuity planning

- » Examine how randomness can affect outcomes and decision making

- » Examine how simulation modeling can be applied to supply chains

- » Analyze a supply chain using simulation modeling

- » Apply simulation modeling to analyze examples of supply chains with multiple tiers under varying assumptions.

*Chapter prepared by Holmes E. Miller, PhD.

Introduction

This chapter discusses how computer simulation, specifically Monte Carlo analysis, can be used as a tool to enhance the business continuity planning process. In particular simulation modeling will be applied to analyze risk in supply chains. Before discussing what Monte Carlo analysis is, the concept of using simulation in business continuity planning will be discussed.

There are various ways that business continuity professionals can address risks associated with supply chains. One is to analyze case studies – for example see Engemann, Miller and Dengler (2010). Case studies may contain both qualitative and quantitative elements that present a decision problem and "facts" necessary for decision making. In a case study, the analyst reviews the situation, reviews the facts, identifies the problem, determines the objectives, evaluates various alternatives and makes a recommendation.

A more "extreme" form of case study analysis is to actually go through an exercise, real or simulated. Business continuity planners are familiar with simulation because a key step in the overall BCP process is a form of simulation: Namely, *exercising the plan*. Exercising a BCP involves developing a scenario that represents a fictitious event and then exercising the plan to ensure that its key components work in practice, as they have been drawn up to work on paper. Why simulate? Obviously, creating a real event is out of the question. No one would suggest burning down a building to see how a plan works or requesting that a key supplier deliberately withhold material from a manufacturer. The potential costs of these events far outweigh any perceived benefit. Rather, simulating these events yields the same insights and knowledge at a far lower cost.

This logic underpins the methodology using simulation as an adjunct to the BCP process. When developing the plan, the planner entertains many situations where the answers to posed questions cannot be obtained by exercising the real-world system but instead, may be obtained by exercising a model of that system. Some examples might include:

▶ Suppose a firm runs out of raw materials – how long can it function if the production system is operating in a "degraded" mode?

▶ If a firm has two plants producing the same product and one is destroyed, can a second plant that produces the same product pick up the slack if a second shift is added?

▶ What would be the impact on production of a strike or work slow down?

▶ What are the effects on production if one of the Tier 3 suppliers in a supply chain has a fire that completely destroys their facility?

▶ Suppose two strategies using offsite vendors are being considered – the more expensive alternative offers capacity similar to the firm's own, while the less expensive vendor's capacity is less than the firm's capacity at full production, but may be acceptable if processing occurred in a degraded mode. What percent of degradation will be expected and will that be acceptable to the firm's customers?

Some questions can be answered analytically – equations or other mathematical relationships can be constructed that represent the underlying system and then solved. Using analytical methods has a long and storied history. The problem with relying on mathematical models, however, is that they are approximations of reality rather than accurate representations of reality. This is especially true for complex, real-world systems where the complexities multiply quickly and no mathematical model can capture the richness of the underlying system. Just as computer models are developed to simulate car crashes or traffic congestion, so can computer models be used to simulate production systems. Once developed, these models can be exercised so to allow the BCP planner to ask many "What if?" questions and in obtaining the answers, develop a more cogent BCP.

Simulation Analysis using Monte Carlo Methods

To understand the benefits of Monte Carlo analysis, consider a simple profit or loss model (ignoring overhead): A company sells x items at a price p, with a fixed cost (assume yearly) F, and a cost of goods sold c. The profit is straightforward:

$$px - (F+cx) = (p-c)x - F$$

For example, if F = \$100,000, p = \$100, and c =\$50, if the company sells 1,000 items it loses \$50,000. If it sells 2,000 items it breaks even and if it sells 2500 items it makes a profit of \$25,000. Suppose however, that the situation is more complicated. Specifically:

▶ The price it can sell its product for varies between \$90 to \$100 depending upon the economy;

▶ The cost of producing the product can range anywhere from \$45 per item to \$65 per item;

▶ The demand for the item follows a Normal distribution with a mean of 2,500 and standard deviation of 500 (which means demand will be between approximately 1,500 to 3,500 units with a probability of 95%).

Putting all this variability together, what is the chance of losing money? Now the answer is not as simple. This is where a simulation model comes in.

In Monte Carlo analysis the computer model in effect "rolls the dice" much the same way the players in a Monopoly game roll the dice, and where the outcome of each game (trial) is different. At the heart of Monte Carlo analysis is the concept of using random numbers (for example, a randomly generated number on the continuum between 0 and 1) to generate a sample from a probability distribution. For example, suppose, as above, that the cost of the item is uniformly distributed between \$45 and \$65 – i.e., any cost in that range is equally likely. If the random number drawn is 0.000 the cost if \$45.00 and if it is 1.000 the cost is \$65.00. Suppose five random numbers between 0 and 1 are drawn and used to generate five costs. Using Excel the formula for the cost is:

=45 + 20 * RAND(), where RAND() is a random number between 0 and 1

The cost results of five simulated trials are given in as follows:

Cost Results from Five Trials

Random Number	Cost
0.3660	\$52.32
0.1284	\$47.57
0.5822	\$56.64
0.1516	\$48.03
0.3617	\$52.23

If five more random numbers were drawn, five other costs would arise. Using Excel functions for doing the same with the price and the demand (assume the fixed costs are known and equal \$50,000 and that price and demand are independent), the following are the profit results for five simulated trials:

Profit Results from Five Trials

Cost	Price	Demand	Profit
$54.48	$94.51	1186	($2,524.42)
$58.65	$94.36	2371	$34,668.41
$64.70	$94.28	3073	$40,899.34
$61.90	$90.85	2539	$23,504.05
$49.35	$95.96	1987	$42,614.07

Even for five trials the results vary significantly, between losing $2,524 to a profit of $42,614. Simulating this for a large number of trials would yield more accurate results. For example in this simple case, the following contains the results from simulating 100 trials:

Statistics from 100 Simulated Trials

Minimum Profit	$(8,822.02)
Maximum Profit	$111,475.51
Average Profit	$52,797.79
# Trials Profit < 0	3

These results are to be contrasted with using the midpoints ($p = \$95$ and $c = \$55$), a fixed cost of $50,000 and the average of the demand (2500) which yield a profit of $50,000. While the average is close (and would be approximately equal if more trials were used), the information about the variability is important.

Hillier and Hillier (2010) discuss the building blocks for constructing a simulation model of a stochastic system i.e., a system involving probabilistic elements). These are:

1. A description of the system's components, including how they operate and interrelate.

2. A simulation clock.

3. A definition of the state of the system.

4. A method for randomly generating the (simulated) events that occur over time.

5. A method for changing the state of the system when an event occurs.

6. A procedure for advancing the time on the simulation clock.

Case 1: Supply Chain Analysis

Simulation modeling can be very useful in business continuity planning. The following illustration extends Case Study C. Each row in the table below lists the number of hours of inventory or raw materials available at each station. The first eight hours of production time are displayed in the table below (assuming that no raw materials are being shipped to the manufacturer due to a disaster event at the supplier). Time 0 represents the "initial conditions" and the values for subsequent hours are the hours of work left at the end of the hour in question:

The First Eight Hours of a Supply Chain Analysis

Time	I1	M1	I2	M2	I3	M3	I4	M4	I5	M5
0	24	4.0	2.0	4.0	1.0	2.0	1.0	1.0	16.0	1.0
1	23	4.0	2.0	4.0	1.0	2.0	1.0	1.0	16.0	1.0
2	22	4.0	2.0	4.0	1.0	2.0	1.0	1.0	16.0	1.0
3	21	4.0	2.0	4.0	1.0	2.0	1.0	1.0	16.0	1.0
4	20	4.0	2.0	4.0	1.0	2.0	1.0	1.0	16.0	1.0
5	19	4.0	2.0	4.0	1.0	2.0	1.0	1.0	16.0	1.0
6	18	4.0	2.0	4.0	1.0	2.0	1.0	1.0	16.0	1.0
7	17	4.0	2.0	4.0	1.0	2.0	1.0	1.0	16.0	1.0
8	16	4.0	2.0	4.0	1.0	2.0	1.0	1.0	16.0	1.0

The relationships are straightforward: Each hour inventory flows to manufacturing and from manufacturing to the downstream (i.e. following) inventory step, where the numbers are the hours of work available. The flow assumption is deterministic, much like the flow of water downstream at a steady, known rate. In Case Study C various scenarios are examined. For example, the first posed question asks: "How long will the finished product be unavailable for shipping to customers if raw material cannot be received for five days?" The answer, under the normal non-accelerated model, is that after five days "there will still be two days of finished product in M5 (Packing and Shipping) and I5 (Warehouse). This can be seen in this analysis looking at hours 38 to 42, specifically hours 40 and 41 (the end of the fifth day and the beginning of the sixth). The following contains the results, where at the end of hour 40 there are 15 hours of work in I5 and 1 hour in M5:

Hours 38-42 of a Supply Chain Analysis

Time	I1	M1	I2	M2	I3	M3	I4	M4	I5	M5
38	0	0.0	0.0	0.0	0.0	0.0	0.0	1.0	16.0	1.0
39	0	0.0	0.0	0.0	0.0	0.0	0.0	0.0	16.0	1.0
40	0	0.0	0.0	0.0	0.0	0.0	0.0	0.0	15.0	1.0
41	0	0.0	0.0	0.0	0.0	0.0	0.0	0.0	14.0	1.0
42	0	0.0	0.0	0.0	0.0	0.0	0.0	0.0	13.0	1.0

The model in Case Study C uses constant time flows that are known with certainty. One way to interpret these is the time flows are *planned hours* of manufacturing. For example at station M1 there are 4 planned manufacturing hours and at M5 there is one planned hour. What if things do not work as planned? In situations where variability is significant (e.g., in waiting line situations), using actual values produces results quite different from planned values.

This is where introducing randomness and probability distributions comes into play. In the deterministic world of the example above, the planned hours equal the actual hours. In the simulated world, rather than each *planned hour* of manufacturing taking in fact, one hour, the *actual* time taken is random following a specified probability distribution. This is true for many cases in manufacturing (e.g., a job shop, other non-repetitive processes, and any operation where machines can malfunction). For example, there may be one hour of manufacturing work planned, but a machine breakdown might result in only one-half hour of "work" actually being performed in that hour. Conversely, in some situations the one hour estimate of work might actually result in more than one hour of work being done – i.e., if a mechanical repair turned out to be less complex than anticipated, one and one-half hours of "planned work" might be completed in one hour. In addition, in the above model the manufacturing stations M1 through M5 might be interpreted as tiers of a supply chain where problems at one level affect tiers upstream (i.e. the tiers of suppliers are "upstream" from the OEM and the customers are "downstream"). In this case simulation may be used to indicate a complete cessation of activity at a node, which would be the case if a supplier ceased to function entirely due to an event such as a fire or earthquake.

How will actual flows being different from planned flows affect the outcome? One probably distribution that can be used to approximate this randomness is the beta distribution, where limits are placed on the maximum and minimum times and where the distribution itself is defined by these limits and characteristic parameters. For events where a machine might or might not break down, the Bernoulli distribution (e.g., an "unfair" coin-flipping type distribution where the probabilities of heads (and tails) sum to 1 but need not each equal 1/2) can be used.

Using the above model, assume that all of the manufacturing flows rather than taking one hour for certain, take an amount of time determined by a beta distribution where the minimum time is 0, the maximum is two hours, and where the beta distribution parameters *alpha* and *beta* equal 1. This creates a case where the outcomes will be uniformly distributed (i.e., have an equal probability of occurring) between the ranges of 0 and 2. Times of zero or near zero can be interpreted as operations scheduled to be performed but not performed due to some unanticipated reason, such as the "machine malfunction" example above. The Excel equation used to generate the values is:

$$=\text{BETAINV}(\text{RAND}(),1,1,0,2),$$

where RAND() is a random number between 0 and 1; the first "1" is the parameter alpha; the second "1" is the parameter beta; the "0" is the lower bound on the output; and the "2" is the upper bound on the output.

These values were chosen for this example; in a real situation, the analyst would research the actual system and come up with numbers representing the actual system being studied. How would this affect the results?

A schematic of the flow relationships (using I2, M2, and I3 as an example) appears below.

Supply Chain Schematic at M2

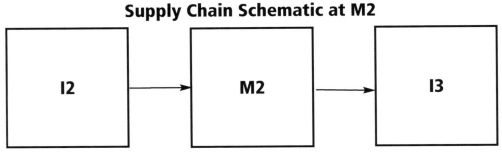

In the figure above the recursive equations used for Manufacturing Station 2 at period t are:

$$M2(t) = M2(t-1) + D2(t) - P2(t).$$
$$D2(t) = \min[I2(t-1),1].$$
$$P2(t) = \min[M2(t-1), \text{BETAINV}(\text{RAND}(),1,1,0,20].$$
$$I2(t) = I2(t-1) + P1(t) - D2(t).$$

where:

M2(t) = available hours of inventory at manufacturing station 2 at the end of period t.

D2(t) = draw from inventory station 2 to manufacturing station 2 during period t.

P2(t) = actual production output in hours for manufacturing station 2 during period t.

I2(t) = inventory level at inventory station 2 at the end of time period 2.

Min (minimum) in D2(t) and P2(t) formulae ensures that no more resources are used than are available.

The following table gives the results for one replication of this simulation for the first eight hours. The numbers represent the "hours of work" values at the end of each period; period 0 represents the initial conditions, i.e., the starting values as in Case E. In Table 6, the actual manufacturing and inventory hours for I1 through I5 and M1 through M5 are on the left and the pure production flows (i.e. the hours of planned work actually produced in one hour of clock time) are labeled P1 through P5 at the right. In the simulation the formulas in Figure 1 were used for the "left hand side" numbers and the "Actual Production Hours Used" were random values generated from the beta distribution (as discussed above). The planned "inventory draw" (i.e., the hours of work flowing from an inventory station to a manufacturing station) always equals 1 (i.e. 1 hour or work) unless the work in the previous period is less than one hour, in which case it equals that value. For example, in period 1, M2 equals 4.0 + 1.0 − 0.7 = 4.3 because I2 in period 0 equals 2.0, a value greater than 1. However, in period 2 M3 equals 1.9 + 0.7 − 0.3 = 2.3 because the value of I3 in period 1 is 0.7 so 0.7 was used as the inventory draw since there was less than one hour of work available. The values in the table are the final values after all flows – i.e. the value of M2 is after the inventory draw into M2 and the production out of M2; the value of I3 is after the production flow from M2 to I3 and after the inventory draw from I3 to M3. Other values are calculated in similar fashion.

Manufacturing and Inventory Hours: Periods 1-8

Time	\multicolumn{10}{c	}{Manufacturing and Inventory Flows}	\multicolumn{5}{c}{Actual Production Hours Used}
	I1	M1	I2	M2	I3	M3	I4	M4	I5	M5	P1	P2	P3	P4	P5
0	24	4.0	2.0	4.0	1.0	2.0	1.0	1.0	16.0	1.0	-	-	-	-	-
1	23	3.7	2.3	4.3	0.7	1.9	1.1	1.9	15.1	1.0	1.3	0.7	1.1	0.1	1.0
2	22	3.5	2.5	4.3	1.0	2.3	0.4	1.7	15.3	1.4	1.2	1.0	0.3	1.2	0.6
3	21	3.9	2.1	4.6	0.7	2.3	1.0	1.7	14.7	1.3	0.6	0.7	1.0	0.4	1.1
4	20	3.9	2.1	4.0	1.6	2.3	0.7	2.1	14.3	1.0	1.0	1.6	0.7	0.6	1.3
5	19	2.9	3.1	4.5	1.1	3.0	0.3	2.5	13.6	1.9	2.0	0.5	0.3	0.3	0.1
6	18	3.7	2.3	3.8	1.8	3.6	0.4	2.7	12.7	1.4	0.2	1.7	0.4	0.1	1.5
7	17	2.7	3.3	4.6	1.0	3.5	1.1	3.0	11.8	1.0	2.0	0.2	1.1	0.1	1.4
8	16	2.1	3.9	4.2	1.4	3.1	1.5	3.5	11.3	1.8	1.6	1.4	1.4	0.5	0.2

Manufacturing and Inventory Hours: Periods 55-62

Time	\multicolumn{9}{c}{Manufacturing and Inventory Flows}		\multicolumn{5}{c}{Actual Production Hours Used}
	I1	M1	I2	M2	I3	M3	I4	M4	I5	M5	P1	P2	P3	P4	P5
55	0.0	0.0	0.0	0.0	0.0	0.0	0.0	0.0	0.0	8.2	0.0	0.0	0.0	0.0	0.6
56	0.0	0.0	0.0	0.0	0.0	0.0	0.0	0.0	0.0	6.6	0.0	0.0	0.0	0.0	1.6
57	0.0	0.0	0.0	0.0	0.0	0.0	0.0	0.0	0.0	5.0	0.0	0.0	0.0	0.0	1.6
58	0.0	0.0	0.0	0.0	0.0	0.0	0.0	0.0	0.0	4.9	0.0	0.0	0.0	0.0	0.1
59	0.0	0.0	0.0	0.0	0.0	0.0	0.0	0.0	0.0	3.0	0.0	0.0	0.0	0.0	1.9
60	0.0	0.0	0.0	0.0	0.0	0.0	0.0	0.0	0.0	1,2	0.0	0.0	0.0	0.0	1.8
61	0.0	0.0	0.0	0.0	0.0	0.0	0.0	0.0	0.0	0.4	0.0	0.0	0.0	0.0	0.8
62	0.0	0.0	0.0	0.0	0.0	0.0	0.0	0.0	0.0	0.0	0.0	0.0	0.0	0.0	0.4

Although in the deterministic case, all work has been exhausted by the end of period 56 (the sum of all the inventory and manufacturing available hours), in this replication of the simulation the end comes later, in period 62. Results are presented in the previous table.

Note that in the final periods the hourly production flows equal zero for all but station M5, since there are no "hours left" at the other stations. This was just one replication. The benefit of using simulation is that one can do many replications and from these results, draw conclusions that can be illuminating and sometimes unexpected. In this example, 1000, replications of the model were run using the Data Table option in Excel.

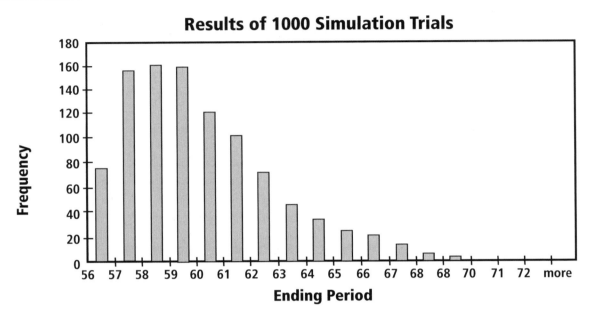

The above figure contains the results. The x-axis is the "ending period", i.e., the period when the last hour of work has been completed. The y-axis represents the frequency (out of 1000 replications) that this occurred. Here the range is from 56 to 72 and the mode is 58, which equals 160 (or 16%) of the 1000 runs. Indeed, slightly less than half (45%) of the trials resulted in "ending hours" over 60, and there is about a 10% chance of taking as long as 63 hours or more. Granted this model was hypothetical, using a distribution (the beta distribution as discussed above) that may not reflect reality. In an actual simulation, the analyst would look at the historical data and from that determine the most appropriate distribution to use as well as the appropriate parameters for that distribution. The message, however, is that using simulation can highlight information that can be used in making a better decision – i.e., that there is a 45% chance the ending period will be 60 or above and a 10% chance it will be 63 or more. In a practical problem this information may be critical.

The model can be used to ask "what if?" questions such as: What if a manufacturing station "goes down completely" for several hours? What if an accelerated model with no inventory were used? What if manufacturing times were "sped up" so work could be done much faster? The information from these can assist the business continuity planner at relatively little cost, and may strengthen the robustness of the BCP itself.

Case 2: A Three Tier Supply Chain

Monte Carlo simulation also can be used to investigate how a larger supply chain can respond to various scenarios that cannot be exercised in practice. Miller and Engemann (2008) discuss this method and discuss an Excel-based model, which consists of a manufacturer (referred to as the "original equipment manufacturer" or OEM) and a supply chain with three tiers. Each tier is supplied by three suppliers at the lower tier supply each agent. The figure below contains a schematic.

Schematic of Three Tier Supply Chain

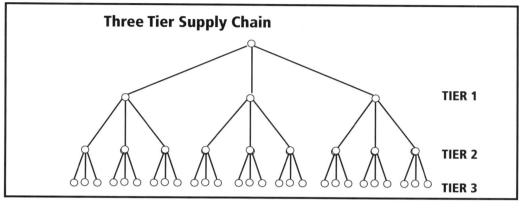

The model allows for random events like the following:

- External natural disasters (e.g., hurricanes, earthquakes) that directly affect the physical production and distribution capabilities of the specific organization in question.

- External infrastructure events (e.g., bridge failures, telecommunications failures) that indirectly affect the production and distribution capabilities of the organization.

- Internal disasters specific to the site that may affect the internal production and distribution capabilities of the organization – e.g., localized fires, and computer and telecommunication failures that do not affect the infrastructure for the firm, but the specific location of the firm itself.

The assumptions for the model include:

- All of the events are statistically independent, so the probability a disaster event affecting one supplier at Tier 3 is independent of the probability of events affecting other suppliers at that tier or other tiers as well (which does not mean that the results of the event will not affect suppliers at higher tiers).

- The output is measured as an "effectiveness index" where 100% is maximum possible output given demand. This index is a proxy for manufacturing output in units produced, and is generic in nature and can represent any manufacturing process.

- The probability of each event occurring is random, according to a discrete probability distribution. In the simulation a multinomial distribution was used with four outcomes: no event, an external disaster, an internal disaster, and an infrastructure event.

- If an event of any type occurs, the level of degradation is calculated using a beta distribution. The level of "degradation" in a tier is random, between 0 and 100. For example there may be 1% chance that an external event occurs but when it does, the beta distribution (defined as appropriate for that type of event) may generate a level of degradation of 25%. If the event did not occur the degradation would equal 0 but if it did occur the degradation would equal 25%.

- For the Tier 3 nodes the production index that measures "effectiveness" equals: 100 minus the degree of "degradation" if an event occurs – for example if "degradation" measured 25, the index would equal 100 - 25 = 75. For subsequent tiers (Tier 2, Tier 1, and the original equipment manufacturer (OEM or "Tier 0") the index equals the index value resulting from random events before considering the effect of upstream events, multiplied by the minimum of the indices for the direct upstream links in the tier below. For example if the index before the upstream events was 90 and if there were three upstream events – i.e. events at the immediate preceding tier of the supply chain – with indices of 100%, 100%, and 50%, the index would be 90 multiplied by 50%, or 45%. The logic behind using the minimum of the three nodes at

Tier 3 stems from a chain being as strong as its weakest link, i.e., the lowest performing step constrains the capacity of the entire system.

Case 2: Results and Discussion

In the simulation, a Base Case was used that assumed that the probability of events occurring at the various nodes throughout the three tiers of the supply chain was statistically independent and that a "perfect" production index for each node would be 100. One thousand replications were run using the Monte Carlo simulation methods and the table below summarizes the Base case results the "joint" events are two tiers of the supply chain taken together):

Results from Three Tier Supply Chain: Base Case

RESULTS FROM BASE CASE				
Output Name	**Minimum**	**Maximum**	**Mean**	**Std. Dev**
Avg Tier 3	88.8	100	97.8	2.0
Avg Tier 2	74.3	100	97.9	3.4
Avg Tier 1	56.9	100	98.0	6.0
Avg: Joint Tier 2 & 3	61.1	100	91.8	6.5
Avg: Joint Tier 1 & 3	18.4	100	76.9	16.0
Avg: Joint OEM & Tier 1	4.3	100	51.1	26.8

The 'Avg Tier 3' is the average final index value after events occurring only for the Tier 3 nodes. 'Minimum' is the smallest average value in the 1000 replications and 'Maximum' is the largest average value. 'Mean' is the average of all 1000 replications and 'Std dev' is the standard deviation for the 1000 replications. For example, if the index for an iteration for a node for the three types of events described above (external, internal, and infrastructure), were 100, 100, and 50 the index for the node would be 50; the average of all nodes at that tier would be one data point out of the 1000 data points for 1000 simulated trials used to develop the output measures just discussed. The values for events just at nodes for Tiers 2 and 1 before considering 'upstream' nodes are defined in a similar fashion (events occurring only at Tier 0 are not included in the output). The output 'Avg: Joint Tier2and3' is the average final index value occurring at Tier 2, adjusted for those at Tier 3 as discussed above. The values for the other tiers are defined in a similar fashion.

We can conclude:

 ▶ The average index for events occurring at a specific node remains relatively constant at about 98, although the standard deviation (and range) grows larger at supply chain tier levels closer to the OEM, because fewer nodes are used (e.g., the standard deviation is 2.0 for the 27 Tier 3 nodes versus 6.0 for the 3 Tier 1 nodes).

 ▶ As one would expect the indices that include events at a level AND prior levels drop as one gets closer to the OEM. Using average values for example at Tier 3, it is 97.8, at Tier 2 and 3 ('Avg: Joint Tier 2&3') it is 91.8, at Tier 1 and 2 ('Avg: Joint Tier 1&2') it is 76.9 and finally at the OEM ('Avg: Joint OEM&Tier 1') the index is 51.1. The ranges and standard deviations also grow wider and the final values exhibit greater dispersion among the 1000 simulated trials

The specifics of this simulation model are less important than what they exemplify: That simulation modeling can be used to highlight risks to a complex supply chain that may arise due to events, however improbable, that occur at one of the suppliers in one of the tiers. If serious enough, the entire production operation may come to a halt. An example of this occurred in China at Honda where a strike at suppliers supplying transmissions halted all production of the automobiles in the four assembly plants in that country (Bradsher 2010).

Using the above simulation model one can examine many other scenarios. For example, some include:

▶ Correlation among events.

▶ The impact of dual sources of supply.

▶ Expanding/contracting the number of Tier 3 suppliers.

▶ Effectiveness of business continuity plans.

The last case will be discussed in more detail to illustrate how the simulation model can illuminate various possibilities. Among the benefits of implementing business continuity plans is mitigating the effects of disasters when they do occur. Using the model the impact of business continuity plans was examined by varying their "bottom-line effectiveness" — measured by what percent they reduced the overall OEM losses. Figure 4 contains a graph of how varying the business continuity plan effectiveness affected the average production index at Tier 0 for 1000 simulated replications:

OEM Production Index from Simulation Runs

As is apparent, the effect for the output of the model is linear. Recall that the Base Case had an OEM production index of about 50, and as the business continuity plan's effectiveness increases from about 20% to 80%, the index increases accordingly from about 60 to 90. The message is having business continuity plans to mitigate the damage does pay off.

Conclusions

Simulation is a valuable tool for any business continuity professional to have in his or her toolbox. Since business continuity itself involves dealing with probabilistic events, what better way to investigate outcomes and the implications of strategic alternatives than to simulate them? Naturally the results of the model are only as good as the assumptions and the details included. This challenges the business continuity professional to judiciously ascertain what is and is not critical and should and should not be included in the model. With the widespread use of computers, simulation methods are available to everyone. The above examples were done using Excel, and the replications were done in Excel itself (using the Data Table option) or using special simulation software available from the Palisade Corporation. Many other simulation packages are available on the marketplace, many very high-powered and oriented to specific business or manufacturing universes.

Review Topics

1. How is simulation modeling useful in supply chain risk analysis?

2. What are some of the elements that are incorporated in a simulation model?

3. What is the benefit and running and analyzing multiple replications of a simulation model? What additional information can it provide?

4. What are some problems that occur in supply chain risk analysis that a simulation model can address?

5. What are some of the challenges in using simulation modeling for supply chain risk analysis?

Bibliography

Bradsher, K. "Strike Forces Honda to Shut Plants in China," *New York Times*, May 27, 2010.

Hillier, F. and M. Hillier; Introduction to Management Science: *A Modeling and Case Studies Approach with Spreadsheets*, McGraw-Hill, 2010.

Engemann, K. J., H. E. Miller, and N. B. Dengler, "Managing Supply Chain Risk in Financial Services," *Emerging Themes in Supply Chain Risk Management: A Collection of Case Studies and Practices*, Editors: Omera Khan and George A. Zsidisin, J. Ross Publishers, 2011.

Miller, H. E., and Engemann, K. J., "A Monte Carlo Simulation Model of Supply Chain Risk due to Natural Disasters," *International Journal of Technology, Policy and Management*, Vol. 8, No. 4, pp. 460–480, 2008.

Miller, H. E., and Engemann, K. J., "A Supply Chain Simulation Model to Examine the Effects of Mitigation and Disaster Recovery Strategies, *Advances in Decision Technology and Intelligent Information Systems, Volume IX* (ed. K. Engemann and G. Lasker), pp. 56-60, The International Institute for Advanced Studies in Systems Research and Cybernetics, 2008.

CHAPTER XVII

Risk and Decision Modeling*

Objectives

» Explore decision making environments

» Examine the concepts of risk and uncertainty

» Review various approaches to decision modeling

» Examine decision modeling with imprecise information.

* Chapter prepared by José M. Merigó PhD.

Introduction

Decision making is a critical undertaking in BCM. In particular, BCM necessitates decisions to be made including selecting strategies, controls, procedures, and suppliers.

Decision making is the process of selecting an action from amongst several alternatives. We can establish four stages of decision making. First, we identify the problem. Second, we develop alternatives for solving the problem. Third, we select the alternative to implement based upon our criteria. And fourth, we evaluate the implemented alternative in order to see how well it has solved the problem.

There are various approaches that may be used in a decision making situation, ranging from utilizing little more than basic intuition to employing sophisticated decision modeling. In this chapter we will introduce some practical decision modeling methodologies.

Decision Making Environments

In order to analyze the available decision making models, first, we have to establish the decision matrix that permit us to consider the different states of nature with the different strategies or actions that the decision maker can take. Note that the information from this matrix can be precise, imprecise, fuzzy, linguistic, etc. More details on how to represent the information will be given later. The graphical representation of this decision matrix is as follows:

Matrix (m x n)	S_1	S_2	... S_j ...	S_n
A_1	a_{11}	a_{12}	a_{1j}	a_{1n}
A_2	a_{21}	a_{22}	a_{2j}	a_{2n}
...	...	...	...	...
A_i	a_{i1}	a_{i2}	a_{ij}	a_{in}
...	...	...	...	...
A_m	a_{m1}	a_{m2}	a_{mj}	a_{mn}

where:

- $S_1, S_2,..., S_n$: The different states of nature that may occur.

- $A_1, A_2,..., A_n$: The different actions or strategies that the decision maker can take.

- $a_{11}, a_{12},..., a_{mn}$: The different results (payoffs) obtained when combining one action with one state of nature.

Note that depending on the type of decision making we are considering, we can present this matrix in different ways. We have presented it by using different states of nature but it is also possible to consider several criteria (multicriteria decision making), attributes (multiattribute decision making), experts (multi-expert decision making), etc.

In general, the decision processes are affected by one of the following environments (Anderson et al., 2011; Render et al., 2009):

1. Decision Making under certainty.

2. Decision Making under risk.

3. Decision Making under uncertainty.

Decision Making under Certainty

Situations where we know the information that will occur in the future. In these situations, we should be able to solve the problem because we can find a unique action that it is the optimal one.

There are different models and techniques for assessing these types of environments. For example, we can use linear programming or other optimization methods. For further information, see for example, Anderson et al. (2011), Render et al. (2009).

Decision Making under Risk

Situations where we do not know the information that it is going to happen in the future but we have some probabilistic information to assess the problem. Thus, the best action is to calculate some kind of expected value for each action available and select the action with the best result.

Note that depending on the available information we can use:

- Objective probabilities: The probability that it is based on historical or experimental data. This information comes from the analysis of the real world.

- Subjective probabilities: The probability that it is based on the beliefs of the experts or the decision makers, where they establish the probability that an event will occur in the future.

- Other types of probabilities: There are a lot of other interpretations that can be developed regarding the concept of probability. For example, we can use complex structures such as the use of the Bayesian analysis or the Dempster-Shafer theory of evidence (Yager and Liu, 2008). Note that in Section 7 and 9 we provide a further discussion on other probabilistic methods.

There are different methods for assessing risk environments but the classical one is the use of the expected value in order to predict the future outcomes. It is formulated as follows:

$$EV = \sum_{i=1}^{n} p_i a_i,$$

where a_i is the ith argument and p_i is the ith probability.

Decision Making under Uncertainty

Situations where we know the future outcomes of the different actions we can follow but we do not know their associated probabilities. That is to say, we know all the states of nature that may occur in the future but we do not know which one will occur. In these cases, we cannot use the expected value and we have to follow more subjective criteria in order to make a decision.

Methods:

- Optimistic approach: Max $\{a_i\}$.

- Pessimistic approach: Min $\{a_i\}$.

- Laplace criteria (Laplace, 1814): $(1 / n) \times (\Sigma a_i)$.

- Hurwicz criteria (Hurwicz, 1951): $\alpha \times$ Max $\{a_i\} + (1 - \alpha) \times$ Min $\{a_i\}$.

These classical methods are particular cases of a more general model called the ordered weighted averaging (OWA) operator. It can be defined as follows.

Definition 1 – An OWA operator of dimension n is a mapping $OWA: R^n$? R that has an associated weighting vector W of dimension n with $w_j \in [0,1]$ and $\sum_{j=1}^{n} w_j = 1$, such that:

$$OWA(a_1, a_2..., a_n) = \sum_{j=1}^{n} w_j b_j,$$

where b_j is the jth largest of the a_i.

As we can see in the OWA, we get:

- The optimistic approach if $w_1 = 1$ and $w_j = 0$ for $j \neq 1 \Rightarrow \text{Max } \{a_i\}$.

- The pessimistic approach if $w_n = 1$ and $w_j = 0$ for $j \neq 1 \Rightarrow \text{Min } \{a_i\}$.

- The Hurwicz criteria if
  $w_1 = \alpha, w_n = (1 - \alpha), \text{ and } w_j = 0 \text{ for } j \neq 1, n \Rightarrow \alpha \times \text{Max } \{a_i\} + (1 - \alpha) \times \text{Min } \{a_i\}$.

- The Laplace criteria if $w_j = 1/n$, for all $j \Rightarrow (1/n) \times (\Sigma a_i)$.

In order to see how to assess decision making problems under uncertainty, we are going to present an illustrative example.

Example – A decision maker wants to select a strategy from 4 possible alternatives: A_1, A_2, A_3 and A_4. The key factor that affects the results (payoffs) obtained with each investment is the state of nature (i.e. which events occur): S_1, S_2, S_3 and S_4

The payoff for each strategy and state of nature combination are displayed in the following payoff matrix.

	S_1	S_2	S_3	S_4	S_5
A_1	80	60	50	30	20
A_2	70	70	40	40	30
A_3	70	60	50	50	40
A_4	60	50	50	50	60

If we now develop the calculations in order to make a decision, we can do the following.

▶ With the optimistic criteria:

- $A_1 = 80$. ←

- $A_2 = 70$.

- $A_3 = 70$.

- $A_4 = 60$.

▶ With the pessimistic criteria:

- $A_1 = 20$.

- $A_2 = 30$.

- $A_3 = 40$.

- $A_4 = 50$. ←

▶ With the Laplace criteria:

- $A_1 = (1/5) (80 + 60 + 50 + 30 + 20) = 48$.

- $A_2 = (1/5) (70 + 70 + 40 + 40 + 30) = 50$.

- $A_3 = (1/5) (70 + 60 + 50 + 50 + 40) = 54$. ←

- $A_4 = (1/5) (60 + 50 + 50 + 50 + 60) = 54$. ←

▶ With the Hurwicz criteria ($\alpha = 0.4$):

- $A_1 = 0.4 \times 80 + 0.6 \times 20 = 44$.

- $A_2 = 0.4 \times 70 + 0.6 \times 30 = 46$.

- $A_3 = 0.4 \times 70 + 0.6 \times 40 = 52$.

- $A_4 = 0.4 \times 60 + 0.6 \times 60 = 60$. ←

▶ With the OWA operator ($W = (0.1, 0.2, 0.2, 0.2, 0.3)$). This means that we are a bit pessimistic because we put more weight at the end of the weighting vector W.

- $A_1 = 0.1 \times 80 + 0.2 \times 60 + 0.2 \times 50 + 0.2 \times 30 + 0.3 \times 20 = 42$.

- $A_2 = 0.1 \times 70 + 0.2 \times 70 + 0.2 \times 40 + 0.2 \times 40 + 0.3 \times 30 = 46$.

- $A_3 = 0.1 \times 70 + 0.2 \times 60 + 0.2 \times 50 + 0.2 \times 50 + 0.3 \times 40 = 51$.

- $A_4 = 0.1 \times 60 + 0.2 \times 60 + 0.2 \times 50 + 0.2 \times 50 + 0.3 \times 50 = 53$. ←

▶ Note that with the OWA:

- Optimistic criteria: $W = (1, 0, 0, 0, 0)$.

- Pessimistic criteria: $W = (0, 0, 0, 0, 1)$.

- Laplace criteria: $W = (0.2, 0.2, 0.2, 0.2, 0.2)$.

- Hurwicz criteria: $W = (0.4, 0, 0, 0, 0.6)$.

▶ Note that in *Decision Making under Risk*, we assume that we have some probabilistic information regarding the states of nature. For example, if $P = (0.1, 0.1, 0.4, 0.3, 0.1)$, we are saying that the probability that economic situation is "regular", is 40%, "bad" 30%, and so on.

Thus:

- $A_1 = 0.1 \times 80 + 0.1 \times 60 + 0.4 \times 50 + 0.3 \times 30 + 0.1 \times 20 = 45.$
- $A_2 = 0.1 \times 70 + 0.1 \times 70 + 0.4 \times 40 + 0.3 \times 40 + 0.1 \times 30 = 45.$
- $A_3 = 0.1 \times 70 + 0.1 \times 60 + 0.4 \times 50 + 0.3 \times 50 + 0.1 \times 40 = 52.$ ←
- $A_4 = 0.1 \times 60 + 0.1 \times 50 + 0.4 \times 50 + 0.3 \times 50 + 0.1 \times 60 = 52.$ ←

As we can see, depending on the particular type of criteria used in the selection process, our decision may be different.

Other Decision Making Models under Uncertainty

There are a lot of other decision making models for dealing with uncertainty that we can use for making a decision. For example:

- Savage criteria (Savage, 1951): Decision making with minimization of regret.
- The Weighted Sum Model (WSM) (Fishburn, 1967).
- The Weighted Product Model (WPM) (Bridgman, 1922; Miller and Starr, 1969).
- The Analytic Hierarchy Process (AHP) (Saaty, 1980).
- The TOPSIS method (Hwang and Yoon, 1981).
- The ELECTRE approach (Roy, 1968).

For a good overview of these and other decision making methods, see for example, (Triantaphyllou, 2000; Figueira et al., 2005).

Recent Approaches

Decision theory under uncertainty is a very active research topic because we can assess the problem from a wide range of perspectives. Therefore, it is not clear which is the most appropriate model for solving the problem. Usually, the conclusion is that the most appropriate model depends on the available information and the particular interests of the decision maker in the specific problem considered. In the following, we consider two general research lines for dealing with uncertainty. The first one is the recent models that have been used for dealing with uncertainty and risk environments in the same formulation. The second one concerns further developments to the OWA operator in order to obtain more general formulations for dealing with uncertainty that might be also used in other type of environments.

Decision Making under Risk and Uncertainty

Decision making under risk and uncertainty is a more general analysis of the decision making problem without certainty. Basically, this environment is found when we know the future outcomes that will occur and we can partially assess them with probabilities. However, some part of the information cannot be assessed with probabilities and therefore, we also need to use more subjective criteria in the analysis. Note that we can use all the classical methods but for simplicity, we will focus on the OWA operator because it represents a more general formulation of these methods.

One of the main methods for dealing with risk and uncertainty in the same problem is the concept of immediate probability (Engemann et al., 1996; Yager et al., 1995). Basically, it is an approach that deals with probabilities and OWA operators in the same formulation. Thus, it is able to assess risk environments with probabilities and the uncertainty with the OWA operators. The main motivation for using it is that sometimes the decision maker does not have full confidence in the probabilistic information and he believes that the final expected result should also reflect a disposition which may be more optimistic (or pessimistic) than the result obtained with the usual expected value method. Therefore, he can use an OWA operator in order to assess these differences because the real situation found in this problem is an environment that fluctuates between risk and uncertainty.

In order to assess the expected value method with immediate probabilities, we can use the following definition.

Definition 2 – An IP-OWA operator of dimension n is a mapping IP-OWA: $R_n \rightarrow R$ that has an associated weighting vector W of dimension n with $w_j \in [0,1]$ and $\sum_{j=1}^{n} w_j = 1$, such that:

$$IP\text{-}OWA\ (a_1, a_2, \ldots, a_n) = \sum_{j=1}^{n} \hat{p}_j b_j,$$

where b_j is the jth largest of the a_i, each a_i has associated a probability p_i, p_j is the associated probability of b_j and

$$\hat{p}_j = (w_j p_j / \sum_{j=1}^{n} w_j p_j).$$

If we apply the previous example with this model, we would get the following results. Note that in this situation we assume that both risk and uncertainty are relevant in the specific problem considered.

First we calculate the immediate probabilities. In this example, the immediate probabilities of the first three actions are equal.

$$\hat{p}_{11} = \hat{p}_{21} = \hat{p}_{31} = \frac{0.1 \times 0.1}{0.1 \times 0.1 + 0.2 \times 0.1 + 0.2 \times 0.4 + 0.2 \times 0.3 + 0.3 \times 0.1} = 0.05$$

$$\hat{p}_{41} = \frac{0.1 \times 0.1}{0.1 \times 0.1 + 0.2 \times 0.1 + 0.2 \times 0.1 + 0.2 \times 0.4 + 0.3 \times 0.3} = 0.045$$

$$\hat{p}_{12} = \hat{p}_{22} = \hat{p}_{32} = \frac{0.2 \times 0.1}{0.1 \times 0.1 + 0.2 \times 0.1 + 0.2 \times 0.4 + 0.2 \times 0.3 + 0.3 \times 0.1} = 0.1$$

$$\hat{p}_{42} = \frac{0.2 \times 0.1}{0.1 \times 0.1 + 0.2 \times 0.1 + 0.2 \times 0.1 + 0.2 \times 0.4 + 0.3 \times 0.3} = 0.09$$

$$\hat{p}_{13} = \hat{p}_{23} = \hat{p}_{33} = \frac{0.2 \times 0.4}{0.1 \times 0.1 + 0.2 \times 0.1 + 0.2 \times 0.4 + 0.2 \times 0.3 + 0.3 \times 0.1} = 0.4$$

$$\hat{p}_{43} = \frac{0.2 \times 0.1}{0.1 \times 0.1 + 0.2 \times 0.1 + 0.2 \times 0.1 + 0.2 \times 0.4 + 0.3 \times 0.3} = 0.09$$

$$\hat{p}_{14} = \hat{p}_{24} = \hat{p}_{34} = \frac{0.2 \times 0.3}{0.1 \times 0.1 + 0.2 \times 0.1 + 0.2 \times 0.4 + 0.2 \times 0.3 + 0.3 \times 0.1} = 0.3$$

$$\hat{p}_{44} = \frac{0.2 \times 0.4}{0.1 \times 0.1 + 0.2 \times 0.1 + 0.2 \times 0.1 + 0.2 \times 0.4 + 0.3 \times 0.3} = 0.36$$

$$\hat{p}_{15} = \hat{p}_{25} = \hat{p}_{35} = \frac{0.1 \times 0.1}{0.1 \times 0.1 + 0.2 \times 0.1 + 0.2 \times 0.4 + 0.2 \times 0.3 + 0.3 \times 0.1} = 0.05$$

$$\hat{p}_{45} = \frac{0.3 \times 0.3}{0.1 \times 0.1 + 0.2 \times 0.1 + 0.2 \times 0.1 + 0.2 \times 0.4 + 0.3 \times 0.3} = 0.409$$

Once we have all the immediate probabilities, we can develop the aggregation process in a similar way as it is done with the OWA operator.

- A_1 = 0.05 × 80 + 0.1 × 60 + 0.4 × 50 + 0.3 × 30 + 0.05 × 20 = 40.
- A_2 = 0.05 × 70 + 0.1 × 70 + 0.4 × 40 + 0.3 × 40 + 0.05 × 30 = 40.
- A_3 = 0.05 × 70 + 0.1 × 60 + 0.4 × 50 + 0.3 × 50 + 0.05 × 40 = 46.5.
- A_4 = 0.045 × 60 + 0.09 × 60 + 0.09 × 50 + 0.36 × 50 + 0.409 × 50 = **51.05.** ←

Another method for dealing with risk and uncertainty in the same formulation is the concept of the probabilistic OWA (POWA) operator (Merigó, 2008). It is very similar to the immediate probabilities. Its main advantage is that it is able to unify the decision making under risk and under uncertainty considering the degree of importance that each environment has in the particular problem considered. Thus, the POWA operator is more flexible than the immediate probabilities because it allows us to use only risk or only uncertainty and consider a wide range of partial situations where we use risk and uncertainty. It can be defined as follows.

Definition 3 – A POWA operator of dimension n is a mapping $POWA: R_n \to R$ that has an associated weighting vector W of dimension n with $w_j \in [0,1]$ and $\sum_{j=1}^{n} w_j = 1$, such that:

$$POWA\,(a_1, a_2, \ldots, a_n) = \sum_{j=1}^{n} \hat{v}_j b_j,$$

where b_j is the jth largest of the a_i, each argument a_i has an associated probability v_i with

$$\sum_{i=1}^{n} v_i = 1 \text{ and } v_i \in [0,1],$$
$$\hat{v}_j = \beta w_j + (1-\beta)v_j \text{ with } \beta \in [0,1]$$

and v_j is the probability v_i ordered according to b_j, that is, according to the jth largest of the a_i.

As we can see, if $\beta = 0$, we get the classical expected value model for dealing with risk environments and if $\beta = 1$, the OWA operator for uncertain environments. The higher is β, the more importance we give to decision making under uncertainty and vice versa.

If we calculate the previous example with the POWA operator, we get the following results. For simplicity, in this example we give the same importance to risk and uncertainty. Thus, $\beta = 0.5$.

First we calculate the new weighting vector that uses probabilities and OWAs. Note that in this example, the three first actions have the same results.

$$\hat{p}_{11} = \hat{p}_{21} = \hat{p}_{31} = 0.5 \times 0.1 + 0.5 \times 0.1 = 0.1$$

$$\hat{p}_{41} = 0.5 \times 0.1 + 0.5 \times 0.1 = 0.1$$

$$\hat{p}_{12} = \hat{p}_{22} = \hat{p}_{32} = 5 \times 0.2 + 0.5 \times 0.1 = 0.15$$

$$\hat{p}_{42} = .5 \times 0.2 + 0.5 \times 0.1 = 0.15$$

$$\hat{p}_{13} = \hat{p}_{23} = \hat{p}_{33} = 0.5 \times 0.2 + 0.5 \times 0.4 = 0.3$$

$$\hat{p}_{43} = 0.5 \times 0.2 + 0.5 \times 0.1 = 0.15$$

$$\hat{p}_{14} = \hat{p}_{24} = \hat{p}_{34} = 5 \times 0.2 + 0.5 \times 0.3 = 0.25$$

$$\hat{p}_{44} = 0.5 \times 0.2 + 0.5 \times 0.4 = 0.3$$

$$\hat{p}_{15} = \hat{p}_{25} = \hat{p}_{35} = 0.5 \times 0.3 + 0.5 \times 0.1 = 0.2$$

$$\hat{p}_{45} = 0.5 \times 0.3 + 0.5 \times 0.3 = 0.3$$

Once we have the new weighting vector, we can develop the aggregation process.

- $A_1 = 0.1 \times 80 + 0.15 \times 60 + 0.3 \times 50 + 0.25 \times 30 + 0.2 \times 20 = 43.5.$

- $A_2 = 0.1 \times 70 + 0.15 \times 70 + 0.3 \times 40 + 0.25 \times 40 + 0.2 \times 30 = 45.5.$

- $A_3 = 0.1 \times 70 + 0.15 \times 60 + 0.3 \times 50 + 0.25 \times 50 + 0.2 \times 40 = 51.5.$

- $A_4 = 0.1 \times 60 + 0.15 \times 60 + 0.15 \times 50 + 0.3 \times 50 + 0.3 \times 50 = 52.5.$ ←

As we can see, in this example it seems that A_4 is the optimal choice.

Extensions and Generalizations of the OWA Operator

The OWA operator was initially introduced for solving decision making problems under uncertainty but as we have seen, further generalizations of the OWA might be able to generalize risk and uncertainty environments in the same formulation. Moreover, in the literature there are a lot of other extensions and generalizations of the OWA operator that can be used in these problems adding some conceptual understanding to the problem. However, it is worth noting that the OWA operator itself is a statistical technique that can be implemented in decision making problems in order to assess the attitudinal character of the decision maker. In the following we present some of these extensions.

The induced OWA (IOWA) operator (Yager and Filev, 1999) is an aggregation operator that uses order inducing variables in order to assess complex reordering processes of the OWA operator. In decision making, it can be useful for reflecting variables not considered when studying the degree of optimism of the decision maker with the OWA operator such as time pressure or personal aspects.

Definition 4 – An IOWA operator of dimension n is a mapping $IOWA: R^n \times R^n \to R$ that has an associated weighting vector W of dimension n with $w_j \in [0,1]$ and $\sum_{j=1}^{n} w_j = 1$, such that:

$$IOWA(\langle u_1, a_1 \rangle, \langle u_2, a_2 \rangle ... \langle u_n, a_n \rangle) = \sum_{j=1}^{n} w_j b_j,$$

where b_j is the a_i value of the IOWA pair $<u_i, a_i>$, having the jth largest u_i, u_i is the order-inducing variable and a_i is the argument variable.

Another interesting generalization is the generalized OWA (GOWA) operator that uses generalized means in the OWA operator.

Definition 5 – A GOWA operator (Yager, 2004) of dimension n is a mapping $GOWA: R^n \to R$ that has an associated weighting vector W of dimension n with $w_j \in [0,1]$ and $\sum_{j=1}^{n} w_j = 1$, such that:

$$GOWA(a_1, a_2, .., a_n) = \left(\sum_{j=1}^{n} w_j b_j^{\lambda} \right)^{1/\lambda}$$

where b_j is the jth largest of the a_i, and λ is a parameter such that $\lambda \in (-\infty, \infty)$.

If we look to different values of the parameter λ, we can obtain other special cases such as the usual OWA operator ($\lambda = 1$), the ordered weighted geometric (OWG) operator ($\lambda = 0$), the ordered weighted harmonic averaging (OWHA) operator ($\lambda = -1$) and the ordered weighted quadratic averaging (OWQA) operator ($\lambda = 2$).

A further interesting extension is the induced generalized OWA (IGOWA) operator (Merigó and Gil-Lafuente, 2009) that uses generalized means and order inducing variables in the OWA operator.

Definition 6 – An IGOWA operator of dimension n is a mapping IGOWA: $R^n \times R^n \to R$ that has an associated weighting vector W of dimension n with $w_j \in [0,1]$ and $\sum_{j=1}^{n} w_j = 1$, such that:

$$IGOWA\big(\langle u_1, a_1 \rangle, \langle u_2, a_2 \rangle, \ldots, \langle u_n, a_n \rangle\big) = \left(\sum_{j=1}^{n} w_j b_j^{\lambda}\right)^{1/\lambda}$$

where b_j is the a_i value of the IGOWA pair $<u_i, a_i>$, having the jth largest u_i, u_i is the order inducing variable, a_i is the argument variable and λ is a parameter such that $\lambda \in (-\infty, \infty)$.

Note that a more general formulation of these formulations can be developed by using quasi-arithmetic means (Merigó and Gil-Lafuente, 2009). For further information on these and other extensions and generalizations, see for example Merigó (2008) and Yager and Kacprzyk (1997).

Other Decision Making Models

More complex decision making models can be used in the analysis depending on the problem we are studying. For example:

- Group decision making: When the decision process depends on more than one person.

- Game theory: When there is an interaction between two or more decision makers in the analysis.

- Utility theory: When the decision depends on the size of the outcomes and how they affect the economy of the decision maker.

- Sequential decision making: A decision process where the final decisions depend on previous ones and so on.

- Decision making with the Dempster-Shafer belief structure: A decision process based on complex probabilities.

Dealing with Imprecise Information

Sometimes, the available information is not clear and we cannot assess it with the "classical" exact numbers. Therefore, a better approach may be the use of other methods such as:

- Interval numbers.

- Fuzzy numbers.

- Linguistic variables.

- Probabilistic sets.

In order to see the motivation for dealing with other techniques rather than the usual exact numbers, let us present the following example.

Example – Do you know the US inflation for the next year?

- Expert 1: 1.7%

- Expert 2: 2%

- Expert 3: 3.2%

- Expert 4: 2.3%.

We don't know the inflation for the next year and we cannot provide a number because our knowledge (information) is imprecise. Thus, we need to use another technique such as the use of interval numbers. In this case, we could assume for simplicity that the inflation could be:

[1.7, 3.2]%

That is, at least 1.7% and no more than 3.2%. With this information, we know at least that the inflation is going to be in this interval. Although we don't know the inflation for the next year, we have this general information that permits us to make further analysis.

In order to see the usefulness of this we can look to the following example. Assume that we want to make an investment and we expect to gain [20, 40] million dollars. Perfect, because independently that the environment fluctuates in an optimistic or pessimistic way, we will gain a lot of money with this investment (although it is obvious that in an optimistic environment we gain more). Thus, although we don't know exactly what is going to happen, it is acceptable to the decision maker because in all the cases he will gain some money.

On the other hand, imagine that the expected benefits are: [−20, 80]. If we use just a classical number, we could expect 30 and this number seems to be positive. However, as we can see the real analysis shows that this investment is not safety because we may lose a lot of money. Therefore, it is strictly necessary to use interval numbers (or related techniques) so we are prepared to all the possible situations that may occur in the future. Otherwise, if we use exact numbers assuming a benefit of 30, we could assume that we are going to obtain profits and not ready for a crisis. Thus, in the case that the crisis occurs, the costs will be higher because we are not ready for them.

When dealing with interval numbers, we find a wide range of different types. For example:

- ▶ Interval (2-tuple): $[a_1, a_2]$.

  Example: [4, 7].
- ▶ Triplet: $[a_1, a_2, a_3]$, where $a_1 \leq a_2 \leq a_3$.

  Example: [2, 4, 9].
- ▶ Quadruplet: $[a_1, a_2, a_3, a_4]$, where $a_1 \leq a_2 \leq a_3 \leq a_4$.

  Example: [2, 4, 6, 9].

In order to deal with interval numbers in mathematical models, we have to be able to develop some mathematical operations. In the following we present some of the very basic ones with intervals (2-tuples). Let $A = [a_1, a_2]$ and $B = [b_1, b_2]$.

- ▶ Addition ($A + B$): $[a_1 + b_1, a_2 + b_2]$.
- ▶ Subtraction ($A - B$): $[a_1 - b_2, a_2 - b_1]$.
- ▶ Multiplication ($A \times B$): $[\min \{a_1 b_1, a_1 b_2, a_2 b_1, a_2 b_2\}, \max \{a_1 b_1, a_1 b_2, a_2 b_1, a_2 b_2\}]$.
  - If R^+: $[a_1 \times b_1, a_2 \times b_2]$.
- ▶ Division ($A \div B$): $[\min \{a_1 \div b_1, a_1 \div b_2, a_2 \div b_1, a_2 \div b_2\}, \max \{a_1 \div b_1, a_1 \div b_2, a_2 \div b_1, a_2 \div b_2\}]$.
  - If R^+: $[a_1 \div b_2, a_2 \ \ b_1]$.

Examples – Let $A = [6, 8]$ and $B = [2, 3]$.

- $A + B = [6 + 2, 8 + 3] = [8, 11]$.
- $A - B = [6 - 3, 8 - 2] = [3, 6]$.
- $A \times B = [6 \times 2, 8 \times 3] = [12, 24]$.
- $A \div B = [6 \div 3, 8 \div 2] = [2, 4]$.

Sometimes it is not clear which interval is higher. Thus, we need to use a method for ranking interval numbers. We recommend to use the average (or weighted average) of the interval. That is: Let $A = [10, 20]$ and $B = [15, 17]$.

- ▶ $A = (10 + 20) / 2 = 15$.
- ▶ $B = (15 + 17) / 2 = 16$.

Thus, in this example we assume that $B > A$.

Another technique for dealing with imprecise information is to use fuzzy numbers. They are similar to interval numbers but more complete because they provide more information concerning the possibility that the internal values of the interval will occur.

There are a lot of types of fuzzy numbers:

- Triangular fuzzy numbers.
- Trapezoidal fuzzy numbers.
- Interval-valued fuzzy numbers.

Triangular fuzzy numbers can be represented as follows:

- $(a_1, a_2, a_3) = (a_1 + (a_2 - a_1) \times \alpha, a_3 - (a_3 - a_2) \times \alpha)$.
- If $\alpha = 0 \Rightarrow (a_1, a_3) \Rightarrow$ the minimum and the maximum values.
- If $\alpha = 1 \Rightarrow (a_2, a_2) = a_2 \Rightarrow$ the most possible value.

Example:

- $(3, 6, 8) = (3 + 3\alpha, 8 - 2\alpha)$.

- $\alpha = 0 \Rightarrow (3, 8)$.

- $\alpha = 1 \Rightarrow (6, 6) = 6$.

- $\alpha = 0.4 \Rightarrow (3 + 3 \times 0.4, 8 - 2 \times 0.4) = (4.2, 7.2)$.

Note that there are a lot of other methods for representing fuzzy numbers. For further information, see for example Gil-Aluja (2004), Gil-Lafuente 2005), Kaufmann and Gupta (1985) and Merigó (2008).

Decision Making under Uncertainty and Imprecise Information

In the following, we are going to analyze a decision making problem under uncertainty where the available information is imprecise. Thus, we have to use a technique for dealing with imprecise information such as the use of interval numbers.

Assume an investment decision making problem:

If we now develop the calculations in order to make a decision, we can do the following.

Payoff Matrix:

	S_1	S_2	S_3	S_4	S_5
A_1	(70, 90)	(50, 70)	(40, 70)	(30, 50)	(10, 30)
A_2	(70, 80)	(60, 70)	(40, 50)	(30, 40)	(20, 30)
A_3	(60, 70)	(50, 60)	(45, 50)	(42, 50)	(35, 45)
A_4	(55, 60)	(50, 53)	(48, 50)	(46, 50)	(52, 60)

▶ With the optimistic criteria:

 - $A_1 = (70, 90)$. ←

 - $A_2 = (70, 80)$.

 - $A_3 = (60, 70)$.

 - $A_4 = (55, 60)$.

▶ With the pessimistic criteria:

  - $A_1 = (10, 30)$.

  - $A_2 = (20, 30)$.

  - $A_3 = (35, 45)$.

  - $A_4 = (46, 50)$. ←

▶ With the Laplace criteria:

- A_1 = (1/5) [(70, 90) + (50, 70) + (40, 70) + (30, 50) + (10, 30)] = (40, 62).

- A_2 = (1/5) [(70, 80) + (60, 70) + (40, 50) + (30, 40) + (20, 30)] = (44, 54).

- A_3 = (1/5) [(60, 70) + (50, 60) + (45, 50) + (42, 50) + (35, 45)] = (46.4, 55).

- A_4 = (1/5) [(55, 60) + (50, 53) + (48, 50) + (46, 50) + (52, 60)] = (50.2, 54.6).

In this case, it is not clear which value is higher, so we have to calculate the average of the interval:

- A_1 = (40 + 62) / 2 = 51.

- A_2 = (44 + 54) / 2 = 49.

- A_3 = (46.4 + 54) / 2 = 50.2.

- A_4 = (50.2 + 54.6) / 2 = **52.4**. ←

▶ With the Hurwicz criteria (α = 0.4):

- A_1 = 0.4 × (70, 90) + 0.6 × (10, 30) = (34, 54).

- A_2 = 0.4 × (70, 80) + 0.6 × (20, 30) = (40, 50).

- A_3 = 0.4 × (60, 70) + 0.6 × (35, 45) = (45, 55).

- A_4 = 0.4 × (55, 60) + 0.6 × (46, 50) = (49.6, 54).

In this case, it is not clear which value is higher, so we have to calculate the average of the interval:

- A_1 = (34 + 54) / 2 = 44.

- A_2 = (40 + 50) / 2 = 45.

- A_3 = (45 + 55) / 2 = 50.

- A_4 = (49.6 + 54) / 2 = **51.8**. ←

▶ With the OWA operator (W = (0.1, 0.2, 0.2, 0.2, 0.3)).

- A_1 = 0.1 × (70, 90) + 0.2 × (50, 70) + 0.2 × (40, 70) + 0.2 × (30, 50) + 0.3 × (10, 30) = (34, 56).

- A_2 = 0.1 × (70, 80) + 0.2 × (60, 70) + 0.2 × (40, 50) + 0.2 × (30, 40) + 0.3 × (20, 30) = (39, 49).

- A_3 = 0.1 × (60, 70) + 0.2 × (50, 60) + 0.2 × (45, 50) + 0.2 × (42, 50) + 0.3 × (35, 45) = (43.9, 52.5).

- A_4 = 0.1 × (55, 60) + 0.2 × (52, 60) + 0.2 × (50, 53) + 0.2 × (48, 50) + 0.3 × (46, 50) = (49.3, 53.6).

In this case, it is not clear which value is higher, so we have to calculate the average of the interval:

- $A_1 = (34 + 56) / 2 = 45$.

- $A_2 = (39 + 49) / 2 = 44$.

- $A_3 = (43.9 + 52.5) / 2 = 48.2$.

- $A_4 = (49.3 + 53.6) / 2 = 51.45$. ←

As we can see, depending on the method used, the results may lead to different decisions. Moreover, by using imprecise information, the decision process becomes more difficult because we have more complexities for ordering the actions (or alternatives). However, by doing this analysis, we are considering all the situations that could occur in the future without losing any information in the analysis.

Review Topics

1. Give some examples of decisions that need to be made in a business continuity program.

2. Describe how the models presented in this chapter can be beneficial to a decision maker involved with a business continuity program.

3. What are some of the limitations of these decisions models? Describe some obstacles in implementing decisions based on these models.

4. How important is it to capture the decision maker's disposition towards risk. How is subjectivity included in the decision modeling process?

Bibliography

Anderson, D.R., Sweeney, D.J., Williams, T.A., Camm, J.D., Martin R.K., *An Introduction to Management Science*, 2011.

Bridgman, P.W., *Dimensional Analysis*, Yale University Press, 1922.

Engemann, K.J., Filev, D.P., Yager, R.R., "Modeling Decision Making Using Immediate Probabilities,"*International Journal of General Systems*, Vol. 24, pp. 281-294, 1996.

Figueira, J., Greco, S., Ehrgott, M., *Multiple Criteria Decision Analysis: State of the Art Surveys*, Springer, Boston, 2005.

Fishburn P.C., "Additive Utilities with Incomplete Product Set: Applications to Priorities and Assignments," *Operations Research Society of America*, 1967.

Gil-Aluja, J., *Fuzzy Sets in the Management of Uncertainty*, Springer, 2004.

Gil-Lafuente, A.M., *Fuzzy Logic in Financial Analysis*, Springer, 2005.

Hurwicz, L., "*Optimality Criteria For decision Making Under Ignorance*," Cowles Communication Discussion paper, Statistics, No. 370, 1951.

Hwang, C.L., Yoon, K., *Multiple Attribute Decision Making: Methods and Applications*, Springer-Verlag, Berlin, 1981.

Kaufmann, A., Gupta, M.M.. *Introduction to Fuzzy Arithmetic*, Publications Van Nostrand, Rheinhold, 1985.

Laplace, P.S., *A Philosophical Essay on Probabilities*, New Cork, Dover Publications, Inc., 1951, first edition 1814.

Merigó, J.M., *New Extensions to the OWA Operators and their Application in Decision Making*, PhD Thesis, Department of Business Administration, University of Barcelona, 2008.

Merigó, J.M., Gil-Lafuente, A.M., "TheInduced Generalized OWA Operator," Information Sciences 179, pp. 729-741, 2009.

Miller, D.W., Starr, M.K., *Executive Decisions and Operations Research*, Prentice-Hall, Inc., 1969.

Render, B., Stair, R.M., Hanna, M.E., *Quantitative Analysis for Management*, Prentice Hall, 2009.

Roy, B., "Classement Et Choix en Présence de Points de Vue Multiples (la Méthode ELECTRE)," *RIRO*, Vol. 8, pp. 57-75, 1968.

Saaty, T.L., *The Analytic Hierarchy Process*, McGraw-Hill, New York, 1980.

Savage, L.J., "The Theory of Statistical Decision," *Journal of American Statistical Association* 46, pp. 55-67, 1951.

Triantaphyllou, E., *Multi-Criteria Decision Making Methods: A Comparative Study*, Kluwer Academic Publishers, 2001.

Yager, R.R., "On Ordered Weighted Averaging Aggregation Operators in Multi-Criteria Decision Making," *IEEE Transactions on Systems, Man and Cybernetics,* Vol. 18, pp. 183-190, 1988.

Yager, R.R., "Generalized OWA Aggregation Operators," *Fuzzy Optimization and Decision Making* 3, pp. 93-107, 2004.

Yager, R.R., Engemann, K.J., Filev, D.P., "On the Concept of Immediate Probabilities," *International Journal of Intelligent Systems*, Vol. 10, pp. 373-397, 1995.

Yager, R.R., Filev, D.P., "Induced Ordered Weighted Averaging Operators," *IEEE Transaction on Systems, Man and Cybernetics*, Vol. B 29, pp. 141-150, 1999.

Yager, R.R., Kacprzyck, J., *The Ordered Weighted Averaging Operators: Theory and Applications,* Kluwer Academic Publishers, Norwell, MA, 1997.

Yager, R.R., Liu L., *Classic Works of the Dempster-Shafer Theory of Belief Functions*, Springer-Verlag, Berlin, 2008.

SECTION V

Case Studies

Six case studies are incorporated in the book to provide a comprehensive view of business continuity management. Two of the case studies describe a typical business; one a service-based business and the other a manufacturing-based business. These two case studies are examined throughout the book and, as topics are introduced, the concepts are applied in a business environment to provide a practical application of the material.

Alpha Investment Services

Operations

General Operations

Alpha Investment Services (AIS) creates technical research materials for institutional investors and individual investors. Institution investors include money managers, broker-dealers and investment advisors. The company produces 20 technical analysis publications with certain publications targeting individual investors and other publications targeting institutional investors. Custom research reports are produced only for large institutional investors.

Publications and custom research reports are produced on a daily, weekly, monthly, quarterly and, for certain custom research reports, on a special time period basis. Information is made available to clients under a variety of media formats including computer downloads, email, Internet, fax and hardcopy reports. Hardcopy reports have become less important over the last several years and is not considered to be as time critical as information released by computer downloads, email or over the Internet. AIS does have a relatively small print shop that produces some hardcopy reports; larger hardcopy reports are externally produced by an outside professional printer.

AIS has four major services: Asset Allocation, Custom Research, Equity Selection and Fixed Income. Each service performs more or less independently of one another. Custom Research accounts for approximately 50% of total profits and many of the custom research projects for institutional money managers require immediate or on-demand delivery. For all operations, the ability of AIS to deliver high quality services on a timely basis is considered to be critical to the business. Customer service and ongoing contact with customers is considered to be critical to the business.

Except for internal hardcopy publications, AIS does not manufacture any item. Although there are several important clients that utilize AIS services, AIS has a well-diversified client base. AIS currently employs approximately 125 individuals. AIS operates out of two buildings with approximately 80 employees working out of the Main Building and with the remainder working out of the Auxiliary Building.

Support Departments and Operational Groups

Operational Groups – capsule summary of responsibilities

▶ **Asset Allocation Services** – research and analysis of asset allocations, reports, customer service and investor contact.

▶ **Custom Research** – research and analysis, custom research projects, reports, customer service and investor contact.

▶ **Equity Selection Services** – research and analysis of equity investments, reports, customer service and investor contact.

▶ **Fixed Income Selection Services** – research and analysis of fixed income investments, reports, customer service and investor contact.

Operational Group	Percent of Revenue	Percent of Profits
Asset Allocation Services	15%	15%
Custom Research	40%	50%
Equity Selection Services	30%	25%
Fixed Income Selection Services	15%	10%

Support Departments – capsule summary of responsibilities

▶ **Data Operations** – data acquisition, data verification and data analysis.

▶ **Facilities** – maintenance of buildings, maintenance of building systems, environmental controls and utility services.

▶ **Finance and Accounting** – accounting, financial reporting, insurance services, external communications and crisis communications, hardcopy publishing operations, legal issues and account management.

▶ **Human Resources (HR)** – payroll, benefits and general workforce issues.

▶ **Information Technology (IT)** – support of technology services including data center operations, data center recovery, alternate site operations, communication technologies, critical data management of electronic information, information security, applications and communications systems.

▶ **Sales and Marketing** – management of the marketing program and direct sales.

▶ **Security** – building protection and threat monitoring.

Interdependencies and Supply Chain

Nearly all operational groups of AIS are completely dependent on computer systems and communication access. The goal of AIS is to provide quality service on a very timely basis and failure in the supply chain and process flow will quickly lengthen processing time to unacceptable levels. The following figure illustrates the supply chain:

Figure Case Study A.1 - AIS Basic Supply Chain

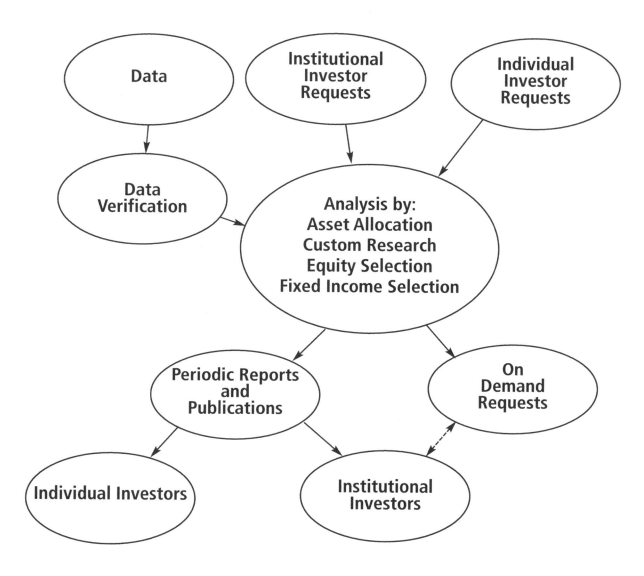

Recovery Time Objectives

The following Recovery Time Objectives have been established by senior management:

Operations that must be maintained at all times:

- Data Operations – data acquisition.
- Information Technology – communication infrastructure.
- Facilities – environmental controls and utility services in the Main Building.
- Finance and Accounting – crisis communication.
- Security – facility protection and threat monitoring.

All critical operations not listed above are to be recovered within one hour.

All non-critical operations are to be recovered within two days.

Resource Requirements

Location

The Main Building and Auxiliary Building are both located within Grand Office Park in central Iowa. The Main Building and the Auxiliary Building are located across the street from one another.

Although protected by a levee, the entire Grand Office Park is located in a 50-year flood plain. There is a single guarded entrance to Grand Office Park and at the entrance there is a railroad spur line. Grand Office Park is essentially bounded by railroad tracks, a river and farmland.

Most of the buildings at Grand Office Park are either office buildings or light industry buildings. Aside from the hazmat threat, most risks from other businesses within Grand Office Park are considered to be low.

Building Environment

Both buildings are two story buildings equipped with an automatic fire suppression system, fire alarms, security systems and adequate exits. Both buildings are of recent construction and meet all building codes.

There is a dual conduit supplying electricity to both buildings and there is a generator to provide electricity during an extended electrical outage for the Main Building but not the Auxiliary Building. Power outages will shutdown virtually all activities in the Auxiliary Building but critical operations can be relocated to conference rooms in the Main Building. Most critical operations including IT are already supported from the Main Building.

Building and Building Systems

AIS essentially requires general office space that can support 125 people. Each operational group can function independently of one another.

Building Contents and Equipment

For the most part, there are no unusual building contents required for operations. The print shop has some expensive equipment but this equipment is insured and would not be that difficult to replace. Moreover, hardcopy reports are no longer considered to be critical to overall operations.

Community Infrastructure

Fire and Police Departments are located a short distance from Grand Office Park. All utility services such as wire communications, electric, natural gas, sewer and water are underground, relatively new and in good condition.

External Dependencies

Several other businesses provide important subcontractor services for facility operations. Most of these services can be secured from multiple providers.

Hazardous Materials

Except for a fairly low level of hazmat in the print shop in the Main Building, there are no significant levels of hazmat in either building.

Personnel Requirements

Employees require workspace, computer, standard office supplies and equipment, high-speed Internet access, email and, to a lesser extent, telephone access. Employees can work from multiple remote locations with proper infrastructure support such as office space, computer, technology services, high speed Internet access and electric power. Many employees can also work individually from home or from other properly supported office environments.

Regional Threats

Man-made: There are no Major Airports, Dams or Nuclear Power Plants in the general area.

Seismic: There are no significant seismic threats in the general area.

Weather:

▶ Grand Office Park floods approximately once every 50 years.

▶ A significant snowfall of six to seven inches occurs approximately every other year. Ice storm events are very rare. Public services are well equipped to clear roadways resulting from typical snowfall events.

▶ Grand Office Park receives approximately 55 thunderstorms per year. The buildings are designed to withstand severe thunderstorm wind, rain and lightning strikes.

▶ Iowa experiences approximately 31 tornadoes in an average year and a few of these tornadoes are of tornado force EF3, EF4 or EF5. EF3, EF4 and EF5 tornadoes will damage or destroy modern buildings.

Security

A very good security system is in place that includes perimeter sensors, cameras, access controls, swipe cards and a sophisticated security monitoring system. There is a security control room in the Main Building. Special security controls are in place for critical areas of each building. Unarmed security guards are present during working hours. During non-working hours, the buildings are monitored and periodic drive-bys are conducted by an outside security subcontractor. The entrance to Grand Office Park is gated and guarded 24/7/365.

Supplies and Raw Materials

There are no special or unusual supplies required for normal operations. Except for print shop operations, raw materials of a physical nature are not a factor for AIS operations.

Raw materials in the form of data information are critical to AIS operations. Data collection is performed automatically without manual intervention and is available free of charge from a variety of worldwide financial markets.

Information Technology (IT)

A detailed analysis of IT will be made later. It is important to note that virtually all AIS operations from data collection to data analysis and ultimately to deliverables are dependent on IT support services.

Information Technology

IT Alternate Site Planning

An IT alternate site has been secured with an outside vendor located in Pennsylvania that specializes in providing these services. The site has standby hardware available and can be classified as a 'co-location site.' All applications and data can be accessed by users from the Internet.

The IT Disaster Recovery Plan is well documented and the IT alternate site is tested annually. Critical applications can be recovered within one hour by activating the site remotely. All applications can be recovered within 12 hours.

Data Center Controls

The data center is well located in an interior section of the Main Building. The data center is equipped with raised floors, fortified walls, a pre-action water based fire suppressant system along with other modern alarms and controls. The data center is monitored 24/7/365 and access to the data center is controlled by a swipe-card security system.

Electrical surge protection and UPS units are provided for all critical computer and communication equipment. Most importantly, the data center has a backup electrical generator capable of running the entire data center and the dedicated air conditioning, heating and ventilation system.

Data Center Recovery

Data center hardware and hardware configuration is well documented. There is a contract with an outside service provider to rapidly replace damaged or destroyed equipment. Information Technology also utilizes the services of an outside consultant who can assist with the data center recovery.

Information Management – Electronic Data

All data files are backed-up daily and secured offsite weekly with quarterly backup files retained indefinitely. Data files are stored at a local bank vault located within the Grand Office Park. Software disks are stored inside the data center in a fire-resistant safe.

Information Management – Hardcopy Data

For AIS, nearly all hardcopy data has backup electronic data. For hardcopy data that are not created or otherwise secured by Information Technology, special precautions are taken. Critical hardcopy data are duplicated and secured with one copy located at each building.

Information Security

Security includes User ID numbers and complex passwords that must be changed regularly. Programs, data and files are all password protected. Firewalls are in place to prevent the introduction of outside viruses, intruders and hackers.

Several years ago, written administrative controls were developed and approved by the Director of Information Technology. Among many other responsibilities, the Director of Information Technology is also responsible for information security.

Revised Recovery Time Objectives

AIS senior management wants to be fully prepared for major crisis events such as a flood and for other crisis events that only temporarily disrupt operations such as a severe winter storm. Senior management is in basic agreement with the analysis and goals presented in the RA and the BIA. However, senior management wants to ensure that data acquisition plus communications between senior management and with investors can be maintained without interruption. Senior management also believes that recovering all critical operations at 100% capability within one hour would require an extremely expensive BCM that is not realistic or cost-justified.

The following Recovery Time Objectives have been established by senior management:

Operations that must be maintained at all times:

- Data Operations – data acquisition.
- Information Technology – communication infrastructure.
- Facilities – environmental controls and utility services in the Main Building.
- Finance and Accounting – crisis communication.
- Security – facility protection and threat monitoring.

Operations that must be recovered within one hour:

- All critical operations not listed above at 50% of normal capability.

Operations that must be recovered within one day:

- All critical operations.
- All non-critical operations at 50% of normal capability.

Operations that must be recovered within five days:

- All non-critical operations.

The prior Recovery Time Objectives was one hour for critical operations and two days for non-critical operations.

Crisis Communication

Communication Infrastructure at Grand Office Park

Both buildings are serviced by dual underground voice and data communication lines. Crisis communication hardware is modern and includes an intercom system in each building. Grand Office Park has a siren system to alert businesses of a tornado, hazardous release or other general threat.

Communication Equipment and Technologies

Emergency team members can be alerted to a crisis simultaneously via cell phone. A voice mail system is in place for disseminating information to employees during non-working hours. The voice mail system hardware is safely located out-of-the-area and can be accessed and updated remotely. The voice mail system is handled by a subcontractor and the system is capable of handling a high volume of calls and there are many redundancies in place. Email can also be used for emergency communications and email servers are located at the data center with redundant email servers at the IT alternate site.

AIS has an emergency webpage link on the home page of the company's website. Information here is accessible to all employees, investors and anyone who accesses the website. AIS also has a special website specifically dedicated to providing crisis information to employees. This special website provides detailed and sometimes confidential information about a crisis situation. Employees may also post information to the special website.

All key management personnel have a PDA and there are six satellite phones that are secured in the data center in the Main Building and available for distribution in a crisis situation. AIS can also text message and instant message crisis information.

Beta Widget Makers

Operations

General Operations

Beta Widget Makers (BWM) manufactures and sells 'widgets' directly to the public throughout the continental USA. The widgets include a wide variety of kitchen and cleaning products. Orders are received by website, phone and, to a lesser extent, facsimile. All shipping is made through the United States Postal Service six days a week. The business currently employs approximately 430 individuals. BWM operates out of two buildings with approximately 280 employees working out of the Central Plant and with the remainder working out of the West Plant.

Support Departments and Operational Groups

Operational (Manufacturing-Related) Groups – capsule summary of business responsibilities

▶ **Manufacturing** – the operation and maintenance of manufacturing equipment, the actual production or manufacturing, fabrication and assembly of product.

▶ **Research and Development** – the design and development of new products, tool and die development, testing and engineering.

▶ **Supply Chain Management** – synchronization of the supply chain, acquisition of raw materials, inventory management, transportation, fulfillment management and quality control.

▶ **Warehouse** – dock operations including receiving, shipping, materials handling, storing and picking.

Support Departments – capsule summary of business responsibilities

▶ **Facilities** – maintenance of physical Plants, maintenance of building systems, hazmat monitoring, environmental controls, utility services, Plant protection and threat monitoring.

▶ **Finance and Accounting** – accounting, financial reporting, insurance services, external communications and crisis communication, legal issues and account management.

▶ **Human Resources (HR)** – payroll, benefits and general workforce issues.

▶ **Information Technology (IT)** – support of technology services (data center operations, data center recovery, alternate site operations, communication technologies, critical data management of electronic information and information security), applications and communications systems.

▶ **Sales and Customer Service** – management of the marketing program, customer service and direct sales.

Information Technology (IT)

A detailed analysis of IT will be made later. It is important to note that virtually all Sales and Customer Service business operations are dependent on IT. Manufacturing and Warehouse related operations utilize IT support services but there are less efficient manual alternatives.

Interdependencies and Supply Chain

As with a typical manufacturing business, BWM business operations are a type of 'supply chain.' The production of the final product is dependent on nearly all operational groups continuously functioning. There is very little buffer stock maintained by BWM. For example, if Fabrication became disabled, then Assembly would be subsequently disabled, Test and Quality Control would be disabled somewhat later and so forth. The following figure illustrates the supply chain:

Figure B.1 - Basic Supply Chain

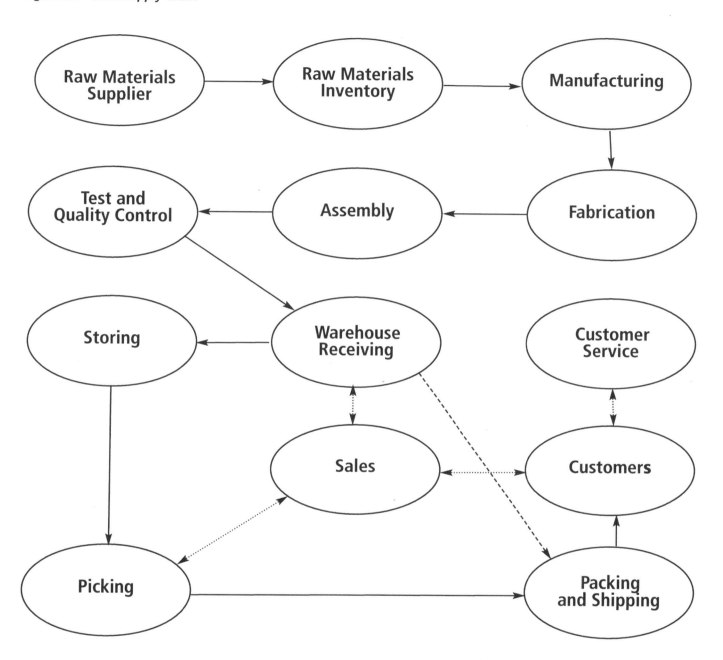

Recovery Time Objectives

The following Recovery Time Objectives have been established by senior management:

Business operations that must be maintained at all times:

▶ Facilities (environmental controls, utility services, facility protection and threat monitoring).

▶ Finance and Accounting (crisis communication).

Manufacturing-related operations:

- Critical operations are assigned a Recovery Time Objective of three days
- Non-Critical operations are assigned a Recovery Time Objective of ten days.

Sales and Customer Service-related operations:

- Critical operations including direct sales order taking are assigned a Recovery Time Objective of one hour.
- Non-Critical operations are assigned a Recovery Time Objective of two days.

Resource Requirements

Location

The Central Plant is located within Grand Office Park in central Iowa. The West Plant is located in another business park approximately 50 miles west of Grand Office Park. The West Plant is not located in a flood plain.

Although protected by a levee, the entire Grand Office Park is located in a 50-year flood plain. There is a single guarded entrance to Grand Office Park and at the entrance there is a railroad spur line (the railroad spur line is not used by BWM). Grand Office Park is essentially bounded by railroad tracks, a river and farmland.

Most of the buildings at Grand Office Park are either office buildings or light industrial buildings. Aside from the hazmat risk, most risks from other businesses within Grand Office Park are considered to be low.

Building Environment

Both the Central Plant and the West Plant are single story buildings that are equipped with an automatic fire suppression system, fire alarms, adequate exits, etc. Both Plants are of recent construction and meet all building codes.

There is a dual conduit supplying electricity to both Plants. There is a diesel powered electric generator to provide electricity during an extended electrical outage in the Central Plant for Information Technology (IT), Sales and Customer Service, and Warehouse. Note that all Information Technology and Sales and Customer Service operations are conducted out of the Central Plant. Power outages will shutdown most manufacturing-related and most support department operations in the Central Plant.

Building and Building Systems

The 'Central Plant' consists of a 30,000-square-foot facility that is used for general office space, manufacturing and warehousing. Critical manufacturing support operations (maintenance, tool and die) are located in the central area of the Plant. Basic specifications are as follows:

- 30,000 sq. ft. of space:
  - ❖ 6,000 sq. ft. general office space.
  - ❖ 6,000 sq. ft. general office space used by Sales and Customer Service.
  - ❖ 13,000 sq. ft. of manufacturing space.
  - ❖ 5,000 sq. ft. of warehouse space (storage, shipping and receiving space).

- Approximately 1,000 sq. ft. of manufacturing and warehouse space must be designated for chemicals.

- Docking bays: three receiving and three shipping.

- Critical building systems include a compressed air system, chilled water systems and high electrical capacity.

The 'West Plant' consists of a 17,000-square-foot facility that is primarily used for manufacturing and warehousing. Critical manufacturing support operations are located in the central area of the Plant primarily surrounded by cement block walls, plywood walls or chain link. Basic specifications are as follows:

- 17,000 sq. ft. of space:
  - ❖ 2,000 sq. ft. general office space.
  - ❖ 11,000 sq. ft. of manufacturing space.
  - ❖ 4,000 sq. ft. of warehouse space (storage, shipping and receiving space).

- Approximately 3,000 sq. ft. of manufacturing and warehouse space must be designated for chemicals and chemical products.

- Docking bays: two receiving and two shipping.

- Critical building systems include a compressed air system, chilled water systems and high electrical capacity.

The critical building systems that support manufacturing-related operations are essentially the same at both Plants. Each Plant contributes approximately 50% of total gross revenue. If a Plant is destroyed, it will take approximately four months to convert a standard warehouse into a Plant suitable for BWM manufacturing operations.

Building Contents and Equipment

The BWM manufacturing business operations require expensive manufacturing equipment. Much of the manufacturing equipment is of custom design and, if destroyed, could take months to replace. The equipment is large, heavy and, in an emergency situation, would take five days to move.

Important equipment necessary for business operations can be summarized as follows:

- Computers, telephones and office supplies for administrative and support staff.

- All manufacturing equipment will be listed as an attachment to the Business Continuity Plan. For our purposes here, it is important to note that some critical manufacturing equipment is highly specialized, expensive and, if destroyed, will take several months to replace.

- All technology systems, equipment and its configuration will be detailed by the IT department.

All tools utilized by BWM are fairly standard and easily replaceable. There are a number of standard and custom made dies that are used in the manufacturing process. Standard dies can be fairly easily replaced. Custom made dies are made by subcontractors according to BWM specifications. BWM retains patents and the engineering drawings for the dies. Custom dies can be replaced by existing or backup subcontractors; however, there is a delay time of two or three weeks for certain dies.

For the most part, each Plant has different manufacturing equipment and produces different products.

Community Infrastructure

Fire and Police Departments are located a short distance from Grand Office Park. All utility services such as wire communications, electric, natural gas, sewer and water are underground, relatively new and in good condition.

External Dependencies

Several other businesses provide important subcontractor services for facility operations. Most of these services can be secured from multiple providers.

Hazardous Materials

There are a number of chemicals used in the manufacturing process. Some of the chemicals are used to manufacture products and some of the chemicals become cleaning products. All of the chemicals are available from multiple suppliers.

BWM has taken a proactive approach to all safety matters and the company has a full-time Director of Environmental Health and Safety. The organization has developed a Safety Procedure Policy and implemented a formal ERP. Teams are trained in emergency response procedures and are provided with the necessary equipment to perform their assignments safely. Hazardous materials, some of which are flammable, are kept in segregated rooms with secondary containment. There were no serious safety deficiencies identified during a recent site inspection.

Personnel Requirements

Most manufacturing-related operations are handled by semi-skilled labor without extensive training. Sales and Customer Service operations are also handled by semi-skilled labor but basic training requires two weeks. Fully trained customer service personnel require several months of experience to be completely proficient. All workers are non-unionized.

Regional Threats

Man-made – There are no Major Airports, Dams or Nuclear Power Plants in the general area.

Seismic – There are no significant seismic threats in the general area.

Weather –
- Grand Office Park floods approximately once every 50 years.
- A significant snowfall of six to seven inches occurs approximately every other year. Ice storm events are very rare. Public services are well equipped to clear roadways resulting from typical snowfall events.
- Grand Office Park receives approximately 55 thunderstorms per year. The buildings are designed to withstand severe thunderstorm wind, rain and lightning strikes.
- Iowa experiences approximately 31 tornadoes in an average year and a few of these tornadoes are of tornado force EF3, EF4 or EF5. EF3, EF4 and EF5 tornadoes will damage or destroy modern

buildings.

Security

There are few security controls in place at both Plants and security services are handled by the Facilities Department. Security controls include standard locking devices on exterior doors and on interior doors with access to very critical areas. Both Plants are monitored for fire. The entrance to Grand Office Park is gated and guarded 24/7/365.

Supplies and Raw Materials

The manufacturing of widgets requires a number of raw materials. Raw materials include chemicals, stainless steel and, in smaller quantities, other metal. All materials needed are available from multiple sources.

From a business continuity planning perspective, it is important to consider inventories and sources of raw materials. BWM maintains fairly low levels of raw materials with inventories sufficient for about three – five days of manufacturing, depending on the type of material. BWM maintains low inventories to maximize cash flow and because the required materials are readily available from outside vendors. Management feels comfortable that BWM is not dependent upon any single vendor for critical supplies that could not otherwise be provided by another vendor.

BWM maintains approximately two to four days of finished product stored in the Warehouse. On occasion, some new products are sold, packed and shipped immediately after they are manufactured but this represents a fairly small percentage of total revenue.

Information Technology

IT Alternate Site Planning

In the event of a crisis at the main data center located in the Central Plant, an alternate data center can be established at the West Plant. The West Plant data center backup area was once an actual operational data center and is located in a separate locked room. Although there is no hardware in place, connectivity is not a problem and the room could be converted into an operational data center.

Information Technology estimates that the West Plant data center can recover most critical operations within 5 to 7 days. Recovering full operations will take 2 weeks or longer. These recovery time periods are contingent upon having a complete Information Technology Disaster Recovery Plan in place. Access should not be a problem as all applications and data can be accessed by users from the Internet. Currently, there is limited written documentation regarding the details of relocating the data center and there are no contractual guarantees to replace hardware on a timely basis.

Data Center Controls

The primary data center is located in the Central Plant in a locked room with a separate dedicated air conditioning, heating and ventilation system. Most hardware is kept on racks. UPS units provide electrical spike protection and temporary power backup. A diesel powered generator provides long-term power backup. Monitoring systems are lacking and thus the data center is not monitored at all during non-business hours.

Data Center Recovery

Documentation of data center hardware, hardware applications and hardware configuration appear to be complete and up-to-date. Information Technology utilizes the services of an outside consultant who can assist with the data center recovery.

Information Management – Electronic Data

Nightly backups of data to tape are performed and the tapes are stored at the home of an employee. Quarterly backup tapes are retained indefinitely. Software disks are stored inside the Central Plant data center area.

Information Management – Hardcopy Data

All important hardcopy data are secured at the Central Plant and historical hardcopy data are stored in a secured room at the West Plant. Critical hardcopy data are duplicated and secured with one copy at each Plant.

Information Security

Security includes User ID's and complex passwords that are regularly changed. Programs, data and files are all password protected. Firewalls are in place to prevent the introduction of outside viruses, intruders and hackers.

Written policies, standards and procedure controls are in place. Security classifications have been established and access controls are in place.

Revised Recovery Time Objectives

Executive management is in basic agreement with the analysis and goals presented in the Risk Analysis and Business Impact Analysis. However, executive management considers the goals presented in the Business Impact Analysis, particularly for sales and customer service-related operations, will require a Business Continuity Management program that is too expensive.

The following Recovery Time Objectives have been established by executive management:

Business operations that must be maintained at all times:

- Facilities (environmental controls, utility services, facility protection and threat monitoring).
- Finance and Accounting (crisis communication).

Manufacturing-related operations:

- Critical operations are assigned a Recovery Time Objective of five days.
- Non-Critical operations are assigned a Recovery Time Objective of ten days.

Sales and customer service-related operations:

- Critical operations including direct sales order taking are assigned a Recovery Time Objective of one day at 25% of normal capacity, 50% of normal capacity within three days and 100% of normal capacity within ten days.
- Non-Critical operations are assigned a Recovery Time Objective of ten days.

Executive management has approved the funding to improve technology services to meet the revised Recovery Time Objectives (hardware and planning at the IT alternate site) and has approved a study to examine improvements to the data center. Executive management has also approved a program to have 25% of the Sales and Customer Service Department work from home.

The prior Recovery Time Objectives for manufacturing-related operations was three days for critical operations and ten days for non-critical operations. The prior Recovery Time Objectives for sales and customer service-related operations was one hour for critical operations and two days for non-critical operations.

Crisis Communication

Communication Infrastructure at Grand Office Park

The Central Plant is serviced by dual underground voice and data communication lines. During business hours, crisis communication can provide information to employees by the phone system. Grand Office Park has a siren system to alert businesses of a tornado, hazardous release or other general threat.

Communication Equipment and Technologies

A voice mail system is in place for employee communications during non-business hours. The voice mail system hardware is located at the Central Plant, can handle up to 12 calls simultaneously and can be accessed and updated remotely. Email can also be used for emergency communications and the email server is located in the data center at the Central Plant and, as a backup, a redundant email server is now located at the West Plant.

All key management personnel at BWM have cell phones and there are also several Blackberries in use. The Facilities Department has two-way radios for internal Plant communications.

Supply Chain Analysis

Supply Chain Analysis

Figure 3.1 in the Business Impact Analysis Chapter illustrated a typical supply chain for a manufacturing business. The business continuity planner can expand this supply chain model to document the manufacturing-related requirements and inventory levels available during the entire product development process. This type of analysis can actually be made for each individual product manufactured.

Manufacturing-related tasks are expressed in terms of the time required to complete the task. Inventory levels are also defined in terms of time – inventory time is equal to the time the next manufacturing-related task will take to process the inventory. For example, if the inventory level in Raw Materials is sufficient to produce ten units of product and Manufacturing can produce two units of product per hour, then there are five hours of Raw Materials inventory available. The entire supply chain manufacturing-related tasks and inventory levels are defined as follows:

1. Raw Materials Inventory – Sufficient quantities of raw materials available for I_1 hours of Manufacturing. Note that time can also be expressed in terms of days, hours, minutes or any other measure of time.

2. Manufacturing Time – M_1 hours to manufacture the product.

3. Work in Progress (WIP) Inventory before Fabrication – Sufficient quantities of manufactured materials available for I_2 hours of Fabrication.

4. Fabrication Time – M_2 hours to fabricate the product.

5. Work in Progress (WIP) Inventory before Assembly – Sufficient quantities of fabricated materials available for I_3 hours of Assembly.

6. Assembly Time – M_3 hours to assemble the product.

7. Work in Progress (WIP) Inventory before Test and Quality Control – Sufficient quantities of assembled materials available for I_4 hours of Test and Quality Control.

8. Test and Quality Control Time – M_4 hours to test and check the product.

9. Warehouse Inventory before Packing and Shipping – I_5 hours of finished product waiting for shipping.

10. Packing and Shipping Time – M_5 hours to pack and ship the finished product.

From Raw Materials to Packing and Shipping, the entire product production time can be expressed as follows:

Production Time = Total Inventory Time + Total Manufacturing-Related Time

Total Inventory Time = $I_1 + I_2 + I_3 + I_4 + I_5$

Total Manufacturing-Related Time = $M_1 + M_2 + M_3 + M_4 + M_5$

Figure C.1 on the next page illustrates this 'normal supply chain' process graphically.

It is evident that there is a disruption in production whenever any one of the manufacturing-related tasks is disabled. Production also is disrupted when inventory is exhausted and when product is unavailable from the prior manufacturing-related task.

The supply chain manager is certainly interested in any disruption of the entire manufacturing process that creates idle equipment and time. However, the business continuity planner is most interested in having finished product to sell. For example, under the normal supply chain model when the M_5 task is disabled, finished product cannot be shipped. Also when the M_4 task is disabled and the I_5 inventory levels are exhausted, new finished product will be unavailable for the M_5 packing and shipping task. This analysis does ignore the fact that, under each of these examples, the product can probably still be sold for a brief period of time and shipped later.

An analysis can be extended all the way up to Raw Materials. If the Supplier of Raw Materials is unable to ship for a period of time greater than I_1 hours, then there will be a disruption of the Manufacturing task.

The business continuity planner must consider the impact of eliminating the inventory component. Note that 'inventory time' is essentially downtime where raw materials or partially completed product is waiting for the next manufacturing-related task. Basically products are now continuously processed from one manufacturing-related task to the next manufacturing-related task and theoretically this process is conducted instantaneously without any inventory time component. This is referred to as the 'JIT supply chain' model.

From Raw Materials to Packing and Shipping, the entire product production time can be expressed as follows:

Production Time = Total Inventory Time + Total Manufacturing-Related Time

Total Inventory Time = $I_1 + I_2 + I_3 + I_4 + I_5 = 0$

Total Manufacturing-Related Time = $M_1 + M_2 + M_3 + M_4 + M_5$

Production Time = Total Inventory Time + Total Manufacturing-Related Time

Production Time = 0 + Total Manufacturing-Related Time

Production Time = Total Manufacturing-Related Time.

Figure C.1 – Normal Supply Chain

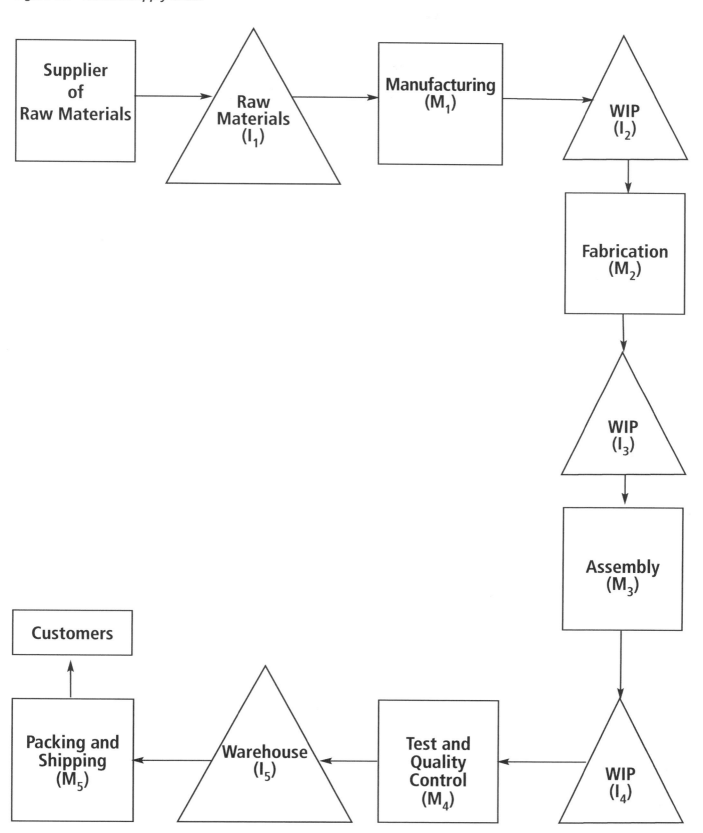

Figure C.2 on the next page illustrates this JIT supply chain process graphically.

This model actually illustrates just-in-time (JIT) and lean manufacturing concepts as well. From the perspective of the business continuity planner, it demonstrates that once any manufacturing-related task is disabled there is an immediate disruption of production. This disruption can be tracked down the supply chain. For example, if Fabrication (M_2) is disabled for 'X hours' then the shipping of finished product will continue for $M_3 + M_4 + M_5$ hours and then be discontinued for X hours.

The business continuity planner should also note that this JIT supply chain model can be utilized to recover production faster after a disruption. The JIT supply chain ignores inventory levels which can be replenished over time at the convenience of the manufacturer.

Figure C.2 – JIT Supply Chain

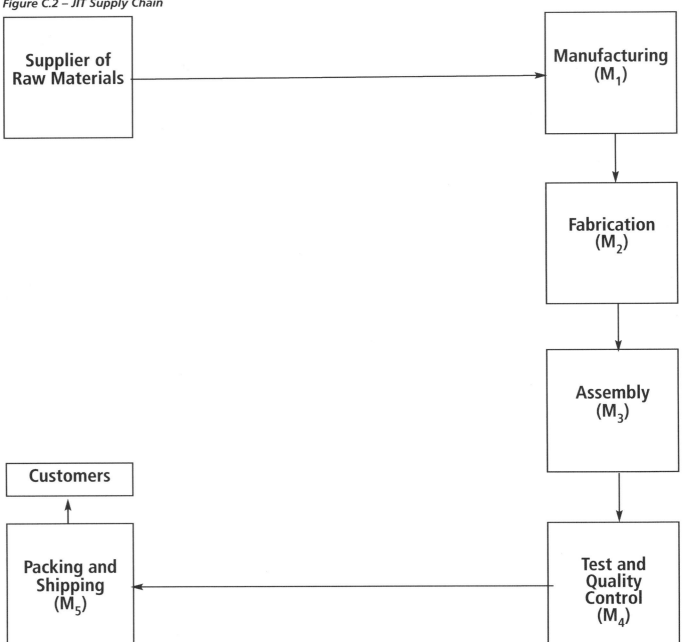

The supply chain analysis can best be illustrated by an example. The following manufacturing-related task times and inventory levels are provided for the product under examination:

1. Inventory/Raw Materials – Sufficient quantities of raw materials available for three days of Manufacturing (I_1).

2. Manufacturing Time – Four hours to manufacture the product (M_1).

3. Inventory/Work in Progress (WIP) before Fabrication – Sufficient quantities of manufactured materials available for two hours of Fabrication (I_2).

4. Fabrication Time – Four hours to fabricate the product (M_2).

5. Inventory/Work in Progress (WIP) before Assembly – Sufficient quantities of fabricated materials available for one hour of Assembly (I_3).

6. Assembly Time – Two hours to assemble the product (M_3).

7. Inventory/Work in Progress (WIP) before Test and Quality Control – Sufficient quantities of assembled materials available for one hour of Test and Quality Control (I_4).

8. Test and Quality Control Time – One hour to test and check the product (M_4).

9. Inventory/Warehouse before Packing and Shipping – Two days of finished product waiting to be packed and shipped (I_5).

10. Packing and Shipping Time – One hour to pack and ship the finished product (M_5).

Under the normal supply chain model, the entire production process takes seven days, including five and one-half days of 'inventory time' and one and one-half days of 'manufacturing-related time.'

Figure C.3 illustrates this process graphically.

This example can be used to analyze when a disruption in the supply chain will result in unavailable finished product for shipment to customers. For simplicity, assume that this manufacturer works one eight-hour shift per day seven days per week. Under the following scenarios, consider these questions, answers and explanations:

Question #1:
How long will finished product be unavailable for shipping to customers if raw materials cannot be received for five days?

Answer:
There should be no disruption in available finished product.

Explanation:
After five days, there will still be two days of finished product in M_5 (Packing and Shipping) and I_5 (Warehouse). Under the JIT supply chain model, new finished product can be shipped after one and one-half days of manufacturing-related time.

Question #2
How long will finished product be unavailable for shipping to customers if raw materials cannot be received for eight days?

Answer:
Finished product will be unavailable for shipping to customers for two and one-half days.

Figure C.3 – Normal Supply Chain

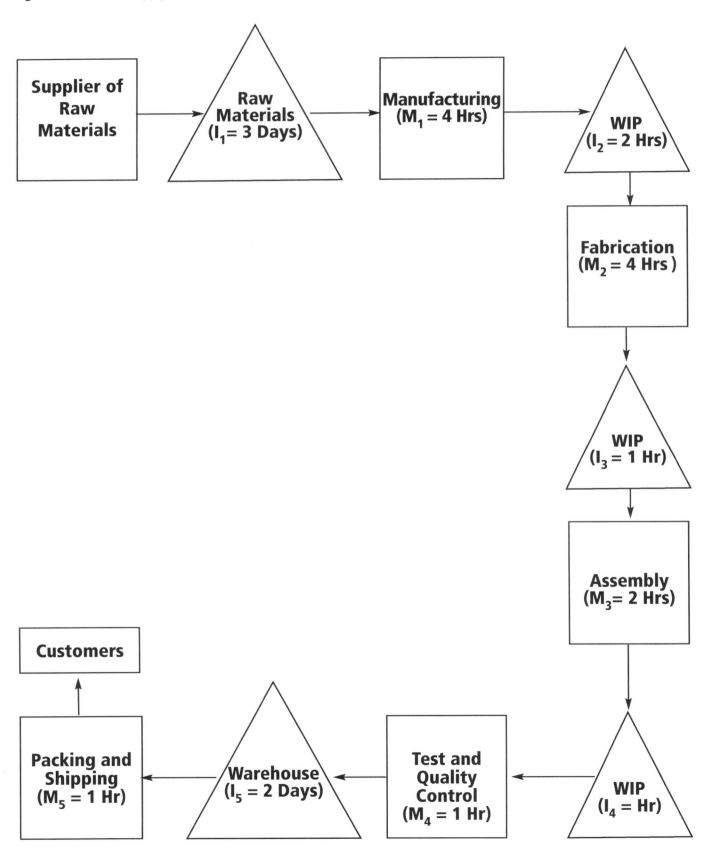

Explanation:
After seven days all product under production will be exhausted. There is one day remaining waiting for raw materials to arrive plus, under the JIT supply chain model, one and one-half days of manufacturing-related time before new finished product can be shipped.

Question: #3.
How long will finished product be unavailable for shipping to customers if Assembly is disabled for two days? Assume that Assembly can immediately forward product at the end of the disablement period.

Answer:
There should be no disruption in available finished product.

Explanation:
After two days, there will still be three hours of finished product in M_5 (Packing and Shipping) and I(Warehouse). Under the JIT supply chain model, new finished product can be shipped after two hours of post-Assembly manufacturing-related time.

Question #4.
How long will finished product be unavailable for shipping to customers if Assembly is disabled for three days? Assume that Assembly can immediately forward product at the end of the disablement period.

Answer:
Finished product will be unavailable for shipping to customers for seven hours.

Explanation:
After two days and three hours $(M_5 + I_5 + M_4 + I_4)$ all finished product under production will be exhausted. There are five hours remaining before Assembly begins to produce product plus, under the JIT supply chain model, two hours of post-Assembly manufacturing-related time before new finished product can be shipped.

Question #5:
Critical Assembly equipment is broken and will take three days to repair. There are manual overrides but Assembly will now take 4 hours. How long will finished product be unavailable for shipping to customer?

Answer:
Finished product will be unavailable for shipping to customers for one hour.

Explanation:
At the time of the equipment breakdown there are two days and three hours of product in the various post-Assembly (M_3) manufacturing tasks and inventory levels $(M_5 + I_5 + M_4 + I_4)$. Moreover, after three days Assembly (M_3 basically working at 25% capacity) will have produced six hours worth of product. Therefore, after three days, there will be one hour of finished product available to be shipped ((2 days and 3 hours) + 6 hours – 3 days) or (19 hours + 6 hours – 24 hours).

Under the JIT supply chain model, at the beginning of the fourth day, new finished product can be shipped after two hours of post-Assembly manufacturing-related time. With only one hour of finished product available for shipment, finished product will be unavailable for one hour.

Case Study Questions

Case Study A-C: Alpha Investment Services (AIS) Supply Chain

For an on-demand Custom Research report referred to as 'Service A', you are provided with the information contained in the supply chain chart below. For simplicity, assume that AIS works from 9:00 am to 5:00 pm, normally takes a full hour for lunch starting at noon and works five days per week Monday through Friday. Also assume that Data Operations starts two hours earlier at 7:00 am than everyone else – assuring that verified data from US markets from the previous day will be available for analysis at the start of normal day.

Questions based on Figure C.4, page 269.

1. Custom Research receives an on-demand custom research report 'Service A' request from a major client on Monday morning at 9:00 am. The report is needed no later than 3:00 pm today. Can Custom Research take a full hour for lunch and still produce the report on time?

2. Custom Research receives an on-demand custom research report 'Service A' request from a major client on Monday morning at 8:00 am. The report is needed no later than 3:00 pm today. However, at 7:00 am a computer malfunction has shutdown Data Operations for 2 hours. Data acquisition and verification can not commence until 9:00 am. Can Custom Research take a full hour for lunch and still produce the report on time?

Case Study B-C: Beta Widget Makers (BWM) Supply Chain

For a product referred to as 'Widget A', you are provided with the information contained in the supply chain chart below. For simplicity, assume that BWM works one eight-hour shift per day seven days per week.

Questions based on Figure C.5, page 270.

1. How long will Widget A be unavailable for shipping to customers if raw materials cannot be received for twelve days?

2. How long will finished Widget A product be unavailable for shipping to customers if raw materials cannot be received for eight days?

3. In order to increase cash flow, new management has decided to keep only 2 days of raw materials in Warehouse Receiving. Question: Under this new scenario, how long will finished Widget A product be unavailable for shipping to customers if raw materials cannot be received for eight days?

4. Critical manufacturing equipment is broken and will take four days to repair. There are manual overrides but Manufacturing for Widget A will now take 16 hours. How long will finished Widget A product be unavailable for shipping to customer?

5. How long will finished Widget A product be unavailable for shipping to customers if Test and Quality Control is disabled for three days?

Figure C.4 - Service A: Supply Chain

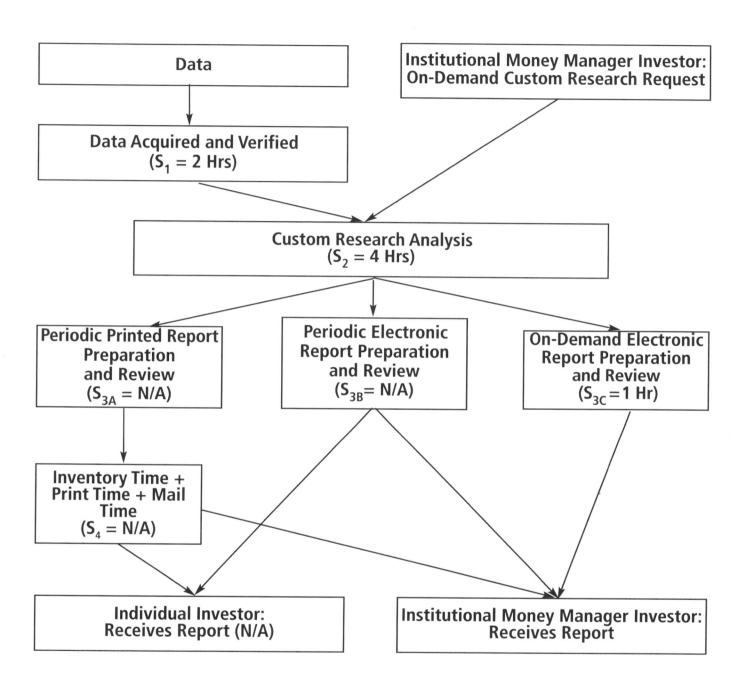

Figure C.5 – Widget A: Supply Chain

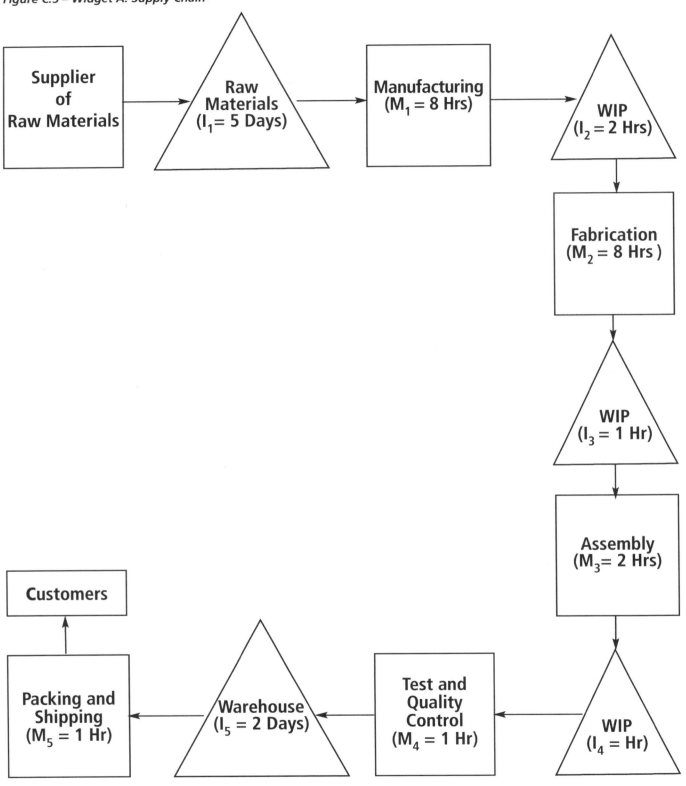

Bibliography

Henderson, D. M., "Supply-Demand Chain Analysis," *Business Survival*, Rothstein Associates Inc. www.rothstein.com/blog/supply-demand-chain-analysis-for-the-business-continuity-planner, June 2009.

Sample Risk Assessment

Introduction

Risk assessment consists of analysis and evaluation, following a process which begins with the identification of threats and proceeds to the prioritization of risks. Case Study D outlines an approach to perform risk assessment using subjective analysis and then illustrates the method with an example. The method described is an effective approach without the cost and time that may be required using more detailed means. While it is important for the assessment to be accurate, needless precision is neither cost-justified nor warranted.

Risk Analysis

Risk analysis follows the risk event chain: threat, crisis, disruption and impact.

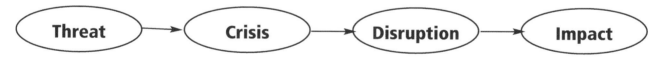

Threat

One approach to identify threats is to analyze an organization from three geographical viewpoints: the general region, the immediate area and the facilities that the organization occupies. Threats may be natural, man-made or accidental and may manifest themselves as crisis events which can cause disruptions and adversely impact the organization.

Crisis

A crisis event is a manifestation of a threat. The following is an example of a numerical scale that may be used to assign a probability classification to each identified crisis event:

- 5 = at least a 10% chance of annual occurrence
- 4 = at least a 5% but less than a 10% chance of annual occurrence
- 3 = at least a 2% but less than a 5% chance of annual occurrence
- 2 = at least a ½% but less than a 2% chance of annual occurrence
- 1 = less than a ½% chance of annual occurrence.

Even though this classification in not a true probability, for the sake of simplicity, it will be referred to as a probability. Even if more rigorous quantitative data were available, judgment is needed when assigning event probabilities.

Disruption

A crisis may create disruptions, in particular due to outages or unavailability of critical resources. The following is an example of a numerical scale that may be used to assign levels of resource unavailability which may cause disruptions in operations:

$$5 = \text{Very High}, 4 = \text{High}, 3 = \text{Medium}, 2 = \text{Low}, 1 = \text{Very Low}$$

The resource unavailability levels are used to assist in making judgments on the resulting disruptions and impacts. The importance of particular resources will vary from business to business. For example, telecommunication capability will be critical for a call center business, as even a short disruption of communication services will cause loss of revenue. On the other hand, a brief telecommunication disruption may have little impact to a manufacturing business. The management team evaluates which resources are most critical.

Impact

For each crisis event under analysis, an impact needs to be determined. In a business environment, impact is most often a function of disruption time as compared to the RTO. The following is an example of an impact classification for a given disruption:

- 4 = Extreme impact – disruption greater than seven days.
- 3 = Serious impact – disruption between two to seven days.
- 2 = Moderate impact – disruption between one hour to two days.
- 1 = Low impact – disruption less than one hour.

The disruptions associated with the impact levels are different for various organizations. In particular, organizations that have time-critical services, such as call centers, would incur adverse impacts rather quickly. Larger businesses have multiple operations, each possibly with a different RTO, therefore it is necessary to analyze impacts for each operation separately. For example, an RTO for manufacturing operations will typically be different than an RTO for sales operations.

Additional Factors

In addition to disruption, additional tangible and intangible factors should be considered when determining impact. Such factors include: life-safety concerns, environmental damage, asset loss and reputation damage.

Consider the following example of impact levels:

- 4 = Extreme impact – significant life-safety threat or significant damage potential or disruption greater than seven days.

- 3 = Serious impact – medium life-safety threat and/or medium damage potential and/or disruption between two to seven days.

- 2 = Moderate impact – some life-safety threat and/or some damage potential and/or disruption between one hour to two days.

- 1 = Low impact – low life-safety threat, low damage potential and disruption less than one hour.

Risk Evaluation

A risk is established with the determination of a probability of occurrence and an impact. A risk measure for each risk can now be determined. Risk Measure (RM) is a quantitative summary value of risk based on probability and impact.

In this case study, the RM formula squares the impact (I) in order to assign it more relative value compared to the probability (P):

$$RM = P \times I^2$$

The RM is used to prioritize risks. The method illustrated is simple, yet incorporates a reasonable level of accuracy. In practice, this analysis is easily understood and meets the needs of many organizations.

Risk Assessment Illustration

The organization under study is a fictitious business named North American Parts and Sales (NAPS). NAPS supplies aircraft parts in North America for Gamma Aircraft. Gamma Aircraft is a European aircraft manufacturer and NAPS is the North American division of Gamma Aircraft located in Norfolk, Virginia.

The primary business of NAPS includes North American aircraft sales, warehouse operations and parts fulfillment. Parts are received by NAPS from Europe via air freight, warehoused in Virginia and distributed throughout North America as needed.

No manufacturing operations are conducted by NAPS; all manufactured products are supplied directly by the parent company. Critical engineering and technical support services are provided directly by the parent company.

Identification of Threats

The following threats have been selected for analysis:

List of Threats

Natural

Hurricane, Category 1

Hurricane, Category 2

Hurricane, Major – Category 3, 4 and 5

Mid-Latitude Storm

Severe Winter Storm

Thunderstorm

Tornado

Man-Made and Accidental

Fire

Hazardous Release

Major Accident

Pandemic Outbreak

Security Breach

Technology Disaster

Terrorist Attack

Transportation Accident

Utility Failure

The NAPS management team has defined the following crisis event classifications:

The probability classification assigned to each crisis event is as follows:

- 5 = at least a 10% chance of annual occurrence
- 4 = at least a 5% but less than a 10% chance of annual occurrence
- 3 = at least a 2% but less than a 5% chance of annual occurrence
- 2 = at least a ½% but less than a 2% chance of annual occurrence
- 1 = less than a ½% chance of annual occurrence.

The impact classification for a given disruption is as follows:

▶ 4 = Extreme impact – expected disruption over seven days.

▶ 3 = Serious impact – expected disruption two to seven days.

▶ 2 = Moderate impact – expected disruption one hour to two days.

▶ 1 = Low impact – expected disruption under one hour.

Shorter disruption periods were initially considered but rejected by executive management. If necessary, critical parts can be supplied by air directly from the manufacturer in Europe.

Natural Crisis Events – Discussion

Hurricane

Hurricanes are a threat to the East Coast of Virginia. Hurricanes can strike the region directly from the southeast or more likely indirectly with somewhat lower intensity from the south. The most likely approach of the hurricane would be from the south forcing the storm to travel over some land. Sea temperatures are also cooler-than-tropical water temperatures. An approaching hurricane will either interact with land and/or travel over some relatively cool water. These factors will limit hurricane intensity making a strike by a category 4 hurricane unlikely and strikes by category 5 hurricanes probably impossible.

Statistically this region will experience hurricane force winds approximately once every 10 years and a major hurricane approximately once every 50 years. The probability of experiencing these wind speeds at any given single location is somewhat less than the probability over the entire region. It is important to note that these statistics are based on long-term trends (over 100 years). The last few years have experienced very active Atlantic Hurricane Seasons and there is credible evidence to suggest that this trend may continue for several years. If anything, this analysis may underestimate the hurricane risk.

All land-falling hurricanes could spawn tornadoes and the entire general area is in a hurricane evacuation zone for a major hurricane. Heavy rainfall could create workforce, utility and transportation disruptions but would not likely flood the building – wind-driven water damage is possible.

If a category 1 hurricane were to strike, there would likely be some brief disruption to the workforce, temporary utility failures and perhaps some physical damage. A category 2 hurricane would result in workforce disruptions, utility failures and possibly physical damage to the buildings.

Damage resulting from a major hurricane is of the greatest concern. For all major hurricanes, the region would experience widespread utility failures, transportation disruptions and residential home damage and destruction. Building damage would also be incurred and there is a possibility of building destruction. None of the company buildings are designed for wind velocities in excess of 120 mph and, depending on the point of actual landfall, storm surge could be a devastating factor.

Category 1 Hurricane: Probability Classification = (4); Impact = Moderate (2)
Category 2 Hurricane: Probability Classification = (3); Impact = Serious (3)
Major Hurricane: Probability Classification = (2); Impact = Extreme (4)

Mid-Latitude Storm

A Mid-Latitude Storm is essentially a flooding event. The Federal Emergency Management Agency (FEMA) provides flood information for the general area. The business location is located outside the 1% annul chance of flooding. In the greater area important transportation roadways are within flood plains; serious area flooding can be expected several times a century.

Floods are a community-wide crisis and can impact workforce availability, disrupt commuting and disable public services. A shutdown of full operations would be unlikely.

Probability Classification = (5); Impact = Low (1)

Severe Winter Storm

Winter snowstorms are a periodic crisis during the cold season. Public services and public utilities are not that well prepared to handle significant winter situations. A severe winter storm, ice storm, or blizzard will swamp public services jeopardizing basic services and making travel dangerous or impossible. Under the most likely scenario, travel will become impossible and a shutdown of normal operations will occur for a period of not longer than two days.

Probability Classification = (5); Impact = Moderate (2)

Thunderstorm

The region regularly experiences strong and sometimes severe thunderstorms (lightning, strong wind, heavy rain and hail). On the average, Virginia receives between 35 and 45 thunderstorms per year.

The greatest threat from a thunderstorm is the disablement of communication and electrical services. Only the IT Department has a backup electric generator and so the business is only partly protected. Nevertheless, power outages from a thunderstorm rarely exceed one hour. There is also a very remote chance that a direct lightning strike could destroy the telephone switch or cable, data center or electrical room equipment. Except when walking in outside open areas, which should not be done, there are few life-safety concerns.

Probability Classification = (5); Impact = Low (1)

Tornado

Land-falling tropical storms and hurricanes could spawn tornadoes. Thunderstorms (especially when preceding an approaching cold front) often spawn tornadoes. Fortunately, tornadoes in Virginia are rarely, if ever, the catastrophic (EF4 and EF5) tornadoes that are possible in the Midwest or central-south United States. A weak/moderate (EF0 and EF1) tornado would probably not significantly damage the buildings. A strong (EF2) tornado could damage and might disable the buildings and a stronger (EF3) tornado would likely disable or destroy the buildings.

Historically between 1950 and 1995 there were seven F1 tornadoes and one F0 tornado in the immediate Norfolk area. During this period there was one F3 tornado in nearby Newport News.

Although tornadoes do not impact an area as large as hurricanes, tornadoes can have a limited community-wide impact. Tornadoes could impact life-safety, workforce availability, disrupt commuting and disable public services. Tornadoes are often assigned an impact of extreme; however, a direct strike by a tornado of sufficient power to disable or destroy the NAPS buildings is incredibly remote. There is a remote probability of a tornado actually striking NAPS and that event would likely have a serious impact.

Probability Classification = (1); Impact = Serious (3)

Note: *On February 1, 2007 the Enhanced Fujita (EF) Scale replaced the Fujita (F) Scale (Appendix I presents additional information). The scales are similar but there is not a simple conversion from one scale to the next. Most historical data are expressed in terms of the Fujita Scale with future projections expressed in terms of the Enhanced Fujita Scale.*

Man-Made, Accidental or Other Crisis Events – Discussion

Fire

Fires are always a risk, even for buildings with automatic fire suppression systems. There is little flammable material stored by NAPS. With an automatic fire suppression system in place, the possibility of the buildings being completely destroyed by fire is very remote. However, a minor fire in any area of a building could create a problem if it resulted in a denial of access for a day or two. There are also asset damage and life-safety concerns that should not be ignored. An impact level of moderate can be justified; however, the life-safety threat factor also justifies a level of serious.

Probability Classification = (2); Impact = Serious (3)

Hazardous Release (Hazmat)

NAPS has few hazardous chemicals stored in the buildings. However, a hazardous release in the general area is a possibility. NAPS is located in an industrial area with roads and railroads that support industrial traffic. Other nearby industries utilize hazardous materials for manufacturing operations. The airport and the close proximity of the seaport both represent a threat. A hazardous release in the general area could shut down operations for several days by forcing a denial of access.

Probability Classification = (3); Impact = Serious (3)

Major Accident

The location at the airport and the nearby industrial business operations all present some level of risk of a major accident (an accident that directly impacts the NAPS). Risk probabilities are difficult to assess and major transportation accidents such as an airplane crash are not common. The NTSB can deny access for an extended period of time. The impact could be extreme but most likely would be serious.

Probability Classification = (2); Impact = Serious (3)

Pandemic Outbreak

An epidemic or pandemic outbreak, whether of accidental or intentional origin, presents a life-threatening crisis of catastrophic proportions. A pandemic outbreak in the general area could necessitate a closing of normal operations quite possibly for an extended period.

Both the probability and the exact impact of a pandemic outbreak are difficult to predict but this threat will need to receive special planning attention. We believe that the probability of a severe life-threatening pandemic outbreak is greater than remote and, if one occurs, the impact could be extreme.

Probability Classification = (2); Impact = Extreme (4)

Security

There are reasonably good security controls in place overall and extra security controls for critical areas of the buildings. NAPS also enjoys a good relationship with individual workers overall. Nevertheless, there is always a risk of a disgruntled employee, former employee or even non-employee intentionally disrupting operations and/or damaging assets. A significant security breach is assigned a medium level of probability. In all likelihood, a serious security breach would not likely disable operations beyond two days. However, there are also life-safety and asset damage concerns that cannot be completely ignored and a serious level of impact has been assigned.

Probability Classification = (3); Impact = Serious (3)

Technology

A disruption of technology services (computer or communication systems) can be a result of events such as a disruption of computers, networks and telephone switches. This could include a hardware malfunction, introduction of a virus, human error, a general 'cyber attack,' activation of the data center's water-based fire suppressant system or intentional hostile security breach. Since the data center is equipped with a standby electric generator and UPS, the risk of a utility failure shutting down technology services is greatly reduced (although not eliminated). Computer systems and communication services are very important to operations.

Software-related problems could occur from a wide variety of sources. Even when excluding very minor shutdowns (which really do not meet our 'crisis' definition), when combined, the probability of software problems is fairly high but software problems would rarely shut down systems for more than a day. Hardware failures are less common than software failures but the impact can be greater.

The lack of an IT alternate site plan and readily available IT alternate site location is a concern. A major technology-related crisis could partially disable normal operations for a week or longer. Critical operations could be maintained manually on a degraded basis without technology support and, as such, a disruption of technology services is considered to be serious rather than extreme.

If management approves funding for IT alternate site planning, this exposure can be reduced.

Probability Classification = (4); Impact = Serious (3)

Terrorist Attack

The intentional release of a chemical, biological, nuclear, high explosive or incendiary device – essentially a Weapon of Mass Destruction (WMD) – is a consideration for all organizations in this century. NAPS does not appear to be a likely terrorist target but the high level of military operations in the general region could be a terrorist target.

There is really no good statistical data for a WMD crisis event and we classify a terrorist attack in the immediate area with probability that is greater than remote but, if one occurs, the impact could be extreme.

Probability Classification = (2); Impact = Extreme (4)

Transportation Accident

We define a 'transportation accident' to be an accident that creates a transportation disruption but does not directly impact the building as a 'major accident' would. The location of the airport, the close proximity of the seaport and industrial operations all present a high level of risk for a transportation accident. The impact would most likely result in a denial of access for a period of less than two days.

Probability Classification = (4); Impact = Moderate (2)

Utility Failure

Utility failures and interruptions can occur from a wide variety of sources. The building is located in an industrial park and NAPS has experienced utility failures in the past.

The most common utility failure is an electrical power outage. There is an electric generator for the data center but not for the rest of the business. Fixed standby generators are extremely expensive but portable generators are much less expensive and could provide electrical power within a few hours. Most utility failures are brief but more serious problems may take one or two days to correct. With all the transportation and industrial risks in the immediate area, utility failures in excess of one hour but fewer than two days have a relatively high probability of annual occurrence.

Probability Classification = (4); Impact = Moderate (2)

Probability

The crisis event that best represents the manifestation of each threat is summarized in the table below.

The Probability Classification (P) assigned to each Crisis Event

Probability Classification (5)
Mid-Latitude Storm
Severe Winter Storm
Thunderstorm

Probability Classification (4)
Category 1 Hurricane
Technology Disaster
Transportation Accident
Utility Failure

Probability Classification (3)
Category 2 Hurricane
Hazardous Release
Security Breach

Probability Classification (2)
Fire
Major Accident
Major Category 3, 4 and 5 Hurricane
Pandemic Outbreak
Terrorist Attack

Probability Classification (1)
Tornado

Expected Disruption

For each crisis event under analysis, the management team considered the following factors:

- Personnel, i.e., unavailability of the workforce.
- Building structure destruction or extended disablement.
- Building denial of access by civil authorities.
- Building content and/or equipment destruction or extended disablement.

- ◗ Loss of IT services.
- ◗ Critical Services:
  - ❖ Loss of computer and communication systems (IT services).
  - ❖ Loss of electrical power.
  - ❖ Loss of police, fire, emergency medical services or other civil resource.
  - ❖ Loss of telecommunications.
  - ❖ Loss of water, gas, sewer, and other utilities.
- ◗ Area-wide or community-wide resource loss:
  - ❖ Transportation disruption.
  - ❖ Workforce disruption.

Levels of Resource Unavailability

Crisis Event	Resources						
	Personnel	Building Structure	Building Access	Building Contents	IT Services	Utility Services	Community Resources
Cat 1 Hurricane	3	1	1	2	3	2	3
Cat 2 Hurricane	4	2	2	3	4	3	4
Maj. Hurricane	5	4	4	5	5	5	5
Mid-Lat. Storm	2	1	2	1	2	2	3
Thunderstorm	2	1	1	2	2	4	4
Tornado	4	4	5	4	5	5	4
Winter Storm	4	1	4	1	2	3	3
Fire	2	5	5	5	5	5	1
Hazmat	3	2	4	2	3	3	2
Major Accident	3	4	4	4	4	4	2
Pandemic	5	1	3	1	5	5	5
Security Breach	2	2	4	4	4	4	2
Tech Disaster	1	1	1	1	5	4	1
Terrorist Attack	4	3	2	3	4	4	4
Transportation	4	1	4	1	2	4	3
Utility Failure	2	1	2	1	2	5	3

5 = Very High, 4 = High, 3 = Medium, 2 = Low, 1 = Very Low

Impact

Based on the life-safety, environmental, disruptions and other factors, the impact classification for each crisis event is summarized in the table below.

Impact (I)

Extreme Impact (4)

Major Category 3, 4 and 5 Hurricane
Pandemic
Terrorist Attack

Serious Impact (3)

Category 2 Hurricane
Fire
Hazardous Release
Major Accident
Security Breach
Technology Disaster
Tornado

Moderate Impact (2)

Category 1 Hurricane
Severe Winter Storm
Transportation Accident
Utility Failure

Low Impact (1)

Mid-Latitude Storm
Thunderstorm

Risk Evaluation

Utilizing the numerical values assigned to impact (I) and probability (P), a prioritization of the most serious risks facing NAPS is determined by using the risk measure: $RM = P \times I^2$.

Risk Prioritization by Risk Measure

Crisis Event	Probability (P)	Impact (I)	$P \times I^2$
Technology Disaster	4	3	36
Major Hurricane	2	4	32
Pandemic Outbreak	2	4	32
Terrorist Attack	2	4	32
Cat 2 Hurricane	3	3	27
Hazardous Release	3	3	27
Security Breach	3	3	27
Severe Winter Storm	5	2	20
Fire	2	3	18
Major Accident	2	3	18
Cat 1 Hurricane	4	2	16
Transportation Accident	4	2	16
Utility Failure	4	2	16
Tornado	1	3	9
Mid-Latitude Storm	5	1	5
Thunderstorm	5	1	5

Significant findings may be summarized as follows:

▶ A Technology failure directly impacts a number of critical services. Without any formal IT alternate site plan, technology services may be unavailable for several days. This risk can be reduced with additional planning and financial commitment.

▶ As expected, a Hurricane (especially a major hurricane) presents a serious risk. As noted in the accompanying discussion, we may be in a period of increased hurricane activity and the hurricane risk may be understated.

▶ Special notice should be given to the Terrorist Attack and Pandemic Outbreak risk due to the extreme impact of the crisis and the difficulty of determining the probability of occurrence.

▶ A Security Breach or a Hazardous Release both present a significant risk.

▶ If a Major Accident and a Transportation Accident are considered together, which arguably they could be, the resulting risk is also significant.

Review Topics

1. Define the major steps involved from identifying threats to ultimately determining risks.

2. Are IT resources more or less important than building structure and building content resources?

3. A computer model might be used to study tornado strike probabilities for an organization located in central Oklahoma. These results may yield more accurate results but is four-decimal-point accuracy necessary?

4. Are there any advantages to use a sophisticated algorithm to assign relative weights to each of the resources in determining impact?

Bibliography

Henderson, D. M., *The Comprehensive Business Continuity Management Program*, Rothstein Associates Inc., 2008.

Phased Pre-Positioning of Employees

Case Study E outlines a plan to pre-position employees in advance of a hurricane strike. With minor modification, this plan will also work well for a flood event that provides sufficient pre-strike time to execute the plan.

Under this plan during the pre-strike period, employees are released from work and return over a staggered period of time. During the period of storm impact, certain employees will be working from designated alternate sites and from other safe distant locations. Other employees that remain in the general area and at the workplace will be available to assist with the emergency response efforts once the storm passes. This process assures that a minimum level of critical operations is maintained at all times.

Although this plan has some application to manufacturing businesses, the plan is most effective for service businesses. A business that relies on large immobile equipment or facilities with special building systems can only partially utilize this plan. The plan requires a great deal of management coordination and is expensive to execute. The plan would only be used by a business with critical operations that must be maintained on an ongoing basis. Simpler versions using the concepts described herein can be less expensive to execute and have application for many organizations.

Objectives

The objectives of this pre-positioning plan are as follows:

- During the pre-strike period, the primary objective is to protect organization assets, employee assets and to relocate employees to safe alternate locations on an orderly basis that minimizes the interruption of normal operations.

- During and immediately surrounding the actual strike period, the primary objective is life-safety, with a secondary objective of protecting assets and maintaining critical operations.

- During the business continuity period, the primary objective is to maintain critical operations at all times and to return to full normal operations as soon as possible under a safe environment.

Employee Release Groups

▶ **Group A:** This group consists of employees who are assigned to travel to alternate sites. There may be subgroups comprised of IT and non-IT employees.

▶ **Group B:** This group consists of employees who intend to travel to locations at least 100 miles away. Group B employees should pre-position themselves at multiple, different and distant locations. Nevertheless, it is acknowledged that some Group B employees may not be able to work during or immediately after the storm.

▶ **Group C:** This group consists of employees who intend to remain in the general area – either at home, in shelters or other nearby safe locations.

▶ **Group D:** This group also consists of employees who intend to remain in the general area – either at home, in shelters or other nearby safe locations.

▶ **Group E:** This group of 'storm personnel' or 'essential personnel' is assigned to stay at the workplace during the storm.

Not every organization will need to assign employees to all Release Groups.

Plan of Action

▶ Group 1 employees are released first, make personal preparations and relocate to the pre-determined and well-supported alternate sites. The alternate sites should be located in regions that do not experience hurricanes.

▶ Group 2 employees are released next, make personal preparations and relocate to other safe distant homes or hotels at least 100 miles away. Supplied with laptop computers, air cards, communication devices and capable of accessing technology services via the Internet, Group 2 will be able to work from laptop computers at distant homes and hotels. Due to possible electric power interruptions and storm damage, it is assumed that some of these employees will be unable to work during and immediately after the hurricane strike.

▶ As Group 1 employees are commencing work from the alternate sites, Group 3 employees are being released. Group 3 employees are given time to make personal preparations and then are expected to return to work before being released again for the actual storm strike. Group 3 employees are expected to work from home to the extent possible.

▶ As Group 3 employees are returning to work, Group 4 employees are being released. Group 4 employees are released in time to make personal preparations and are subsequently expected to work from home to the extent possible.

▶ Group 5 employees are released in time to make personal preparations and are subsequently expected to return to work. Group 5 employees are most likely Facility or Security personnel. Organizations that intend to designate Group 5 employees should be certain that a safe environment can be maintained and that legal counsel approves the plan. It is important to assess the hurricane wind, flood and storm surge risk levels carefully.

Figure E.1 graphically illustrates this process.

Figure E.1 - Continuous Processing of Critical Operations

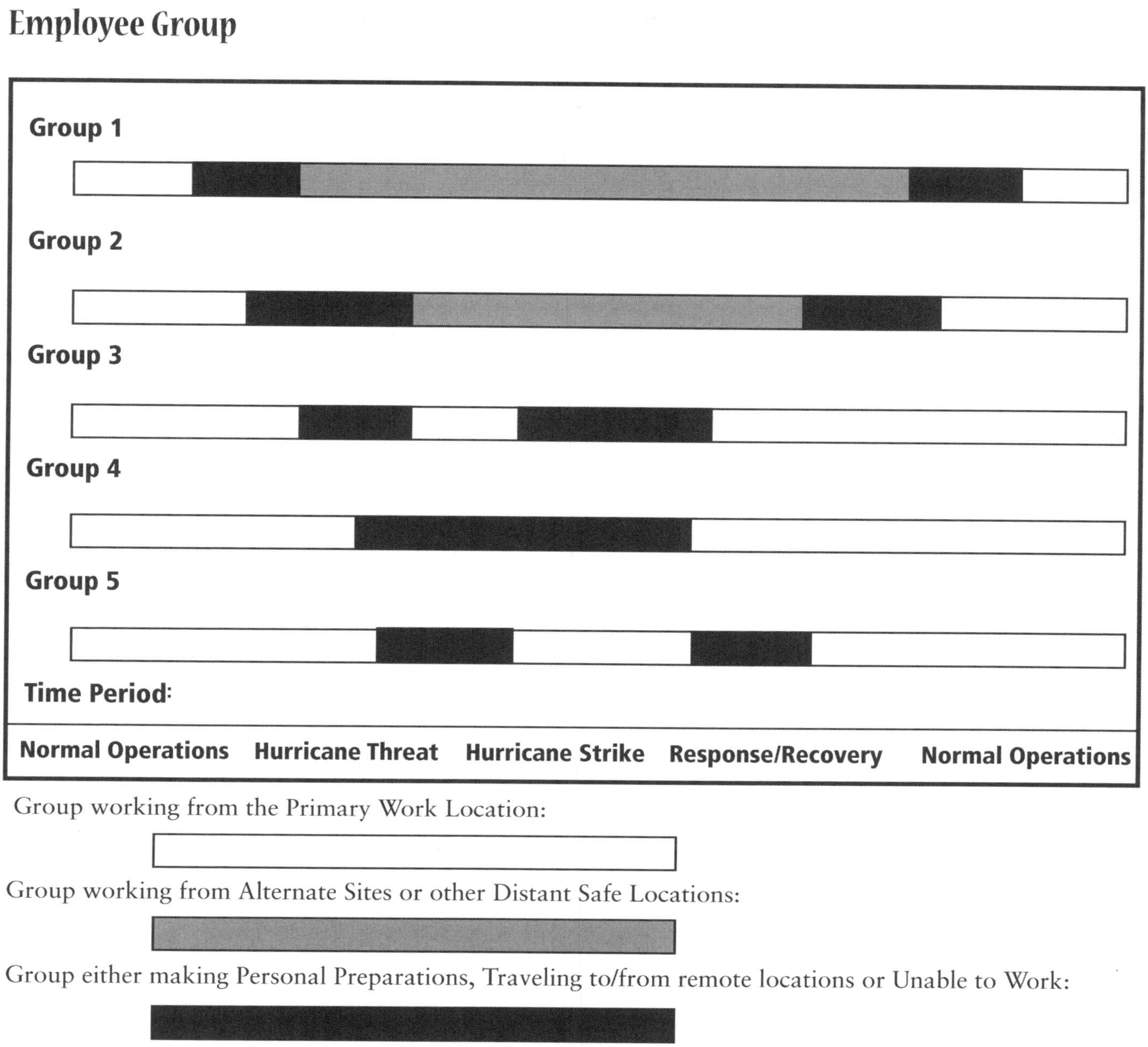

Employee Group

Group 1

Group 2

Group 3

Group 4

Group 5

Time Period:

| Normal Operations | Hurricane Threat | Hurricane Strike | Response/Recovery | Normal Operations |

Group working from the Primary Work Location:

Group working from Alternate Sites or other Distant Safe Locations:

Group either making Personal Preparations, Traveling to/from remote locations or Unable to Work:

Review Topics

1. What could go wrong with the personnel aspects of executing the strategy?

2. What could go wrong with the logistical aspects of executing the strategy?

3. How could weather forecasting inaccuracies interfere with executing the strategy?

Bibliography

Henderson, D. M., *The Complete Hurricane and Flood Plan for Business,* Rothstein Associates Inc., 2006.

Tabletop Exercise

Tabletop Exercise Overview

A Tabletop exercise is a paper-type exercise and the participants do not evacuate a building, start a fire or perform anything of a physical nature. The Tabletop exercise is typically a two-hour to one-half-day exercise that will involve participation from the Emergency Response Team (ERT) and ideally the Crisis Management Team (CMT). The Tabletop exercise should include an Exercise Workbook describing a crisis scenario and defining specific questions to be answered.

The Exercise Workbook will describe a realistic crisis scenario event and incorporate as much detail regarding the event as possible. This approach will help to insure participant buy-in.

The participants are broken into small groups and each group will work on the questions as a team. Note that this typically is a 'closed book' type exercise for two reasons. First of all, in an actual emergency response there will not likely be time to read documentation; it is necessary for everyone to respond immediately and correctly. The second reason is that individuals will tend to just copy responses out of the plan; it is important for everyone to 'think out of the box' possibly inspiring some new solutions that were not initially envisioned. Sometimes after the initial emergency response is completed, participants will be allowed to refer to the planning documentation.

In a Tabletop exercise, a crisis event is described and questions regarding the proper responses that should be taken are addressed. In the first section of the exercise the initial crisis situation is described. Specific questions regarding the initial response are then asked. Each group will review the situation and then record answers to the questions. The participants will then meet and discuss the responses as one team. The crisis situation is then updated and the process is repeated.

Purpose

There are multiple purposes of a Tabletop exercise. Ensuring that every member of the ERT is aware of their roles and responsibilities is an important objective. The exercise should also check and verify the accuracy and completeness of the BCM program. New ideas and procedures frequently emerge from these exercises.

Overall Approach

A 'Project Manager' needs to be selected to coordinate the exercise. Ideally a senior level officer such as the CEO, CFO, CIO or other c-level executive can function in this position; however, the BCM Coordinator often will function in this capacity. In any event, the Project Manager must be familiar with the plan, the actual execution of the plan plus must also have sufficient time to prepare for the exercise. The Project Manager should be the only employee of the organization who knows the Exercise Scenario in advance.

The Project Manager might also function as the 'Facilitator' to actually guide and conduct the exercise. Consideration should also be given to utilizing the services of an outside consultant who is experienced in this area to work with the Project Manager and to function as the Facilitator.

Selecting a Scenario

The following Exercise Workbook describes a fire crisis scenario. This is a frequently used scenario since virtually all organizations have at least some level of fire risk. This exercise can be used to test both the emergency response and business continuity aspects of BCM.

Another good crisis scenario is some type of community-wide crisis such as a hurricane, earthquake or terrorist act. A community-wide crisis will test how well the BCM program performs when local support services are unavailable or limited. In the case of certain crisis events such as a hurricane, tornado or flood, the actions during the pre-strike watch and warning periods can also be exercised.

Conducting the Tabletop Exercise

The Tabletop exercise is conducted chronologically as follows:

1. The participants are divided into 2-4 groups of 4-8 individuals.
2. The crisis situation is described by the Facilitator and documented in the Exercise Workbook.
3. Specific questions are asked in the Exercise Workbook regarding the proper emergency response action steps.
4. Each group meets independently to discuss the questions as a group. The questions are answered and recorded, typically on a flip-chart.
5. Once the set of questions is answered, individual groups can make a brief presentation regarding the actions that should be taken at this juncture:
   A. The Facilitator will discuss alternative actions / alternate approaches
   B. The entire group should then discuss the issues
   C. Attending executive management personnel should make final comments, observations and conclusions.

The Tabletop exercise is conducted at several points in time or 'segments' with a set of facts being submitted to the ERT. Typically there will be three segments involved with the Tabletop Exercise as follows:

▶ **First Segment** – Will largely focus on the emergency response. We have already noted that when the crisis situation is described, sufficient detail should be presented; however, there should also be some uncertain or conflicting information. Keep in mind that in an actual crisis situation the initial reports are rarely 100% accurate or complete.

▶ **Second Segment** – Now the situation is described a few hours later, or the next day depending on the selected crisis scenario, and the exercise is continued. At this second stage some additional facts or 'twists' to the initial description can be introduced. At this second segment the questions transition from the initial focus of emergency response to the longer-term objective of business continuity.

▶ **Third Segment** – The focus is now on business continuity. This third segment of the process can be extended to a point in time several days or longer from the initial event, as appropriate. This last evaluation point will be to examine if the actions taken have met the established Recovery Time Objectives and maintained critical services at a reasonable level?

Completing the Tabletop Exercise

Some time should be devoted to discussing the entire exercise at the end of the Third Segment. Discussion questions often include the following:

▶ What have we learned today?

▶ How did we do?

▶ Did the BCM program meet the stated objectives?

▶ What changes are needed in the BCM program?

▶ Are any additional assets or resources needed?

▶ Is any additional training needed?

▶ When do we run another exercise?

A formal report documenting the proceedings is often prepared. Proposed changes presented to senior management for approval and subsequently incorporated into the documentation.

Two example Tabletop exercises follow.

Alpha Investment Services Tabletop Exercise

For AIS, the following specific information is provided:

Chain-of-Command:

1. President/CEO

2. Vice President of Finance/CFO

3. Vice President of Operations/COO

4. Vice President of Information Technology/CIO.

Spokesperson:

1. President/CEO

2. Vice President of Finance/CFO.

Status of improvements to the BCM program:

▶ The overall BCM program is well documented and tested.

▶ Employees have been trained, provided the necessary resources and assigned alternate work locations.

▶ Information Technology has added redundant data collection and communication infrastructure to the co-location site.

Crisis Scenario – Monday Morning
Time Situation

9:01 AM

▶ A fire breaks out in the in the northwest corner of the Main Building.

▶ The fire evacuation alarm is immediately sounded and an evacuation commences.

▶ The weather conditions are fine; mild and dry conditions prevail.

9:07 AM

▶ The evacuation may be complete; no one has left the building during the last minute.

▶ Several employees appear to be suffering from smoke inhalation.

▶ There is a great deal of confusion at the gathering areas.

▶ Although the fire and smoke appears to be confined to a small area, there is an unconfirmed report that a small explosion, loud noise or 'bang' was heard.

▶ The Auxiliary Building is unaffected.

9:12 AM

▶ The Fire Department arrives on the scene, assumes incident command and enters the building to engage the fire and to seek out anyone who needs assistance in evacuating.

9:13 AM

▶ All employees are present except for the CEO who is the designated Incident Commander and the CFO who is the primary backup Incident Commander. The CEO is on an airplane and is effectively out of contact for several hours. The CFO is in Chicago and is now in contact by cell phone; the CFO will immediately return and should be back by this afternoon.

▶ The Police Department and Emergency Medical Services arrive at the scene.

9:19 AM

▶ The fire is under control and nearly out. It is unclear when the building can be re-entered.

9:20 AM

▶ The news media is arriving and seeking answers.

Questions
Monday Morning – 9:20 AM

1. What do we know at this time?

2. What don't we know at this time?

3. Who is in charge of the overall crisis scene? Who is the Incident Commander?

4. Who is in charge of AIS business matters?

        A. President/CEO

        B. Vice President of Finance/CFO

        C. Vice President of Information Technology/CIO

        D. Vice President of Operations/COO.

5. What are the immediate priorities?

6. What business continuity actions, if any, should be taken?

        A. Should we activate the BCM program?

        B. What crisis level should be declared?

        C. What should we tell the employees to do?

        D. Should we activate the IT alternate site?

7. What actions should be taken an hour from now if the Fire Department informs us that we cannot get back in the building at least until tomorrow at the earliest?

8. Who should be speaking with the news media?

9. Should we contact clients at this time and, if so, what do we tell them?

10. Should anyone else be contacted at this time and, if so, what do we tell them?

11. What, if anything, should key team members be doing?

        A. President/CEO

        B. Vice President of Finance/CFO

        C. Vice President of Information Technology/CIO

        D. Vice President of Operations/COO.

Note: The preceding questions should be completed before continuing with the exercise.

Crisis Scenario Update
Monday Afternoon – 2:00 PM

The team assembles at the Emergency Operations Center (EOC) at 2:00 PM; the situation is as follows:

▶ Three employees were hospitalized; one has been treated and released. All other employees have been accounted for.

▶ The fire is out. The exact cause of the fire is still under investigation but it appears to have been accidental.

▶ The Fire Department has left and the Police Department is providing access control.

▶ There apparently was no structural damage to the building but hazardous materials were released and water damage appears certain.

▶ General access to the building is currently being denied by Civil Authorities and it is expected that the building will be closed until Thursday morning for decontamination.

▶ The Fire Department did allow a Facilities employee in hazmat gear to briefly enter the building with a Fire Department Official and determine:

❖ The employee Print Shop and Custom Research Department area appears to be badly damaged.

❖ The Data Center appears to be completely unaffected.

❖ The rest of the building may have some smoke and water damage.

❖ The CEO should be back by 4:00 PM.

❖ The CFO has now returned and, except for the CEO, all team members are present at the EOC.

Questions
Monday Afternoon – 2:00 PM

1. What do we know at this time?

2. What don't we know at this time?

3. Who is in charge of the overall crisis scene? Who is the Incident Commander?

4. Who is in charge of AIS business matters?

       A. President/CEO

       B. Vice President of Finance/CFO

       C. Vice President of Information Technology/CIO

       D. Vice President of Operations/COO.

5. What are the immediate priorities?

6. What business continuity actions, if any, should be taken?

7. Who should be speaking with the news media?

8. Should we contact clients at this time and, if so, what do we tell them?

9. Should we contact employees at this time and, if so, what do we tell them?

10. Should anyone else be contacted at this time and, if so, what do we tell them?

Note: The preceding questions should be completed before continuing with the exercise.

Crisis Scenario Update
Early Tuesday Morning; 1-Day Later

The building is being decontaminated and can be reentered on Thursday. The known status of the building and employees are as follows:

- All hospitalized employees have been released; they should be able to return to work shortly.
- There is the following damage:
    - ❖ The employee lounge and the Custom Research Offices will be unusable for two weeks.
    - ❖ The Print Shop was destroyed.
- There was no structural damage to the building.
- The fire started in an employee lounge and was accidental. The explosion, loud noise or 'bang' may have been a coffee pot that was dropped when the fire commenced.
- The Police Department is no longer providing access control.

Questions
Early Tuesday Morning; 1-Day Later

1. What should key members of the ERT be doing?

        A. President/CEO

        B. Vice President of Finance/CFO

        C. Vice President of Information Technology/CIO

        D. Vice President of Operations/COO.

2. Where are Custom Research and Print Shop employees going to work?
3. Describe the business continuity steps that will need to take place.

Beta Widget Makers Tabletop Exercise

For BWM, the following specific information is provided:

Chain-of-Command:

1. President/CEO
2. Vice President of Operations/COO

3. Vice President of Finance/CFO

4. Vice President of Information Technology/CIO.

Spokesperson:

1. President/CEO

2. Vice President of Finance/CFO.

Status of improvements to the BCM program:

▶ The overall BCM program is well documented.

▶ Approximately 25% of Sales and Customer Service representatives now work from home.

▶ Information Technology has made a number of improvements:

    ❖ Planning is well documented, tested and adequate subcontractor services have been secured.

    ❖ A complete analysis of proposed improvements to the data center in the Central Plant is being developed.

    ❖ Redundant hardware has been added to IT alternate site in the West Plant to support communication infrastructure and sales and customer service-related operations.

    ❖ Information Technology is now capable of recovering communication infrastructure and sales and customer service-related support within one day and can recover all technology services within five days.

Crisis Scenario – Monday Morning
Time Situation

9:01 AM

▶ A fire breaks out in the in the northwest corner of the Central Plant.

▶ The fire evacuation alarm is immediately sounded and an evacuation commences.

▶ The weather conditions are fine; mild and dry conditions prevail.

9:07 AM

▶ The evacuation may be complete; no one has left the Plant during the last minute.

▶ Several employees appear to be suffering from smoke inhalation.

▶ There is a great deal of confusion at the gathering areas.

▶ Although the fire and smoke appears to be confined to a small area, there is an unconfirmed report that a small explosion, loud noise or 'bang' was heard.

9:12 AM

▶ The Fire Department arrives on the scene, assumes incident command and enters the Plant to engage the fire and to seek out anyone who needs assistance in evacuating.

▶ The Police Department and Emergency Medical Services arrive at the scene.

9:13 AM

▶ All employees are present except for the CEO who is the designated Incident Commander and the CFO. The CEO is on an airplane and is effectively out of contact for several hours. The CFO is in

Chicago and is now in contact by cell phone; the CFO will immediately return and should be back by this afternoon.

9:19 AM
▶ The fire is under control and nearly out. It is unclear when the building can be re-entered.

9:20 AM
▶ The news media is arriving and seeking answers.

Questions
Monday Morning – 9:20 AM

1. What do we know at this time?

2. What don't we know at this time?

3. Who is in charge of the overall crisis scene? Who is the Incident Commander?

4. Who is in charge of BWM business matters?

      A. President/CEO

      B. Vice President of Finance/CFO

      C. Vice President of Information Technology/CIO

      D. Vice President of Operations/COO.

5. What are the immediate priorities?

6. What business continuity actions, if any, should be taken now?

      A. Should we activate the BCM program?

      B. What crisis level should be declared?

      C. What should we tell the employees to do?

      D. Should we activate the IT alternate site?

7. What actions should be taken an hour from now if the Fire Department informs us that we cannot get back in the Plant at least until tomorrow at the earliest?

8. Who should be speaking with the news media?

9. Should we contact customers at this time and, if so, what do we tell them?

10. Should anyone else be contacted at this time and, if so, what do we tell them?

11. What, if anything, should key team members be doing?

      A. President/CEO

      B. Vice President of Finance/CFO

      C. Vice President of Information Technology/CIO

      D. Vice President of Operations/COO.

Note: The preceding questions should be completed before continuing with the exercise.

Crisis Scenario Update
Monday Afternoon – 2:00 PM

The team assembles at the Emergency Operations Center (EOC) at 2:00 PM; the situation is as follows:

- Three employees were hospitalized; one has been treated and released. All other employees have been accounted for.

- The fire is out. The exact cause of the fire is still under investigation but it appears to have been accidental.

- The Fire Department has left and the Police Department is providing access control.

- There apparently was no structural damage to the Plant but hazardous materials were released and water damage appears certain.

- General access to the building is currently being denied by Civil Authorities and it is expected that the building will be closed until Thursday morning for decontamination.

- The Fire Department did allow a Facilities employee in hazmat gear to briefly enter the Plant with a Fire Department Official and determine:

  - ❖ The main data center appears to be badly damaged.

  - ❖ The rest of the Plant may have some smoke and water damage.

- The CEO should be back by 4:00 PM.

- The CFO has now returned and, except for the CEO, all team members are present at the EOC.

Questions
Monday Afternoon – 2:00 PM

1. What do we know at this time?

2. What don't we know at this time?

3. Who is in charge of the overall crisis scene? Who is the Incident Commander?

4. Who is in charge of BWM business matters?

> A. President/CEO
>
> B. Vice President of Finance/CFO
>
> C. Vice President of Information Technology/CIO
>
> D. Vice President of Operations/COO.

5. What are the immediate priorities?

6. What business continuity actions, if any, should be taken?

7. Who should be speaking with the news media?

8. Should we contact customers at this time and, if so, what do we tell them?

9. Should we contact employees at this time and, if so, what do we tell them?

10. Should anyone else be contacted at this time and, if so, what do we tell them?

Note: The preceding questions should be completed before continuing with the exercise.

Crisis Scenario Update
Early Tuesday Morning; 1-Day Later

The Plant is being decontaminated and can be reentered on Thursday. The known status of the Plant and employees are as follows:

▶ All hospitalized employees have been released; they should be able to return to work shortly.

▶ There is the following damage:

❖ The employee lounge and the main data center will be unusable for two weeks.

▶ There was no structural damage to the Plant.

▶ The fire started in an employee lounge and was accidental. The explosion, loud noise or 'bang' may have been a coffee pot that was dropped when the fire commenced.

▶ The Police Department is no longer providing access control.

Questions
Early Tuesday Morning; 1-Day Later

1. What should key members be doing?

       A. President/CEO

       B. Vice President of Finance/CFO

       C. Vice President of Information Technology/CIO

       D. Vice President of Operations/COO.

2. Where are Information Technology employees going to work?

3. Describe the business continuity steps that will need to take place.

SECTION VI

Additional Information

Additional Information includes a Glossary, a set of Appendices and an Index. Most of the Appendices provide important supplementary information that tie the text with the actions taken by an organization. The remaining Appendices provide important background or terminology information.

Business Continuity refers to the actions taken to sustain and/or resume operations impacted by crisis events. Frequently the term business continuity by itself also implies recovery.

Business Continuity Management (BCM) – BCM is a holistic management program that identifies potential events that threaten an organization and provides a framework for building resilience with the capability for an effective response that safeguards the interests of its key stakeholders, the environment, reputation, brand and value creating activities. Essentially BCM is the overall or total collective sum of all the emergency response and business continuity planning components and activities. BCM is a program consisting of the following three major stages:

- **Development** includes senior management's commitment to a BCM program and the determination of business continuity strategies based upon an understanding of the organization.

- **Implementation** includes putting the strategies in place, finalizing, documenting and, as necessary, activating the plans.

- **Maintenance** includes creating an education and awareness culture of BCM and ongoing testing, auditing and change management to ensure the plans remain operable and current.

Business Continuity Management (BCM) Coordinator – The Business Continuity Management Coordinator (BCM Coordinator) has overall responsibility for BCM at each specific location.

Business Continuity Management (BCM) Steering Committee – The BCM Steering Committee is the primary decision making group for the BCM program, has oversight for BCM at the corporate level, and reviews and approves the BCM program.

Business Continuity Phases – Business Continuity Phases are the steps to be taken before during and after a crisis and include prevention, mitigation, response, recovery and restoration.

- **Prevention** steps are designed to lessen the likelihood of a crisis event.

- **Mitigation** steps are designed to make the impact of an event less severe.

- **Response** is the reaction of an organization to an event to address immediate effects.

- **Recovery** is the stabilization and resumption of operations.

- **Restoration** is the process of returning to normal operations at a permanent location.

Business Continuity Plan (BCP) – The BCP is the central plan that documents continuity and recovery procedures for crisis events. The BCP provides sufficient detail regarding the deployment of appropriate strategies for the resumption of operations according to predetermined priorities.

Business Continuity Planning Team – The Business Continuity Planning Team is the team responsible for providing professional guidance throughout the development, implementation and maintenance of the BCM program. The Business Continuity Planning Team develops the guidelines, methodologies, standards and best practices to be used in the BCM program.

Business Impact Analysis (BIA) – BIA is a process that identifies and analyzes controls, exposures and operations to establish planning needs, strategies and recovery objectives. Also, the senior management report that documents this process is frequently referred to as the Business Impact Analysis.

Catastrophe – Catastrophe is an extreme disaster.

Chain-of-Command – The chain-of-command is the order of authority within the organization.

Cloud Computing – Cloud computing is anything that entails the delivery of hosted services over the Internet and a 'Private Cloud' is a proprietary network that delivers hosted services to designated users.

Co-location Site – A co-location site is an alternate site where the vendor provides the facility and infrastructure support and the organization provides the hardware.

Crisis (crisis event) – A crisis is a manifestation of a threat. If not handled properly, a crisis may have a severe negative impact. Crisis events may be classified as follows:

- **Minor crisis** has limited impact and does not affect the overall functioning capacity of an organization.
- **Major crisis** has the potential to seriously disrupt the overall operation of an organization.

Crisis Communication – Crisis Communication is the process of obtaining and disseminating information regarding crisis events.

Crisis Communication Team – The Crisis Communication Team is a team of senior managers at the corporate level assigned to communicate with interested parties, conduct all media communications and chaired by an individual who is in-charge of overall communications.

Crisis Management Team (CMT) – The CMT is the team with overall responsibility to manage crisis events.

Crisis Phases include the following three phases:

- **Pre-Strike phase** – The period of time when there are indications that the manifestation of a threat is credible. Crisis events may have an extended, brief or nonexistent pre-strike phase.
- **Strike phase** – The period of time when the crisis has the most direct impact to the organization.
- **Post-Strike phase** – The period of time after the crisis has been contained and controlled, and before all operations are fully recovered.

Critical Operations (Mission Critical Activities) – Critical operations are the activities necessary to safely support the primary mission of the organization. Critical operations are determined based on two variables: the importance of the operation and the time sensitivity of the operation.

Damage Assessment Team – The Damage Assessment Team is a team that assesses damages caused by a crisis.

Department Plans – Department plans should be prepared by departments to document critical BCM planning, response or recovery responsibilities and actions.

Disaster – A disaster is a major crisis event which imperils an organization. An event may be deemed a disaster due to factors such as loss of life, environmental damage, asset damage and duration of disruption.

Disaster Declaration (Invocation, Activation) – Disaster declaration is the statement used to announce the activation of BCM. The term is commonly used to activate an alternate site frequently sponsored by an outside vendor.

Disaster Recovery – Disaster recovery is the term generally used in the IT area to indicate business continuity activity.

Disaster Recovery Plan (DRP) – A DRP is a plan for the Information Technology (IT) Department to provide continuation and recovery of the systems and communication capabilities of the organization.

Disruption – Disruption is an interruption of operations.

Emergency – Emergency is a crisis that requires immediate action.

Emergency Command Post (ECP) – The ECP is a designated area near the site of the crisis but located a safe distance from and generally upwind of the crisis site where the Incident Commander will direct response activities.

Emergency Operations Center (EOC) – The EOC is the central location where the management team(s) gathers and executes the ERP and the BCP.

Emergency Response – Emergency response is the set of immediate actions taken during a crisis event with the prioritized objectives of life-safety, environmental protection and asset protection.

Emergency Response Plan (ERP) – The ERP is a plan that documents the actions to be taken to respond to hazard-specific crisis events with the prioritized objectives of life-safety, environmental protection and asset protection.

Emergency Response Team (ERT) – The ERT is an assembly of primary and alternate members at each major location responsible for the response to a crisis.

Essential Personnel (Storm Personnel) – Essential Personnel are employees who are assigned to remain at the organization's location during a crisis.

Event (incident) – An event is an occurrence that could have an impact upon the organization.

Exercise – Exercise is a planned or unannounced testing of personnel and/or equipment used in BCM. There are several categories of exercises as follows:

- **Talk Through** is a presentation and discussion of a particular topic.
- **Walk Through** is a Talk Through exercise but is more physical.

▶ **Tabletop** describes a crisis situation followed by questions regarding the proper actions that should be taken.

▶ **Drills or Full Scale** actually requires the organization or a segment of the organization to cease normal operations and practice a response to a crisis.

Green BCM – Green BCM is the conducting of the BCM program in a manner that is consistent with the objectives of reducing environmental impact, promoting sustainability, and conserving energy and other resources.

Impact (consequences) – Impact is the effect of an event. The level of impact depends on factors such as loss of life, environmental damage, asset damage and duration of disruption.

Incident Commander – The Incident Commander for the organization is a senior member of the Emergency Management Committee who is in charge of the Emergency Response Team. The Incident Commander will relinquish incident command to responding civil authorities.

Information Technology (IT) – IT is the hardware, software, telecommunications and other technologies used in computer based information systems.

Initial Responder – An initial responder to a crisis is an individual who encounters the crisis and is the first to take action.

IT Alternate Site (IT Recovery Site) – The IT alternate site is a backup data center where technology services can be performed in the event of the destruction or disablement of the primary data center. There are several categories of sites that need to be identified as follows:

▶ **Redundant Site** is a completely functional separate backup data center that continually duplicates every activity of the primary data center. Also referred to as a Mirror Site.

▶ **Hot Site** is a separate backup data center that is ready on a standby status.

▶ **Co-location Site** is a backup site where the organization provides the hardware and a vendor provides the location and infrastructure support. Typically this is a type of Hot or Redundant Site.

▶ **Cold Site** is a separate backup data center that is not operational but can be made operational within a reasonable period of time. As features and hardware are added, the cold site becomes a **Warm Site**.

Material Safety Data Sheet (MSDS) – MSDS is a summary of information regarding hazardous materials.

Mutual Aid Agreement – A mutual aid agreement is a service level agreement between two or more organizations to provide a resource when one of the organizations experiences an outage.

Office Alternate Site (Office Recovery Site) – The office alternate site is a backup site where non-technology services can be performed in the event of the destruction or disablement of the primary facility. The office alternate site and the IT alternate site are sometimes the same physical location.

Outage – An outage is the unavailability of a resource which may cause a disruption in operations. This may be due to destruction, disablement or denial of use of a resource.

Phases of Emergency Management – As defined by the Post-Katrina Emergency Management Reform Act of 2006, Title VI National Emergency Management, FEMA utilizes Phases of Emergency Management defined as follows:

- ▶ **Phase 1 – Mitigation** actions include taking sustained actions to reduce or eliminate long-term risks to people and property from hazards and their effects.

- ▶ **Phase 2 – Preparedness** actions include planning, training and building the emergency management profession to prepare effectively for, mitigate against, respond to and recover from any hazard.

- ▶ **Phase 3 – Response** actions include conducting emergency operations to save lives and property through positioning emergency equipment, personnel and supplies; through evacuating potential victims, through providing food, water, shelter and medical care to those in need and through restoring critical public services.

- ▶ **Phase 4 – Recovery** actions include rebuilding communities so individuals, businesses and governments can function on their own, return to normal life and protect against future hazards.

Probability – Probability is the measure of the likelihood of occurrence of an event.

Process Flow (internal supply chain) – Process flow is the sequence of operations by which an organization creates a deliverable.

Recovery Point Objective (RPO) – The RPO is the retrospective point in time to which information must be recovered to ensure objectives can be met. The RPO establishes the period of acceptable information loss.

Recovery Team – The Recovery Team is the team designated to recover operations caused by a disaster.

Recovery Time Objective (RTO) – The RTO is the prospective point in time when an operation must be resumed before a disruption compromises the ability of the organization to achieve its objectives.

Resilience – Resilience is the ability of an organization to withstand the impact of a crisis event.

Resource – Resource is an asset used to conduct operations. Resources include personnel, facilities, equipment, inventory, utilities and systems.

Risk – Risk is the possibility of experiencing an event, measured in terms of probability and impact.

Risk Analysis – Risk analysis is the process of identifying events, determining causes, and estimating probabilities and impact.

Risk Assessment (RA) – RA is the process of risk analysis and risk evaluation.

Risk Communication – Risk communications is the exchange of risk information among stakeholders.

Risk Evaluation – Risk evaluation is the process of comparing risk levels with established risk criteria.

Risk Event Chain – Risk event chain is a description of the transition from threat to crisis to disruption to impact.

Risk Management – Risk management is comprised of the processes of risk assessment, risk communication and risk treatment.

Risk Measure – Risk measure is a quantitative summary value of risk based on probability and impact.

Risk Tolerance – Risk tolerance is the amount of risk that an organization is prepared to accept.

Risk Treatment – Risk treatment is the selection of procedures for managing risk that include the following:

- **Acceptance** – the risk is retained.
- **Avoidance** – the activities causing the risk are eliminated.
- **Reduction** – the likelihood and/or impact of the risk is reduced.
- **Transfer** – the risk in part or in totality is assigned to another.

Service Level Agreements – Written documents between organizations that specify services and performance levels to be provided.

Single-Point-of-Failure – A single-point-of-failure is a unique resource, the failure of which will interrupt critical operations.

Strategy – An approach used by an organization to treat risk to accomplish resiliency objectives.

Supply Chain – Supply chain is a sequence of operations conducted by a system of organizations involved in the creation and distribution of a deliverable.

Threat (hazard) – Threat is a source of potential negative impact.

Vulnerability – Vulnerability is a measure of exposure to a threat that increases as the probability and impact of the event increases.

Organizational Functions

All organizations include the three primary functions of operations, finance and marketing. The responsibilities of these functions are:

▶ Operations – The operations function is responsible for producing the goods and services of an organization.

▶ Finance – The finance function is responsible for managing an organization's financial assets and financial records.

▶ Marketing – The marketing function is responsible for selling an organization's goods and services.

Organizational support functions include information technology, human resources and communications. The responsibilities of these functions are:

▶ Information Technology – The IT function is responsible for the technologies used in an organization's computer based information systems.

▶ Human Resources – The human resources function is responsible for maintaining an organization's workforce.

▶ Communications – The communications function is responsible for managing the communication and public image of an organization.

The need for organizational support functions depend on the nature of the organization. Some other organizational support functions include compliance and legal, and research and development.

Effective management is needed for all organizations. The functions of management are: planning, organizing, staffing, directing, and controlling.

▶ Planning is the process of developing an organization's objectives and determining how they will be accomplished.

▶ Organizing is establishing an organizational structure.

▶ Staffing is maintaining qualified employees in an organization.

▶ Directing is influencing people's behavior.

▶ Controlling is the process of taking action to meet standards.

The management functions are applicable within all organizational functions. Organizational functions involve key decision areas including:

▶ **Operations**

- ❖ Assembly
- ❖ Capacity
- ❖ Design
- ❖ Equipment
- ❖ Fabrication
- ❖ Facilities
- ❖ Hazardous materials
- ❖ Inventory
- ❖ Job design
- ❖ Layout
- ❖ Location
- ❖ Logistics
- ❖ Maintenance
- ❖ Manufacturing
- ❖ Materials requirements
- ❖ Outsourcing
- ❖ Physical security
- ❖ Processing
- ❖ Product design
- ❖ Quality
- ❖ Reliability
- ❖ Scheduling
- ❖ Supply chain

▶ **Finance**

- ❖ Accounting
- ❖ Auditing
- ❖ Capitalization
- ❖ Cash control
- ❖ Credit
- ❖ Debt
- ❖ Disbursements
- ❖ Engineering
- ❖ Financial assets
- ❖ Financial records
- ❖ Flow of funds
- ❖ Funds management
- ❖ Insurance
- ❖ Investments
- ❖ Payments
- ❖ Payroll
- ❖ Profit planning
- ❖ Purchasing
- ❖ Real estate
- ❖ Receivables
- ❖ Return on investment
- ❖ Financial Securities

▶ **Marketing**

- ❖ Advertising
- ❖ Competitor analysis
- ❖ Customer satisfaction
- ❖ Customer service
- ❖ Distribution channel
- ❖ Market research
- ❖ Opportunity identification
- ❖ Order processing
- ❖ Packaging
- ❖ Personal selling
- ❖ Place
- ❖ Positioning
- ❖ Pricing
- ❖ Product branding
- ❖ Product design
- ❖ Product differentiation
- ❖ Promotions
- ❖ Prospects
- ❖ Sales

▶ **Information Technology**

- ❖ Application software
- ❖ Computer hardware
- ❖ Data center
- ❖ Data resources
- ❖ Data retrieval
- ❖ Data storage
- ❖ Decision support systems
- ❖ Electronic commerce
- ❖ End user support
- ❖ Enterprise systems
- ❖ Information controls
- ❖ Information security
- ❖ Information systems
- ❖ IT infrastructure
- ❖ Networks
- ❖ Peripherals
- ❖ Security and control
- ❖ System software
- ❖ Systems development
- ❖ Telecommunications
- ❖ Web systems

▶ **Human Resources**

- ❖ Compensation
- ❖ Employee benefits
- ❖ Employee evaluation
- ❖ Employee recruitment
- ❖ Employee relations
- ❖ Hiring
- ❖ Labor relations
- ❖ Performance evaluation
- ❖ Placement
- ❖ Record keeping requirements
- ❖ Recruitment
- ❖ Safety and health
- ❖ Termination
- ❖ Training

▶ **Communications**

- ❖ Analyst relations
- ❖ Consumer public relations
- ❖ Corporate communications
- ❖ Crisis communications
- ❖ Financial public relations
- ❖ Government relations
- ❖ Industry relations
- ❖ Internal communications
- ❖ Investor relations
- ❖ Labor relations
- ❖ Media relations
- ❖ Public relations
- ❖ Publicity.

Disaster Assistance Plan

Mission Statement

The organization intends to do everything reasonably possible to provide a place of employment and make every reasonable effort to maintain the health, safety and well being of all employees.

Payroll and Workforce Policies

After a community-wide crisis strike, some employees may not be able to work, there may not be work available, travel to work may be impossible or a wide-variety of other conditions may preclude work. In the event of a community-wide crisis that forces the organization to close, the following policies will apply:

Work Hours

- Overtime may be authorized to the extent needed to bring critical operations back to normal levels.
- Vacations and holidays may be canceled.
- If the event is of extended duration, special policies may be implemented.

Payroll

- Non-Exempt employees who are required to work (essential employees) will be compensated at time-and-a-half.
- If the event is of extended duration, special compensation will be considered for exempt employees who are required to work (essential employees).
- Full expense reimbursements will be provided to all employees who are required to relocate to alternate sites in order to maintain critical operations.
- Employees who are not seriously affected by the crisis are expected to work to the extent that work is available.
- If no work is available, employees will be compensated for a period of time as long as reasonably practical.

Employee Assistance

For employees who have been affected by a crisis, management will make every reasonable effort to assist employees as follows:

- Time off for personal matters.
- Psychological assistance.
- Working from home (to the extent possible).
- Flexible work hours (to the extent possible).

Essential Personnel

Essential Personnel are expected to work 12-hour shifts and will be compensated a 'time-and-a-half' rate for all hours.

Employees Pre-Storm Policy

It is the policy of the company to release all employees prior to a storm impact. Employees will be given adequate time to travel home, secure their residences and travel to safe locations.

Compensation options for Exempt Employees

Salaried employees often receive extra compensation as a discretionary bonus rather than as time-and-a-half. It is very important to maintain the normal compensation balance. Normally higher compensated salaried employees could conceivably be compensated at a lower rate than hourly employees receiving time-and-a-half.

Families of Relocated Employees

Should families also be relocated? If the crisis is a community-wide crisis, such as a hurricane, the environment may be dangerous and relocated employees will be extremely concerned about their families being left alone.

Families of Essential Personnel

Should families of Essential Personnel be provided shelter at the workplace location?

Employees Who Work Additional Pre-Storm Hours

Some organizations will release a group of employees early and require another group of employees to work longer to maintain critical operations. It is important to provide extra compensation (or extra time off) to the employee group that is required to work longer.

Note: This sample Disaster Assistance Plan is more of a 'personnel policy' than a 'plan.' As such, the policy provisions are typically drafted by the Human Resources department then submitted for examination and approval by senior management.

Building Fortification

Non-Structural Aspects

To protect the non-structural aspects of a building, the following should be considered:

Earthquakes – Secure all objects that could fall or move and identify objects that could spill, rupture or break. For each object, consider the risk to life or injury, replacement cost and downtime. There is no reliable prediction of when an earthquake could strike. Without a watch or warning period, much more emphasis must be placed in the continual planning phase.

Common non-structural building hazards include the following:

- Building exterior – windows and signs.
- Interior overhead objects – pipes, ducts, light fixtures, signs, hanging plants, etc.
- Storage items – shelves, cabinets, bookcases, etc.
- Desktop equipment – computers, printers, telephones, etc.
- Heavy equipment – photocopiers, computers, printers, shredders, refrigerators, etc.
- Utility items – heaters, air conditioners, water heaters, etc.
- Miscellaneous – hazmat material containers, fire extinguishers, elevators, room dividers, lunchroom appliances, etc.

Floods – Typically there will be some warning of a pending flood, therefore significant protection measures can take place during the warning period. Consider the following steps:

- Move equipment off the floor.
- Move equipment to a higher level in the building.

- Move equipment to a higher location.
- Cover and secure or encase and seal equipment with plastic.

Wind – As with floods, typically there will be some warning of a pending severe windstorm, therefore significant protection measures can take place during the warning period. In addition to the flood protection measures, consider the following steps:

- Close and lock or secure all doors, files, cabinets, etc.
- Move equipment away from windows.
- Move equipment to interior areas of the building.

A glossary of weather and seismic terms is presented in Appendices M and N.

Structural Aspects

Consideration should be given to the modifications that can be made to a building to improve the ability of the structure to withstand a disaster. These procedures need to be reviewed with a structural engineer or other qualified professional. To protect the structural aspects of a building, the following should be considered:

Earthquakes
- Add steel bracing to walls and ceilings.
- Reinforce building columns and foundations.
- Secure all equipment with braces and bolts.

Floods
- Install watertight barriers.
- Construct flood walls or levees.
- Build watertight walls and reinforce those walls.
- Install sump pumps.
- Install check valves to prevent water entry from sewer and utility lines.

Wind
- Install storm shutters or wind resistant glass.
- Structurally reinforce roofs.
- Brace walls and doors.
- Secure/anchor equipment on roofs.

Pandemic Outbreak Planning and Response

Overview

A pandemic outbreak is a very different crisis that does not involve damage to physical property. Instead, the impact of a pandemic outbreak is focused on fatalities and high absentee rates. In an extreme situation, a pandemic outbreak could also involve the loss of critical services and create major long-term socioeconomic changes. Crisis-specific planning is needed to respond to a pandemic outbreak.

Typical planning for an organization focuses on site-specific or area-specific natural and man-made hazards – earthquakes, fires, hurricanes, tornadoes, etc. Much of this planning is still applicable for pandemic outbreak planning. Additional planning needs to be made in the following areas:

- Social distancing policies.
- Personal hygiene practices.
- Personal protective equipment.
- Special time-off and compensation policies.

Social distancing policies, personal hygiene practices and personal protective equipment are designed to reduce the possibility of contracting the virus. Special time-off policies will be necessary for employees who either cannot work or who are not allowed to work for an extended period of time. Special compensation policies will also be necessary for essential personnel who must work during an outbreak.

Expected Impact

- Fatalities:
  - ❖ Possible within the workforce and possibly at significant levels.
  - ❖ Numerous (in the thousands or much more) nationwide/worldwide.

- High absentee rates.
- Areas will almost certainly be quarantined.
- Even with quarantines, widespread impact is possible.
- Not a physically damaging crisis.
- Duration would not likely be short, hampering any rapid recovery efforts.
- Areas would likely be affected in waves lasting several weeks.
- There may be multiple waves of the same or slightly mutated virus.
- Medical facilities swamped.
- Effective vaccines would not likely be readily available.
- Some general warning period is likely, but it may be a brief warning.
- General panic likely.
- Enormous post-crisis socioeconomic changes are possible.
- For some organizations, physical assets may be commandeered by civil authorities.

Evaluating the Risk Level

To determine the level of vulnerability to a pandemic outbreak, an organization should evaluate the following:

- Is the organization located in an urban environment?
- Do the employees use mass transportation?
- Does the organization share the facility with other organizations?
- Can the organization suspend receiving all guests and visitors?
- Can the organization suspend all travel?
- Can employees work from home?
- Does the organization have multiple locations where minimum levels of mission-critical production and services can be maintained in non-affected areas?
- Can the organization function if all employees, guests and visitors are required to wear personal protective equipment?
- Does the medical plan cover vaccines?
- Does the organization have medical staff?
- Does the organization have on-site sanitizing equipment?
- Does the organization have on-site medical supplies such as gloves, masks, etc.?
- Is the organization in a high-impacted industry such as Food Handling (especially Poultry), Travel/Transportation, Medical/Health Care, Hospitality, Entertainment, Retail, and any organization that relies on dealing directly with the general public or Education related?

Pre-Event Actions

The organization should consider the following pre-event actions:

- Identify a group to monitor the situation.
- Develop plans to maintain mission-critical operations:
    - ❖ Plans to function with a skeleton workforce of essential personnel.
    - ❖ Back-up plans to maintain critical communication and technology services.
- If possible, develop plans for employees to work from home.
- Collaborate with health plan insurers and public health agencies.
- Store personal protection equipment and supplies.
- Develop liberal time-off policies and establish special compensation policies:
    - ❖ Essential employees who must work.
    - ❖ Employee sick leave.
- Educate employees on hygiene habits and work policies.
- Require employees to practice good hygiene habits.
- Place 'Wash Hands' and other hygiene messages in bathrooms and in other areas.
- Install hand sanitizer stations.
- Install 'touch-less' bathrooms.
- Install speakerphones at all workstations.

Actions Levels

Fundamentally the response to a pandemic outbreak can be broadly classified as follows:

- Level 1 – 'Monitor and prepare.'
- Level 2 – Implement 'social distancing policies' plus 'personal protection equipment' requirements and keep the organization open.
- Level 3 – Close the organization facility and work from home or other safe remote locations.

Key Factors

The primary factors involved in determining a course of action are the 'severity' of the outbreak, the availability of an 'effective vaccine' and the 'location(s)' of the outbreak. The severity of the outbreak is determined by the 'contagiousness' and 'mortality rate' associated with the virus. The location can be sub-classified as either 'overseas,' within 'North America' or within the 'immediate area.'

Current Pandemic Planning and Response Efforts

The current status of the H5N1 'bird flu' virus is that the virus is very deadly but not easily contracted. There is also no effective vaccine available and the virus is located overseas. In a large sense, the virus is actually difficult for humans to contract; the current planning status in the United States is Level 1.

The current status of the H1N1 'swine flu' is that the virus is easily contracted but (except for certain vulnerable groups) the virus does not have a particularly high rate of mortality. Moreover, in the United States there is an effective vaccine available and in sufficient quantities at least for the high risk groups. For most organizations the current planning status in the United States is either Level 1 or Level 2.

An Outbreak Scenario

If a contagious/airborne strain does develop (many experts would argue that this is a matter of 'when' rather than a matter of 'if'). An effective vaccine will not be available for several months (medical experts indicate that with current technologies this is the likely scenario). The critical factors now become the mortality rate associated with the virus and the location(s) of the outbreak.

The mortality rate will be the primary factor in determining what actions (Level 2 or Level 3) will be taken. The location(s) of the outbreak will be the primary factor in determining when these actions are taken.

Response

If the mortality rate is not too high, the organization should consider executing Level 2 actions – remaining open and implementing social distancing plus personal protection equipment policies as needed. In particular, if the outbreak is overseas there may be some time to develop an effective vaccine before the virus reaches the immediate area.

Depending on the location(s) of the outbreak, social distancing policies would likely be gradually introduced. If the outbreak is not in the immediate area, certain travel and visitor restrictions would likely be effective immediately. If the outbreak is in the immediate area, full social distancing and personal protection equipment policies would become effective.

If the mortality rate is high, an organization should consider executing Level 3 actions – closing the organization facility and working from home or other safe remote locations. A contingent of essential personnel may remain on site to provide security and, if applicable, to maintain environmental controls for sensitive materials . Figure App.D.1 illustrates the response actions.

Initial actions – Outbreak not in the Immediate Area

- Activate or maintain the Emergency Operations Center (EOC):
  - ❖ Closely monitor the location(s) and mortality rate of the outbreak
  - ❖ Closely monitor absentee rates.
  - ❖ Meetings should be held at 5:30 a.m. (meetings may be conducted by telephone among selected members) and at 5:30 p.m. or more frequently as necessary.
  - ❖ The emergency hotline and the emergency webpage should be updated at 6:00 a.m. and at 6:00 p.m. or more frequently if necessary.
- Track vaccination programs.
- Assist employees with access to vaccination programs.
- Implement travel and organization facility access restriction policies.
- Restrict travel to any affected areas.
- Consider eliminating all travel.

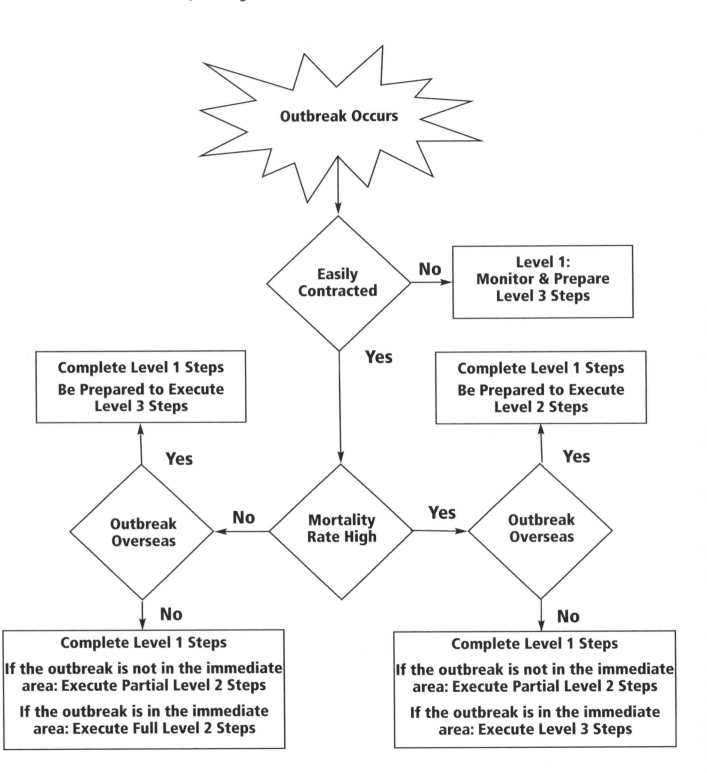

Figure App.D.1 - Situation – Response
(Assuming that an effective vaccine is not available)

- Complete all pre-event preparation steps.
- Do not allow access to anyone who has traveled to an infected area.

Full Activation – Outbreak in the Immediate Area

- If possible, do not allow any guests or visitors.
- If possible, allow employees to work from home.
- Consider activating alternate sites.
- Consider working from other safe locations.
- Limit, but preferably eliminate, all type of face-to-face contact.
- Avoid meetings, shared offices, handshaking, etc.
- Limit, but preferably eliminate, all face-to-face talking.
- Utilize speakerphones, and avoid any face contact with communication equipment.
- Disallow smoking breaks.
- Cancel any social gathering/events.
- Allow employees to eat lunch alone at their workstations.
- Organizations with work shifts should consider leaving an interval of inactivity between shifts.
- Any employee with symptoms:
  - ❖ If at work, should be sent home or, if available, to medical facilities, wearing a face mask.
  - ❖ If at home, should not report to work.
- Maintain contact with employees at home by phone, website and email.
- When not working alone at their workstation require everyone to wear face masks, eye goggles, gloves and other protective equipment.
- Insist that employees wash hands frequently.
- Maintain employee, client, customer, etc. contact by phone, website and email.

Personal Safety – In Advance of an Outbreak

- Have sufficient nonperishable food, water, medications and other survival supplies available for as long a period as reasonably possible.
- In particular, maintain an adequate supply of:
  - ❖ Soap for frequent hand washing.
  - ❖ Face masks, latex gloves, tissue, etc.
  - ❖ Antiviral medications.
- Do not travel to any areas where an outbreak is occurring.

Personal Safety –

If an Epidemic or Pandemic Outbreak occurs in the Immediate Area

▶ Try to avoid contamination by taking the following general precautions:

  ❖ Avoid public transportation.

  ❖ Eliminate all unnecessary travel.

  ❖ Eliminate shopping, entertainment, etc.

  ❖ Do not allow guests or visitors.

▶ Try to avoid contamination by taking the following medical precautions:

  ❖ Wash hands frequently with soap and water.

  ❖ Wash sheets and clothes in hot water.

  ❖ Do not touch your face with your hands (eyes, nose and mouth are the most likely points of virus entry into the body).

  ❖ Coughs and sneezes:

      ❑ Into tissue and dispose of tissue.

      ❑ Into elbows.

  ❖ Wear face masks, eye goggles and other personal protection equipment.

  ❖ Dispose of all used face masks, tissue, etc., and afterwards wash hands.

  ❖ Stop smoking.

  ❖ Stay away from others as much as possible, in particular:

      ❑ People with symptoms.

      ❑ Children.

      ❑ Chronically ill people.

  ❖ Limit any touching or face contact with others.

  ❖ Keep children out of school.

▶ If infected:

  ❖ Do not report to work.

  ❖ Quarantine yourself.

  ❖ Wear a face mask.

Note: Communicate this information to all family members.

Emergency Operations Center (EOC)

Physical Requirements	Number/Specifications/Notes
Size	
Large Table	
Small Table(s)	
Chairs	
Equipment	
Personal Computers	*
Cell Phones, PDA	*
Hardwire Phones	
Two-Way Radios	
Satellite Phones	
Printers	
Fax Machines	
TV Sets	
AM/FM Radios	
Weather Radios	
Flipcharts	
Markers	
Supplies	
First Aid Kits	
Safety Glasses	
Hard Hats	
Flashlights	
Extra Batteries	
Work Gloves	
Work Clothes	*
Extra Work Clothes	*
Drinking Water	
Non-perishable Food	
Manual Bottle Openers	
Manual Can Openers	

Team members are to bring their own laptops, cell phones, PDAs, etc. However, extra laptops and communication devices should be available.

Evacuation Procedures

When an evacuation of a building is ordered, the evacuation will be performed in an orderly and safe manner.

1. If a fire is discovered, immediately pull the closest fire alarm switch.

2. When a fire alarm is activated, all occupants will evacuate the building in an orderly and safe manner. Fire Deputies should be the last occupants to leave the building to ensure everyone has exited the building.

3. Should a person have to remain in the building due to circumstances beyond his/her control, the Fire Deputy will notify the arriving fire officials of the person's location and the condition of the individual (e.g., handicapped, wheelchair bound, injured, etc.).

4. The alarm systems should be designed to notify the fire alarm monitoring company of a fire condition at the location in which the alarm was activated. Security will immediately contact the Incident Commander and inform him/her of the situation.

5. When feasible, Security will respond to the alarm panel of the building that has been activated and determine the exact location of the activation. Security will then go to that location to determine the response needed, inform the arriving emergency personnel of their findings and assist with traffic and crowd control.

Note: These are standard evacuation procedures for typical buildings. For example, high-rise buildings generally do not immediately evacuate floors above the floor where the fire occurs. Evacuation procedures will be different for high-rise buildings, hospitals and other special buildings. Evacuation procedures should be reviewed with local fire department officials.

Fire Deputies

Fire Deputies are to:

1. Conduct a sweep of assigned areas and be certain that everyone has evacuated. Close doors once everyone has evacuated the area.

2. Initiate evacuation procedures, as necessary.

3. Close doors as areas are evacuated.

4. Assist with the extraction of any physically challenged personnel. If necessary, record the location of any individuals who require emergency personnel to assist with the extraction.

5. Maintain an orderly evacuation.

6. Record inappropriate actions (panic, use of elevators, etc.).

7. Assemble personnel at a designated safe location and account for personnel.

8. Record any missing personnel and their last known location.

9. Document evacuation time.

10. In the most minor of incidents, only employees with training in the use of fire extinguishers are permitted to actually fight a fire.

11. Be the last ones out.

Someone in each general area should be designated as a Fire Deputy. Some organizations supply Fire Deputies with special hard hats, badges, jackets, etc. for identification purposes. Fire Deputy backup personnel should also be identified.

Evacuation Procedures

When an evacuation of a building is ordered, the evacuation will be performed in an orderly and safe manner.

1. Everyone should become familiar with work areas and exit locations.

2. When the fire alarm sounds, prepare to evacuate immediately.

3. Do not panic but walk quickly to the closest emergency exit.

4. Do not use elevators. Do not use cell phones.

5. Walk in a single file to the right through corridors and stairwells.

6. Avoid unnecessary talking and keep the lines moving.

7. Individuals requiring assistance in evacuation should proceed to stairwell entrance areas and wait for assistance.

8. If smoke is encountered, drop to the floor and crawl along the wall to the nearest exit.

9. When approaching a closed door, feel the door with the back of your hand. If the door is cool, carefully open the door and (if safe) proceed with the evacuation.

10. No one is to return to the building until the Incident Commander authorizes permission.

Shelter-in-Place Procedures

Communications

▶ A shelter-in-place will be announced by siren, intercom or other voice communication.

▶ If a situation that may require a shelter-in-place is discovered, the individual making the discovery shall immediately move to a safe location, contact Security and provide as much information as possible.

▶ Fire evacuation alarms are not to be sounded.

Depending on the type of hazard, there are subtle but important differences between the various response steps. It is important for an organization to develop procedures to alert everyone to conduct a shelter-in-place procedure and to inform everyone of the exact nature of the hazard.

Procedures – Earthquake

▶ If an earthquake strikes while you are in a building, take cover immediately under a sturdy object:

❖ Cover your head, neck and face.

❖ Be prepared to move with the object.

❖ To the extent possible, stay away from windows and items that might fall.

▶ Do not attempt an evacuation during the earthquake.

▶ Once the shaking stops; evacuate and remain prepared for aftershocks:

❖ Do not move seriously injured individuals.

❖ Provide search and rescue personnel with the last known location of any missing victim.

- Once outdoors, stay away from power lines, buildings and any objects that might fall.

- There is no warning period; therefore, all attention should be directed towards life-safety procedures.

Note: If high-rise buildings are in the general area, falling debris may make open areas more dangerous than buildings.

Procedures – Hazardous Release Outside

- Employees in hallways or open areas are to seek shelter in the nearest room.

- Close windows and window treatments.

- Everyone is to remain quiet and not enter hallways or open areas.

- Crouch down in areas that are away from windows.

- Air ventilation systems will be shut down.

- A vertical evacuation may be considered.

- Should the fire alarm sound, do not evacuate the building unless:

  - ❖ You have firsthand knowledge that there is a fire in the building, or

  - ❖ You have been advised by Police/Security to evacuate the building, or

  - ❖ There is imminent danger in the immediate area.

Some organizations will have plastic and tape available to seal windows and doors. Most organizations will not go to these lengths and it should be noted that the employees who deploy the materials may be exposed to some risk.

Procedures – Hostile Intruder/Violent Employee

- Everyone in hallways or open areas is to seek shelter in the nearest room.

- A silent evacuation should be considered if it can be conducted safely.

- Lock and barricade doors.

- Close windows and window treatments.

- Turn off lights.

- Everyone is to remain quiet (quietly contact 911) and not enter hallways or open areas.

- Crouch down in areas that are out of sight from doors and windows.

- Should the fire alarm sound, do not evacuate the building unless:

  - ❖ You have firsthand knowledge that there is a fire in the building, or

  - ❖ You have been advised by Police/Security to evacuate the building, or

  - ❖ There is imminent danger in the immediate area.

Procedures – Tornado

▶ At the onset of a tornado warning:

  ❖ Everyone in outdoor areas is to seek shelter in secure buildings.

  ❖ Trailers and temporary structures are to be evacuated.

▶ Everyone is to go to interior areas/hallways or designated safe areas of the building.

▶ Close doors.

▶ If possible, take cover under a sturdy object.

▶ Cover your head, neck and face.

▶ Stay away from windows and objects that might fall.

▶ Do not seek cover in large open rooms (auditoriums, cafeterias, etc.)

▶ Remain quiet.

Hurricane Preparation Steps

Action Steps:

At the Alert Point (72 hours from expected impact)

▶ Open the EOC and conduct regular meetings of the ERT:

- ❖ Meetings should be held at 5:30 am (early morning meetings may be conducted by telephone among selected ERT members) and 5:30 pm or more frequently as necessary.

- ❖ The National Hurricane Center will update forecasts at 5:00 am and at 5:00 pm.

- ❖ Government officials will generally announce evacuation orders in either the late afternoon or pre-dawn hours following weather updates.

▶ Communications and Public Relations provides updated messages for the emergency hotline (voicemail) and webpage.

▶ Facilities checks:

- ❖ Emergency equipment

- ❖ Fuel levels

- ❖ Vehicles

- ❖ Generators

- ❖ Emergency supply quantities.

▶ Secure any needed fuel, emergency food and water, tools and other needed supplies.

▶ The Facilities Department secures the grounds/remove or secure loose items.

▶ The Facilities Department secures the building structure(s)/deploys shutters, water barricades, etc.

▶ Both Facilities and Security Departments continuously monitor the weather.

▶ If applicable, essential personnel (individuals who are to remain at the workplace during the storm) are released to conduct personal preparations and are instructed to report back at a later time.

▶ If applicable, activate the alternate sites and release alternate site personnel (individuals who are to activate and maintain the alternate site) to conduct personal preparations and to travel to their alternate site.

At the Watch Point (36-hours from expected impact) or earlier
▶ Maintain the EOC and conduct regular meetings of the ERT:

❖ Meetings should be held at 5:30 am (early morning meetings may be conducted by telephone among selected ERT members) and 5:30 pm or more frequently as necessary.

❖ The National Hurricane Center will update forecasts at 5:00 am and at 5:00 pm.

❖ Government officials will generally announce evacuation orders in either the late afternoon or pre-dawn hours following weather updates.

▶ Communications and Public Relations provides updated messages for the emergency hotline and webpage.

▶ The Facilities Department distributes supplies to secure building contents.

▶ Facilities secures the work areas for employees who are assigned to work from alternate sites and were unable to secure their work areas.

▶ Certain employees secure their work areas and are then released for personal preparations.

▶ The Facilities Department secures building contents located in common areas.

▶ The Facilities Department is to secure special assets and, as necessary, backup equipment required to maintain environmental controls. Give special attention to:

❖ Assets of high value.

❖ Perishable assets.

❖ Non-replaceable assets.

▶ Both the Facilities and Security Departments monitor the weather continuously.

▶ Outdoor activities are cancelled.

▶ Operations are established at the alternate sites.

At the Warning Point (24-hours from expected impact)
▶ Essential personnel return to work (only if life-threatening conditions are not expected).

▶ Communications and Public Relations provides updated messages for the emergency hotline and webpage.

▶ Operations are maintained at the alternate sites.

▶ Alternate site personnel are working from the alternate sites.

▶ Remaining employees secure their work areas and are then released for personal preparations.

▶ Normal activities are conducted from alternate sites.

▶ The Facilities and Security Departments make a final inspection of the building and secure the perimeter.

Note: Organizations that face a serious hurricane hazard often develop more detailed special hurricane plans.

Tornado Preparation Steps

Action Steps:

At the Watch Point (Tornadoes are Possible)

▶ Both Facilities and Security Departments continuously monitor the weather.

▶ The Incident Commander is contacted.

At the Warning Point (Tornadoes are Occurring or are about to Occur)

▶ Security dispatches someone to observe approaching weather conditions (tornadoes generally travel from the southwest to the northeast in the USA).

▶ The Incident Commander is contacted.

▶ Employees conduct a shelter-in-place:

❖ Outdoor activities are cancelled.

❖ Temporary structures are evacuated.

❖ Auditoriums, gyms and other large open structures are evacuated.

❖ Employees relocate to the safest building locations.

Typically there will generally be a brief warning period, providing insufficient time to take major emergency protection measures for buildings but hopefully sufficient time for last-minute survival efforts. The most life-threatening situation occurs at night when storms are difficult to spot and people may be asleep. For organizations with nighttime operations, it is important to consider weather monitoring and warning alert procedures during nighttime hours.

Note: Organizations that face a serious tornado hazard often develop more detailed special tornado plans.

Severe Winter Storm Preparation Steps

Blizzards/Ice Storms/Major Snow Events

Action Steps:

At the Watch Point (36 hours from expected impact)

- Conduct a meeting of the ERT/Open the EOC.
- Communications and Public Relations provides updated messages for the emergency hotline and webpage.
- Certain organizations with highly time-critical operations may activate recovery sites in advance of the storm.
- The Facilities Department checks:
  - ❖ Emergency equipment
  - ❖ Fuel levels
  - ❖ Vehicles
  - ❖ Generators
  - ❖ Emergency supply quantities
  - ❖ Salt, sand and ice-melting chemicals
  - ❖ Emergency heaters.
- Secure any needed fuel, supplies, etc.
- The Facilities Department secures the grounds.
- The Facilities Department secures building contents located in common areas.
- The Facilities Department secures special assets and, as necessary, backup equipment required to maintain environmental controls. Give special attention to:

❖ Assets of high value.

❖ Perishable assets.

❖ Non-replaceable assets.

◗ Both the Facilities and Security Departments monitor the weather continuously.

◗ Human Resources secures water and non-perishable foods – enough for 72 hours for the ERT and essential personnel (as applicable).

Note: *If employees are to be pre-positioned at distant alternate sites, travel preparations should commence prior to the 36 hour Watch Point.*

At the Warning Point (24 hours from expected impact)

◗ Conduct regular meetings of the ERT:

❖ Meetings should be held at 5:30 am (early morning meetings may be conducted by telephone among selected ERT members) and 5:30 pm or more frequently as necessary.

◗ Communications and Public Relations provides updated messages for the emergency hotline and webpage.

◗ The Facilities Department secures special assets and, as necessary, backup equipment required to maintain environmental controls. Special attention for:

❖ Assets of high value.

❖ Perishable assets.

❖ Non-replaceable assets.

◗ Take precautions to avoid frozen pipes.

◗ Outdoor activities will likely be cancelled.

◗ Employees will be released before travel conditions become dangerous.

Note: *Unlike many other weather hazards, winter storms generally cause little damage. They can cause major disruptions of transportation and utility services.*

DHS Advisory Code System

National Terrorism Advisory System

Alert

DATE & TIME ISSUED: XXXX

SUMMARY

The Secretary of Homeland Security informs the public and relevant government and private sector partners about a potential or actual threat with this alert, indicating whether there is an "imminent" or "elevated" threat.

DURATION

An individual threat alert is issued for a specific time period and then automatically expires. It may be extended if new information becomes available or the threat evolves.

DETAILS

• This section provides more detail about the threat and what the public and sectors need to know.

• It may include specific information, if available, about the nature and credibility of the threat, including the critical infrastructure sector(s) or location(s) that may be affected.

• It includes as much information as can be released publicly about actions as being taken or planned by authorities to ensure public safety, such as increased protective actions and what the public may expect to see.

AFFECTED AREAS

▪ This section includes visual depictions (such as maps or other graphics) showing the affected location(s), sector(s), or other illustrative detail about the threat itself.

HOW YOU CAN HELP

• This section provides information on ways the public can help authorities (e.g. camera phone pictures taken at the site of an explosion), and reinforces the importance of reporting suspicious activity.

• It may ask the public or certain sectors to be alert for a particular item, situation, person, activity or developing trend.

STAY PREPARED

• This section emphasizes the importance of the public planning and preparing for emergencies before they happen, including specific steps individuals, families and businesses can take to ready themselves and their communities.

• It provides additional preparedness information that may be relevant based on this threat.

STAY INFORMED

• This section notifies the public about where to get more information.

• It encourages citizens to stay informed about updates from local public safety and community leaders.

• It includes a link to the DHS NTAS website http://www.dhs.gov/alerts and http://twitter.com/NTASAlerts

If You See Something, Say Something™. Report suspicious activity to local law enforcement or call 911.

The National Terrorism Advisory System provides Americans with alert information on homeland security threats. It is distributed by the Department of Homeland Security. More information is available at: **www.dhs.gov/alerts.** To receive mobile updates **www.twitter.com/NTASAlerts**
If You See Something Say Something™ used with permission of the NY Metropolitan Transportation Authority.

www.dhs.gov/xlibrary/assets/ntas/ntas-sample-alert.pdf

Assigning Actions by Department

Department Identification

Departments are the operational groups and support departments that comprise an organization. The following departments along with a capsule summary of department responsibilities are referred to in this appendix:

▶ **Communications and Public Relations** – public announcements and internal communications.

▶ **Facilities** – maintenance of buildings, maintenance of building systems, environmental controls and utility services.

▶ **Finance and Accounting** – accounting, financial reporting, insurance services, legal issues and account management.

▶ **Human Resources (HR)** – payroll, benefits and general workforce issues.

▶ **Information Technology (IT)** – support of technology services including data center operations, data center recovery, IT alternate site operations, communication technologies, critical data management of electronic information, information security, applications and communication systems.

▶ **Operational Groups** – comprise the departments that are responsible for the production of products and/or completion of services that produce revenue. It is not possible to precisely state the exact responsibilities of the individual operational groups as the responsibilities vary from one organization to the next.

▶ **Sales and Customer Service** – management of the marketing program, direct sales and customer service.

▶ **Security** – building protection and threat monitoring.

Note: The support department titles and responsibilities referred to by any individual organization, such as the AIS and BWM case studies, are sometimes slightly different.

Department Plans and Responsibilities

The major operational groups and support departments of the organization need to be identified, department responsibilities assigned and a department plan should be documented as necessary. Sometimes these department plans are developed independently under a 'silo' approach. This often leads to plans that are poorly coordinated and vary widely in terms of detail and quality. It is important to develop department plans using an 'enterprise-wide' approach to ensure that all important responsibilities are assigned, assignments are not duplicated, planning is coordinated and no 'weak-links' exist among the plans. Thus it is important for senior management to assign responsibilities to each major department.

Emergency Response and Business Continuity Actions

'Emergency response' and 'business continuity' are two separate but closely integrated topics. After a major crisis event, the immediate actions are focused on life-safety and environmental issues first and asset protection second. Some organizations with good planning in place can also direct attention to maintaining or rapidly recovering critical operations during certain crisis events. Once the initial crisis is contained or controlled, the primary focus becomes business continuity.

After a major crisis, buildings may be damaged and the general environment will likely be dangerous. Emergency response priorities focus on the protection of human life and safety first, protection of the environment second and the protection of organization assets third. Business continuity priorities focus on maintaining or rapidly restoring operations. Sample combined emergency response and business continuity actions by department include the following:

Actions during the Pre-Crisis Strike Phase

- Communications and Public Relations
    - Assemble the Crisis Communication Team.
    - Coordinate information for employees.
    - Coordinate information for customers.
    - Coordinate information for the press, the public and other interested parties.
- Facilities
    - Shut down any utility service that presents a danger.
    - Activate the EOC.
    - Deploy equipment designed to maintain environmental controls and give special attention to:
        - Assets of high value.
        - Perishable assets.
        - Non-replaceable assets.
    - Monitor utility services.
    - Monitor the weather.
    - Test emergency equipment.
    - Secure building plans, architectural drawings and other important building documents.

> ❖ Maintain contact with utility providers.

◗ Finance and Accounting

> ❖ Insurance services – contact the insurance company.

> ❖ Contact legal counsel.

> ❖ Secure an adequate level of cash.

◗ Human Resources

> ❖ Distribute safety information to employees.

> ❖ If necessary, accelerate payroll processing.

◗ Information Technology

> ❖ Be prepared to activate IT alternate site operations.

◗ Sales and Customer Service

> ❖ Be prepared to maintain critical sales and customer service operations from remote locations.

◗ Security

> ❖ Monitor and communicate warnings and threats.

> ❖ Maintain contact with county and state police, fire, emergency and other government entities.

◗ All Employees

> ❖ Employees assigned to alternate sites will be instructed to travel to those sites if the alternate sites are activated.

> ❖ Secure work areas.

Actions during the Strike Phase

◗ Teams and individuals responsible for emergency response should assemble at the EOC

1. Determine if an evacuation or shelter-in-place order should be given.

2. Address injuries and life-safety issues.

3. Contact police, fire, EMS and other emergency responders as necessary.

4. Take steps to contain the incident.

5. Cordon off any dangerous areas.

6. If applicable, direct the Facilities Department to shut down utility services.

7. Take a count of all employees.

8. For any missing employees:

> ❑ Note the place they were last seen.
> ❑ Activate search and rescue teams ASAP.

9. Determine if employees should be released.

10. Assist with any search and rescue efforts.

11. Provide access control.

12. Conduct a preliminary damage assessment, focusing on critical operations first.

13. Address physical damage and operational issues.

14. Determine if the IT alternate site and the office alternate site should be activated.

▶ Communications and Public Relations

❖ Disseminate emergency messages.

❖ Assemble the Crisis Communication Team.

❖ Establish contact with:

❑ Alternate site operations.

❑ Responsible teams and individuals.

❑ Employees.

❑ Other interested parties.

❖ Update the emergency hotline message.

❖ Update emergency webpage message.

❖ Prepare for media contact.

▶ Facilities

❖ Activate the EOC.

❖ Deploy equipment designed to maintain environmental controls and give special attention to:

❑ Assets of high value.

❑ Perishable assets.

❑ Non-replaceable assets.

❖ Shut down any utility service that presents a danger.

❖ Establish contact with civil authorities and utility companies.

❖ Determine if the building environment is safe.

❖ Secure hazardous materials.

❖ Direct Security to cordon off any dangerous areas.

❖ Conduct a preliminary damage assessment:

❑ Building structure.

❑ Building systems.

❑ Building contents and equipment.

❑ Grounds.

- Finance and Accounting
  - ❖ Insurance services – contact the insurance company.
  - ❖ Contact legal counsel.

- Human Resources
  - ❖ Update the emergency hotline message as directed by Communications and Public Relations.
  - ❖ Establish contact with employees.
  - ❖ Make a preliminary workforce assessment.
  - ❖ Address travel logistics for employees who travel to alternate sites.
  - ❖ Maintain payroll processing.

- Information Technology
  - ❖ Update the emergency webpage message as directed by Communications and Public Relations.
  - ❖ Maintain or restore the operation of voice, Internet, data, video and communications access/services.
  - ❖ Establish communications and applications support from the IT alternate site
  - ❖ Make a preliminary damage assessment of the main data center.

- Sales and Customer Service
  - ❖ Establish critical operations from remote locations such as office alternate sites, homes and/or hotels.

- Security
  - ❖ Secure the workplace.
  - ❖ Cordon off any dangerous areas.
  - ❖ Establish contact with police departments and other civil authorities.
  - ❖ Control access to the property.
  - ❖ Assist with search and rescue efforts.

- Operational Groups
  - ❖ Assist the Facilities Department with preliminary damage assessments.
  - ❖ Direct/redirect shipments in transit.
  - ❖ Maintain quality controls.
  - ❖ Maintain security controls for proprietary information.

- All Employees
  - ❖ Do not congregate around crisis scenes:
    - ❑ They are often dangerous.
    - ❑ Employees may interfere with recovery efforts.

❖ All employees should make contact with their supervisor and (once their personal situation has stabilized) report to work or follow the instructions on the emergency hotline and webpage.

❖ Employees assigned to alternate sites will be instructed to travel to those sites if the alternate sites are activated.

❖ Non-relocated employees:

❑ Work from home, or

❑ Assist with damage assessments and cleanup efforts.

Comprehensive Damage Assessment and Resumption of Critical Operations Actions

▶ Teams and individuals responsible for initial recovery efforts

❖ Establish a regular meeting schedule at the EOC.

❖ Direct organization resources.

❖ Develop a recovery plan and timeframe.

❖ Based on a comprehensive damage assessment, determine if the building is repairable:

❑ Direct the Facilities Department to make repairs, or

❑ Secure alternate facilities or temporary structures or modules.

❖ Maintain critical operations at the alternate sites.

❖ In an extreme situation it may be necessary to relocate more employees to the alternate sites.

❖ Maintain contact with the Home Office and the Board of Trustees.

❖ If serious injuries or fatalities have occurred, become involved with family and relative contact.

▶ Communications and Public Relations

❖ Disseminate emergency messages.

❖ Maintain regular meetings of the Crisis Communication Team.

❖ Together with the Incident Commander, establish an accurate description of the crisis.

❖ Coordinate all communications.

❖ Develop messages and maintain contact with the media, employees and other interested parties.

❖ Direct HR to update the emergency hotline message.

❖ Direct IT to update the emergency webpage.

❖ Together with HR, contact relatives of affected employees.

▶ Facilities

❖ Complete a comprehensive damage assessment:

- ❑ Building structure.
- ❑ Building systems.
- ❑ Building contents and equipment.
- ❑ Grounds.

- ❖ Assess critical utility services:
  - ❑ Provide critical utility services.
  - ❑ Shut down any utility service that presents a danger.
  - ❑ Contact utility providers.
  - ❑ Commence repairs.
- ❖ Maintain a safe building environment.
- ❖ Maintain the EOC and distribute supplies, tools and equipment to the ERT.
- ❖ Commence cleanup and debris removal activities.
- ❖ Account for and secure all known hazardous materials.
- ❖ Provide building information to civil authorities.
- ❖ Contact cleanup, restoration and repair subcontractors.
- ❖ Supervise the repair of buildings.

◗ Finance and Accounting
  - ❖ Establish payroll processing.
  - ❖ Maintain contact with legal counsel.
  - ❖ Contact parties with a financial interest.
  - ❖ Insurance services:
    - ❑ Collect and analyze damage assessments.
    - ❑ Take pictures.
    - ❑ Maintain contact with the insurance company.

◗ Human Resources
  - ❖ Maintain the emergency hotline message as directed by Communications and Public Relations.
  - ❖ Execute the post-crisis section of the Disaster Assistance Plan:
    - ❑ Contact all employees – in person if necessary.
    - ❑ Provide survival supplies to employees seriously affected by the crisis.
    - ❑ Maintain logistical support to employees at recovery locations.
  - ❖ Assess workforce capabilities.
  - ❖ Contact relatives of affected employees.
  - ❖ Establish payroll processing.

❖ Establish critical employee benefit services.

▌ Information Technology

    ❖ Maintain communications and applications support from the IT alternate site.

    ❖ Maintain the emergency webpage as directed by Communications and Public Relations.

    ❖ Complete a comprehensive damage assessment of the main data center.

    ❖ Commence repair of the main data center:

        ❑ Repair salvageable hardware.

        ❑ Order replacement hardware.

        ❑ Secure and supervise subcontractors.

▌ Sales and Customer Service

    ❖ Maintain critical operations from remote locations such as office alternate sites, homes and/or hotels.

    ❖ Establish and maintain contact with clients, customers, advertisers, subcontractors and prospects.

▌ Security

    ❖ Maintain workplace security.

    ❖ Cordon off any dangerous areas.

    ❖ Maintain contact with police departments and other civil authorities.

    ❖ Control access to the property.

▌ Operational Groups

    ❖ Assist the Facilities Department with comprehensive damage assessments.

    ❖ Repair damaged equipment:

        ❑ Make temporary repairs.

        ❑ Instigate the replacement of equipment that cannot be repaired.

    ❖ Secure and supervise subcontractors.

    ❖ Assist with cleanup, reconstruction and/or relocation efforts.

    ❖ Direct and redirect shipments in transit.

    ❖ Maintain inventory control.

    ❖ Maintain quality controls.

    ❖ Maintain security controls for proprietary information.

▌ All Employees

    ❖ Maintain contact with supervisors or the Human Resources Department.

    ❖ Relocated employees should continue to work from alternate sites and not return until instructed to do so.

❖ To the extent possible, non-relocated employees are to:

❑ Assist with the building content damage assessment and cleanup.

❑ Work from home until the facility is operational or temporary structures or modules are secured.

Resumption of General Operations Actions

▌ Teams and individuals responsible for general recovery efforts

❖ Maintain a regular meeting schedule.

❖ Direct organization resources.

❖ Execute the BCM program recovery efforts.

❖ Gradually shift critical operations from the alternate sites to the repaired facility, new facility or temporary structure(s) or modules.

▌ Communications and Public Relations

❖ Coordinate all communications.

❖ Maintain a consistent message for the media, clients, employees and other interested parties.

▌ Facilities

❖ Maintain a safe environment.

❖ Maintain environmental controls.

❖ Complete the cleanup and debris removal activities.

❖ Supervise the repair or reconstruction of the building.

▌ Finance and Accounting

❖ Maintain payroll processing.

❖ Maintain contact with legal counsel.

❖ Maintain contact with parties who have a financial interest.

❖ Insurance services:

❑ Collect and analyze damage assessments.

❑ File insurance claims.

▌ Human Resources

❖ Maintain the emergency hotline message as directed by Communications and Public Relations.

❖ Execute the disaster assistance to employees:

❑ Maintain contact with all employees – in person if necessary.

❑ Provide recovery supplies to employees seriously affected by the crisis.

❑ Maintain logistical support to employees at alternate site locations.

- ❖ Continually assess workforce capabilities.

- ❖ Maintain contact with relatives of affected employees.

- ❖ Maintain payroll processing.

- ❖ Maintain critical employee benefit services.

▶ Information Technology

   - ❖ Complete the repair of the main data center:

      - ❏ Repair salvageable hardware.

      - ❏ Install replacement hardware.

      - ❏ Supervise subcontractors.

   - ❖ Maintain the emergency webpage as directed by Communications and Public Relations.

   - ❖ Shift critical operations from the IT alternate site to the main data center.

▶ Sales and Customer Service

   - ❖ Shift critical operations from remote locations such as, office alternate sites, homes and/or hotels.

   - ❖ Maintain contact with clients, customers, advertisers, subcontractors and prospects.

▶ Security

   - ❖ Maintain workplace security and access controls.

▶ Operational Groups

   - ❖ Assist with cleanup, reconstruction and/or relocation efforts.

   - ❖ Repair damaged equipment:

      - ❏ Make permanent repairs.

      - ❏ Replacement of equipment that cannot be repaired.

   - ❖ Supervise subcontractors.

▶ All Employees

   - ❖ Maintain contact with supervisors or the Human Resources Department.

   - ❖ Relocated employees should return to work once the facility is operational or temporary structures or modules are secured.

   - ❖ Non-relocated employees are to return to work once the facility is operational or temporary structures or modules are secured.

National Weather Service Terms

Floods:

Flood Watch – Flooding is possible.

Flash Flood Watch – Flash flooding is possible.

Flood Warning – Flooding is occurring or will occur soon.

Flash Flood Warning – Flash flooding is occurring.

Urban and Small Stream Advisory – Flooding of small streams, streets and low areas is occurring.

Cold Weather:

Blizzard Warning – Heavy snow, strong winds, extreme wind chill, etc. are expected.

Frost/Freeze Warnings – Below freezing temperatures are expected.

Travelers Advisory – Severe weather may make driving conditions difficult or dangerous.

Winter Storm Advisory – Cold temperatures, ice and/or heavy snow accumulations is expected.

Winter Storm Watch – Severe winter weather is possible within the next 24 to 48 hours.

Winter Storm Warning – Severe winter weather is about to begin.

Tornadoes:

Tornado Watch – Tornadoes are possible.

Tornado Warning – Tornadoes are occurring.

Severe Thunderstorm – A thunderstorm that produces a tornado, has winds of at least 58 mph and/or produces hail of ¾" in diameter or more.

Severe Thunderstorm Watch – Severe thunderstorms are possible.

Severe Thunderstorm Warning – Severe thunderstorms are occurring.

Fujita Scale and Enhanced Fujita Scale (of tornado force)

F	Fujita Scale Wind Speed (mph)	EF	Enhanced Fujita Scale Wind Speed (mph)
0	40 – 72	0	65 – 85
1	73 – 112	1	86 – 110
2	113 – 157	2	111 – 135
3	158 – 207	3	136 – 165
4	208 – 260	4	166 – 200
5	Over 260	5	Over 200

Hurricanes:

Hurricane Watch – A hurricane hazard exists for the next 24 to 36 hours.

Hurricane Warning – A hurricane strike is expected within the next 24 hours.

Hurricane Categories (Saffir-Simpson Scale)
     Tropical Storm – Wind speed 39 to 73mph, isolated damage.
     Category 1 – Wind speed 74 to 95 mph, minor damage.
     Category 2 – Wind speed 96 to 110 mph, moderate damage.
     Category 3 – Wind speed 111 to 130 mph, extensive damage.
     Category 4 – Wind speed 131 to 155 mph, extreme damage.
     Category 5 – Wind speed over 155 mph, catastrophic damage.

Wind Speed – This is really sustained wind speed; higher gusts may (probably will) be present.

Major Hurricanes – Category 3, 4 and 5 hurricanes.

Seismic Terms

Epicenter – The point of origin of an earthquake is known as the focus. Shock waves spread out from the focus and the point on the surface directly above the focus is known as the epicenter.

Fault – A fracture plane in the surface of the earth.

Ground Movement – Ground vibration or other aspects of motion that occurs during an earthquake.

Uplift and Subsidence – The uplifting or sinking of land during an earthquake.

Liquefaction – The process by which certain soils behave as a liquid during an earthquake. Water-saturated sands and compact soils (landfills) lose their load-bearing capacity.

Modified Mercalli Scale – The intensity of an earthquake indicates the effects on people and structures. Intensity is determined by reports of observers and not by instruments. The Modified Mercalli Scale measures intensity on a scale of I (least intense) to XII (most intense).

Richter Scale – The size of an earthquake is a measure of the total energy released and is referred to as its magnitude. The Richter Scale is a logarithmic scale used to measure earthquake magnitude. Each increase of one number corresponds to a ten-fold increase in ground motion. Expected annual frequency and is as follows:

Richter Magnitude	Worldwide Annual Frequency	Comments
2	–	
3	–	
4	10,000	
5	1,000	
6	100	
7	10	A "major" earthquake
8	1	A "great" earthquake

Tsunami – A large ocean wave (or series of waves) usually created by the sudden dislocation of the sea bottom.

INDEX

DO THE MATH

Combine more than 30 expert authors,
with 1,000 years of experience, and countless
problems solved for companies like yours…

Your definitive, current, comprehensive Business Continuity textbook and reference – based on international standards and grounded in best practices.

Business Continuity Management: Global Best Practices, 4th Edition
by Andrew Hiles
©2014
494 pages + 200 pages of free downloads, illustrations, glossary, index, and instructional teaching materials.

ISBN 978-1-931332-35-4, paperback

ISBN 978-1-931332-76-7, eBook

ISBN 978-1-931332-83-5, ePub

Root Cause Analysis Handbook, Third Edition: A Guide to Efficient and Effective Incident Investigation
by ABS Consulting
©2008
320 pages, plus accompanying downloads, glossary.

ISBN 978-1-931332-51-4, paperback

ISBN 978-1-931332-72-9, eBook

ISBN 978-1-931332-82-8, ePub

Complete all-in-one package for root cause analysis, including 600+ pages of book and downloads, color-coded, 17" x 22" Root Cause Map™, and licensed access to online resources.

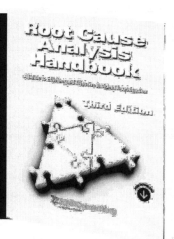

Be prepared! Follow this tested six-phase method to create a plan that you can activate at a moment's notice – to get everyone to safety from any workplace.

Emergency Evacuation Planning for Your Workplace: From Chaos to Life-Saving Solutions
by Jim Burtles
©2013
340 pages + 300 pages of free downloads, illustrations, glossary, index, and instructional teaching materials.

ISBN 978-1-931332-56-9, casebound

ISBN 978-1-931332-67-5, eBook

ISBN 978-1-931332-85-9, ePub

...and you have Rothstein Publishing – books with the *answers* you're looking for.

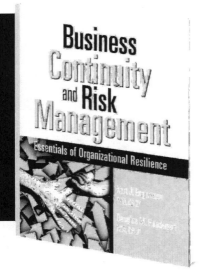
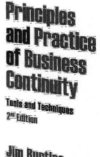

New eBooks
From The Rothstein Publishing eBook Collection

The Manager's Guide to Simple, Stategic, Service-Oriented Business Continuity

Rachelle Loyear, MBCP, AFBCI, CISM, PMP Kristen Noakes-Fry, ABCI, Editor
(A Rothstein Publishing Collection eBook) May 2017
ISBN: 978-1-944480-38-7 (EPUB)
ISBN: 978-1-944480-39-4 (PDF)
145 pages

(For more info go to Rothstein Pubishing) (To purchase go to Amazon)

You have the knowledge and skill to create a workable Business Continuity Management (BCM) program –but too often, your projects are stalled while you attempt to get the right information from the right person. Rachelle Loyear takes you through the practical steps to get your program back on track.

The Manager's Guide to Risk Assessment: Getting It Right

Douglas M. Henderson, FSA, CBCP Kristen Noakes-Fry, ABCI, Editor
(A Rothstein Publishing Collection eBook) March 2017
ISBN: 978-1-944480-38-7 (EPUB)
ISBN: 978-1-944480-39-4 (PDF)
114 pages

(For more info go to Rothstein Pubishing) (To purchase go to Amazon)

Risk assessment is required for just about all business plans or decisions. As a responsible manager, you need to consider threats to your organization's resilience. But to determine probability and impact – and reduce your risk – can be a daunting task. Guided by Henderson's The Manager's Guide to Risk Assessment: Getting It Right, you will confidently follow a clearly explained, step-by-step process to conduct a risk assessment.

The Manager's Guide to Cybersecurity Law: Essentials for Today's Business

Teri Schreider, SSCP, SISM, C | CISO, ITIL Foundation Kristen Noakes-Fry, ABCI, Editor
(A Rothstein Publishing Collection eBook) February 2017
ISBN: 978-1-944480-30-1 (EPUB)
ISBN: 978-1-944480-31-8 (PDF)
168 pages

(For more info go to Rothstein Pubishing) (To purchase go to Amazon)

In today's litigious business world, cyber-related matters could land you in court. As a computer security professional, you are protecting your data, but are you protecting your company? While you know industry standards and regulations, you may not be a legal expert, but fortunately, in a few hours of reading rather than months of classroom study you could be.

ROTHSTEIN PUBLISHING
A Division of Rothstein Associates Inc.
Brookfield, Connecticut USA
www.rothstein.com

www.facebook.com/RothsteinPublishing

www.linkedin.com/company/rothsteinpublishing

www.twitter.com/rothsteinpub

I

New eBooks
From The Rothstein Publishing eBook Collection

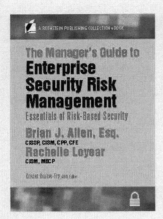

The Manager's Guide to Enterprise Security Risk Management: Essentials of Risk-Based Security
Brian J. Allen, Esq., CISSP, CISM, CPP, CFE
Rachelle Loyear MBCP, AFBCI, CISM, PMP Kristen Noakes-Fry, ABCI, Editor
(A Rothstein Publishing Collection eBook) November 2016
ISBN: 978-1-944480-24-0 (EPUB)
ISBN: 978-1-944480-25-7 (PDF)

For more info go to Rothstein Pubishing | To purchase go to Amazon

Is security management changing so fast that you can't keep up? Perhaps it seems like those traditional "best practices" in security no longer work? One answer might be that you need better best practices!

The Manager's Guide to Business Continuity Exercises: Testing Your Plan
Jim Burtles, KLT, MMLT, Hon FBCI Kristen Noakes-Fry, ABCI, Editor
(A Rothstein Publishing Collection eBook) November 2016
ISBN: 978-1-944480-32-5 (EPUB)
ISBN: 978-1-944480-33-2 (PDF)
100 pages

For more info go to Rothstein Pubishing | To purchase go to Amazon

Your challenge is to maintain a good and effective plan in the face of changing circumstances and limited budgets. If your situation is like that in most companies, you really cannot depend on the results of last year's test or exercise of the plan.

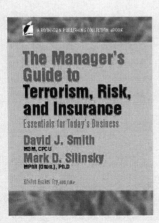

The Manager's Guide to Terrorism, Risk, & Insurance: Essentials for Today's Business
David J. Smith, MSM, CPCU Mark D. Silinsky, MPhol (Oxon.), Ph.D
Kristen Noakes-Fry, ABCI, Editor
(A Rothstein Publishing Collection eBook) October 2016
ISBN: 978-1-944480-26-4 (EPUB)
ISBN: 978-1-944480-27-1 (PDF)
120 pages

For more info go to Rothstein Pubishing | To purchase go to Amazon

As a manager, you're aware of terrorist acts, are considering the risks, but sense that you need more background. How might terrorism occur?

ROTHSTEIN PUBLISHING
A Division of Rothstein Associates Inc.
Brookfield, Connecticut USA
www.rothstein.com

www.facebook.com/RothsteinPublishing

www.linkedin.com/company/rothsteinpublishing

www.twitter.com/rothsteinpub

New eBooks
From The Rothstein Publishing eBook Collection

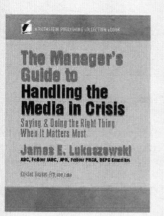

The Manager's Guide to Handling the Media in a Crisis: Saying & Doing the Right Thing When It Matters Most
James E. Lukaszewski, ABC, Fellow IABC, Fellow PRSA, BEPS Emeritus
Kristen Noakes-Fry, ABCI, Editor
(A Rothstein Publishing Collection eBook) September 2016
ISBN: 978-1-944480-28-8 (EPUB)
ISBN: 978-1-944480-29-5 (PDF)
120 pages

(For more info go to Rothstein Pubishing)   (To purchase go to Amazon)

Attracting media attention is surprisingly easy – you just want it to be the right kind! If an event causes the phone to ring and TV cameras to appear in your lobby, you need confidence that the people who happen to be at your worksite that day are prepared.

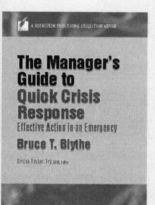

The Manager's Guide to Quick Crisis Response: Effective Action in an Emergency
Bruce T. Blythe Kristen Noakes-Fry, ABCI, Editor
(A Rothstein Publishing Collection eBook) August 2016
ISBN: 978-1-944480-23-3 (EPUB)
ISBN: 978-1-944480-22-6 (PDF)
117 pages

(For more info go to Rothstein Pubishing)   (To purchase go to Amazon)

Avoid being "blindsided" by an unexpected emergency or crisis in the workplace – violence, natural disaster, or worse!

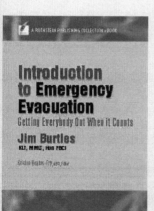

Introduction to Emergency Evacuation: Getting Everybody Out When It Counts
Bruce T. Blythe Kristen Noakes-Fry, ABCI, Editor
(A Rothstein Publishing Collection eBook) July 2016 ISBN: 978-1-944480-14-1 (EPUB)
ISBN: 978-1-944480-15-8 (PDF)
120 pages

(For more info go to Rothstein Pubishing)   (To purchase go to Amazon)

When it's not just a drill, you need to get it right the first time. If an emergency alert sounds, are you ready to take charge and get everyone out of the office, theater, classroom, or store safely?

ROTHSTEIN PUBLISHING
A Division of Rothstein Associates Inc.
Brookfield, Connecticut USA
www.rothstein.com

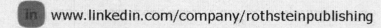

f www.facebook.com/RothsteinPublishing

in www.linkedin.com/company/rothsteinpublishing

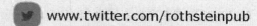
www.twitter.com/rothsteinpub

New eBooks
From The Rothstein Publishing eBook Collection

The Manager's Guide to Bullies in the Workplace: Coping with Emotional Terrorists

Vali Hawkins Mitchell, Ph.D, LMHC, REAT, CEAP Kristen Noakes-Fry, ABCI, Editor
(A Rothstein Publishing Collection eBook) July 2016
ISBN: 978-1-944480-12-7 (EPUB)
ISBN: 978-1-944480-13-4 (PDF)
120 pages

(For more info go to Rothstein Pubishing) (To purchase go to Amazon)

As a manager, you can usually handle disruptive employees. But sometimes, their emotional states foster workplace tension, even making them a danger to others.

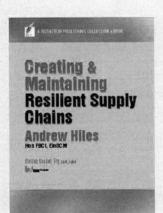

Creating & Maintaining Resilient Supply Chains

Andrew Hiles, Hon FBCI, EloSCM Kristen Noakes-Fry, ABCI, Editor
(A Rothstein Publishing Collection eBook) July 2016
ISBN: 978-1-944480-07-3 (EPUB)
ISBN: 978-1-944480-08-0 (PDF)
120 pages

(For more info go to Rothstein Pubishing) (To purchase go to Amazon)

Will your supply chain survive the twists and turns of the global economy? Can it deliver mission-critical supplies and services in the face of disaster or other business interruption?

ROTHSTEIN PUBLISHING
A Division of Rothstein Associates Inc.
Brookfield, Connecticut USA
www.rothstein.com

www.facebook.com/RothsteinPublishing

www.linkedin.com/company/rothsteinpublishing

www.twitter.com/rothsteinpub

Cause Analysis Manual:
Incident Investigation Method & Techniques

by: Fred Forck (Author), Kristen Noakes-Fry ABCI (Editor)

"One significant difference in Fred's approach to Cause Analysis is that he starts with success, not failure. You need to be able to clearly define success using objective criteria, not only in results (dollars, product) but also in behaviors."

> – John D. Schnack,
> Manager,
> Nuclear Corporate
> Oversight, Ameren

"...the distillation of the wisdom of vast knowledge and experience into a finely tuned instrument for evoking and capturing the invisible influences that shape the human side of events. This sort of virtuosity is routine throughout the book."

> – Ben Whitmer, Event Cause Analyst,
> STP Nuclear Operating Company

A failure or accident brings your business to a sudden halt. How did it happen? Good investigative work is needed – but how do you go about it? In this new book, industry pioneer Fred Forck's seven-step cause analysis methodology guides you to the roots of the incident, enabling you to act effectively to avoid loss of time, money, productivity, and quality.

From 30+ years of experience as a performance improvement consultant, self-assessment team leader, and trainer, Fred Forck, CPT, understands what you need to get the job done. He leads you through a clear step-by-step process cause evaluation and corrective action development. Using these straightforward tools, you can avoid errors, increase reliability, enhance performance, and improve bottom-line results - while creating a resilient culture that avoids repeat failures.

The key phases of a successful cause analysis include:

- ✦ Scoping the Problem
- ✦ Investigating the Factors
- ✦ Reconstructing the Story
- ✦ Reporting Learnings
- ✦ Validating Underlying Factors
- ✦ Planning Corrective Actions
- ✦ Establishing Contributing Factors
- ✦ References for further reading
- ✦ Hundreds of illustrative figures, tables, and diagrams
- ✦ A full glossary of terms and acronyms
- ✦ Professional index

At each stage, *Cause Analysis Manual: Incident Investigation Method and Techniques* gives you a wealth of real-world examples, models, thought-provoking discussion questions, and ready-to-use checklists and forms.

You know that identifying causes and preventing business-disrupting events aren't always easy. By following Fred Forck's proven steps you will be able to identify contributing factors, align organizational behaviors, take corrective action, and improve business performance!

A Division of Rothstein Associates Inc.

www.rothsteinpublishing.com
info@rothstein.com
203.740.7400

4 Arapaho Road
Brookfield, Connecticut
06804-3104 USA

ISBN: 978-1-944480-09-7 (Print) $99.99
ISBN: 978-1-944480-10-3 (ePub) $49.99
ISBN: 978-1-944480-11-0 (Web PDF eBook) $49.99

https://www.amazon.com/Cause-Analysis-Manual-Investigation-Techniques/dp/1944480099

https://www.rothstein.com/product/cause-analysis-manual/

65584237R00210